365 days with Spurgeon

A unique collection of 365 daily
readings from sermons preached
by **Charles Haddon Spurgeon**
from his New Park Street Pulpit.

Selected and arranged by
Terence Peter Crosby

Day One

© Day One Publications 1998
First printed 1998
Reprinted 2004

Scripture quotations are from the King James Version.

British Library Cataloguing in Publication Data available
ISBN 0 902548 84 0 Casebound

Published by Day One Publications
Ryelands Road Leominster HR6 8NZ
☎ 01565 613 740 **FAX** 01568 611 473
email address: sales@dayone.co.uk

Chief Sub-Editor: David Simm
Designed by Steve Devane. Printed by CPD Wales

Dedication

In memory of Pastor Bob Sheehan, at
whose suggestion this book was compiled

Charles Haddon Spurgeon
photographed during his time at
New Park Street

There are golden moments in the history of the Christian Church, occasions which always renew and refresh. Luther standing his ground before the illustrious Charles V at the City of Worms in 1521 or George Whitefield preaching the Gospel to the Kingswood miners in the open air at Bristol in 1739.[1] These are times that we treasure. Another such moment was September 23rd 1857 when six people attended a prayer meeting at Fulton Street, New York, organised by Jeremiah Lamphier a humble city missionary to office workers. The next week twenty came and the next forty. Six months later in New York alone 50,000 were attending daily lunch time prayer meetings. This proved to be the watershed of a nation-wide spiritual awakening in which a million were added to the churches in America. [2]

During that same year of 1857 when the Holy Spirit was moving so powerfully in New York and beginning a work across America Spurgeon declared, 'In one year it was my happiness personally to see not less than a thousand who had then been converted.'[3] Spurgeon was only nineteen the first time he preached at New Park Street on December 18th 1853. During 1854 he became the pastor at New Park Street and in January 1855 the publication of the weekly sermon began. By the autumn of 1854, 500 were attending the weekly prayer meeting. The church was enlarged but it was inadequate and Exeter Hall seating 5,000 was hired. That in turn gave way to the hiring for three years of the Surrey Gardens Music Hall capable of holding 10,000. During 1861 the building of The Metropolitan Tabernacle was completed.

A wonderful unction attended the preaching in those early years.[4] Extraordinary vitality characterised all of Spurgeon's preaching. This shows in the demand for his printed sermons which have exceeded and continue to exceed all records for popularity. As we read these daily notes extracted from the New Park Street era we recall the opposition and fierce criticism that was levelled at the young preacher. The popular press depicted him as the most abominable buffoon that ever climbed the stairs of a pulpit. He was described as a spoiled boy, vulgar, theatrical, 'an over-ripe cucumber soon to return to the nility from whence it sprang.' That one so young, so unconventional, so new from the country, could present so effectively and uncompromisingly the grand doctrines of man's depravity and God's peerless grace to such great crowds, was infuriating to his critics.

An outstanding feature of these extracts chosen by Terence Crosby is the amazing diversity of subjects covered. How is it that Spurgeon who was completely moulded by the Puritans of the 16th and 17th centuries[5] did not preach in the systematic way that they did going text by text, section by section, through books of the Bible? The answer is that Spurgeon esteemed every occasion as a unique evangelistic opportunity and so needed total freedom.[6] The Holy Spirit used a wide range of biblical truth to convert and build up. May that rich ministry continue to edify and inspire through these pages is my prayer.

Erroll Hulse
Leeds

1   George Whitefield's Journals, Banner of Truth, 1965, pages 223ff.
2   When Heaven Touched Earth, Roy J Fish, Need of the Times Publishers, Azle, USA, 1997.
3   C H Spurgeon , The Early Years, Banner of Truth, 1967, page 452.
4   The story is told briefly yet wonderfully by Iain Murray in his The Forgotten Spurgeon, Banner of Truth 1966, and in much more detail and in a way which draws tears by Lewis Drummond, Spurgeon - Prince of Preachers, Kregel, 1992.
5   Ernest W Bacon, Spurgeon - Heir of the Puritans, Eerdmans, 1968, page 102ff.
6   A Marvellous Ministry - How the all-round ministry of C H Spurgeon speaks to us today, Tim Curnow, Geoff Thomas, David Kingdon and Erroll Hulse, Soli Deo Gloria, USA, 1993, page 72.

Spurgeon's youthful New Park Street Pulpit sermons constitute a preface to the great series of Metropolitan Tabernacle Pulpit sermons. Due in part to their tiny close type (caused by the need to avoid heavy paper-tax) they are probably less read than the later and larger series.

These daily readings are designed to provide a glimpse of the riches to be found and to whet the reader's appetite. In all there are 368 numbers in the New Park Street Pulpit, consisting of 6 volumes and about a quarter of a seventh volume which continues as The Metropolitan Tabernacle Pulpit. However, there are not 368 sermons! A few of the occasional double numbers consist of a single extra-long sermon with or without supplements (nos. 7-8; 39-40; 41-42; 61-62; 66-67; 81-82; 141-142; 154-155; 297-298). Nos. 268-270 cover the services in connection with the laying of the first stone of the new Tabernacle on August 16th 1859, while nos. 331-332 give accounts of the first meetings to be held in the still incomplete building on August 21st 1860.

The majority of the readings have been arranged to coincide with the actual dates on which the sermons were preached. Duplication of dates due to two leap years and/or publication of both morning and evening sermons have led to the displacement of readings to an adjacent day, where possible or to an unrepresented date in the same month where possible. Both July and October are poorly represented by sermons preached in those months. To provide some variation, the holiday month of July has been filled out by readings from expositions and tracts attached to the long sermons mentioned above, by a four day series from the account of Spurgeon's Continental Tour given during the first meeting at the Metropolitan Tabernacle and by the insertion of readings from Spurgeon's first two sermons at New Park Street preached on his visit on December 18th 1853. Each reading indicates Spurgeon's text and sermon-title; the suggested further readings and footnotes for meditation have been added by the arranger.

I would like to express my thanks to all at Day One who helped to turn my original draft into this final publication. I am particularly grateful for the hard work of David Simm, who as Chief Sub-Editor has helped to remove and update some of the antiquated language and terminology of the original material without losing Spurgeon's distinctive style. Paul Sayer's guidance and advice has also been very much appreciated. I must also thank Steve Devane and John Roberts who have both offered helpful advice and encouragement. Pastor Erroll Hulse kindly agreed to write the Foreword and I would like to express my gratitude to him for providing such a helpful introduction. Finally, I thank my wife, Daphne for previewing these readings with me day by day.

Terence Peter Crosby
Wandsworth, London

A New Year's benediction

"But the God of all grace, who hath called us unto his eternal glory by Christ Jesus, after that ye have suffered a while, make you perfect, stablish, strengthen, settle you." 1 Peter 5: 10

SUGGESTED FURTHER READING: Revelation 21: 1-6

Oh, beloved, when you hear of Christ, when you know that this grace comes through Christ, and the calling through Christ, and the glory through Christ, then you say, "Lord, I can believe it now, if it is through Christ." It is not a hard thing to believe that Christ's blood was sufficient to purchase every blessing for me. If I go to God's treasury without Christ, I am afraid to ask for anything, but when Christ is with me I can then ask for everything. For sure I think he deserves it, though I do not. If I can claim his merits then I am not afraid to plead. Is perfection too great a boon for God to give to Christ? No. Is the keeping, the stability, the preservation of the blood-bought ones too great a reward for the terrible agonies and sufferings of the Saviour? No. Then we may with confidence plead, because everything comes through Christ. I would in concluding make this remark. I wish, my brothers and sisters, that during this year you may live nearer to Christ than you have ever done before. Depend upon it, it is when we think much of Christ that we think little of ourselves, little of our troubles, and little of the doubts and fears that surround us. Begin from this day, and may God help you. Never let a single day pass over your head without a visit to the garden of Gethsemane, and the cross of Calvary. And as for some of you who are not saved, and know not the Redeemer, I would to God that this very day you would come to Christ.

FOR MEDITATION: The New Year may not always be as "Happy" as we would wish, but the Christian is blessed in Christ with every spiritual blessing in the heavenly places (Ephesians 1: 3) and can look forward to a "Blessed New Year" throughout the problems that may come.

SERMON NO. 292

Faith in perfection

"The Lord will perfect that which concerneth me: thy mercy, O Lord, endureth for ever: forsake not the works of thine own hands."
Psalm 138: 8

SUGGESTED FURTHER READING: Deuteronomy 31: 1-8

There is yet another confession in the text—the Psalmist's confession that all he has, he has from God. "Forsake not the works of thine own hands." I will not, however, dwell upon it, but urge you who are believers to go home and cry aloud to God in prayer. Let this be a New Year's day prayer. "Forsake not the work of thine hands. Father, forsake not thy little child, lest he die by the hand of the enemy. Shepherd, forsake not thy lamb, lest the wolves devour him. Great husbandman, forsake not thy little plant, lest the frost should nip it, and it should be destroyed. Forsake me not, O Lord now, and when I am old and grey headed, O Lord, forsake me not. Forsake me not in my joys, lest I curse God. Forsake me not in my sorrows, lest I murmur against him. Forsake me not in the day of my repentance, lest I lose the hope of pardon, and fall into despair; and forsake me not in the day of my strongest faith, lest my faith degenerate into presumption, and so I perish by my own hand." Cry out to God, that he would not forsake you in your business, in your family; that he would not forsake you either upon your bed by night or in your business by day. And may God grant, when you and I shall come to the end of this year, we may have a good tale to tell concerning the faithfulness of God in having answered our prayers, and having fulfilled his promise.

FOR MEDITATION: Do you open up every area of your life to the One who has promised never to forsake his people? Are there any aspects of your relationship with him which are not all that they should be (Malachi 1: 6)?

SERMON NO. 231

The immutability of Christ

"Jesus Christ the same yesterday, and to day, and for ever." Hebrews 13: 8
SUGGESTED FURTHER READING: Hebrews 1: 5-13

It is well that there is one person who is the same. It is well that there is one stable rock amidst the changing billows of this sea of life; for how many and how grievous have been the changes of last year? How many of you who commenced in affluence, have by the panic, which has shaken nations, been reduced almost to poverty? How many of you, who in strong health marched into this place on the first Sabbath of last year, have had to come tottering here, feeling that the breath of man is in his nostrils, and wherein is he to be accounted of? Many of you came to this hall with a numerous family, leaning upon the arm of a choice and much loved friend. Alas! for love, if that were all, and nought beside, O earth! For you have buried those you loved the best. Some of you have come here childless, or widows, or fatherless, still weeping your recent affliction. Changes have taken place in your estate that have made your heart full of misery. Your cups of sweetness have been dashed with draughts of gall; your golden harvests have had tares cast into the midst of them, and you have had to reap the noxious weed along with the precious grain. Your much fine gold has become dim, and your glory has departed; the sweet feelings at the commencement of last year became bitter ones at the end. Your raptures and your ecstasies were turned into depression and forebodings. Alas! for our changes, and hallelujah to him that has no change.

FOR MEDITATION: Change is part and parcel of everything in a fallen creation (Genesis 3: 16-19). The Lord Jesus Christ is not part of creation, not even the very first part, but is Lord over all creation and not subject to any change. In him God's children can look forward to glorious liberty from creation's present bondage to decay (Romans 8: 21-23).

A mighty Saviour

"Mighty to save." Isaiah 63: 1
SUGGESTED FURTHER READING: Hebrews 7: 23-28

Remember the case of John Newton, the great and mighty preacher of St. Mary, Woolnoth,—an instance of the power of God to change the heart, as well as to give peace when the heart is changed. Ah! dear hearers, I often think within myself, "This is the greatest proof of the Saviour's power." Let another doctrine be preached: will it do the same? If it will, why not let every man gather a crowd round him and preach it? Will it really do it? If it will, then the blood of men's souls must rest upon the man who does not boldly proclaim it. If he believes his gospel does save souls, how does he account for it that he stands in his pulpit from the first of January till the last of December, and never hears of a harlot made honest, nor of a drunkard reclaimed? Why? For this reason, that it is a poor dilution of Christianity. It is something like it, but it is not the bold, broad Christianity of the Bible; it is not the full gospel of the blessed God, for that has power to save. But if they do believe that theirs is the gospel, let them come out to preach it, and let them strive with all their might to win souls from sin, which is rife enough, God knows. We say again, that we have proof positive in cases even here before us, that Christ is mighty to save even the worst of men—to turn them from follies in which they have too long indulged, and we believe that the same gospel preached elsewhere would produce the same results. The best proof you can ever have of God's being mighty to save, dear hearers, is that he saved you.

FOR MEDITATION: Does the church today lack the fullness of the blessing of the gospel of Christ (Romans 15: 29) because the church is ashamed of the fullness of the gospel, which is God's power to save all who believe (Romans 1: 16)?

A sermon for the week of prayer

"Continue in prayer, and watch in the same with thanksgiving."
Colossians 4: 2

SUGGESTED FURTHER READING: Luke 18: 1-8

Continue in prayer once more, because prayer is a great weapon of attack against the error and wickedness of the world. I see before me the strong bastions of the castle of sin. I note the host of men who have surrounded it. They have brought the battering-ram, they have dashed it many times against the gate; it has fallen with tremendous force against it, and you would have supposed that the timbers would be split asunder the first time. But they are staunch and strong; he who made them was a cunning architect, he who depends upon them for his protection is one who knew how to make the gate exceeding massive,—is one who knew the struggle full well which he would have to endure—prince of darkness as he is. If he knew of his defeat, yet well he knew how to guard against it if it were possible. But I see this ponderous battering-ram as it has been hurled with giant force again and again upon the gate, and how as often seemed to recoil before the massive bars. Many of the saints of God are ready to say, "Let us withdraw the instrument. Let us take away the besieging artillery, we shall never be able to storm this castle, we shall never effect an entrance." Oh, be not craven, sirs, be not craven. The last time the battering-ram thundered in its course, I saw the timbers shake. The very gate did reel, and the posts did rock to and fro; see now they have moved the earth around their sockets. Hell is howling from within because it knows how soon its end must come. Now, Christian warriors, use your battering-rams once more, for the gates begin to shake, and the walls are tottering. They will reel, they will fall before long.

FOR MEDITATION: Are your prayers stuck in defensive mode as you seek God's protection? Does your prayer-life ever venture out on the attack? Remember the Saviour's powerful promise that the gates of hell would be unable to stand up against the advance of his church (Matthew 16: 18). May these words before a special week of prayer encourage us to continue in prayer all year round.

SERMON NO. 354

Life for a look

"Look unto me, and be ye saved, all the ends of the earth; for I am God, and there is none else." Isaiah 45: 22
SUGGESTED FURTHER READING: Acts 26:1-29

Six years ago, today, as nearly as possible at this very hour of the day, I was "in the gall of bitterness and in the bond of iniquity," but had yet, by divine grace, been led to feel the bitterness of that bondage, and to cry out by reason of the soreness of its slavery. Seeking rest, and finding none, I stepped within the house of God, and sat there, afraid to look upward, lest I should be utterly cut off, and lest his fierce wrath should consume me. The minister rose in his pulpit, and, as I have done this morning, read this text—"Look unto me, and be ye saved, all the ends of the earth: for I am God, and there is none else." I looked that moment; the grace of faith was vouchsafed to me in the self-same instant; and now I think I can say with truth:

"E'er since by faith I saw the stream His flowing wounds supply,
Redeeming love has been my theme, And shall be till I die."

I shall never forget that day, while memory holds its place; nor can I help repeating this text, whenever I remember that hour when first I knew the Lord. How strangely gracious! How wonderfully and marvellously kind, that he who heard these words so little time ago for his own soul's profit, should now address you from the same text, in the full and confident hope that some poor sinner may hear the glad tidings of salvation for himself also, and may today, on this 6th of January, be "turned from darkness to light, and from the power of Satan unto God."

FOR MEDITATION: Even if you cannot pinpoint an exact time or place, can you recall your conversion when the Lord Jesus Christ became real to you and you trusted him to be your Saviour? If you can, are the memories of that great event still as precious as they should be? If you have no such memories, Spurgeon, though dead, speaks to you today. Read again his testimony, obey his text and look to his Saviour so that you too may be saved.

SERMON NO. 60

The immutability of God

"I am the Lord, I change not; therefore ye sons of Jacob are not consumed"
Malachi 3: 6

SUGGESTED FURTHER READING: Romans 11: 33-12: 2

It has been said by some that "the proper study of mankind is man." I will not oppose the idea, but I believe it is equally true that the proper study of God's elect is God; the proper study of a Christian is the Godhead. The highest science, the loftiest speculation, the mightiest philosophy, which can ever engage the attention of a child of God, is the name, the nature, the person, the work, the doings and the existence of the great God whom he calls his Father. There is something exceedingly improving to the mind in a contemplation of the Divinity. It is a subject so vast, that all our thoughts are lost in its immensity; so deep that our pride is drowned in its infinity. Other subjects we can compass and grapple with; in them we feel a kind of self-content, and go our way with the thought, "Behold I am wise." But when we come to this master-science, finding that our plumb-line cannot sound its depth, and that our eagle eye cannot see its height, we turn away with the thought, that vain man would be wise, but he is like a wild ass's colt; and with the solemn exclamation, "I am but of yesterday, and know nothing." No subject of contemplation will tend more to humble the mind, than thoughts of God. We shall be obliged to feel:

"Great God, how infinite art thou,
What worthless worms are we!"

But while the subject humbles the mind it also expands it. He who often thinks of God, will have a larger mind than the man who simply plods around this narrow globe.

FOR MEDITATION: "In the beginning God" (Genesis 1: 1) could well describe these opening sentences of Spurgeon's "New Park Street Pulpit". But who or what comes first in our thoughts and lives?

SERMON NO. 1

The King's highway opened and cleared

"And they said, Believe on the Lord Jesus Christ, and thou shalt be saved, and thy house." Acts 16: 31

SUGGESTED FURTHER READING: Matthew 16: 21-23

I remember a certain narrow and crooked lane in a certain country town, along which I was walking one day while I was seeking the Saviour. On a sudden the most fearful oaths that any of you can conceive rushed through my heart. I put my hand to my mouth to prevent the utterance. I had not, that I know of, ever heard those words; and I am certain that I had never used in my life from my youth up so much as one of them, for I had never been profane. But these things sorely beset me; for half an hour together the most fearful imprecations would dash through my brain. Oh, how I groaned and cried before God! That temptation passed away; but before many days it was renewed again; and when I was in prayer, or when I was reading the Bible, these blasphemous thoughts would pour in upon me more than at any other time. I consulted with an aged godly man about it. He said to me, "Oh, all this many of the people of God have proved before you. But," said he, "do you hate these thoughts?" "I do," I truly said. "Then," said he, "they are not yours; serve them as the old parishes used to do with vagrants—whip them and send them on to their own parish. So," said he, "do with them. Groan over them, repent of them, and send them on to the devil, the father of them, to whom they belong—for they are not yours." Do you not recollect how John Bunyan hits off the picture? He says, when Christian was going through the Valley of the Shadow of Death, that one stepped up softly to him, and whispered blasphemous thoughts into his ear, so that poor Christian thought they were his own thoughts; but they were not his thoughts at all, but the injections of a blasphemous spirit.

FOR MEDITATION: The Lord Jesus Christ heard things that were temptations to him, but he always resisted them and never sinned. As long as we hate and resist them, temptations remain temptations only—they become sins only when we enjoy them and give in to them.

SERMON NO. 293

Free grace

"Not for your sakes do I this, saith the Lord God, be it known unto you: be ashamed and confounded for your own ways, O house of Israel."
Ezekiel 36: 32
SUGGESTED FURTHER READING: 1 Timothy 1: 12-17

My God! I have rebelled against thee, and yet thou hast loved me, unworthy me! How can it be? I cannot lift myself up with pride, I must bow down before thee in speechless gratitude. Remember, my dear brethren, that not only is the mercy which you and I have received undeserved, but it was unasked. It is true you sought for mercy, but not till mercy first sought you. It is true you prayed, but not till free grace made you pray. You would have been still today hardened in heart, without God, and without Christ, had not free grace saved you. Can you be proud then?—proud of mercy which, if I may use the term, has been forced upon you?—proud of grace which has been given you against your will, until your will was changed by sovereign grace? And think again—all the mercy you have you once refused. Christ sups with you; be not proud of his company. Remember, there was a day when he knocked, and you refused—when he came to the door and said, "My head is wet with dew, and my locks with the drops of the night; open to me, my beloved;" and you barred it in his face, and would not let him enter. Be not proud, then of what you have, when you remember that you once rejected him. Does God embrace you in his arms of love? Remember, once you lifted up your hand of rebellion against him. Is your name written in his book? Ah! there was a time when, if it had been in your power, you would have erased the sacred lines that contained your own salvation. Can we, dare we, lift up our wicked heads with pride, when all these things should make us hang our heads down in the deepest humility?

FOR MEDITATION: Whatever we have become or achieved in the Christian life must always be attributed to God's grace and directed to his glory. The apostle Paul needed no reminder (1 Corinthians 15: 10).

Paul's sermon before Felix

"And as he reasoned of righteousness, temperance, and judgment to come, Felix trembled, and answered, Go thy way for this time; when I have a convenient season, I will call for thee." Acts 24: 25

SUGGESTED FURTHER READING: Acts 17: 30-18: 1

Felix, unhappy Felix! why is it that thou dost rise from thy judgment-seat? Is it that thou hast much business to do? Stop, Felix; let Paul speak to thee a minute longer. Thou hast business; but hast thou no business for thy soul? Stop, unhappy man! Art thou about again to be extortionate, again to make thy personal riches greater? Oh! stop: canst thou not spare another minute for thy poor soul? It is to live for ever: hast thou nought laid up for it—no hope in heaven, no blood of Christ, no pardon of sin, no sanctifying Spirit, no imputed righteousness? Ah! man, there will be a time when the business that seems so important to thee will prove to have been but a day-dream, a poor substitute for the solid realities thou hast forgotten. Dost thou reply, "Nay, the king has sent me an urgent commission; I must attend to Caesar." Ah! Felix, but thou has a greater monarch than Caesar, there is one who is Emperor of heaven and Lord of earth: canst thou spare no time to attend to his commands? Before his presence Caesar is but a worm. Man! wilt thou obey the one, and wilt thou despise the other? Ah! no; I know what thou durst not say. Felix, thou art turning aside again to indulge in thy lascivious pleasures. Go, and Drusilla with thee! But stop! Darest thou do that, with that last word ringing in thy ears, "Judgment to come?" What! Wilt thou repeat that wanton dalliance that hath damned thee already, and wilt thou go again to stain thy hands in lust, and doubly damn thy spirit, after warnings heard and felt? O man! I could weep o'er thee.

FOR MEDITATION: When you hear the Word of God preached, do you get impatient for the sermon to finish and forget about it as soon as you can? That can be a very dangerous habit. We need to act upon it there and then—receive, remember, repent (Revelation 3: 3; Luke 8: 18).

The war of truth

"And Moses said unto Joshua, Choose us out men, and go out, fight with Amalek: tomorrow I will stand on the top of the hill with the rod of God in mine hand." Exodus 17: 9
SUGGESTED FURTHER READING: 2 Timothy 2: 1-7

There are many things that should make you valiant for God and for his truth. The first thing I will bring to your remembrance is the fact, that this warfare in which you are engaged is an hereditary warfare; it is not one which you began, but it is one which has been handed to you from the moment when the blood of Abel cried aloud for vengeance. Each martyr that has died has passed the blood-red flag to the next, and he in his turn has passed it on to another. Every confessor who has been nailed to the stake to burn, has lit his candle, and handed it to another, and said, "Take care of that!" And now here is the old "sword of the Lord and of Gideon." Remember what hands have handled the hilt; remember what arms have wielded it; remember how often it has "pierced to the dividing asunder of the joints and marrow." Will you disgrace it? There is the great banner: it has waved in many a breeze; long ere the flag of this our land was made, this flag of Christ was borne aloft. Will you stain it? Will you not hand it to your children, still unsullied, and say, "Go on, go on; we leave you the heritage of war; go on, and conquer. What your fathers did, do you again, still keep up the war, till time shall end." I love my Bible because it is a Bible baptized with blood; I love it all the better, because it has the blood of Tyndale on it; I love it, because it has on it the blood of John Bradford, and Rowland Taylor, and Hooper; I love it, because it is stained with blood.

FOR MEDITATION: The Christian faith does not change with the course of time; we are still to contend for the truth (Jude 3). The church today has no right to insult the memory of the martyrs by making friends with unbiblical teaching which they bravely opposed with their lives.

The bed and its covering

"For the bed is shorter than that a man can stretch himself on it: and the covering narrower than he can wrap himself in it." Isaiah 28: 20
SUGGESTED FURTHER READING: Hebrews 4: 3-10

What a glorious thing, it is to be a Christian, to have faith in Christ. Come my soul, take thy rest, the great High Priest has full atonement made. Thou hast much good laid up, not for many years, but for eternity; take thine ease; eat spiritual things; drink wine on the lees and be merry; for it cannot be said of thee, "tomorrow thou shalt die," for thou shalt never die, for "thy life is hid with Christ in God." Thou art no fool to take thy ease and rest, for this is legitimate ease and rest, the rest which the God of Sabaoth hath provided for all his people. And then, O Christian! march boldly to the river of death, march calmly up to the throne of judgment, enter placidly and joyfully into the inheritance of thy Lord, for thou hast about thee an armour that can keep thee from the arrows of death, a wedding garment that makes thee fit to sit down at the banquet of the Lord. Thou hast about thee a royal robe that makes thee a fit companion even for Jesus, the King of kings, when he shall admit thee into his secret chambers, and permit thee to hold holy and close fellowship with him. I cannot resist quoting that verse of the hymn:

"With his spotless vesture on,
Holy as the Holy One."

That is the sum and substance of it all. And on this bed let us take our rest, and during this week let us make Christ's work our only garment, and we shall find it long enough, and broad enough, for us to wrap ourselves up in it.

FOR MEDITATION: The Christian's sufficiency is not his own but comes from God (2 Corinthians 3: 5).

Portraits of Christ

"For whom he did foreknow, he also did predestinate to be conformed to the image of his Son." Romans 8: 29
SUGGESTED FURTHER READING: 1 John 2: 28-3:5

That image is so perfect I can never reach it. It is high as heaven, what can I know? It surpasses my thoughts, I cannot conceive the ideal, how, then, can I reach the fact? If I were to be like David I might hope it; if I were to be made like Josiah, or some of the ancient saints, I might think it possible; but to be like Christ, who is without spot or blemish, and the chief among ten thousand, and altogether lovely, I cannot hope it. I look, sir; I look, and look, and look again, till I turn away, tears filling my eyes, and I say, "Oh, it is presumption for such a fallen worm as I, to hope to be like Christ." And did you know it, that while you were thus speaking, you were really getting the thing you thought to be impossible? Or did you know that, while you were gazing on Christ, you were using the only means which can be used to effect the divine purpose? And when you bowed before that image overawed, do you know it was because you began to be made like it? When I come to love the image of Christ, it is because I have some measure of likeness to it. It was said of Cicero's works, if any man could read them with admiration, he must be in a degree an orator himself. And if any man can read the life of Christ, and really love it, methinks there must be somewhat—however little—that is Christ-like within himself. And if you as believers will look much at Christ, you will grow like him; you shall be transformed from glory to glory as by the image of the Lord.

FOR MEDITATION: Getting to know Christ now is the process by which the Christian will become like Christ in the future. (Philippians 3: 8,10,20,21). We may say "Such knowledge is too wonderful for me; it is high, I cannot attain unto it." (Psalm 139: 6), but the image of Christ in the believer is no more impossible to God than the conception of Christ in a virgin (Luke 1: 37).

SERMON NO. 355

The sin of unbelief

"And that lord answered the man of God, and said, Now, behold, if the Lord should make windows in heaven, might such a thing be? And he said, Behold, thou shalt see it with thine eyes, but shalt not eat thereof."
2 Kings 7: 19
SUGGESTED FURTHER READING: John 20: 24-29

"Thou shalt shall see it with thine eyes, but shalt not eat thereof." It is so often with God's own saints. When they are unbelieving, they see the mercy with their eyes, but do not eat it. Now, here is corn in this land of Egypt, but there are some of God's saints who come here on the Sabbath, and say, "I do not know whether the Lord will be with me or not." Some of them say, "Well, the gospel is preached, but I do not know whether it will be successful." They are always doubting and fearing. Listen to them when they get out of the chapel. "Well, did you get a good meal this morning?" "Nothing for me." Of course not. Ye could see it with your eyes, but did not eat it, because you had no faith. If you had come up with faith, you would have had a morsel. I have found Christians, who have grown so very critical, that if the whole portion of the meat they are to have, in due season, is not cut up exactly into square pieces, and put upon some choice dish of porcelain, they cannot eat it. Then they ought to go without, until they are brought to their appetites. They will have some affliction, which will act like quinine upon them: they will be made to eat by means of bitters in their mouths; they will be put in prison for a day or two until their appetite returns, and then they will be glad to eat the most ordinary food, off the most common platter, or no platter at all. But the real reason why God's people do not feed under a gospel ministry, is because they have not faith. If you believed, if you heard only one promise, that would be enough.

FOR MEDITATION: The unbeliever needs to hear in order to believe (Romans 10:14); the believer needs to believe in order to hear.

A home question

"But are there not with you, even with you, sins against the Lord your God?" 2 Chronicles 28: 10

SUGGESTED FURTHER READING: Matthew 7: 1-5

Tell him that his sins deserve the wrath of hell. Make him feel that it is an awful thing to fall into the hands of our God, for he is a consuming fire. Then throw him down on a bed of spikes, and make him sleep there if he can. Roll him on the spikes, and tell him that bad as he is, he is worse by nature than by practice. Make him feel that the leprosy lies deep within. Give him no rest. Treat him as cruelly as he could treat another. It would only be his deserts. But who is this that I am telling you to treat so? Yourself, my hearer, yourself. Be as severe as you can, but let the culprit be yourself. Put on the wig, and sit upon the judgment-seat. Read the king's commission. There is such a commission for you to be a judge. It says— Judge thyself—though it says judge not others. Put on, I say, your robes; sit up there Lord Chief Justice of the Isle of Man, and then bring up the culprit. Make him stand at the bar. Accuse him; plead against him; condemn him. Say: "Take him away, jailor." Find out the hardest punishment you can discover in the statute book, and believe that he deserves it all. Be as severe as ever you can on yourself, even to the putting on the black cap, and reading the sentence of death. When you have done this, you will be in a hopeful way for life, for he that condemns himself God absolves. He that stands self-convicted, may look to Christ hanging on the cross, and see himself hanging there, and see his sins for ever put away by the sacrifice of Jesus on the tree.

FOR MEDITATION: Does your heart condemn you before God? The Lord Jesus Christ is your defence lawyer, but only if you are trusting in him as your Saviour, and he can silence even the condemnation coming from your own heart (1 John 2: 1; 3: 19-23).

Corn in Egypt

"Now when Jacob saw that there was corn in Egypt, Jacob said unto his sons, Why do ye look one upon another? And he said, Behold, I have heard that there is corn in Egypt: get you down thither, and buy for us from thence; that we may live, and not die." Genesis 42: 1,2
SUGGESTED FURTHER READING: Matthew 13: 24-34

God in his wisdom has made the outward world, so that it is a strange and wonderful picture of the inner world. Nature has an analogy with grace. The wonders that God does in the heart of man, each of them finds a parallel, a picture, a metaphor, an illustration, in the wonders which God performs in providence. It is the duty of the minister always to look for these analogies. Our Saviour did so. He is the model preacher: his preaching was made up of parables, pictures from the outer world, accommodated to teach great and mighty truths. And so is man's mind constituted, that we can always see a thing better through a picture than in any other way. If you tell a man a simple truth, he does not see it nearly so well as if you told it to him in an illustration. If I should attempt to describe the flight of a soul from sin to Christ, you would not see it one half so readily as if I should picture John Bunyan's pilgrim running out of the city of destruction, with his fingers in his ears, and hastening with all his might to the wicket gate. There is something tangible in a picture, a something which our poor flesh and blood can lay hold of; and therefore the mind, grasping through the flesh and the blood, is able to understand the idea, and to appropriate it. Hence the necessity and usefulness of the minister always endeavouring to illustrate his sermon, and to make his discourse as much as possible like the parables of Jesus Christ.

FOR MEDITATION: How observant are you? The world around us is always teaching us lessons and underlining the truths of God's Word (Matthew 6: 26-30; Mark 13: 28,29; Romans 1: 20; 1 Corinthians 11: 14,15).

SERMON NO. 234

Search the Scriptures

"To the law and to the testimony: if they speak not according to this word, it is because there is no light in them." Isaiah 8: 20
SUGGESTED FURTHER READING: Acts 17: 10-15

I teach that all men by nature are lost by Adam's fall. See whether that is true or not. I hold that men have so gone astray that no man either will or can come to Christ except the Father draw him. If I am wrong, find me out. I believe that God, before all worlds, chose to himself a people, whom no man can number, for whom the Saviour died, to whom the Holy Spirit is given, and who will infallibly be saved. You may dislike that doctrine; I do not care: see if it is not in the Bible. See if it does not there declare that we are "elect according to the foreknowledge of God the Father," and so on. I believe that every child of God must assuredly be brought by converting grace from the ruins of the fall, and must assuredly be "kept by the power of God, through faith, unto salvation," beyond the hazard of ever totally falling away. If I am wrong there, get your Bibles out, and refute me in your own houses. I hold it to be a fact that every man who is converted will lead a holy life, and yet at the same time will put no dependence on his holy life, but trust only in the blood and righteousness of Jesus Christ. And I hold, that every man that believes, is in duty bound to be immersed. I hold the baptism of infants to be a lie and a heresy; but I claim for that great ordinance of God, Believer's Baptism, that it should have the examination of Scripture. I hold, that to none but believers may immersion be given, and that all believers are in duty bound to be immersed. If I am wrong, well and good; do not believe me; but if I am right, obey the Word with reverence. I will have no error, even upon a point which some men think to be unimportant; for a grain of truth is a diamond, and a grain of error may be of serious consequence to us, to our injury and hurt. I hold, then, that none but believers have any right to the Lord's Supper; that it is wrong to offer the Lord's Supper indiscriminately to all, and that none but Christians have a right either to the doctrines, the benefits, or the ordinances of God's house. If these things are not so, condemn me as you please; but if the Bible is with me, your condemnation is of no avail.

FOR MEDITATION: This is how to use these daily readings—according to the Bible, Spurgeon must have made some mistakes (James 3: 1,2).

SERMON NO. 172

Confession of sin – a sermon with seven texts

"I have sinned." Exodus 9: 27; Numbers 22: 34; 1 Samuel 15: 24; Joshua 7: 20; Matthew 27: 4; Job 7: 20; Luke 15: 18.
SUGGESTED FURTHER READING: Psalm 51

Unless there be a true and hearty confession of our sins to God, we have no promise that we shall find mercy through the blood of the Redeemer. "Whoso confesseth (his sins) and forsaketh them shall have mercy." But there is no promise in the Bible to the man who will not confess his sins. Yet, as upon every point of Scripture there is a liability of being deceived, so more especially in the matter of confession of sin. There are many who make a confession, and a confession before God, who notwithstanding receive no blessing, because their confession has not in it certain marks which are required by God to prove it genuine and sincere, and which demonstrate it to be the work of the Holy Spirit.

THE HARDENED SINNER – PHARAOH. It is of no use for you to say, "I have sinned," merely under the influence of terror, and then to forget it afterwards.

THE DOUBLE-MINDED MAN—BALAAM. It is idle and useless for you to say, "I have sinned," unless you mean it from your heart.

THE INSINCERE MAN—SAUL. To say, "I have sinned," in an unmeaning manner, is worse than worthless, for it is a mockery of God thus to confess with insincerity of heart.

THE DOUBTFUL PENITENT—ACHAN. The most we can say is, that we hope their souls are saved at last, but indeed we cannot tell.

THE REPENTANCE OF DESPAIR—JUDAS. If you have such a repentance as that, it will be a warning to generations yet to come.

THE REPENTANCE OF THE SAINT—JOB. This is the repentance of the man who is a child of God already, an acceptable repentance before God.

THE BLESSED CONFESSION—THE PRODIGAL. Here is that which proves a man to be a regenerate character – "Father, I have sinned."

FOR MEDITATION: All have sinned. (Romans 3: 23) "Thou art the man" (2 Samuel 12: 7); but which one?

SERMON NO. 113

The beatific vision

"We shall see him as he is." 1 John 3: 2
SUGGESTED FURTHER READING: 1 Peter 1: 3-9

Not think about him, and dream about him; but we shall positively "see him as he is." How different that sight of him will be from that which we have here. For here we see him by reflection. Now, I have told you before, we see Christ "through a glass darkly;" then we shall see him face to face. Good Doctor John Owen, in one of his books, explains this passage, "Here we see through a glass darkly;" and he says that means, "Here we look through a telescope, and we see Christ only darkly through it." But the good man had forgotten that telescopes were not invented till hundreds of years after Paul wrote; so that Paul could not have intended telescopes. Others have tried to give other meanings to the word. The fact is, glass was never used to see through at that time. They used glass to see by, but not to see through. The only glass they had for seeing was a glass mirror. They had some glass which was no brighter than our black common bottle-glass. "Here we see through a glass darkly." That means, by means of a mirror. As I have told you, Jesus is represented in the Bible; there is his portrait; we look on the Bible, and we see it. We see him "through a glass darkly." Just as sometimes, when you are looking in your looking glass, you see somebody going along in the street. You do not see the person; you only see him reflected. Now, we see Christ reflected; but then we shall not see him in the looking-glass; we shall positively see his person. Not the reflected Christ, not Christ in the sanctuary, not the mere Christ shining out of the Bible, not Christ reflected from the sacred pulpit; but "we shall see him as he is."

FOR MEDITATION: The sight of Jesus will distress many (Revelation 1: 7); are you positively looking forward to seeing him (John 12: 21)?

Words of expostulation

"And now what hast thou to do in the way of Egypt, to drink the waters of Sihor? or what hast thou to do in the way of Assyria, to drink the waters of the river?" Jeremiah 2: 18
SUGGESTED FURTHER READING: 2 Corinthians 6: 14 -7: 1

In the life of Madame Guyon, who, though professedly a Papist, one must ever receive as being a true child of God, I have read an anecdote something to this effect. She had been invited by some friends to spend a few days at the palace of St. Cloud. She knew it was a place full of pomp, and fashion, and, I must add, of vice also; but being over-persuaded by her friend, and being especially tempted with the idea that perhaps her example might do good, she accepted the invitation. Her experience afterwards should be a warning to all Christians. For some years that holy woman had walked in constant fellowship with Christ; perhaps none ever saw the Saviour's face, and kissed his wounds more truly than she had done. But when she came home from St. Cloud, she found her usual joy was departed; she had lost her power in prayer; she could not draw near to Christ as she should have done. She felt in going to the lover of her soul as if she had played the harlot against him. She was afraid to hope that she could be received again to his pure and perfect love, and it took some months before the equilibrium of her peace could be restored, and her heart could yet again be wholly set upon her Lord. He that wears a white garment must mind where he walks when the world's streets are as filthy as they are. He that has a thousand enemies must take care how he shows himself. He that has nothing on earth to assist him towards heaven should take care that he does not go where the world can help towards hell. O believer, keep clear of fellowship with this world, for the love of this world is enmity against God.

FOR MEDITATION: Commonsense should tell us that when something clean and something unclean brush against one another, the unclean object is not improved but the clean object is changed for the worse (Haggai 2: 11-14).

The personality of the Holy Spirit

"And I will pray the Father, and he shall give you another Comforter, that he may abide with you for ever: Even the Spirit of truth; whom the world cannot receive, because it seeth him not, neither knoweth him: but ye know him: for he dwelleth with you, and shall be in you." John 14: 16,17
SUGGESTED FURTHER READING: Acts 2: 32-39

Observe here, that each person is spoken of as performing a separate office. "I will pray," says the Son—that is intercession. "I will send," says the Father—that is donation. "I will comfort," says the Holy Spirit—that is supernatural influence. Oh! if it were possible for us to see the three persons of the Godhead, we should behold one of them standing before the throne with outstretched hands crying day and night, "O Lord, how long?" We should see one girt with Urim and Thummim, precious stones, on which are written the twelve names of the tribes of Israel; we should behold him crying unto his Father, "Forget not thy promises, forget not thy covenant;" we should hear him make mention of our sorrows, and tell forth our griefs on our behalf, for he is our intercessor. And if we could behold the Father, we should not see him a listless and idle spectator of the intercession of the Son, but we should see him with attentive ear listening to every word of Jesus, and granting every petition. Where is the Holy Spirit all the while? Is he lying idle? Oh, no; he is floating over the earth, and when he sees a weary soul, he says, "Come to Jesus, he will give you rest." When he beholds an eye filled with tears, he wipes away the tears, and bids the mourner look for comfort on the cross. When he sees the tempest-tossed believer, he takes the helm of his soul and speaks the word of consolation; he helps the broken in heart, and binds up their wounds; and ever on his mission of mercy, he flies around the world, being everywhere present. Behold how the three persons work together.

FOR MEDITATION: Salvation is all of God—the work is all done by him. And yet he grants to believers the privilege of being co-opted as his fellow-workers to advertise the gospel on his behalf (2 Corinthians 5: 18-6: 1).

SERMON NO. 4

The treasure of grace

"The forgiveness of sins, according to the riches of his grace." Ephesians 1:7
<small>SUGGESTED FURTHER READING:</small> 1 Corinthians 15: 5-11

Paul proclaimed the grace of God—free, full, sovereign, eternal grace—beyond all the glorious company of the apostles. Sometimes he soared to such amazing heights, or dived into unsearchable depths, that even Peter could not follow him. He was ready to confess that "our beloved brother Paul, according to the wisdom given unto him," had written "some things hard to be understood." Jude could write of the judgments of God, and reprove with terrible words, "ungodly men, who turned the grace of God into lasciviousness." But he could not tell out the purpose of grace as it was planned in the eternal mind, or the experience of grace as it is felt and realized in the human heart, like Paul. There is James again: he, as a faithful minister, could deal very closely with the practical evidences of Christian character. And yet he seems to keep very much on the surface; he does not bore down deep into the substratum on which must rest the visible soil of all spiritual graces. Even John, most favoured of all those apostles who were companions of our Lord on earth—sweetly as the beloved disciple writes of fellowship with the Father and his Son Jesus Christ—even John does not speak of grace so richly as Paul, in whom God first showed forth "all long-suffering as a pattern to them which should hereafter believe on him to life everlasting." Not, indeed, that we are at liberty to prefer one apostle above another. We may not divide the Church, saying, I am of Paul, I of Peter, I of Apollos; but we may acknowledge the instrument which God was pleased to use; we may admire the way in which the Holy Ghost fitted him for his work; we may, with the churches of Judea, glorify God in Paul.

<small>FOR MEDITATION:</small> Paul always looked back with amazement when he recalled God's grace to him, the chief of sinners, who so persecuted the Church (1 Corinthians 15: 9-10; Galatians 1: 13,15; Ephesians 3: 7,8; 1 Timothy 1: 13-15). Our gratitude and love to God can sadly be limited by our failure to realise how sinful we really are and how much he has forgiven us (Luke 7: 41-47).

The fainting warrior

"O wretched man that I am! Who shall deliver me from the body of this death? I thank God through Jesus Christ our Lord." Romans 7: 24,25
SUGGESTED FURTHER READING: Galatians 2: 1-13

It is Paul the apostle, who was not less than the very greatest of the apostles—it is Paul, the mighty servant of God, a very prince in Israel, one of the King's mighty men—it is Paul, the saint and the apostle, who here exclaims, "O wretched man that I am!" Now, humble Christians are often the dupes of a very foolish error. They look up to certain advanced saints and able ministers, and they say, "Surely, such men as these do not suffer as I do; they do not contend with the same evil passions as those which vex and trouble me." Ah! if they knew the hearts of those men, if they could read their inward conflicts, they would soon discover that the nearer a man lives to God, the more intensely has he to mourn over his own evil heart, and the more his Master honours him in his service, the more also does the evil of the flesh vex and tease him day by day. Perhaps, this error is more natural, as it is certainly more common, with regard to apostolic saints. We have been in the habit of saying, Saint Paul, and Saint John, as if they were more saints than any other of the children of God. They are all saints whom God has called by his grace, and sanctified by his Spirit; but somehow we very foolishly put the apostles and the early saints into another list, and do not venture to look on them as common mortals. We look upon them as some extraordinary beings, who could not be men of like passions with ourselves. We are told in Scripture that our Saviour was "tempted in all points like as we are;" and yet we fall into the serious error of imagining that the apostles, who were far inferior to the Lord Jesus, escaped these temptations, and were ignorant of these conflicts.

FOR MEDITATION: Are there Christians—missionaries perhaps—to whom you look up in the wrong way? These deserve your respect, but they need your prayers, not your pedestals. They surely feel their own weakness and very probably look up to their own Christian heroes! The apostles knew their own and one another's weaknesses and pointed away from themselves to their God (Acts 14: 15).

SERMON NO. 235

The death of Christ

"Yet it pleased the Lord to bruise him; he hath put him to grief: when thou shalt make his soul an offering for sin, he shall see his seed, he shall prolong his days, and the pleasure of the Lord shall prosper in his hand."
Isaiah 53: 10
SUGGESTED FURTHER READING: Acts 4: 23-31

He who reads the Bible with the eye of faith, desiring to discover its hidden secrets, sees something more in the Saviour's death than Roman cruelty or Jewish malice: he sees the solemn decree of God fulfilled by men, who were the ignorant, but guilty instruments of its accomplishment. He looks beyond the Roman spear and nail, beyond the Jewish taunt and jeer, up to the sacred fount, whence all things flow, and traces the crucifixion of Christ to the breast of deity. He believes with Peter—"Him, being delivered by the determinate counsel and foreknowledge of God, ye have taken, and by wicked hands have crucified and slain." We dare not impute to God the sin, but at the same time the fact, with all its marvellous effects in the world's redemption, we must ever trace to the sacred fountain of divine love. So does our prophet. He says, "It pleased Jehovah to bruise him." He overlooks both Pilate and Herod, and traces it to the heavenly Father, the first person in the divine trinity. "It pleased the Lord to bruise him; he hath put him to grief." Now, beloved, there be many who think that God the Father is at best but an indifferent spectator of salvation. Others belie him still more. They look upon him as an unloving, severe being, who had no love to the human race, and could only be made loving by the death and agonies of our Saviour. Now, this is a foul libel upon the fair and glorious grace of God the Father, to whom for ever be honour: for Jesus Christ did not die to make God loving, but he died because God was loving.

> " 'Twas not to make Jehovah's love
> Towards his people flame,
> That Jesus from the throne above,
> A suff'ring man became.

> 'Twas not the death which he endured,
> Nor all the pangs he bore,
> That God's eternal love procured,
> For God was love before."

FOR MEDITATION: Who so loved the world that he gave his only begotten Son (John 3:16)?

SERMON NO. 173

Preaching for the poor

"The poor have the gospel preached to them." Matthew 11: 5
SUGGESTED FURTHER READING: Amos 7: 10-17

There was a tinker once, who never so much as brushed his back against the walls of a college, who wrote a Pilgrim's Progress. Did ever a doctor in divinity write such a book? There was a pot-boy once—a boy who carried on his back the pewter pots for his mother, who kept the Old Bell. That man drove men mad, as the world had it, but led them to Christ, as we have it, all his life long, until, loaded with honours, he sank into his grave, with the good will of a multitude round about him, with an imperishable name written in the world's records, as well as in the records of the church. Did you ever hear of any mighty man, whose name stood in more esteem among God's people than the name of George Whitefield? And yet these were poor men, who, as Wycliffe said, were taking to the preaching of the gospel. If you will read the life of Wycliffe, you will find him saying there, that he believed that the Reformation in England was more promoted by the labours of the poor men whom he sent out from Lutterworth than by his own. He gathered around him a number of the poor people whom he instructed in the faith, and then he sent them two and two into every village, as Jesus did. They went into the market-place, and they gathered the people around; they opened the book and read a chapter, and then they left them a manuscript of it, which for months and years after the people would assemble to read, and would remember the gospellers that had come to tell them the gospel of Christ. These men went from market-place to market-place, from town to town, and from village to village, and though their names are unknown to fame, they were the real reformers.

FOR MEDITATION: Wycliffe's translation of the text was "Poor men are taking to the preaching of the gospel." A small percentage of Christians would be regarded as great in worldly terms (1 Corinthians 1: 27)—only a tiny fraction of preachers would be so described. Are your preachers suitably honoured and supported by your church (1 Corinthians 9: 11; Galatians 6: 6; 1 Timothy 5: 17,18)?

SERMON NO. 114

Marvellous increase of the church

"Who are these that fly as a cloud, and as the doves to their windows?"
Isaiah 60: 8
SUGGESTED FURTHER READING: Matthew 10: 5-16

They were not doves by nature; they were ravens; but they are doves now. They are changed from ravens into doves, from lions into lambs. Beloved, it is very easy for you to pretend to be the children of God; but it is not easy for you to be so. The old fable of the jackdaw dressed up in peacock's feathers often takes place now. Many a time have we seen coming to our church, a fine strutting fellow, with long feathers of prayer behind him. He could pray gloriously; and he has come strutting in, with all his majesty and pride, and said, "Surely I must come; I have everything about me; am I not rich and polite: have I not learning and talent?" In a very little while we have found him to be nothing but an old prattling jackdaw, having none of the true feathers belonging to him; by some accident one of his borrowed feathers has dropped out, and we have found him to be a hypocrite. I beseech you, do not be hypocrites. The glory of the gospel is not that it paints ravens white, and whitewashes blackbirds, but that it turns them into doves. It is the glory of our religion not that it makes a man seem what he is not, but that it makes him something else. It takes the raven and turns him into a dove; his ravenish heart becomes a dove's heart. It is not the feathers that are changed, but the man himself. Glorious gospel, which takes a lion, and does not cut the lion's mane off, and then cover him with a sheep's skin, but makes him into a lamb! O church of God! these that have come like doves to their windows are trophies of regenerating grace, which has transformed them, and made them as new creatures in Christ Jesus.

FOR MEDITATION: We should expect to be among wolves in the world, but beware of them when they are in the church, undetected and unconverted (Matthew 7: 15).

SERMON NO. 63

The Christ of Patmos

"... one like unto the Son of man,... His head and his hairs were white like wool, as white as snow... And when I saw him, I fell at his feet as dead."
Revelation 1: 12-18
SUGGESTED FURTHER READING: Matthew 22: 41-46

"His head and his hairs were white like wool, as white as snow." When the Church described him in the Canticles she said "His locks are bushy and black as a raven's." How do we understand this apparent discrepancy? My brethren, the Church in the Canticles looked forward, she looked forward to days and ages that were to come, and she perceived his perpetual youth; she pictured him as one who would never grow old, whose hair would ever have the blackness of youth. And do we not bless God that her view of him was true? We can say of Jesus, "Thou hast the dew of thy youth;" but the Church of to-day looks backward to his work as complete; we see him now as the ancient of eternal days. We believe that he is not the Christ of 1800 years ago merely, but, before the day-star knew its place, he was one with the Eternal Father. When we see in the picture his head and his hair white as snow, we understand the antiquity of his reign. "In the beginning was the Word, and the Word was with God, and the Word was God." When all these things were not, when the old mountains had not lifted their hoary heads into the clouds, when the yet more hoary sea had never roared in tempest; ere the lamps of heaven had been lit, when God dwelt alone in his immensity, and the unnavigated waves of ether, if there were such, had never been fanned by the wings of seraphim, and the solemnity of silence had never been startled by the song of cherubim, Jesus was of old in eternity with God. We know how he was despised and rejected of men, but we understand, too, what he meant when he said, "Before Abraham was, I am." We know how he who died, when but a little more than thirty years of age, was verily the Father of the everlasting ages, having neither beginning of days nor end of years.

FOR MEDITATION: Glory in the paradoxes of Christ—seen as old, yet young; God and man; A.D. yet B.C.; David's Son, yet David's Lord; a Shepherd, yet a Lamb; the Master, yet a Servant; the Great High Priest, yet the Sacrifice; the Immortal who died and rose again!

The kingly priesthood of the saints

"And hast made us unto our God kings and priests: and we shall reign on the earth." Revelation 5: 10
SUGGESTED FURTHER READING: Mark 14: 32-42

Jesus said, "I will take the cup of salvation;" and he did take it—the cup of our deliverance. Bitter were its drops; gall lay in its depths; there were groans, and sighs, and tears, within the red mixture; but he took it all, and drank it to its dregs, and swallowed all the awful draught. All was gone. He drank the cup of salvation, and he ate the bread of affliction. See him, as he drinks the cup in Gethsemane, when the fluid of that cup did mingle with his blood, and make each drop a scalding poison. Mark how the hot feet of pain did travel down his veins. See how each nerve is twisted and contorted with his agony. Behold his brow covered with sweat; witness the agonies as they follow each other into the very depths of his soul. Speak, you lost, and tell what hell's torment means; but you cannot tell what the torments of Gethsemane were. Oh! the deep unutterable! There was a depth which couched beneath, when our Redeemer bowed his head, when he placed himself between the upper and nether millstones of his Father's vengeance, and when his whole soul was ground to powder. Ah! that wrestling God-man—that suffering man of Gethsemane! Weep o'er, saints—weep o'er him; when you see him rising from that prayer in the garden, marching forth to his cross; when you picture him hanging on his cross four long hours in the scorching sun, overwhelmed by his Father's passing wrath—when you see his side streaming with gore—when ye hear his death-shriek, "It is finished,"—and see his lips all parched, and moistened by nothing save the vinegar and the gall,—ah! then prostrate yourselves before that cross, bow down before that sufferer, and say, "Thou hast made us—thou hast made us what we are; we are nothing without thee."

FOR MEDITATION: Creating us could not have been easier for God—it took just a word. (Genesis 1: 26,27). Making us right with himself could not have given him more trouble. The work of salvation was terribly hard for the Lord Jesus Christ, but he completed it. It would have been absolutely impossible for us.

SERMON NO. 10

A revival sermon

"Behold, the days come, saith the Lord, that the plowman shall overtake the reaper, and the treader of grapes him that soweth seed; and the mountains shall drop sweet wine, and all the hills shall melt." Amos 9: 13
SUGGESTED FURTHER READING: Psalm 44

Pharaoh's dream has been enacted again in the last century. About a hundred years ago, if I may look back in my dream, I might have seen seven ears of corn upon one stalk, firm and strong; anon, the time of plenty went away, and I have seen, and you have seen, in your lifetime, the seven ears of corn thin and withered in the east wind. The seven ears of withered corn have eaten up and devoured the seven ears of fat corn, and there has been a sore famine in the land. Lo, I see in Whitefield's time, seven bullocks coming up from the river, fat and well-favoured, and since then we have lived to see seven lean kine come up from the same river; and lo! the seven lean kine have eaten up the seven fat kine, yet have they been none the better for all that they have eaten. We read of such marvellous revivals a hundred years ago, that the music of their news has not ceased to ring in our ears; but we have seen alas, a season of lethargy, of soul-poverty among the saints, and of neglect among the ministers of God. The product of the seven years has been utterly consumed, and the Church has been none the better. Now, I take it, however, we are about to see the seven fat years again. God is about to send times of surprising fertility to his Church. When a sermon has been preached in these modern times, if one sinner has been converted by it, we have rejoiced with a suspicious joy; for we have thought it something amazing. But, brethren, where we have seen one converted, we may yet see hundreds; where the Word of God has been powerful in scores, it shall be blessed to thousands.

FOR MEDITATION: The prayer of Habakkuk during a period of lean years (Habakkuk 3: 2). Will you join him in prayer?

SERMON NO. 296

The shameful sufferer

"Who for the joy that was set before him endured the cross, despising the shame, and is set down at the right hand of the throne of God."
Hebrews 12: 2
SUGGESTED FURTHER READING: Luke 9: 18-22, 51-53

You have an enemy who all his life long has been your enemy. His father was your enemy, and he is your enemy too. There is never a day passes but you try to win his friendship; but he spits upon your kindness, and curses your name. He does injury to your friends, and there is not a stone he leaves unturned to do you damage. As you are going home to-day, you see a house on fire; the flames are raging, and the smoke is ascending up in one black column to heaven. Crowds gather in the street, and you are told there is a man in the upper chamber who must be burnt to death. No one can save him. You say, "Why that is my enemy's house;" and you see him at the window. It is your own enemy—the very man; he is about to be burnt. Full of lovingkindness, you say, "I will save that man if I can." He sees you approach the house; he puts his head from the window and curses you. "An everlasting blast upon you!" he says; "I would rather perish than that you should save me." Do you imagine yourself, then, dashing through the smoke, and climbing the blazing staircase to save him; and can you conceive that when you get near him he struggles with you, and tries to roll you in the flames? Can you conceive your love to be so potent, that you can perish in the flames rather than leave him to be burned? You say, "I could not do it; it is above flesh and blood to do it." But Jesus did it. We hated him, we despised him, and, when he came to save us, we rejected him. When his Holy Spirit comes into our hearts to strive with us, we resist him; but he will save us; nay, he himself braved the fire that he might snatch us as brands from eternal burning.

FOR MEDITATION: The wonderful determination of Christ and his insistence on carrying out his Father's will despite all the attempts to distract him (Matthew 16: 21-23; 26: 51-54; Luke 13: 31-33).

SERMON NO. 236

The two talents

"He also that had received two talents came and said, Lord, thou deliveredst unto me two talents: behold, I have gained two other talents beside them. His lord said unto him, Well done, good and faithful servant; thou hast been faithful over a few things, I will make thee ruler over many things: enter thou into the joy of thy Lord." Matthew 25: 22-23
SUGGESTED FURTHER READING: 1 Chronicles 29: 1-17

If by divine grace—(and it is only by divine grace that this can ever be accomplished)—our two talents be rightly used, the fact that we did not have five, will be no injury to us. You say, when such a man dies, who stood in the midst of the church, a triumphant warrior for the truth, the angels will crowd to heaven's gates to see him, for he has been a mighty hero, and done much for his Master. A Calvin or a Luther, with what plaudits shall they be received!—men with talents, who have been faithful to their trust. Yes, but know ye not, that there is many a humble village pastor whose flock scarcely numbers fifty, who toils for them as for his life, who spends hours in praying for their welfare, who uses all the little ability he has in his endeavour to win them to Christ; and do ye imagine that his entry into heaven shall be less triumphant than the entry of such a man as Luther? If so, ye know not how God dealeth with his people. He giveth them rewards, not according to the greatness of the goods with which they were entrusted, but according to their fidelity thereunto, and he that hath been faithful in the least, shall be as much rewarded, as he that hath been faithful in much. I want you briefly to turn to the chapter to see this. You will note first, that the man with two talents came to his Lord with as great a confidence as the man that had five. "And he said, Lord, thou deliveredst unto me two talents; behold, I have gained two talents beside them."

FOR MEDITATION: These words, spoken exactly 34 years before the day on which Spurgeon died, remind us not to covet the gifts of a Spurgeon. Our concern, as believers, should not be how much we have got from God, but how much we gladly use whatever we have got for God (1 Corinthians 4: 2; 2 Corinthians 8: 12).

SERMON NO. 175

Why are men saved?

"Nevertheless he saved them for his name's sake." Psalm 106: 8
SUGGESTED FURTHER READING: 1 Peter 1: 1,2

Jesus Christ is the Saviour; but not more so than God the Father, or God the Holy Spirit. Some persons who are ignorant of the system of divine truth think of God the Father as being a great being full of wrath, and anger, and justice, but having no love, they think of God the Spirit perhaps as a mere influence proceeding from the Father and the Son. Now, nothing can be more incorrect than such opinions. It is true the Son redeems me, but then the Father gave the Son to die for me, and the Father chose me in the everlasting election of his grace. The Father blots out my sin; the Father accepts me and adopts me into his family through Christ. The Son could not save without the Father any more than the Father without the Son; and as for the Holy Spirit, if the Son redeems, do you not know that the Holy Spirit regenerates? It is he that makes us new creatures in Christ, who "begets us again unto a lively hope," who purifies our soul, who sanctifies our spirit, and who, at last, presents us spotless and faultless before the throne of the Most High, accepted in the beloved. When you say, "Saviour," remember there is a Trinity in that word—the Father, the Son, and the Holy Spirit, this Saviour being three persons under one name. You cannot be saved by the Son without the Father, nor by the Father without the Son, nor by Father and Son without the Spirit. But as they are one in creation, so are they one in salvation, working together in one God for our salvation, and unto that God be glory everlasting, world without end. Amen.

FOR MEDITATION: We are to be baptised in the name of the Father and of the Son and of the Holy Spirit (Matthew 28: 19) in acknowledgement of the fact that all three persons of the Trinity have accomplished our salvation.

The enchanted ground

"Therefore let us not sleep, as do others; but let us watch and be sober."
1 Thessalonians 5: 6
SUGGESTED FURTHER READING: Matthew 26: 31-47

You never read that Christian went to sleep when lions were in the way; he never slept when he was going through the river of death, or when he was in Giant Despair's castle, or when he was fighting with Apollyon. Poor creature! He almost wished he could sleep then. But when he had got half way up the Hill Difficulty, and came to a pretty little arbour, in he went, and sat down and began to read his roll. Oh, how he rested himself! How he unstrapped his sandals and rubbed his weary feet! Very soon his mouth was open, his arms hung down, and he was fast asleep. Again the Enchanted Ground was a very easy smooth place, and liable to send the pilgrim to sleep. You remember Bunyan's description of some of the arbours: "Then they came to an arbour, warm, and promising much refreshing to the weary pilgrims; for it was finely wrought above head, beautified with greens, and furnished with benches and settles. It had also in it a soft couch, where the weary might lean." "The arbour was called the Slothful's Friend, and was made on purpose to allure, if it might be, some of the pilgrims to take up their rest there when weary." Depend upon it, it is in easy places that men shut their eyes and wander into the dreamy land of forgetfulness. Old Erskine said a good thing when he remarked: "I like a roaring devil better than a sleeping devil." There is no temptation half so bad as not being tempted. The distressed soul does not sleep; it is after we get into confidence and full assurance that we are in danger of slumbering.

FOR MEDITATION: What would have happened to the disciples in Gethsemane if Christ had not woken them up? Are you oblivious to spiritual danger even when God warns you in his Word (Revelation 3: 2,3)?

The earnest of heaven

"That holy Spirit of promise, which is the earnest of our inheritance."
Ephesians 1:13-14
SUGGESTED FURTHER READING: 1 Corinthians 2:6-16

You remember the day, some of you, when you first learned the doctrines of grace. When we were first converted, we did not know much about them, we did not know whether God had converted us, or we had converted ourselves; but we heard a discourse one day in which some sentences were used, which gave us the clue to the whole system, and we began at once to see how God the Father planned, and God the Son carried out, and God the Holy Spirit applied, and we found ourselves suddenly brought into the midst of a system of truths, which we might perhaps have believed before, but which we could not have clearly stated, and did not understand. Well, the joy of that advance in knowledge was exceeding great. I know it was to me. I can remember well the day and hour, when first I received those truths in my own soul—when they were burnt into me, as John Bunyan says—burnt as with a hot iron into my soul; and I can recollect how I felt I had grown suddenly from a babe into a man—that I had made progress in Scriptural knowledge, from having got a hold once and for all of the clue to the truth of God. Well, now, in that moment when God the Holy Spirit increased your knowledge, and opened the eyes of your understanding, you had the earnest, that you shall one day see, not through a glass darkly, but face to face, and then you shall know the whole truth, even as you are known.

FOR MEDITATION: The best teacher and interpreter of Scripture is God the Holy Spirit who moved chosen men to record his Word (2 Peter 1:20-21). Do you always seek his help when you are reading or studying God's Word?

SERMON NO. 358

Sweet comfort for feeble saints

"A bruised reed shall he not break, and smoking flax shall he not quench, till he send forth judgment unto victory." Matthew 12: 20
SUGGESTED FURTHER READING: 1 John 2: 12-14

Man of business, toiling and striving in this world, he will not quench you when you are like smoking flax; he will not break you when you are like the bruised reed, but will deliver you from your troubles, you shall swim across the sea of life, and stand on the happy shore of heaven, and shall sing, "Victory" through him that loved you. Young people! I speak to you, and have a right to do so. You and I often know what the bruised reed is, when the hand of God blights our fair hopes. We are full of giddiness and waywardness, it is only the rod of affliction that can bring folly out of us, for we have much of it in us. Slippery paths are the paths of youth, and dangerous are the ways of the young, but God will not break or destroy us. Men, by their overcaution, bid us never tread a step lest we fall; but God bids us go, and makes our feet like hind's feet, that we may tread upon high places. Serve God in early days; give your hearts to him, and then he will never cast you out, but will nourish and cherish you. Let me not finish without saying a word to little children. You who have heard of Jesus, he says to you, "The bruised reed I will not break; the smoking flax I will not quench." I believe there is many a little prattler, not six years old, who knows the Saviour. I never despise youthful piety; I love it. I have heard little children talk of mysteries that grey-headed men knew not. Ah! little children who have been brought up in Sabbath-schools, and love the Saviour's name, if others say you are too forward, do not fear, love Christ still.

FOR MEDITATION: God will bring down those who are proud before him, but he will raise up those who are aware of and willing to admit to him their weakness (Luke 1: 50-53).

Mr Evil Questioning tried and executed

"Are not Abana and Pharpar, rivers of Damascus, better than all the waters of Israel? may I not wash in them, and be clean?" 2 Kings 5: 12
SUGGESTED FURTHER READING: Mark 12: 18-27

Mr Evil Questioning often boasts that he is the child of Human Reason; but I will let you know a secret or two about his parentage. Mr Human Reason was once a very respectable man. He had a country-seat in the garden of Paradise, and he was then great and honourable. He served his God with all his might, and many a great and marvellous thing did he discover for the good of mankind; at that time he had a family, and they were all like himself, right good and loyal. But after the fall this man married again, and he took to himself one called Sin to be his partner, and this old Evil Questioning was one that was born after the fall. He does not belong to the first family at all. The first family was not so numerous as the last. There was one called Right Judgment born at that time. I hope he is still alive, and I believe he is. But the second family was very black and of tainted blood. They did not take at all after the father, except in one point, that at the time of the fall Mr Human Reason lost his country-seat at Paradise, and together with the rest of the servants of Adam fell from his high estate and became perverted and depraved. His children are like him in their depravity, but not in their power of reasoning. They take after their mother, and they always have a predilection for sin, so that they "put darkness for light and light for darkness, bitter for sweet and sweet for bitter." The old gentleman never mentions his mother's name if he can help it. He always likes to boast that he is a lineal descendant of Human Reason, and so indeed he is, but he is a descendant of fallen Human Reason, not of Human Reason as it was in its glorious perfection. Now, all the powers of Adam were by the fall spoiled and ruined.

FOR MEDITATION: Always beware of human philosophies and traditions (Colossians 2: 8).

SERMON NOS. 297-298

Hypocrisy

"Beware ye of the leaven of the Pharisees, which is hypocrisy." Luke 12: 1
SUGGESTED FURTHER READING: Matthew 23: 23-28

Some people I know of are like inns, which have an angel hanging outside for a sign, but they have a devil within for a landlord. There are many men of that kind; they take good care to have an excellent sign hanging out; they must be known by all men to be strictly religious; but within, which is the all-important matter, they are full of wickedness. But I have sometimes heard persons mistake this matter. They say, "Ah! well, poor man, he is a sad drunkard, certainly, but he is a very good-hearted man at bottom." Now, as Rowland Hill used to say, that is a most astonishing thing for any man to say of another, that he was bad at top and good at bottom. When men take their fruit to market they cannot make their customers believe, if they see rotten apples at the top, that there are good ones at the bottom. A man's outward conduct is generally a little better than his heart. Very few men sell better goods than they put in the window. Therefore, do not misunderstand me. When I say we must attend more to the inward than the outward, I would not have you leave the outward to itself. "Make clean the outside of the cup and platter"—make it as clean as you can, but take care also that the inward is made clean. Look to that first. Ask yourself such questions as these— "Have I been born again? Am I passed from darkness to light? Have I been brought out of the realms of Satan into the kingdom of God's dear Son? Do I live by private communion near to the side of Jesus? Can I say that my heart panteth after the Lord, even as the hart does after the water-brooks?"

FOR MEDITATION: A true work of God both starts on the inside and shows on the outside (Philippians 2: 12-13). The Christian is one who is "inside out"; the hypocrite is only "out".

The prodigal's return

"But when he was yet a great way off, his father saw him and had compassion, and ran, and fell on his neck, and kissed him." Luke 15: 20
SUGGESTED FURTHER READING: John 3: 16-21

When the light of God's grace comes into your heart, it is something like the opening of the windows of an old cellar that has been shut up for many days. Down in that cellar, which has not been opened for many months, are all kinds of loathsome creatures, and a few sickly plants blanched by the darkness. The walls are dark and damp with the trail of slugs and snails; it is a horrid filthy place into which no one would willingly enter. You may walk there in the dark very securely, and except now and then for the touch of some slimy creature, you would not believe the place was so bad and filthy. Open those shutters, clean a pane of glass, let a little light in, and now see how a thousand noxious things have made this place their habitation. It was not the light that made this place so horrible, but it was the light that showed how horrible it was before. So let God's grace just open a window and let the light into a man's soul, and he will stand astonished to see at what a distance he is from God. Yes, sir, today you think yourself second to none but the Eternal; you fancy that you can approach his throne with steady step; it is but a little that you have to do to be saved; you imagine that you can accomplish it at any hour, and save yourself upon your dying bed as well as now. Ah! sir, if you could be made to be in appearance what you are in reality, then you would see that you are far enough from God even now, and so far from him that unless the arms of his grace were stretched out to bring you to himself; you must perish in your sin.

FOR MEDITATION: Even the believer has sins of which he is ignorant (Psalm 19: 12). God knows all about them. Thank him that he came in the person of his only-begotten Son to meet us when we were far off and to bring us back to himself (Ephesians 2: 13).

SERMON NO. 176

Secret sins

"Cleanse thou me from secret faults." Psalm 19: 12
SUGGESTED FURTHER READING: 2 Kings 5: 15-27

You do not think there is any evil in a thing unless somebody sees it, do you? You feel that it is a very great sin if your master finds you out in robbing the till—but there is no sin if he should not discover it—none at all. And you, sir, you fancy it to be very great sin to play a trick in trade, in case you should be discovered and brought before the court; but to play a trick and never be discovered, that is all fair—do not say a word about it. "Mr Spurgeon, it is all business; you must not touch business; tricks that are not discovered, of course you are not to find fault with them." The common measure of sin is the notoriety of it. But I do not believe in that. A sin is a sin, whether done in private or before the wide world. It is singular how men will measure guilt. A railway servant puts up a wrong signal, there is an accident; the man is tried, and severely reprimanded. The day before he put up the wrong signal, but there was no accident, and therefore no one accused him for his neglect. But it was just the same, accident or no accident, the accident did not make the guilt, it was the deed which made the guilt, not the notoriety nor yet the consequence of it. It was his business to have taken care—and he was as guilty the first time as he was the second, for he negligently exposed the lives of men. Do not measure sin by what other people say of it; but measure sin by what God says of it, and what your own conscience says of it. Now, I hold that secret sin, if anything, is the worst of sin; because secret sin implies that the man who commits it has atheism in his heart.

FOR MEDITATION: "Be sure your sin will find you out" (Numbers 32: 23)— one day God is going to reveal the secrets of men (Romans 2: 16). There is a world of difference between being truly sorry for our sin itself and just feeling sorry for ourselves when we get found out (Hebrews 12: 17).

Lions lacking – but the children satisfied

"The young lions do lack, and suffer hunger: but they that seek the Lord shall not want any good thing." Psalm 34: 10
SUGGESTED FURTHER READING: Matthew 7: 7-11

We take it concerning things spiritual. Are we wanting a sense of pardon? We shall not want it long. Are we desiring stronger faith? We shall not want it long. Do you wish to have more love to your Saviour, to understand more concerning inward communion with Jesus? You shall have it. "They that seek the Lord shall not want any good thing." Do you desire to renounce your sins, to be able to overcome this corruption or that, to attain this virtue, or that excellency? "They that seek the Lord shall not want any good thing." Is it adoption, justification, sanctification that you want? "You shall not lack any good thing." But are your wants temporal? Do you want bread and water? No, I know you do not, for it is said, "Bread shall be given, and water shall be sure." Or, if you do want it somewhat, it shall come before long; it shall not be to starvation. David said, "I have been young, and now am old; yet I have not seen the righteous forsaken, nor his seed begging bread." Do you want clothes? You shall have them. "He that clothes the lilies of the valley, will he not much more clothe you, O ye of little faith?" Do you need temporary supplies? You shall receive them, for "your heavenly Father knoweth that ye have need of these things." Whatever your desire, there is the promise, only go and plead it at the throne, and God will fulfil it. We have no right to look for the fulfilment of the promises unless we put the Promiser in mind of them, although truly, at times, he exceeds our desires or wishes.

FOR MEDITATION: A true seeking of God will mould our desires to the things which we need and which please him—as such he cannot but answer when we call (Psalm 37: 3-5).

The Tabernacle—without the camp

"And Moses took the tabernacle, and pitched it without the camp, afar off from the camp, and called it the Tabernacle of the congregation. And it came to pass, that every one which sought the Lord went out unto the tabernacle of the congregation, which was without the camp." Exodus 33:7
SUGGESTED FURTHER READING: Hebrews 13:9-16

This going out of the camp will involve much inconvenience. Some try to get over the inconvenience in the way Joshua did, they think they will come out of the camp altogether and live in the tabernacle, and then there will be no difficulty. You know there are many pious minds, a little over-heated with imagination, who think, that if they have never mixed with the world they could be holy. No doubt they would like to have a building erected, in which they could live, and pray, and sing all day, and never go to business, nor have anything at all to do with buying and selling. Thus they think by going without the camp they should become the people of God. In this however, they mistake the aim and object of the Christian religion—"I pray not that thou shouldest take them out of the world, but that thou shouldest keep them from the evil." That were an easy, lazy subterfuge, for getting rid of the hard task of having to fight for Christ. To go out of the battle in order that you may win the victory, is a strange method indeed of seeking to become "more than conquerors!" No, no, we must be prepared, like Moses, to go into the camp and to come out of it; always to come out of it when we seek fellowship with God, but still to be in it; to be mixed up with it, to be in the midst of it doing the common acts of man, and yet never being tainted by its infection, and never having the spirit troubled by that sin and evil which is so rampant there. I counsel you, not that you should come out of the world, but that being in it, you should be so distinctly not of it, that all men may see that you worship the Father outside the camp of their common association and their carnal worship.

FOR MEDITATION: As in everything the Lord Jesus Christ is our perfect example—not of the world, but most certainly in it (John 17: 14-18), separate from sinners (Hebrews 7: 26) and yet able to be called the friend of sinners (Luke 7: 34 and 15: 2).

SERMON NO. 359

Christ crucified

"But we preach Christ crucified, unto the Jews a stumblingblock, and unto the Greeks foolishness; But unto them which are called, both Jews and Greeks, Christ the power of God, and the wisdom of God."
1 Corinthians 1: 23,24
SUGGESTED FURTHER READING: Galatians 1: 1-9

I do not believe it is preaching Christ and him crucified, to give our people a batch of philosophy every Sunday morning and evening, and neglect the truth of this Holy Book. I do not believe it is preaching Christ and him crucified, to leave out the main cardinal doctrines of the Word of God, and preach a religion which is all a mist and a haze, without any definite truths whatever. I take it that a man does not preach Christ and him crucified, who can get through a sermon without mentioning Christ's name once; nor does that man preach Christ and him crucified who leaves out the Holy Spirit's work, who never says a word about the Holy Ghost, so that indeed the hearers might say, "We do not so much know whether there be a Holy Ghost." And I have my own private opinion that there is no such thing as preaching Christ and him crucified, unless you preach what nowadays is called Calvinism. I have my own ideas, and those I always state boldly. It is a nickname to call it Calvinism; Calvinism is the gospel, and nothing else. I do not believe we can preach the gospel, if we do not preach justification by faith, without works; nor unless we preach the sovereignty of God in his dispensation of grace; nor unless we exalt the electing, unchangeable, eternal, immutable, conquering, love of Jehovah; nor do I think we can preach the gospel, unless we base it upon the peculiar redemption which Christ made for his elect and chosen people; nor can I comprehend a gospel which lets saints fall away after they are called, and suffers the children of God to be burned in the fires of damnation after having believed. Such a gospel I abhor. The gospel of the Bible is not such a gospel as that.

FOR MEDITATION: To "know nothing among you except Jesus Christ and him crucified" (1 Corinthians 2: 2) may sound very limited. In fact it is a vast and glorious subject upon which everything else should be based and for which God should be given all the glory (1 Corinthians 1: 30,31).

SERMON NOS. 7/8

Sin immeasurable

"Who can understand his errors?" Psalm 19: 12
SUGGESTED FURTHER READING: Matthew 5: 21-30

With every commandment—the bare letter is nothing, compared with the whole stupendous meaning and severe strictness of the rule. The commandments, if I may so speak, are like the stars. When seen with the naked eye, they appear to be brilliant points; if we could draw near to them, we should see them to be infinite worlds, greater than even our sun, stupendous though it is. So is it with the law of God. It seems to be but a luminous point, because we see it at a distance, but when we come nearer where Christ stood, and estimate the law as he saw it, then we find it is vast, immeasurable. "Thy commandment is exceeding broad." Think then for a moment of the spirituality of the law, its extent and strictness. The law of Moses condemns for offence, without hope of pardon, and sin, like a millstone, is bound around the sinner's neck, and he is cast into the depths. Moreover, the law deals with sins of thought,—the imagination of evil is sin. The transit of sin across the heart, leaves the stain of impurity behind it. This law, too, extends to every act,—tracks us to our bed-chamber, goes with us to our house of prayer, and if it discovers so much as the least sign of wavering from the strict path of integrity, it condemns us. When we think of the law of God we may well be overwhelmed with horror, and sit down and say, "God be merciful to me, for to keep this law is utterly beyond power; even to know the fulness of its meaning is not within finite capacity. Therefore, great God, cleanse us from our secret faults—save us by thy grace, for by the law we never can be saved."

FOR MEDITATION: "All that the Lord has spoken we will do." (Exodus 19: 8)—we should admire the spirit of the Israelites, but not their self-confidence. Only one slip-up spells condemnation (Galatians 3: 10; James 2: 10). Praise God for his Son who came to fulfil the law perfectly (Matthew 5: 17) and then to die in our place to save us from the curse of the law (Galatians 3: 13).

SERMON NO. 299

Reform

"Now when all this was finished, all Israel that were present went out to the cities of Judah, and brake the images in pieces, and cut down the groves, and threw down the high places and the altars out of all Judah and Benjamin, in Ephraim also and Manasseh, until they had utterly destroyed them all." 2 Chronicles 31: 1
SUGGESTED FURTHER READING: Ecclesiastes 12: 9-12

There are many books that are to be so esteemed by the Christian man, that they must be cut down like the groves of trees, not because they are bad in themselves, but because there false gods are worshipped. Novel-reading is the rage of the present day. I go to a railway bookstall, and I cannot see a book that I can read, I get one, and it is all trash. I search to find something that would be really valuable, but I am told, "It would not sell here." The fact is, nothing will sell but that which is light, and frothy, and frivolous; so every traveller is compelled to consume such food as that, unless he carry something better with him. Do I, therefore, say, that the Christian man must condemn all reading of fiction and novels? No, I do not, but I do say, that the mass of popular books published under the name of light literature, is to be eschewed and cut down, for the simple reason that the moral of it is not that of piety and goodness; the tendency of the reading is not to bring the Christian towards heaven, but rather to retard and impede him in his good course. I lift up my axe against many a work that I cannot condemn, if I look at it abstractedly in itself, but which must come down, because I recollect how much of my own precious time I wasted in such trivial reading, how many years in which I might have had fellowship with Christ have been cast away, whilst I have been foolishly indulging a vicious taste for the romantic and the frivolous. No, there are many things which are not wrong in themselves, but which nevertheless must be given up by the true Christian, because they have had, and do have association with things positively wrong. Just as these groves must be cut down—not because there can be a sin in trees, but because the trees have been associated with the worship of idols.

FOR MEDITATION: 1 Corinthians 10: 23. "The best book to read is the Bible … It will help you on your way".

God, the all-seeing One

"Hell and destruction are before the Lord: how much more then the hearts of the children of men?" Proverbs 15: 11
SUGGESTED FURTHER READING: Jeremiah 17: 9,10

God knows the heart so well that he is said to 'search' it. We all understand the figure of a search. There is a search-warrant out against some man who is supposed to be harbouring a traitor in his house. The officer goes into the lower room, opens the door of every cupboard, looks into every closet, peers into every cranny, takes the key, descends into the cellar, turns over the coals, disturbs the wood, lest anyone should be hidden there. Up stairs he goes: there is an old room that has not been opened for years,—it is opened. There is a huge chest: the lock is forced and it is broken open. The very top of the house is searched, lest upon the slates or upon the tiles some one should be concealed. At last, when the search has been complete, the officer says, "It is impossible that there can be anybody here, for, from the tiles to the foundation, I have searched the house thoroughly; I know the very spiders well, for I have seen the house completely." Now, it is just so God knows our heart. He searches it—searches into every nook, corner, crevice and secret part; and the figure of the Lord is pushed further still. "The candle of the Lord," we are told, "searches the inward parts of the belly." As when we wish to find something, we take a candle, and look down upon the ground with great care, and turn up the dust. If it is some little piece of money we desire to find, we light a candle and sweep the house, and search diligently till we find it. Even so it is with God. He searches Jerusalem with candles, and pulls everything to daylight. No partial search, like that of Laban, when he went into Rachel's tent to look for his idols. She put them in the camel's furniture and sat upon them; but God looks into the camel's furniture, and all.

FOR MEDITATION: God does not need a search-warrant or a torch to search your heart (Hebrews 4: 13). What does he see there?

Distinguishing grace

"For who maketh thee to differ from another?" 1 Corinthians 4: 7
SUGGESTED FURTHER READING: Luke 22: 31-34

If thou leave me, Lord, for a moment, I am utterly undone.

"Leave, ah! leave me not alone, Still support and comfort me."

Let Abraham be deserted by his God, he equivocates and denies his wife. Let Noah be deserted, he becomes a drunkard, and is naked to his shame. Let Lot be left awhile, and, filled with wine, he revels in incestuous embraces, and the fruit of his body becomes a testimony to his disgrace. Nay, let David, the man after God's own heart, be left, and Uriah's wife shall soon show the world that the man after God's own heart still has an evil heart of unbelief in departing from the living God. Oh! the poet puts it well -

"Methinks I hear my Saviour say, 'Wilt thou forsake me too?'"

And now let our conscience answer:-

"Ah, Lord! with such a heart as mine,
Unless thou hold me fast,
I feel I must, I shall decline,
And prove like them at last."

Oh be not rashly self-confident, Christian man. Be as confident as you can in your God, but be distrustful of yourself. You may yet become all that is vile and vicious, unless sovereign grace prevent and keep you to the end. But remember if you have been preserved, the crown of your keeping belongs to the Shepherd of Israel, and you know who that is. For he has said "I the Lord do keep it; I will water it every moment: lest any hurt it, I will keep it night and day." You know "who is able to keep you from falling, and to present you faultless before the presence of his glory with exceeding joy." Then give all glory to the King immortal, invisible, the only wise God your Saviour, who has kept you thus.

FOR MEDITATION: Those who think they can stand by themselves are taught by being allowed to fall by themselves (1 Corinthians 10: 12; Ecclesiastes 4: 10).

The resurrection of the dead

"There shall be a resurrection of the dead, both of the just and unjust."
Acts 24: 15
SUGGESTED FURTHER READING: 1 Corinthians 15: 35-44

There are some faint glimmerings in men of reason which teach that the soul is something so wonderful that it must endure for ever. But the resurrection of the dead is quite another doctrine, dealing not with the soul, but with the body. The doctrine is that this actual body in which I now exist is to live with my soul; that not only is the "vital spark of heavenly flame" to burn in heaven, but the very censer in which the incense of my life smokes is holy unto the Lord, and is to be preserved for ever. The spirit, every one confesses, is eternal; but how many there are who deny that the bodies of men will actually start up from their graves at the great day! Many of you believe you will have a body in heaven, but you think it will be an airy fantastic body, instead of believing that it will be a body like to this—flesh and blood (although not the same kind of flesh, for all flesh is not the same flesh), a solid, substantial body, even such as we have here. And there are yet fewer of you who believe that the wicked will have bodies in hell; for it is gaining ground everywhere that there are to be no positive torments for the damned in hell to affect their bodies, but that it is to be metaphorical fire, metaphorical brimstone, metaphorical chains, metaphorical torture. But if you were Christians as you profess to be, you would believe that every mortal man who ever existed shall not only live by the immortality of his soul, but his body shall live again, that the very flesh in which he now walks the earth is as eternal as the soul, and shall exist for ever. That is the peculiar doctrine of Christianity. The heathens never guessed or imagined such a thing.

FOR MEDITATION: Spurgeon went on to quote Job 19: 25,26; Psalm 16: 10; Isaiah 26: 19; Daniel 12: 2; Hosea 6: 1,2; Hebrews 11: 19,35. Does your hope match up to the hope of the Old Testament saints and the experience of Enoch and Elijah who rose bodily into heaven without suffering death?

None but Jesus

"He that believeth on him is not condemned." John 3: 18
SUGGESTED FURTHER READING: Acts 15: 5-11

When I stand at the foot of the cross, I do not believe in Christ because I have got good feelings, but I believe in him whether I have good feelings or not.

"Just as I am, without one plea,
But that Thy blood was shed for me,
And that Thou bidd'st me come to Thee,
O Lamb of God, I come."

Mr Roger, Mr Sheppard, Mr Flavell, and several excellent divines, in the Puritan age, and especially Richard Baxter, used to give descriptions of what a man must feel before he may dare to come to Christ. Now, I say in the language of good Mr Fenner, another of those divines, who said he was but a babe in grace when compared with them—"I dare to say it, that all this is not Scriptural. Sinners do feel these things before they come, but they do not come on the ground of having felt it; they come on the ground of being sinners, and on no other ground whatever." The gate of Mercy is opened, and over the door it is written, "This is a faithful saying and worthy of all acceptation, that Christ Jesus came into the world to save sinners." Between that word "save" and the next word "sinners," there is no adjective. It does not say, "penitent sinners," "awakened sinners," "sensible sinners," "grieving sinners," or "alarmed sinners." No, it only says, "sinners" and I know this, that when I come, I come to Christ today, for I feel it as much a necessity of my life to come to the cross of Christ today as it was to come ten years ago,—when I come to him, I dare not come as a conscious sinner or an awakened sinner, but I have to come still as a sinner with nothing in my hands.

FOR MEDITATION: We have no more right to complicate the Gospel than we have to water it down. Feelings are good and proper, but Satan can use them not only to give false assurance of salvation, but also to make sinners feel too bad to obey the Gospel and come to Christ.

SERMON NO. 361

Spiritual liberty

"Where the Spirit of the Lord is, there is liberty." 2 Corinthians 3: 17
SUGGESTED FURTHER READING: Isaiah 53: 1-6

Do you understand how it is that the very guilt of the sinner is taken away? Here I stand today a guilty and condemned traitor; Christ comes for my salvation, he bids me leave my cell. "I will stand where you are; I will be your substitute; I will be the sinner; all your guilt is to be imputed to me; I will die for it, I will suffer for it, I will have your sins." Then stripping himself of his robes, he says, "There, put them on; you shall be considered as if you were Christ; you shall be the righteous one. I will take your place, you take mine." Then he casts around me a glorious robe of perfect righteousness; and when I behold it, I exclaim, "Strangely, my soul, art thou arrayed", with my elder brother's garments on. Jesus Christ's crown is on my head, his spotless robes are round my loins, and his golden sandals are the shoes of my feet. And now is there any sin? The sin is on Christ; the righteousness is on me. Ask for the sinner, Justice! Let the voice of Justice cry, "Bring forth the sinner!" The sinner is brought. Who does the executioner lead forth? It is the incarnate Son of God. True, he did not commit the sin; he was without fault; but it is imputed to him: he stands in the sinner's place. Now justice cries, "Bring forth the righteous, the perfectly righteous." Whom do I see? Lo, the Church is brought; each believer is brought. Justice says, "Are these perfectly righteous?" "Yes they are. What Christ did is theirs; what they did is laid on Christ; his righteousness is theirs; their sins are his."

FOR MEDITATION: The substitutionary atonement of Christ (2 Corinthians 5: 21; 1 Peter 2: 24; 3: 18). Are you a beneficiary?

Spiritual peace

"Peace I leave with you, my peace I give unto you." John 14: 27
SUGGESTED FURTHER READING: Ephesians 2: 11-21

If you would maintain unbroken peace, take advice from God's minister this morning, young though he be in years. Take advice, which he can warrant to be good, for it is Scriptural. If you would keep your peace continual and unbroken, look always to the sacrifice of Christ; never permit your eye to turn to anything but Jesus. When you repent, my hearer, still keep your eye on the cross; when you labour, labour in the strength of the crucified One. Everything you do, whether it be self-examination, fasting, meditation, or prayer, do all under the shadow of Jesus' cross; or otherwise, no matter how you live, your peace will be but a sorry thing; you shall be full of disquiet and of sore trouble. Live near the cross and your peace shall be continual. Another piece of advice. Walk humbly with your God. Peace is a jewel; God puts it on your finger; be proud of it, and he will take it off again. Peace is a noble garment; boast of your dress, and God will take it away from you. Remember the hole of the pit whence you were digged, and the quarry of nature whence you were hewn; and when you have the bright crown of peace on your head, remember your black feet; nay, even when that crown is there, cover it and your face still with those two wings, the blood and right-eousness of Jesus Christ. In this way shall your peace be maintained. And again, walk in holiness, avoid every appearance of evil. "Be not conformed to this world." Stand up for truth and rectitude. Suffer not the maxims of men to sway your judgment. Seek the Holy Spirit that you may live like Christ, and live near to Christ, and your peace shall not be interrupted.

FOR MEDITATION: The Christian has permanent peace with God (Romans 5:1). The ruling peace of Christ in the heart is not supposed to be an optional extra (Colossians 3: 15).

The great reservoir

"Keep thy heart with all diligence; for out of it are the issues of life."
Proverbs 4: 23
SUGGESTED FURTHER READING: Matthew 12: 33-37

If I should vainly attempt to fashion my discourse after lofty models, I should this morning compare the human heart to the ancient city of Thebes, out of whose hundred gates multitudes of warriors were wont to march. As was the city such were her armies, as was her inward strength, such were they who came forth of her. I might then urge the necessity of keeping the heart, because it is the metropolis of our manhood, the citadel and armoury of our humanity. Let the chief fortress surrender to the enemy, and the occupation of the rest must be an easy task. Let the principal stronghold be possessed by evil, the whole land must be overrun thereby. Instead, however, of doing this, I shall attempt what possibly I may be able to perform, by a humble metaphor and a simple figure, which will be easily understood; I shall endeavour to set forth the wise man's doctrine, that our life issues from the heart, and thus I shall labour to show the absolute necessity of keeping the heart with all diligence. You have seen the great reservoirs provided by our water companies, from which the water which is to supply hundreds of streets and thousands of houses comes. Now, the heart is just the reservoir of man, and our life is allowed to flow in its proper season. That life may flow through different pipes—the mouth, the hand, the eye; but still all the issues of hand, of eye, of lip, derive their source from the great fountain and central reservoir, the heart; and hence there is no difficulty in showing the great necessity that exists for keeping the reservoir, the heart, in a proper state and condition, since otherwise that which flows through the pipes must be tainted and corrupt.

FOR MEDITATION: God is the only one who knows the natural wickedness of our hearts (Jeremiah 17: 9), the only one who can renew them (Ezekiel 36: 25-26) and the only one who can produce good from them (John 7: 38-39).

SERMON NO. 179

How to keep the heart

"The peace of God, which passeth all understanding, shall keep your hearts and minds through Christ Jesus." Philippians 4:7
SUGGESTED FURTHER READING: Mark 4: 35-41

Cast your troubles where you have cast your sins; you have cast your sins into the depth of the sea, there cast your troubles also. Never keep a trouble half an hour on your own mind before you tell it to God. As soon as the trouble comes, quick, the first thing, tell it to your Father. Remember, that the longer you take telling your trouble to God, the more your peace will be impaired. The longer the frost lasts, the more thick the ponds will be frozen. Your frost will last till you go to the sun; and when you go to God—the sun, then your frost will soon become a thaw, and your troubles will melt away. But do not be long, because the longer you are in waiting, the longer will your trouble be in thawing afterwards. Wait a long while till your trouble gets frozen thick and firm, and it will take many a day of prayer to get your trouble thawed again. Away to the throne as quick as ever you can. Do as the child did, when he ran and told his mother as soon as his little trouble happened to him; run and tell your Father the first moment you are in affliction. Do this in everything, in every little thing—"in everything by prayer and supplication" make known your wants unto God. Take your husband's headache, take your children's sicknesses, take all things, little family troubles as well as great commercial trials—take them all to God; pour them all out at once. And so by an obedient practice of this command in everything making known your wants unto God, you shall preserve that peace "which shall keep your heart and mind through Jesus Christ."

FOR MEDITATION: If the God of peace is with you (Philippians 4: 9), you have open access to the peace of God—but check carefully all the conditions in Philippians 4: 6.

SERMON NO. 180

The blood-shedding

"Without shedding of blood is no remission" Hebrews 9: 22
SUGGESTED FURTHER READING: John 6: 52-59

Here is a garden dark and gloomy; the ground is crisp with the cold frost of midnight; between those gloomy olive trees I see a man, I hear him groan out his life in prayer; hearken, angels, hearken, men, and wonder; it is the Saviour groaning out his soul! Come and see him. Behold his brow! O heavens! Drops of blood are streaming down his face, and from his body; every pore is open, and it sweats! but not the sweat of men that toil for bread; it is the sweat of one that toils for heaven—he sweats "great drops of blood!" That is the blood-shedding, without which there is no remission. Follow that man further; they have dragged him with sacrilegious hands from the place of his prayer and his agony, and they have taken him to the hall of Pilate; they mock him; a robe of purple is put on his shoulders in mockery; and mark his brow—they have put about it a crown of thorns, and the crimson drops of gore are rushing down his cheeks! Ye angels! the drops of blood are running down his cheeks! But turn aside that purple robe for a moment. His back is bleeding. Tell me, demons, who did this. They lift up the thongs, still dripping clots of gore; they scourge and tear his flesh, and make a river of blood to run down his shoulders! That is the shedding of blood without which there is no remission. Not yet have I done: they hurry him through the streets; they fling him on the ground; they nail his hands and feet to the transverse wood, they hoist it in the air, they dash it into its socket, it is fixed, and there he hangs the Christ of God. Blood from his head, blood from his hands, blood from his feet! In agony unknown he bleeds away his life; in terrible throes he exhausts his soul. "Eloi, Eloi, lama sabachthani." And then see! they pierce his side, and forthwith runneth out blood and water. This is the shedding of blood, sinners and saints; this is the awful shedding of blood, the terrible pouring out of blood, without which for you, and for the whole human race, there is no remission.

FOR MEDITATION: Even with the shedding of Christ's blood there is still no forgiveness of sins unless we eat his flesh and drink his blood (John 6: 53); that is by coming to him and trusting in him (John 6: 35).

SERMON NO. 118

A solemn warning for all churches

"Thou hast a few names even in Sardis which have not defiled their garments; and they shall walk with me in white: for they are worthy."
Revelation 3: 4
SUGGESTED FURTHER READING: John 14: 18-24

Do you meet with many men who hold communion with Christ? Though they may be godly men, upright men, ask them if they hold communion with Christ, and will they understand you? If you give them some of those sweetly spiritual books, that those who hold fellowship love to read, they will say they are mystical, and they do not love them. Ask them whether they can spend an hour in meditation upon Christ, whether they ever rise to heaven and lay their head on the breast of the Saviour, whether they ever know what it is to enter into rest and get into Canaan; whether they understand how he has raised us up together and made us sit together in heavenly places in Christ Jesus; whether they can often say,

"Abundant sweetness while I sing
Thy love, my ravish'd heart o'erflows;
Secure in thee my God and King
Of glory that no period knows."

Ask them that, and they will say, "We don't comprehend you." Now, the reason of it is in the first part of my sermon—they have defiled their garments, and therefore Christ will not walk with them. He says "Those that have not defiled their garments shall walk with me." Those who hold fast the truth, who take care to be free from the prevailing sins of the times, "These," he says, "shall walk with me; they shall be in constant fellowship with me; I will let them see that I am bone of their bone, and flesh of their flesh; I will bring them into the banqueting 'a house and the banner over them shall be love; they shall drink wine on the lees well refined; they shall have the secrets of the Lord revealed unto them, because they are the people who truly fear me: they shall walk with me in white."

FOR MEDITATION: Do you have to confess that you have no idea what Spurgeon is talking about? If so, he must be talking about you!

SERMON NO. 68

The glorious right hand of the Lord

"And the Lord said unto Moses, Is the Lord's hand waxed short? thou shalt see now whether my word shall come to pass unto thee or not." Numbers 11: 23

SUGGESTED FURTHER READING: Luke 12: 22-31

Which of his people have found the riches of his grace drained dry? Which of his children has had to mourn that the unsearchable riches of Christ had failed to supply his need? In grace, as well as in providence and nature, the unanimous verdict is that God is still Almighty, that he does as he wills, and fulfils all his promises and his counsels. How is it, then, that such a question as this ever came from the lips of God himself? Who suggested it? What suggested it? What could there have been that should lead him or any of his creatures to say, "Is the Lord's hand waxed short?" We answer, there is but one creature that God has made that ever doubts him. The little birds doubt not: though they have no barn nor field, yet they sweetly sing at night as they go to their roosts, though they know not where tomorrow's meal shall be found. The very cattle trust him; and even in days of drought, ye have seen them when they pant for thirst, how they expect the water; how the very first token of it makes them show in their very animal frame, by some dumb language, that they felt that God would not leave them to perish. The angels never doubt him, nor the devils either: devils believe and tremble. But it was left for man, the most favoured of all creatures, to mistrust his God. This high, this black, this infamous sin, of doubting the power and faithfulness of Jehovah, was reserved for the fallen race of rebellious Adam, and we alone, out of all the beings that God has ever fashioned, dishonour him by unbelief, and tarnish his honour by mistrust.

FOR MEDITATION: Man is good at taming and training animals (James 3: 7) but they still have a thing or two to teach him about God (2 Peter 2: 15-16; Luke 12: 24).

SERMON NO. 363

The people's Christ

"I have exalted one chosen out of the people." Psalm 89: 19
SUGGESTED FURTHER READING: Acts 1: 1-11

How exalted was he in his ascension! He went out from the city to the top of the hill, his disciples attending him while he waited the appointed moment. Mark his ascension! Bidding farewell to the whole circle, up he went gradually ascending, like the exaltation of a mist from the lake, or the cloud from the streaming river. Aloft he soared; by his own mighty buoyancy and elasticity he ascended up on high—not like Elijah, carried up by fiery horses; nor like Enoch of old, of whom it could be said he was not, for God took him. He went himself; and as he went, I think I see the angels looking down from heaven's battlements, and crying, "See the conquering hero comes!" while at his nearer approach again they shouted, "See the conquering hero comes!" So his journey through the plains of ether is complete—he nears the gates of heaven—attending angels shout, "Lift up your heads, ye everlasting gates; and be ye lift up, ye everlasting doors!" The glorious hosts within scarce ask the question, "Who is this king of glory?" when from ten thousand thousand tongues there rolls an ocean of harmony, beating in mighty waves of music on the pearly gates and opening them at once, "The Lord strong and mighty, the Lord mighty in battle." Lo! heaven's barriers are thrown wide open and cherubim are hastening to meet their monarch,

"They brought his chariot from afar,
To bear him to his throne;
Clapp'd their triumphant wings and said,
"The Saviour's work is done."

Behold he marches through the streets. See how kingdoms and powers fall down before him! Crowns are laid at his feet, and his Father says, "Well done, my Son, well done!" while heaven echoes with the shout, "Well done! Well done!" Up he climbs to that high throne, side by side with the Paternal Deity. "I have exalted one chosen out of the people."

FOR MEDITATION: Our ascended Lord Jesus Christ—his principal posture (he sits), his persistent pleading (he intercedes), his patient preparation (he waits to return)—Hebrews 10: 11-13.

SERMON NO. 11

A blast of the trumpet against false peace

"Peace, peace, when there is no peace." Jeremiah 6: 14
SUGGESTED FURTHER READING: 1 Corinthians 1: 18-25

Many of the people of London enjoy peace in their hearts, because they are ignorant of the things of God. It would positively alarm many of our sober orthodox Christians, if they could once have an idea of the utter ignorance of spiritual things that reigns throughout this land. Some of us, when moving about here and there, in all classes of society, have often been left to remark, that there is less known of the truths of religion than of any science, however obscure that science may be. Take as a lamentable instance, the ordinary effusions of the secular press, and who can avoid remarking the ignorance they manifest as to true religion. Let the papers speak on politics, it is a matter they understand, and their ability is astonishing; but, once let them touch religion, and our Sabbath-school children could convict them of entire ignorance. The statements they put forth are so crude, so remote from the fact, that we are led to imagine that the presentation of a fourpenny testament to special correspondents, should be one of the first efforts of our societies for spreading the gospel among the heathen. As to theology, some of our great writers seem to be as little versed in it as a horse or a cow. Go among all ranks and classes of men, and since the day we gave up our catechism, and old Dr Watts' and the Assemblies' ceased to be used, people have not a clear idea of what is meant by the gospel of Christ. I have frequently heard it asserted, by those who have judged the modern pulpit without severity, that if a man attended a course of thirteen lectures on geology, he would get a pretty clear idea of the system, but that you might hear not merely thirteen sermons, but thirteen hundred sermons and you would not have a clear idea of the system of divinity that was meant to be taught.

FOR MEDITATION: The unconverted by themselves cannot understand the truths of the Gospel when they hear them unless God enlightens them (1 Corinthians 2: 14; 2 Corinthians 4: 4). But there are parts of the country where they would find it very hard to hear the truths of the Gospel being preached (Amos 8: 11,12).

SERMON NO. 301

Prayer answered, love nourished

"I love the Lord, because he hath heard my voice and my supplication."
Psalm 116: 1
SUGGESTED FURTHER READING: Ephesians 6: 18-24

If a beggar comes to your house, and you give him alms, you will be greatly annoyed if within a month he shall come again; and if you then discover that he has made it a rule to wait upon you monthly for a contribution, you will say to him, "I gave you something once, but I did not mean to establish it as a rule." Suppose, however, that the beggar should be so impudent and impertinent that he should say, "But I intend sir, to wait upon you every morning and every evening," then you would say, "I intend to keep my gate locked that you shall not trouble me." And suppose he should then look you in the face and add still more, "Sir, I intend waiting upon you every hour, nor can I promise that I won't come to you sixty times in an hour; but I just vow and declare that as often as I want anything so often will I come to you: if I only have a wish I will come and tell it to you; the least thing and the greatest thing shall drive me to you; I will always be at the post of your door." You would soon be tired of such importunity as that, and wish the beggar anywhere, rather than that he should come and tease you so. Yet recollect, this is just what you have done to God, and he has never complained of you for doing it; but rather he has complained of you the other way. He has said, "Thou hast not called upon me, O Jacob." He has never murmured at the frequency of your prayers, but has complained that you have not come to him enough.

FOR MEDITATION: In his unchanging willingness and desire to hear his childrens' requests, God is unlike any person we know. Jesus had to teach this lesson by contrast, rather than by comparison (Luke 11: 5-13; 18: 1-8).

SERMON NO. 240

Particular redemption

"Even as the Son of man came not to be ministered unto, but to minister, and to give his life a ransom for many." Matthew 20: 28
SUGGESTED FURTHER READING: Matthew 27: 45-54

See the Saviour's limbs, how they quiver! Every bone has been put out of joint by the dashing of the cross into that socket! How he weeps! How he sighs! How he sobs! Indeed, how at last he shrieks in agony, "My God, my God, why hast thou forsaken me?" O sun, no wonder thou didst shut thine eye, and look no longer upon a deed so cruel! O rocks! no wonder that ye did melt and rend your hearts with sympathy, when your Creator died! Never man suffered as this man suffered. Even death itself relented, and many of those who had been in their graves arose and came into the city. This however, is but the outward. Believe me, brethren, the inward was far worse. What our Saviour suffered in his body was nothing, compared with what he endured in his soul. You cannot guess, and I cannot help you to guess, what he endured within. Suppose for one moment—to repeat a sentence I have often used—suppose a man who has passed into hell—suppose his eternal torment could all be brought into one hour; and then suppose it could be multiplied by the number of the saved, which is a number past all human enumeration. Can you now think what a vast aggregate of misery there would have been in the sufferings of God's people, if they had been punished through all eternity? And recollect that Christ had to suffer an equivalent for all the hells of all his redeemed. I can never express that thought better than by using those oft-repeated words: it seemed as if hell was put into his cup; he seized it, and, "At one tremendous draught of love, he drank damnation dry." So that there was nothing left of all the pangs and miseries of hell for his people ever to endure.

FOR MEDITATION: The secret things of the sufferings of Christ belong to the Lord our God (Deuteronomy 29: 29)—we could never begin to take them in. But God has given us a glimpse behind the scenes—meditate on the alternate torment and trust recorded in Psalm 22: 1-21.

SERMON NO. 181

Rahab's faith

"By faith the harlot Rahab perished not with them that believed not, when she had received the spies with peace." Hebrews 11: 31

SUGGESTED FURTHER READING: James 2: 18-26

Rahab's faith was a sanctifying faith. Did Rahab continue a harlot after she had faith? No, she did not. I do not believe she was a harlot at the time the men went to her house, though the name still stuck to her, as such ill names will; but I am sure she was not afterwards, for Salmon the prince of Judah married her, and her name is put down among the ancestors of our Lord Jesus Christ. She became after that a woman eminent for piety, walking in the fear of God. Now, you may have a dead faith which will ruin your soul. The faith that will save you is a faith which sanctifies. "Ah!" says the drunkard, "I like the gospel, sir; I believe in Christ:" then he will go over to the Blue Lion tonight, and get drunk. Sir, that is not the believing in Christ that is of any use. "Yes," says another, "I believe in Christ;" and when he gets outside he will begin to talk lightly, frothy words, perhaps lascivious ones, and sin as before. Sir, you speak falsely; you do not believe in Christ. That faith which saves the soul is a real faith, and a real faith sanctifies men. It makes them say, "Lord, thou hast forgiven me my sins; I will sin no more. Thou hast been so merciful to me, I will renounce my guilt; so kindly hast thou treated me, so lovingly hast thou embraced me, Lord, I will serve thee till I die; and if thou wilt give me grace, and help me so to be, I will be as holy as thou art." You cannot have faith, and yet live in sin. To believe is to be holy. The two things must go together. That faith is a dead faith, a corrupt faith, a rotten faith, which lives in sin that grace may abound. Rahab was a sanctified woman.

FOR MEDITATION: Faith has to be seen to be believed (Joshua 2: 17-21).

The allegories of Sarah and Hagar

"These are the two covenants." Galatians 4: 24
SUGGESTED FURTHER READING: Galatians 3: 19-24

Hagar was not intended to be a wife; she never ought to have been anything but a hand-maid to Sarah. The law was never intended to save men: it was only designed to be a hand-maid to the covenant of grace. When God delivered the law on Sinai, it was apart from his ideas that any man would ever be saved by it; he never conceived that men would attain perfection thereby. But you know that the law is a wondrous handmaid to grace. Who brought us to the Saviour? Was it not the law thundering in our ears? We should never have come to Christ if the law had not driven us there; we should never have known sin if the law had not revealed it. The law is Sarah's handmaid to sweep our hearts, and make the dust fly so that we may cry for blood to be sprinkled so that the dust may be laid. The law is, so to speak, Jesus Christ's dog, to go after his sheep, and bring them to the shepherd; the law is the thunderbolt which frightens ungodly men, and makes them turn from the error of their ways, and seek after God. Ah! if we know rightly how to use the law, if we understand how to put her in her proper place, and make her obedient to her mistress, then all will be well. But this Hagar will always be wishing to be mistress, as well as Sarah; and Sarah will never allow that, but will be sure to treat her harshly, and drive her out. We must do the same; and let none murmur at us, if we treat the Hagarenes harshly in these days— if we sometimes speak hard things against those who are trusting in the works of the law.

FOR MEDITATION: God's law will never have the power to save us (Romans 8: 3); but thank God that it points us to a Man who can.

SERMON NO. 69

The fruitless vine

"And the word of the Lord came unto me, saying, Son of man, What is the vine tree more than any tree, or than a branch which is among the trees of the forest?" Ezekiel 15: 1-2
SUGGESTED FURTHER READING: John 15: 1-8

In looking upon all the various trees, we observe, that the vine is distinguished amongst them—so that, in the old parable of Jotham, the trees waited upon the vine tree, and said unto it, "Come thou and reign over us." But merely looking at the vine, without regard to its fruitfulness, we should not see any kingship in it over other trees. In size, form, beauty, or utility, it has not the slightest advantage. We can do nothing with the wood of the vine. "Shall wood be taken thereof to do any work? or will men take a pin of it to hang a vessel thereon?" It is a useless plant apart from its fruitfulness. We sometimes see it in beauty, trained up by the side of our walls, and in the east it might be seen in all its luxuriance, and great care is bestowed in its training; but leave the vine to itself, and consider it apart from its fruitfulness, it is the most insignificant and despicable of all things that bear the name of trees. Now beloved, this is for the humbling of God's people. They are called God's vine; but what are they by nature more than others? Others are as good as they; yea, some others are even greater and better than they. They, by God's goodness, have become fruitful, having been planted in a good soil; the Lord has trained them upon the walls of the sanctuary, and they bring forth fruit to his glory. But what are they without their God? What are they without the continual influence of the Spirit, begetting fruitfulness in them? Are they not the least among the sons of men, and the most to be despised of those that have been brought forth of women?

FOR MEDITATION: It is only by the grace of God that we become different from others and useful to God (1 Corinthians 15: 10).

SERMON NO. 125

The peculiar sleep of the beloved

"So he giveth his beloved sleep." Psalm 127: 2
SUGGESTED FURTHER READING: Psalm 4

It is God who steeps the mind in drowsiness, and bids us slumber, that our bodies may be refreshed, so that for tomorrow's toil we may rise reinvigorated and strengthened. O my friends, how thankful should we be for sleep. Sleep is the best physician that I know of. Sleep has healed more pains of wearied bones than the most eminent physicians upon earth. It is the best medicine; the choicest thing of all the names which are written in all the lists of pharmacy. There is nothing like sleep! What a mercy it is that it belongs alike to all! God does not make sleep the boon of the rich man, he does not give it merely to the noble, or the rich, so that they can keep it as a peculiar luxury for themselves; but he bestows it upon all. Yes, if there is a difference, the sleep of the labouring man is sweet, whether he eat little or much. He who toils, sleeps all the sounder for his toil. While luxurious effeminacy cannot rest, tossing itself from side to side upon a bed of soft down, the hard-working labourer, with his strong and powerful limbs, worn out and tired, throws himself upon his hard couch and sleeps; and waking, thanks God that he has been refreshed. You know not, my friends, how much you owe to God, that he gives you rest at night. If you had sleepless nights, you would then value the blessing. If for weeks you lay tossing on your weary bed, you then would thank God for this favour. But as it is the gift of God, it is a gift most precious, one that cannot be valued until it is taken away; yea, even then we cannot appreciate it as we ought.

FOR MEDITATION: Possession of spiritual blessings in Christ should not make us forget to thank God for our continued enjoyment of his common grace (Matthew 5: 45; Acts 14: 17).

Jesus about his Father's business

"Jesus saith unto them, My meat is to do the will of him that sent me, and to finish his work." John 4: 34
SUGGESTED FURTHER READING: John 18: 33-40

Satan took him to the brow of a hill, and offered him all the kingdoms of this world—a mightier dominion even than Caesar had—if he would bow down and worship him. That temptation was substantially repeated in Christ's life a thousand times. You remember one practical instance as a specimen of the whole. "They would have taken him by force and would have made him a king." And if he had but pleased to accept that offer, on the day when he rode into Jerusalem upon a colt, the foal of an ass, when all cried "Hosanna!" when the palm branches were waving, he had needed to have done nothing but just to have gone into the temple, to have commanded with authority the priest to pour the sacred oil publicly upon his head, and he would have been king of the Jews. Not with the mock title which he wore upon the cross, but with a real dignity he might have been monarch of nations. As for the Romans, his omnipotence could have swept away the intruders. He could have lifted up Judaea into a glory as great as the golden days of Solomon: he might have built Palmyras and Tadmors in the desert: he might have stormed Egypt and have taken Rome. There was no empire that could have resisted him. With a band of zealots such as that nation could have furnished, and with such a leader capable of working miracles walking at the head, the star of Judaea might have risen with resplendent light, and a visible kingdom might have come, and his will might have been done on earth, from the river unto the ends of the earth. But he came not to establish a carnal kingdom upon earth, else would his followers fight: he came to wear the thorn-crown, to bear our griefs and to carry our sorrows.

FOR MEDITATION: Of what profit would it have been to any man, if Christ had gained the whole world and lost all our souls?

SERMON NO. 302

Predestination and calling

"Moreover whom he did predestinate, them he also called." Romans 8: 30
SUGGESTED FURTHER READING: 1 John 3: 19-24

The testimony of sense may be false, but the testimony of the Spirit must be true. We have the witness of the Spirit within, bearing witness with our spirits that we are born of God. There is such a thing on earth as an infallible assurance of our election. Let a man once get that, and it will anoint his head with fresh oil, it will clothe him with the white garment of praise, and put the song of the angel into his mouth. Happy, happy man, who is fully assured of his interest in the covenant of grace, in the blood of atonement, and in the glories of heaven! Such men there are here this very day. Let them "rejoice in the Lord alway, and again I say rejoice." What would some of you give if you could arrive at this assurance? Mark, if you anxiously desire to know, you may know. If your heart pants to read its title clear it shall do so before long. No man ever desired Christ in his heart with a living and longing desire, who did not find him sooner or later. If you have a desire, God has given it to you. If you pant, and cry, and groan after Christ, even this is his gift; bless him for it. Thank him for little grace, and ask him for great grace. He has given you hope, ask for faith; and when he gives you faith, ask for assurance; and when you get assurance, ask for full assurance; and when you have obtained full assurance, ask for enjoyment; and when you have enjoyment, ask for glory itself; and he shall surely give it to you in his own appointed season.

FOR MEDITATION: Are you content with a logical possession of God's salvation, or do you long for a heart-felt assurance? Both head knowledge and heart knowledge are important.
(1 John 2: 3-5; 3: 14,19,24; 4: 13; 5: 2,13,19-20).

SERMON NO. 241

Human inability

"No man can come to me, except the Father which hath sent me draw him." John 6: 44
SUGGESTED FURTHER READING: 1 Timothy 4: 1-5

When man fell in the garden, manhood fell entirely; there was not one single pillar in the temple of manhood that stood erect. It is true, conscience was not destroyed. The pillar was not shattered; it fell, and it fell in one piece, and there it lies along, the mightiest remnant of God's once perfect work in man. But that conscience is fallen, I am sure. Look at men. Who among them is the possessor of a "good conscience towards God," but the regenerated man? Do you imagine that if men's consciences always spoke loudly and clearly to them, they would live in the daily commission of acts, which are as opposed to the right as darkness is to light? No, beloved; conscience can tell me that I am a sinner, but conscience cannot make me feel that I am one. Conscience may tell me that such and such a thing is wrong, but how wrong it is conscience itself does not know. Did any man's conscience, unenlightened by the Spirit, ever tell him that his sins deserved damnation? Or if conscience did do that, did it ever lead any man to feel an abhorrence of sin as sin? In fact, did conscience ever bring a man to such a self-renunciation, that he did totally abhor himself and all his works and come to Christ? No, conscience, although it is not dead, is ruined, its power is impaired, it has not that clearness of eye and that strength of hand, and that thunder of voice, which it had before the fall; but has ceased to a great degree, to exert its supremacy in the town of Mansoul. Then, beloved, it becomes necessary for this very reason, because conscience is depraved, that the Holy Spirit should step in, to show us our need of a Saviour, and draw us to the Lord Jesus Christ.

FOR MEDITATION: Our consciences need to be cleansed by the blood of Christ, like every other part of our being (Titus 1: 15; Hebrews 9: 9,14; 10: 22). The Christian now has the ability to seek to maintain a good conscience (Acts 24: 16; 1 Timothy 1: 5,19; 1 Peter 3: 16).

SERMON NO. 182

A faithful friend

"There is a friend that sticketh closer than a brother." Proverbs 18: 24
SUGGESTED FURTHER READING: Proverbs 27: 6-10

You have a friend, have you? Yes; and he keeps a pair of horses, and has a good establishment. Ah! but your best way to prove your friend is to know that he will be your friend when you have not so much as a mean cottage; and when homeless and without clothing, you are driven to beg for your bread. Thus you would make true proof of a friend. Give me a friend who was born in the winter time, whose cradle was rocked in the storm; he will last. Our fair weather friends shall flee away from us. I had rather have a robin for a friend than a swallow; for a swallow abides with us only in the summer time, but a robin cometh to us in the winter. Those are tight friends that will come the nearest to us when we are in the most distress; but those are not friends who speed themselves away when ill times come. Believer, have you reason to fear that Christ will leave you now? Has he not been with you in the house of mourning? You found your friend where men find pearls, "In caverns deep, where darkness dwells;" you found Jesus in your hour of trouble. It was on the bed of sickness that you first learned the value of his name; it was in the hour of mental anguish that you first did lay hold of the hem of his garment; and since then, your nearest and sweetest intercourse has been held with him in hours of darkness. Well then, such a friend, proved in the house of sorrow—a friend who gave his heart's blood for you, and let his soul run out in one great river of blood—such a friend never can and never will forsake you; he sticketh closer than a brother.

FOR MEDITATION: God offered us the hand of friendship when we were his enemies (Romans 5: 10)—it cost the Lord Jesus Christ his life to make us his friends (John 15: 13-15). How much do you display your side of the friendship in a world which has no time for the cause of Christ (James 4: 4)?

The leafless tree

"But yet in it shall be a tenth, and it shall return, and shall be eaten: as a teil tree, and as an oak, whose substance is in them, when they cast their leaves: so the holy seed shall be the substance thereof." Isaiah 6: 13
SUGGESTED FURTHER READING: Romans 11: 11-24

"The race of Abraham shall endure for ever, and his seed as many generations." But why is it that the Jewish race is preserved? We have our answer in the text: "The holy seed is the substance thereof." There is something within a tree mysterious, hidden and unknown, which preserves life in it when everything outward tends to kill it. So in the Jewish race there is a secret element which keeps it alive. We know what it is; it is the 'remnant according to the election of grace;' in the worst of ages there has never been a day so black but there was a Hebrew found to hold the lamp of God. There has always been found a Jew who loved Jesus; and though the race now despise the great Redeemer, yet there are not a few of the Hebrew race who still love Jesus the Saviour of the uncircumcised, and bow before him. It is these few, this holy seed, that are the substance of the nation; and for their sake, through their prayers, because of God's love to them, he still says of Israel to all nations, "Touch not these mine anointed, do my prophets no harm. These are the descendants of Abraham, my friend. I have sworn and will not repent; I will show kindness unto them for their father's sake, and for the sake of the remnant I have chosen." Let us think a little more of the Jews than we have been wont; let us pray oftener for them. "Pray for the peace of Jerusalem; they shall prosper that love her." As truly as any great thing is done in this world for Christ's kingdom, the Jews will have more to do with it than any of us have dreamed.

FOR MEDITATION: Do you attach anything like the same priority to the Jews as God does (Romans 1: 16; 2: 9,10)? "How odd of God to choose the Jews" (William Norman Ewer)—but not as odd as those who choose a Jewish God and hate the Jews.

Effectual calling

"When Jesus came to the place, he looked up, and saw him, and said unto him, Zaccheus, make haste, and come down; for today I must abide at thy house." Luke 19: 5
SUGGESTED FURTHER READING: Ephesians 5: 21— 6: 4

"I will come into thy house and give thee a blessing." Oh! what affection there was in that! Poor sinner, my Master is a very affectionate Master. He will come into your house. What kind of a house have you got? A house that you have made miserable with your drunkenness—a house you have defiled with your impurity—a house you have defiled with your cursing and swearing—a house where you are carrying on an ill-trade that you would be glad to get rid of. Christ says, "I will come into thy house." And I know some houses now that once were dens of sin, where Christ comes every morning; the husband and wife who once could quarrel and fight, bend their knees together in prayer. Christ comes there at dinner-time, when the workman comes home for his meals. Some of my hearers can scarce come for an hour to their meals but they must have a word of prayer and reading of the Scriptures. Christ comes to them. Where the walls were once plastered up with the lascivious song and idle picture, there is a Christian calendar in one place, there is a Bible on the chest of drawers; and though it is only one room they live in, if an angel should come in, and God should say, "What hast thou seen in that house?" he would say, "I have seen good furniture, for there is a Bible there; here and there a religious book; the filthy pictures are pulled down and burned; there are no cards in the man's cupboard now; Christ has come into his house." Oh! what a blessing that we have our household God as well as the Romans! Our God is a household God. He comes to live with his people; he loves the tents of Jacob.

FOR MEDITATION: What a difference Christ makes to a household (Acts 16: 31-34). How do you regard him? As an occasional visitor or Head of the house?

Consolation proportionate to spiritual sufferings

"For as the sufferings of Christ abound in us, so our consolation also aboundeth by Christ." 2 Corinthians 1: 5
SUGGESTED FURTHER READING: 2 Corinthians 4: 7-18

I have sometimes heard religion described in such a way that its high colouring has displeased me. It is true "her ways are ways of pleasantness;" but it is not true that a Christian never has sorrow or trouble. It is true that light-eyed cheerfulness, and airy-footed love, can go through the world without much depression and tribulation: but it is not true that Christianity will shield a man from trouble; nor ought it to be so represented. In fact, we ought to speak of it in the other way. Soldier of Christ, if thou enlisteth, thou wilt have to do hard battle. There is no bed of down for thee; there is no riding to heaven in a chariot; the rough way must be trodden; mountains must be climbed, rivers must be forded, dragons must be fought, giants must be slain, difficulties must be overcome, and great trials must be borne. It is not a smooth road to heaven, believe me; for those who have gone but a very few steps therein, have found it to be a rough one. It is a pleasant one; it is the most delightful in all the world, but it is not easy in itself, it is only pleasant because of the company, because of the sweet promises on which we lean, because of our Beloved who walks with us through all the rough and thorny breaks of this vast wilderness. Christian, expect trouble: "Think it not strange concerning the fiery trial.... as though some strange thing happened unto you;" for as truly as you are a child of God, your Saviour has left you for his legacy,—"In the world, ye shall have tribulation; in me ye shall have peace."

FOR MEDITATION: The man who proclaims that the Christian life is an easy one is not only contradicting the Lord Jesus Christ and the apostles, but also exposing his own ignorance of true Christianity. Jesus promised his followers blessings now "with persecutions" and eternal life to come (Mark 10: 29-30).

Election and holiness

"Behold, the heaven and the heaven of heavens is the Lord's thy God, the earth also, with all that therein is. Only the Lord had a delight in thy fathers to love them, and he chose their seed after them, even you above all people, as it is this day. Circumcise therefore the foreskin of your heart, and be no more stiffnecked." Deuteronomy 10: 14-16
SUGGESTED FURTHER READING: Isaiah 45: 1-13

Preaching a few months ago in the midst of a large congregation of Methodists, the brethren were all alive, giving all kinds of answers to my sermon, nodding their heads and crying, "Amen!" "Hallelujah!" "Glory be to God!" and the like. They completely woke me up. My spirit was stirred, and I preached away with an unusual force and vigour; and the more I preached the more they cried, "Amen!" "Hallelujah!" "Glory be to God!" At last, a part of text led me to what is styled high doctrine. So I said, this brings me to the doctrine of election. There was a deep drawing of breath. "Now, my friends, you believe it;" they seemed to say "No, we don't." But you do, and I will make you sing "Hallelujah!" over it. I will so preach it to you that you will acknowledge it and believe it. So I put it thus: Is there no difference between you and other men? "Yes, yes; glory be to God, glory!" There is a difference between what you were and what you are now? "Oh, yes! oh, yes!" There is sitting by your side a man who has been to the same chapel as you have, heard the same gospel, he is unconverted, and you are converted. Who has made the difference, yourself or God? "The Lord!" said they, "the Lord! Glory! Hallelujah!" Yes, cried I, and that is the doctrine of election; that is all I contend for, that if there is a difference the Lord makes the difference. Some good man came up to me and said, "Thou'rt right, lad! thou'rt right. I believe thy doctrine of election; I do not believe it as it is preached by some people, but I believe that we must give the glory to God; we must put the crown on the right head."

FOR MEDITATION: The doctrines of God give God all the glory. The doctrines of man seek to steal some of God's glory to give to man instead (Isaiah 42: 6-8).

SERMON NO. 303

Christ precious to believers

"Unto you therefore which believe he is precious." 1 Peter 2: 7
SUGGESTED FURTHER READING: 1 Peter 1: 18-21

This text calls to my recollection the opening of my ministry. It is about eight years since as a lad of sixteen, I stood up for the first time in my life to preach the gospel in a cottage to a handful of poor people, who had come together for worship. I felt my own inability to preach, but I ventured to take this text, "Unto you therefore which believe he is precious." I do not think I could have said anything upon any other text, but Christ was precious to my soul and I was in the flush of my youthful love, and I could not be silent when a precious Jesus was the subject. I had but just escaped from the bondage of Egypt, I had not forgotten the broken fetter; still did I recollect those flames which seemed to burn about my path, and that devouring gulf which opened its mouth as if ready to devour me. With all these things fresh in my youthful heart, I could but speak of his preciousness who had been my Saviour; and had plucked me as a brand from the burning, and set me upon a rock, and put a new song in my mouth, and established my goings. And now, at this time what shall I say? "What hath God wrought?" How hath the little one become a thousand, and the small one a great people? And what shall I say concerning this text, but that if the Lord Jesus was precious then, he is as precious now? And if I could declare then, that Jesus was the object of my soul's desire, that for him I hoped to live, and for him I would be prepared to die, can I not say, God being my witness, that he is more precious to me this day than ever he was?

FOR MEDITATION: Is the Lord Jesus Christ precious to you? If so, the feeling is mutual (Isaiah 43: 4; Psalm 116: 15).

SERMON NO. 242

The solar eclipse

"I form the light, and create darkness." Isaiah 45:7
SUGGESTED FURTHER READING: Ecclesiastes 1:1-10

Since God has made the ecliptic, or the circle, the great rule of nature, it is impossible but that eclipses should occur. Now, did you ever notice that in providence the circle is God's rule still. The earth is here to-day; it will be in the same place this day next year; it will go round the circle; it gets no further. It is just so in providence. God began the circle of his providence in Eden. That is where he will end. There was a paradise on earth, when God began his providential dealings with mankind; there will be a paradise at the end. It is the same with your providence. Naked you came forth from your mother's womb, and naked you must return to the earth. It is a circle. Where God has begun, there will he end; and as God has taken the rule of the circle in providence, as well as in nature, eclipses must be sure to occur. Moving in the predestined orbit of divine wisdom, the eclipse is absolutely and imperatively necessary in God's plan of government. Troubles must come; afflictions must befall; it must needs be that for a season you should be in heaviness, through manifold temptations. But I have said, that eclipses must also occur in grace, and it is so. God's rule in grace is still the circle. Man was originally pure and holy; that is what God's grace will make him at last. He was pure when he was made by God in the garden. That is what God shall make him, when he comes to fashion him like unto his own glorious image, and present him complete in heaven. We begin our piety by denying the world, by being full of love to God; we often decline in grace, and God will bring us back to the state in which we were when we first began.

FOR MEDITATION: This sermon was occasioned by the anticipation of the solar eclipse on the following day. Meditate on the significance of the most important solar eclipse in all history. Remember this was not an astronomical eclipse, since it occurred at Passover—full moon (Luke 23: 44-46)!

SERMON NO. 183

Christ about his Father's business

"Wist ye not that I must be about my Father's business?" Luke 2: 49
SUGGESTED FURTHER READING: Ephesians 4: 32-5: 10

You never find Christ doing a thing which you may not imitate. You would scarcely think it necessary that he should be baptised; but lo, he goes to Jordan's stream and dives beneath the wave, that he may be buried in baptism unto death, and may rise again—though he needed not to rise—into newness of life. You see him healing the sick to teach us benevolence; rebuking hypocrisy to teach us boldness; enduring temptation to teach us hardness, wherewith, as good soldiers of Christ, we ought to war a good warfare. You see him forgiving his enemies to teach us the grace of meekness and of forbearance; you behold him giving up his very life to teach us how we should surrender ourselves to God, and give up ourselves for the good of others. Put Christ at the wedding; you may imitate him. Yes, sirs, and you might imitate him, if you could, in turning water into wine, without a sin. Put Christ at a funeral; you may imitate him—"Jesus wept." Put him on the mountain top; he shall be there in prayer alone, and you may imitate him. Put him in the crowd; he shall speak so, that if you could speak like him you should speak well. Put him with enemies; he shall so confound them, that he shall be a model for you to copy. Put him with friends, and he shall be a "friend that sticketh closer than a brother," worthy of your imitation. Exalt him, cry hosanna, and you shall see him riding upon a "colt, the foal of an ass," meek and lowly. Despise and spit upon him; you shall see him bearing disgrace and contempt with the same evenness of spirit which characterised him when he was exalted in the eye of the world. Everywhere you may imitate Christ.

FOR MEDITATION: The imitation of Christ is an impossible way to obtain salvation, but it is an excellent way of follow-up after conversion (John 13: 15; 1 Corinthians 11: 1; 1 Peter 2: 21).

Good works

"Zealous of good works" Titus 2: 14
SUGGESTED FURTHER READING: 1 Timothy 2: 8-15

It would be a good thing, perhaps, if we went back to Wesley's rule, to come out from the world in our apparel, and to dress as plainly and neatly as the Quakers, though alas! they have sadly gone from their primitive simplicity. I am obliged to depart a little sometimes, from what we call the high things of the gospel; for really the children of God cannot now be told by outward appearance from the children of the devil, and they really ought to be; there should be some distinction between the one and the other; and although religion allows distinction of rank and dress, yet everything in the Bible cries out against our arraying ourselves, and making ourselves proud, by reason of the goodliness of our apparel. Some will say, "I wish you would leave that alone!" Of course you do, because it applies to yourself. But we let nothing alone which we believe to be in the Scriptures; and while I would not spare any man's soul, honesty to every man's conscience, and honesty to myself, demands that I should always speak of that which I see to be an evil breaking out in the Church. We should always take care that in everything we keep as near as possible to the written Word. If you want ornaments here they are. Here are jewels, rings, dresses, and all kinds of ornament; men and women, you may dress yourselves up till you shine like angels. How can you do it? By dressing yourselves out in benevolence, in love to the saints, in honesty and integrity, in uprightness, in godliness, in brotherly-kindness, in charity. These are the ornaments which angels themselves admire, and which even the world will admire; for men must give admiration to the man or the woman who is arrayed in the jewels of a holy life and godly conversation. I beseech you, brethren, "adorn the doctrine of God our Saviour in all things."

FOR MEDITATION: Isaiah 3: 16-23: God is concerned about our outward appearance and our attitude to it. He wants spirituality, not showing off (1 Peter 3: 3-4).

SERMON NO. 70

Humility

"Serving the Lord with all humility." Acts 20: 19
SUGGESTED FURTHER READING: Philippians 2: 3-11

Pride can shut the door in the face of Christ. Only let us take out our tablets and write down "God is for me, therefore let me be proud;" only let us say with Jehu, "Come, and I will show thee my zeal for the Lord of Hosts," and God's presence will soon depart from us, and Ichabod be written on the front of the house. And let me say to those of you who have already done much for Christ as evangelists, ministers, teachers, or what not, do not sit down and congratulate yourselves upon the past. Let us go home and think of all the mistakes we have made; all the errors we have committed, and all the follies into which we have been betrayed, and I think instead of self-congratulation we shall say, "I have heard of thee by the hearing of the ear: but now mine eye seeth thee. Wherefore I abhor myself, and repent in dust and ashes." Let us humble ourselves before God. You know there is a deal of difference between being humble and being humbled. He that will not be humble shall be humbled. Humble yourselves therefore under the mighty hand of God and he shall lift you up, lest he leave you because you hold your head so high. And should I be addressing any here this morning who are very much exalted by the nobility of rank, who have what the poet calls "The pride of heraldry, the pomp of power," be humble, I pray you. If any man would have friends, let him be humble. Humility never did any man any hurt. If you stoop down when you pass through a doorway, if it should be a high one, you will not be hurt by stooping; but if it should be a low one, you might have knocked your head if you had held it up.

FOR MEDITATION: We have no end of sins to be ashamed of. Let us be proud only of the Gospel of our Saviour, who so humbled himself for our sakes. We ought to boast only of the Lord (2 Corinthians 10: 17), otherwise boasting is groundless (Romans 3: 27).

The victory of faith

"For whatsoever is born of God overcometh the world; and this is the victory that overcometh the world, even our faith." 1 John 5: 4
SUGGESTED FURTHER READING: Matthew 4: 1-11

Faith helps Christians to overcome the world. It always does it homoeopathically. You say, "That is a singular idea." So it may be. The principle is that "like cures like." So does faith overcome the world by curing like with like. How does faith trample upon the fear of the world? By the fear of God, "Now," says the world, "if you do not do this I will take away your life. If you do not bow down before my false god, you shall be put in yonder burning fiery furnace." "But," says the man of faith, "I fear him who can destroy both body and soul in hell. True, I may dread you, but I have a greater fear than that. I fear lest I should displease God; I tremble lest I should offend my Sovereign." So the one fear counterbalances the other. How does faith overthrow the world's hopes? "There," says the world, "I will give you this, I will give you that, if you will be my disciple. There is a hope for you; you shall be rich, you shall be great." But, faith says, "I have a hope laid up in heaven; a hope which fadeth not away, eternal, incorrupt, a golden hope, a crown of life;" and the hope of glory overcomes all the hopes of the world. "Ah!" says the world, "Why not follow the example of your fellows?" "Because," says faith, "I will follow the example of Christ." If the world puts one example before us, faith puts another. "Oh, follow the example of such an one; he is wise, and great, and good," says the world. Says faith, "I will follow Christ; he is the wisest, the greatest, and the best." It overcomes example by example; "Well," says the world, "since you will not be conquered by all this, come, I will love you; you shall be my friend." Faith says, "He that is the friend of this world, cannot be the friend of God. God loves me."

FOR MEDITATION: Faith can say to society, self, Satan and sin, "Anything you can give, Christ can give better" (Ephesians 2: 1-8).

The Bible

"I have written to him the great things of my law, but they were counted as a strange thing." Hosea 8: 12

SUGGESTED FURTHER READING: 2 Peter 1: 16-21

Who is the author of it? Do these men jointly claim the authorship? Are they the compositors of this massive volume? Do they between themselves divide the honour? Our holy religion answers, No! This volume is the writing of the living God: each letter was penned with an Almighty finger; each word in it dropped from the everlasting lips, each sentence was dictated by the Holy Spirit. Albeit, that Moses was employed to write his histories with his fiery pen, God guided that pen. It may be that David touched his harp and let sweet psalms of melody drop from his fingers, but God moved his hands over the living strings of his golden harp. It may be that Solomon sang canticles of love, or gave forth words of consummate wisdom, but God directed his lips, and made the preacher eloquent. If I follow the thundering Nahum when his horses plough the waters, or Habbakuk when he sees the tents of Cushan in affliction; if I read Malachi, when the earth is burning like an oven; if I turn to the smooth page of John, who tells of love, or the rugged fiery chapters of Peter, who speaks of the fire devouring God's enemies; if I turn to Jude, who launches forth curses upon the foes of God, everywhere I find God speaking: it is God's voice, not man's; the words are God's words, the words of the Eternal, the Invisible, the Almighty, the Jehovah of this earth. This Bible is God's Bible; and when I see it, I seem to hear a voice springing up from it, saying, "I am the book of God: man, read me. I am God's writing: open my leaf, for I was penned by God; read it, for he is my author, and you will see him visible and manifest everywhere."

FOR MEDITATION: We all have our favourite Bible writers and passages, but we must never limit ourselves to them, otherwise we will miss some of the great things God has said.

Weak hands and feeble knees

"Strengthen ye the weak hands, and confirm the feeble knees." Isaiah 35: 3
SUGGESTED FURTHER READING: Ezekiel 34: 1-16

In all flocks there must be lambs, and weak and wounded sheep, and among
the flock of men, it seems that there must necessarily be some who should
more than others prove the truth of Job's declaration, "man is born to
trouble, even as the sparks fly upwards." It is the duty then of those of us
who are more free than others from despondency of spirit, to be very tender
to these weak ones. Far be it from the man of courageous disposition, of
stern resolve, and of unbending purpose, to be hard towards those who are
timid and despairing. If we have a lion-like spirit, let us not imitate the king
of beasts in his cruelty to those timid fallow deer that fly before him, but let
us place our strength at their service for their help and protection. Let us
with downy fingers bind up the wounded heart; with oil and wine let us
nourish their fainting spirits. In this battle of life, let the unwounded
warriors bear their injured comrades to the rear, bathe their wounds, and
cover them from the storm of war. Be gentle with those that are despondent.
Alas, it is not every man that has learned this lesson. There are some who
deal with others with rough-handed thoughtlessness. "Ah," they say, "if
such a one be so foolish as to be sensitive let him be." O speak not thus; to be
sensitive, timid, and despondent, is ill enough in itself, without our being
hard and harsh towards those who are so afflicted. Go forth, and "do to
others as ye would that they should do to you" and as ye would that others
should in your hours of despondency deal with you tenderly and
comfortably, so deal tenderly and comfortably with them.

FOR MEDITATION: It is not very clever to add insult to injury. "Don't be so
silly; cheer up, it may never happen," is not much help to someone when it
has already happened! God has told us what to do with the weak (Romans
12: 15; 1 Thessalonians 5: 14).

SERMON NO. 243

The glorious gospel

"This is a faithful saying, and worthy of all acceptation, that Christ Jesus came into the world to save sinners; of whom I am chief." 1 Timothy 1: 15
SUGGESTED FURTHER READING: Luke 5: 17-32

Do you see that spirit yonder—foremost among the ranks, most sweetly singing the praises of God? Do you mark it robed in white, an emblem of its purity? Do you see it as it casts its crown before the feet of Jesus, and acknowledges him the Lord of all? Hark! Do you hear it as it sings the sweetest song that ever charmed Paradise itself? Listen to it, its song is this:

"I, the chief of sinners am,
But Jesus died for me."

"Unto him that loved me, and washed me from my sins in his blood, unto him be glory and honour, and majesty, and power, and dominion, world without end." And who is that whose song thus emulates the seraph's strain? The same person who a little while ago was so frightfully depraved, the self-same man! But he has been washed, he has been sanctified, he has been justified. If you ask me, then, what is meant by salvation, I tell you that it reaches all the way from that poor, desperately fallen piece of humanity, to that high-soaring spirit up yonder, praising God. That is to be saved—to have our old thoughts made into new ones; to have our old habits broken off, and to have new habits given; to have our old sins pardoned, and to have righteousness imputed; to have peace in the conscience, peace to man, and peace with God; to have the spotless robe of imputed righteousness cast about our loins, and ourselves healed and cleansed. To be saved is to be rescued from the gulf of perdition; to be raised to the throne of heaven; to be delivered from the wrath, and curse, and the thunders of an angry God, and brought to feel and taste the love, the approval, and applause of Jehovah, our Father and our Friend. And all this Christ gives to sinners.

FOR MEDITATION: Do you get tired of the simple Gospel? Are you saved?

SERMON NO. 184

Particular election

"Wherefore the rather, brethren, give diligence to make your calling and election sure: for if ye do these things, ye shall never fall. For so an entrance shall be ministered unto you abundantly into the everlasting kingdom of our Lord and Saviour Jesus Christ." 2 Peter 1: 10,11

SUGGESTED FURTHER READING: Revelation 6: 12 - 7: 12

There are the two things which you and I are to prove to be sure for ourselves—whether we are called and whether we are elected. And oh, dear friends, this is a matter about which you and I should be very anxious. For consider what an honourable thing it is to be elected. In this world it is thought a mighty thing to be elected to the House of Parliament; but how much more honourable to be elected to eternal life; to be elected to "the Church of the first born, whose names are written in heaven;" to be elected to be an equal with angels, to be a favourite of the living God, to dwell with the Most High, amongst the fairest of the sons of light, nearest the eternal throne! Election in this world is but a short-lived thing, but God's election is eternal. Let a man be elected to a seat in the House; five years must be the longest period that he can hold his election; but if you and I are elected according to the Divine purpose, we shall hold our seats when the day-star shall have ceased to burn, when the sun shall have grown dim with age, and when the eternal hills shall have bowed themselves with weakness. If we are chosen of God and precious, then are we chosen for ever; for God changeth not in the objects of his election. Those whom he hath ordained he hath ordained to eternal life, "and they shall never perish, neither shall any man pluck them out of his hand." It is worth while to know ourselves elect, for nothing in this world can make a man more happy or more valiant than the knowledge of his election. "Nevertheless," said Christ to his apostles, "rejoice not in this, but rather rejoice that your names are written in heaven."

FOR MEDITATION: It is far more important to make sure of our standing in God's sight than to obtain high office in man's sight (Acts 26: 27-29).

Note: Spurgeon preached this sermon during the run-up to an election.

SERMON NO. 123

A bottle in the smoke

"For I am become like a bottle in the smoke; yet do I not forget thy statutes." Psalm 119: 83
SUGGESTED FURTHER READING: Job 1: 13-22

Let me give a word of consolation. If you have been persecuted, and still hold fast by God's word—if you have been afflicted, and still persevere in the knowledge of our Lord and Master, you have every reason to believe yourself a Christian. If under your trials and troubles you remain just what you were when at ease, you may then hope, and not only so, but steadfastly believe and be assured that you are a child of God. Some of you, however, are very much like Christians, when you hear sermons full of promises; when I preach to you about bruised reeds, or address you with the invitation, "Come unto me, all ye that labour;" but when I give you a smoky sermon— one which you cannot endure—if you then can say, guilty, weak, and helpless I may be, but still I fall into his arms; sinful I know I am, and I have grave cause for doubt, but still:

"There, there, unshaken will I rest,
Till this vile body dies;"

I know, poor, weak, and helpless though I am, that I have a rich Almighty Friend; if you can stand a little smoke, then you may believe yourself to be a child of God. But there are some fantastic people we know of, who are shocked with a very puff of smoke, they cannot endure it, they go out at once, just like rats out of the hold of a ship when they begin to smoke it; but if you can live in the smoke and say, "I feel it, and still can endure it,"—if you can stand a smoky sermon, and endure a smoky trial, and hold fast to God under a smoky persecution, then you have reason to believe that you are certainly a child of God.

FOR MEDITATION: In the parable of the sower, the true believer is the one who hears the word and accepts it; those making a false profession are found out in time either as a result of troubles or of worldly success (Mark 4: 16-20). Job passed both tests (Job 1).

SERMON NO. 71

The silver trumpet

"Come now, and let us reason together, saith the Lord: though your sins be as scarlet, they shall be as white as snow; though they be red like crimson, they shall be as wool." Isaiah 1: 18
SUGGESTED FURTHER READING: Zechariah 3: 1-6

When a man believes in Christ, he is in that moment, in God's sight, as though he had never sinned in all his life. Nay, I will go further, he is that day in a better position than though he had never sinned; for if he had never sinned, he would have had the perfect righteousness of man; but by believing, he is made the righteousness of God in Christ. We had once a cloak that is taken away: when we believe, Christ gives us a robe; but it is an infinitely better one. We lost but a common garment, but he arrays us royally. Strangely indeed is that man clothed who believes in Jesus. Yon thief who is hanging on the cross, is black as hell: he believes, and he is as white as heaven's own purity. Faith takes away all sin, through the precious blood of Jesus. When a man has once gone down into that sacred laver which is filled with Jesus' blood, there "is no spot, or wrinkle, or any such thing," left upon him. His sin has ceased to be; his iniquity is covered; his transgressions have been carried into the wilderness, and are gone. This is the most wonderful thing about the gospel. This does not take away part of our sin, but the whole of it; it does not remove it partially, but entirely; not for a little time, but for ever. "He that believeth on him is not condemned." And though today you should have committed every crime in the world, yet the moment you believe in Jesus, you are saved; the Spirit of God shall dwell in you to keep you from sin in the future, and the blood of Christ shall plead for you, that sin shall never be laid to your charge.

FOR MEDITATION: How Satan must hate the doctrine of justification by faith in Christ alone! Never give him the satisfaction of seeing you grow weary of it. "Being justified by faith, we have peace with God through our Lord Jesus Christ." (Romans 5: 1).

SERMON NO. 366

Paul's first prayer

"For, behold, he prayeth." Acts 9: 11
SUGGESTED FURTHER READING: Colossians 4: 2-12

Whenever a Christian backslides, his wandering commences in his closet. I speak what I have felt. I have often gone back from God—never so as to fall finally, I know, but I have often lost that sweet savour of his love which I once enjoyed. I have had to cry:

"What peaceful hours I once enjoyed! How sweet their memory still!
But they have left an aching void, The world can never fill."

I have gone up to God's house to preach, without either fire or energy; I have read the Bible, and there has been no light upon it, I have tried to have communion with God, but all has been a failure. Shall I tell you where that commenced? It commenced in my closet. I had ceased, in a measure, to pray. Here I stand, and do confess my faults; I do acknowledge that whenever I depart from God it is there it begins. Oh Christians, would you be happy? Be much in prayer. Would you be victorious? Be much in prayer.

"Restraining prayer, we cease to fight; Prayer makes the Christian's armour bright."

Mrs Berry used to say, "I would not be hired out of my closet for a thousand worlds." Mr Jay said, "If the twelve apostles were living near you, and you had access to them, if this intercourse drew you from the closet, they would prove a real injury to your souls." Prayer is the ship which brings home the richest freight. It is the soil which yields the most abundant harvest. Brother, when you rise in the morning your business so presses, that with a hurried word or two, down you go into the world, and at night, jaded and tired, you give God the fag end of the day. The consequence is, that you have no communion with him.

FOR MEDITATION: Jonah's backsliding was accompanied by a total lack of prayer, even when pagans were trying to pray (Jonah 1: 5,6,14). God sometimes resorts to drastic measures to bring the believer back to himself and to prayer (Jonah 2: 1).

SERMON NO. 16

Separating the precious from the vile

"That ye may know how that the Lord doth put a difference between the Egyptians and Israel." Exodus 11: 7
SUGGESTED FURTHER READING: Ephesians 4: 17-32

A stern rough argument might move us to be separate from the world. But once again, how is it possible for us to honour Jesus Christ, while there is no difference between us and the world? I can imagine that a man may not profess to be a Christian, and yet he may honour his master; that however is a matter of imagination, I do not know of an instance; but I cannot imagine a man professing to be a Christian, and then acting as the world acts, and yet honouring Christ. Methinks I see my Master now; he stands before me. He has more than those five blessed wounds. I see his hands running with blood. "My Master! My Master!" I cry, "where didst thou get those wounds? Those are not the piercings of the nails, nor the gash of the spear-thrust; whence come those wounds?" I hear him mournfully reply, "These are the wounds which I have received in the house of my friends; such-and-such a Christian fell, such-and-such a disciple followed me afar off, and at last Peter-like denied me altogether. Such a one of my children is covetous, such another of them is proud, such another has taken his neighbour by the throat, and said, "Pay me what thou owest," and I have been wounded in the house of my friends." O, blessed Jesus, forgive us, forgive us, and give us thy grace that we may do so no more, for we would follow thee whithersoever thou goest; thou knowest Lord we would be thine, we would honour thee and not grieve thee. O give us now of thine own Spirit, that we may come out from the world and be like thyself,—holy, harmless, undefiled, and separate from sinners.

FOR MEDITATION: Does the Lord have to ask you "Will ye also go away?" May he enable us to reply as Simon Peter did (John 6: 67-69).

SERMON NO. 305

The way to God

"No man cometh unto the Father, but by me." John 14: 6
SUGGESTED FURTHER READING: Genesis 28: 10-17

From the moment when Adam touched the forbidden fruit, the way from God to man became blocked up, the bridge was broken down, a great gulf was fixed, so that if it had not been for the divine plan of grace, we could not have ascended to God, neither could God in justice come down to us. Happily, however, the everlasting covenant, ordered in all things and sure, had provided for this great catastrophe. Christ Jesus the Mediator had in eternity past been ordained to become the medium of access between man and God. If you want a figure of him, remember the memorable dream of Jacob. He lay down in a solitary place, and he dreamed a dream, which had in it something more substantial than anything he had seen with his eyes wide open. He saw a ladder, the foot whereof rested upon earth, and the top thereof reached to heaven itself. Upon this ladder he saw angels ascending and descending. Now this ladder was Christ. Christ in his humanity rested upon the earth, he is bone of our bone, and flesh of our flesh. In his divinity he reaches to the highest heaven, for he is very God of very God. When our prayers ascend on high they must tread the staves of this ladder; and when God's blessings descend to us, the rounds of this marvellous ladder must be the means of their descent. Never has a prayer ascended to God save through Jesus Christ. Never has a blessing come down to man save through the same Divine Mediator. There is now a highway, a way of holiness wherein the redeemed can walk to God, and God can come to us. The king's highway:

"The way the holy prophets went-
The road that leads from banishment."

Jesus Christ, the way, the truth, and the life.

FOR MEDITATION: The crucifixion of God the Son was the opening ceremony of the way to the Father. As soon as the Son announced "It is finished", the Father marked the occasion by cutting the veil of the temple from top to bottom (Mark 15: 37,38; Hebrews 10:19,20).

SERMON NO. 245

The great revival

"The Lord hath made bare his holy arm in the eyes of all the nations; and all the ends of the earth shall see the salvation of our God." Isaiah 52: 10
SUGGESTED FURTHER READING: 1 Corinthians 14: 26-40

In the old revivals in America a hundred years ago, commonly called "the great awakening," there were many strange things, such as continual shrieks and screams, and knockings, and twitchings, under the services. We cannot call that the work of the Spirit. Even the great Whitefield's revival at Cambuslang, one of the greatest and most remarkable revivals ever known, was attended by some things that we cannot but regard as superstitious wonders. People were so excited, that they did not know what they did. Now, if in any revival you see any of these strange contortions of the body, always distinguish between things that differ. The Holy Spirit's work is with the mind, not with the body in that way. It is not the will of God that such things should disgrace the proceedings. I believe that such things are the result of Satanic malice. The devil sees that there is a great deal of good doing; "Now," says he, "I'll spoil it all. I'll put my hoof in there, and do a world of mischief. There are souls being converted; I will let them get so excited that they will do ludicrous things, and then it will all be brought into contempt." Now, if you see any of these strange things arising, look out. There is that old Apollyon busy, trying to mar the work. Put such vagaries down as soon as you can, for where the Spirit works, he never works against his own precept, and his precept is, "Let all things be done decently and in order." It is neither decent nor orderly for people to dance under the sermon, nor howl, nor scream, while the gospel is being preached to them, and therefore it is not the Spirit's work at all, but mere human excitement.

FOR MEDITATION: The Holy Spirit produces self-control, not loss of control (1 Corinthians 14: 32; Galatians 5: 22,23; 2 Timothy 1: 7).

The snare of the fowler

"Surely he shall deliver thee from the snare of the fowler." Psalm 91: 3
SUGGESTED FURTHER READING: 2 Corinthians 11: 1-20

It was once said by a talented writer, that the old devil was dead, and that there was a new devil now; by which he meant to say, that the devil of old times was a rather different devil from the deceiver of these times. We believe that it is the same evil spirit; but there is a difference in his mode of attack. The devil of five hundred years ago was a black and grimy thing, well portrayed in our old pictures of that evil spirit. He was a persecutor, who cast men into the furnace, and put them to death for serving Christ. The devil of this day is a well-spoken gentleman: he does not persecute—he rather attempts to persuade and to beguile. He is not now the furious Romanist, so much as the insinuating unbeliever, attempting to overturn our religion, whilst at the same time he pretends he would but make it more rational, and so more triumphant. He would only link worldliness with religion; and so he would really make religion void, under the cover of developing the great power of the gospel, and bringing out secrets which our forefathers had never discovered. Satan is always a fowler; whatever his tactics may be, his object is still the same—to catch men in his net. Men are here compared to silly, weak birds, that have not skill enough to avoid the snare, and have not strength enough to escape from it. Satan is the fowler; he has been so and is so still; and if he does not attack us as the roaring lion, roaring against us in persecution, he attacks us as the adder, creeping silently along the path, endeavouring to bite our heel with his poisoned fangs, and weaken the power of grace and ruin the life of godliness within us. Our text is a very comforting one to all believers, when they are beset by temptation.

FOR MEDITATION: We should be on our guard against falling into the snare of the devil (1 Timothy 3: 7), but take courage from the fact that God is able to enable us to escape from it (2 Timothy 2: 26).

Israel at the Red Sea

"He rebuked the Red sea also, and it was dried up: so he led them through the depths, as through the wilderness." Psalm 106: 9
SUGGESTED FURTHER READING: Psalm 136

How sweet is providence to a child of God, when he can reflect upon it! He can look out into this world, and say, "However great my troubles, they are not so great as my Father's power; however difficult may be my circumstances, yet all things around me are working together for good. He who holds up the starry heavens can also support my soul without a single apparent prop; he who guides the stars in their well-ordered courses, even when they seem to move in mazy dances, surely he can overrule my trials in such a way that out of confusion he will bring order; and from seeming evil produce lasting good. He who bridles the storm, and puts the bit in the mouth of the tempest, surely he can restrain my trial, and keep my sorrows in subjection. I need not fear while the lightnings are in his hands, and the thunders sleep within his lips; while the oceans gurgle from his fist, and the clouds are in the hollow of his hands; while the rivers are turned by his foot, and while he digs the channels of the sea. Surely he whose might wings an angel, can furnish a worm with strength; he who guides a cherub will not be overcome by the trials of a worm like myself. He who makes the greatest star roll in dignity, and keeps its predestined orbit, can make a little atom like myself move in my proper course, and conduct me as he pleases." Christian! There is no sweeter pillow than providence; and when providence seems adverse, believe it still, lay it under your head, for depend upon it there is comfort in its bosom. There is hope for you, child of God!

FOR MEDITATION: You may find it easy to think like this when all seems to be going well. The Christian is still able to look up spiritually when circumstances would make him look down naturally (Romans 8: 28,31,35-39).

The march

"And it came to pass, when the ark set forward, that Moses said, Rise up, Lord, and let thine enemies be scattered; and let them that hate thee flee before thee." Numbers 10: 35
SUGGESTED FURTHER READING: 2 Chronicles 20: 1-30

"Rise up, Lord, Father, Son, and Spirit, we can do nothing without thee; but if thou wilt arise, thine enemies shall be scattered, and they that hate thee shall flee before thee." Will you and I go home and pray this prayer by ourselves, fervently laying hold upon the horns of God's altar? I charge you, my brethren in Christ, do not neglect this private duty. Go, each one of you, to your chambers; shut your doors; cry to him who hears in secret, and let this be the burden of your cry—"Rise up, Lord, and let thine enemies be scattered." And at your altars tonight, when your families are gathered together, still let the same cry ring up to heaven. And then tomorrow, and all the days of the week, and as often as we shall meet together to hear his word and to break bread, cry, "Rise up, Lord, and let thine enemies be scattered; and let them that hate thee flee before thee." Pray for your children, your neighbours, your families, and your friends, and let your prayer be—"Rise up, Lord; rise up, Lord." Pray for this neighbourhood; pray for the dense darkness of Southwark, and Walworth, and Lambeth. And oh! If you cannot pray for others because your own needs come so strongly before your mind, remember sinner, all you need is by faith to look to Christ, and then you can say, "Rise up, Lord; scatter my doubts; kill my unbelief; drown my sins in thy blood; let these thine enemies be scattered; let them that hate thee flee before thee."

FOR MEDITATION: This call to prayer, which comes at the very end of the "New Park Street Pulpit" reminds us of some important lessons—the battle is the Lord's, the armour is God's, but the responsibility to pray still rests with us, God's people (Ephesians 6:10-20).

SERMON NO. 368

I shall rise again

"But some man will say, How are the dead raised up? and with what body do they come? Thou fool, that which thou sowest is not quickened, except it die: And that which thou sowest, thou sowest not that body that shall be, but bare grain, it may chance of wheat, or of some other grain: But God giveth it a body as it hath pleased him, and to every seed his own body." 1 Corinthians 15: 35-38
SUGGESTED FURTHER READING: Luke 21: 25-33

The seasons are four evangelists, each of them having his testimony to utter to us. Does not summer preach to us of God's bounty, of the richness of his goodness, of that lavish generosity with which he has been pleased to supply the earth, not simply with food for man, but with delights for both ear and eye in the beauteous landscape, the melodious birds, and the flowers of various hue? Have you never heard the still small voice of autumn, who bears the wheatsheaf, and whispers to us in the rustling of the withered leaf? He bids us prepare to die. "All we" saith he, "do fade as a leaf," and "all our righteousnesses are as filthy rags." Then comes winter, crowned with snow, and he thunders out a most mighty sermon, which, if we would but listen to it, might well impress us with the terrors of God's vengeance, and let us see how soon he can strip the earth of all its pleasantries, and enrobe it in storm, when he shall come himself to judge the earth with righteousness, and the people with equity. But it seems to me that spring reads us a most excellent discourse upon the grand doctrine of revelation. This very month of April, which, if it be not the very entrance of spring, yet certainly introduces us to the fulness of it; this very month, bearing by its name the title of the opening month, speaks to us of the resurrection. As we have walked through our gardens, fields, and woods, we have seen the flower-buds ready to burst upon the trees, and the fruit-blossoms hastening to unfold themselves; we have seen the buried flowers rising from the sod, and they have spoken to us with sweet, sweet voice, the words, "Thou too shalt rise again, thou too shalt be buried in the earth like seeds that are lost in winter, but thou shalt rise again, and thou shalt live and blossom in eternal springs."

FOR MEDITATION: Only a fool ignores the lessons of creation (Romans 1: 20-22).

SERMON NO. 306

Joseph attacked by the archers

"The archers have sorely grieved him, and shot at him, and hated him: But his bow abode in strength, and the arms of his hands were made strong by the hands of the mighty God of Jacob; (from thence is the shepherd, the stone of Israel)." Genesis 49: 23,24
SUGGESTED FURTHER READING: Acts 4: 1-12

"The stone which the builders refused is become the headstone of the corner." It is said that when Solomon's temple was being built, all the stones were brought from the quarry ready cut and fashioned, and there was marked on all the blocks the places where they were to be put. Amongst the stones was a very curious one; it seemed of no describable shape, it appeared unfit for any portion of the building. They tried it at this wall, but it would not fit; they tried it in another, but it could not be accommodated; so, vexed and angry, they threw it away. The temple was so many years building, that this stone became covered with moss, and grass grew around it. Everybody passing by laughed at the stone; they said Solomon was wise, and doubtless all the other stones were right; but as for that block, they might as well send it back to the quarry, for they were quite sure it was meant for nothing. Year after year rolled on, and the poor stone was still despised, the builders constantly refused it. The eventful day came when the temple was to be finished and opened, and the multitude was assembled to see the grand sight. The builders said, "Where is the top-stone? Where is the pinnacle?" they little thought where the crowning marble was, until some one said, "Perhaps that stone which the builders refused is meant to be the top-stone." They then took it, and hoisted it to the top of the house; and as it reached the summit, they found it well adapted to the place. Loud hosannas made the heavens ring, as the stone which the builders refused became the headstone of the corner. So is it with Christ Jesus.

FOR MEDITATION: To begin with, man saw to it that the first shall be last; in the end God saw to it that the last shall be first. Where do you place the Lord Jesus Christ?

Mr Fearing comforted

"O thou of little faith, wherefore didst thou doubt?" Matthew 14: 31
SUGGESTED FURTHER READING: Isaiah 51: 9-16

Why did Simon Peter doubt? He doubted for two reasons. First, because he looked too much to second causes, and secondly, because he looked too little at the first cause. The answer will suit you also, my trembling brother. This is the reason why you doubt, because you are looking too much to the things that are seen, and too little to your unseen Friend who is behind your troubles, and who shall come forth for your deliverance. See poor Peter in the ship—his Master bids him come; in a moment he casts himself into the sea, and to his own surprise he finds himself walking the billows. His foot is upon a crested wave, and yet he stands erect; he treads again, and yet his footing is secure. "Oh!" thinks Peter, "this is marvellous." He begins to wonder within his spirit what manner of man he must be who has enabled him thus to tread the treacherous deep; but just then, there comes howling across the sea a terrible blast of wind; it whistles in the ear of Peter, and he says within himself, "Ah! Here comes an enormous billow driven forward by the blast; now, surely, I must, I shall be overwhelmed." No sooner does the thought enter his heart than down he goes; and the waves begin to enclose him. So long as he shut his eye to the billow, and to the blast, and kept it only open to the Lord who stood there before him, he did not sink; but the moment he shut his eye on Christ, and looked at the stormy wind and treacherous deep, down he went.

FOR MEDITATION: The Christian is in a battle against unseen enemies. The shield of faith helps us to fight and, having done all, to stand (Ephesians 6: 12-16); to put it down for a moment and to rely on sight is to risk falling in battle.

The form and spirit of religion

"Let us fetch the ark of the covenant of the Lord out of Shiloh unto us, that, when it cometh among us, it may save us out of the hand of our enemies." 1 Samuel 4: 3

<small>SUGGESTED FURTHER READING:</small> 1 Corinthians 1: 13-17

How vain are the hopes that men build upon their good works, and ceremonial observances! How frightful is that delusion which teaches for the gospel a thing which is not "the gospel", nor "another gospel"; but it is a thing that would pervert the gospel of Christ. Let me ask thee solemnly, what is thy ground of hope? Dost thou rely on baptism? O man, how foolish thou art! What can a few drops of water, put upon an infant's forehead, do? Some lying hypocrites tell us that children are regenerated by drops of water. What kind of regeneration is that? We have seen people hanged that were regenerated in this fashion. There have been men that have lived all their lives as whoremongers, adulterers, thieves, and murderers, who have been regenerated in their baptism by that kind of regeneration. Oh, be not deceived by a regeneration so absurd, so palpable even to flesh and blood, as one of the lying wonders that have come from hell itself. But maybe thou sayest, "Sir, I rely upon my baptism, in after life." Ah, my friends, what can washing in water do? As the Lord liveth, if thou trustest in baptism thou trustest in a thing that will fail thee at last. For what is washing in water, unless it is preceded by faith and repentance? We baptize you, not in order to wash away your sins, but because we believe they are washed away beforehand; and if we did not think you believed so, we would not admit you to a participation in that ordinance. But if you will pervert this to your own destruction, by trusting in it, take heed; you are warned this morning. For as "circumcision availeth nothing, nor uncircumcision, but a new creature," so baptism availeth nothing.

<small>FOR MEDITATION:</small> Baptism is supposed to illustrate the gospel, not to replace it. The command to be baptised follows the new birth, repentance and faith in Christ (Mark 16: 16; Acts 2: 38; 8: 12,36-38; 9: 17-18; 10: 47-48; 16: 14-15,31-34; 18: 8).

<small>SERMON NO.186</small>

Justification by grace

"Being justified freely by his grace through the redemption that is in Christ Jesus." Romans 3: 24

SUGGESTED FURTHER READING: Hebrews 10: 11-18

God demanded of Christ the payment for the sins of all his people; Christ stood forward, and to the utmost farthing paid whate'er his people owed. The sacrifice of Calvary was not a part payment; it was not a partial exoneration, it was a complete and perfect payment, and it obtained a complete and perfect remission of all the debts of all believers that have lived, do live, or shall live, to the very end of time. On that day when Christ hung on the cross, he did not leave a single farthing for us to pay as a satisfaction to God. The whole of the demands of the law were paid down there and then by Jehovah Jesus, the great high priest of all his people. And blessed be his name, he paid it all at once too. So priceless was the ransom, so princely and generous was the price demanded for our souls, one might have thought it would have been marvellous if Christ had paid it by instalments; some of it now, and some of it then. Kings' ransoms have sometimes been paid part at once, and part in dues afterwards, to run through years. But not so our Saviour: once for all he gave himself a sacrifice; at once he counted down the price, and said, "It is finished," leaving nothing for him to do, nor for us to accomplish. He did not drivel out a part-payment, and then declare that he would come again to die, or that he would again suffer, or that he would again obey; but down upon the nail, to the utmost farthing, the ransom of all people was paid, and a full receipt given to them, and Christ nailed that receipt to his cross.

FOR MEDITATION: Those who attempt to complete or repeat a finished piece of work insult its maker and render it useless to themselves (Galatians 5: 2).

Effects of sound doctrine

"For there shall arise false Christs, and false prophets, and shall shew great signs and wonders; insomuch that, if it were possible, they shall deceive the very elect." Matthew 24: 24

SUGGESTED FURTHER READING: 1 Peter 2: 4-10

What effect does election have on our actions? If this doctrine be fully received and known, it breathes with all gratitude to God, an earnest desire to show forth his praise. It leads to all kinds of holy activity, and a hearty endeavour for the service of God. We are told continually by philosophic writers, that the idea of necessity—the idea that anything is fixed or decreed—tends at once to damp activity. Never was there a grosser misrepresentation. Look abroad, everything that has been great in the spirit of the age has had a Necessitarian at the bottom of it. When Mohammed preached predestination, he took a necessitarian view. Did that doctrine of predestination make his followers idle? Did it not make them dash into the battle, declaring they must die when the appointed time came, and while they lived they must fight, and earnestly defend their faith? Or to take an instance from the history of our own country. Did the Calvinism of Oliver Cromwell make his Ironsides idle? Did they not keep their powder dry? They believed that they were chosen men of God, and were they not men of valour? Did this doctrine mar their energy? So in every good enterprise our churches are never behind. Are we backward in missionary enterprise? Are we slow to send forth men of God to preach in foreign lands? Are we deficient in our efforts? Are we the people who would preach to a select few?—who would erect buildings for worship that the poor scarcely dare to enter? Are we the people who would keep our religious services for a privileged circle? The fact is, the most zealous, the most earnest, and the most successful of men, have been those who have held this truth.

FOR MEDITATION: The doctrine of election is not supposed to turn us in upon ourselves, but to send us out to others (John 15: 16; Acts 9: 15).

SERMON NO.324

The tomb of Jesus

"Come, see the place where the Lord lay." Matthew 28: 6
SUGGESTED FURTHER READING: John 20: 1-10

Come, Christian, for angels are the porters to unbar the door; come, for a cherub is thy messenger to usher thee into the death-place of death himself. Nay, start not from the entrance; let not the darkness frighten thee; the vault is not damp with the vapours of death, nor does the air contain anything of contagion. Come, for it is a pure and healthy place. Fear not to enter that tomb. I will admit that catacombs are not the places where we, who are full of joy, would love to go. There is something gloomy and offensive about a vault. There are noxious smells of corruption; often pestilence is born where a dead body has lain; but fear it not, Christian, for Christ was not left in hell, in hades, neither did his body see corruption. Come, there is no foul smell, but rather a perfume. Step in here, and, if thou didst ever breathe the gales of Ceylon, or winds from the groves of Arabia, thou shalt find them far excelled by that sweet holy fragrance left by the blessed body of Jesus, that alabaster vase which once held divinity, and was rendered sweet and precious thereby. Think not thou shalt find anything obnoxious to thy senses. Corruption Jesus never saw; no worms ever devoured his flesh; no rottenness ever entered into his bones; he saw no corruption. Three days he slumbered, but not long enough to putrify; he soon arose, perfect as when he entered, uninjured as when his limbs were composed for their slumber. Come then, Christian, summon up thy thoughts, gather all thy powers; here is a sweet invitation, let me press it again. Let me lead thee by the hand of meditation, my brother; let me take thee by the arm, and let me again say to thee, "Come, see the place where the Lord lay."

FOR MEDITATION: "Come, see .... Go ...and tell." (Matthew 28: 6,7).

SERMON NO.18

Importance of small things in religion

"The Lord our God made a breach upon us, for that we sought him not after the due order." 1 Chronicles 15: 13
SUGGESTED FURTHER READING: 1 Samuel 13: 8-14

When we come before God, it will be no excuse for us to say, "My Lord, I did wrong, but I thought I was doing right." "Yes, but I gave you my law, but you did not read it; or, if you read it, you read it so carelessly that you did not understand it, and then you did wrong, and you tell me you did it with a right motive. Yes, but it is of no avail whatever." Just as in Uzzah's case, did it not seem the rightest thing in the world to put out his hand to prevent the ark from slipping off? Who could blame the man? But God had commanded that no unpriestly hand should ever touch it, and inasmuch as he did touch it, though it was with a right motive, yet Uzzah must die. God will have his laws kept. Besides, my dear brethren, I am not sure about the rightness of your motives after all. The State has issued a proclamation, it is engraven, according to the old Roman fashion, in brass. A man goes up with his file, and he begins working away upon the brass; erases here, and amends there. Says he, "I did that with a right motive; I didn't think the law a good one, I thought it was too old-fashioned for these times, and so I thought I would alter it a little, and make it better for the people." Ah, how many have there been who have said, "The old puritanic principles are too rough for these times; we'll alter them, we'll tone them down a little." What are you at, sir? Who are you that dares to touch a single letter of God's Book?

FOR MEDITATION: Sincerity needs to be allied to truth (Joshua 24: 14). It is possible to be sincerely wrong (John 16: 2; Acts 26: 9; Romans 10: 2).

The jeer of sarcasm, and the retort of piety

"Then David returned to bless his household. And Michal... came out to meet David, and said, How glorious was the king of Israel today, who uncovered himself today in the eyes of the handmaids of his servants, as one of the vain fellows shamelessly uncovereth himself! And David said unto Michal, It was before the Lord, which chose... to appoint me ruler... over Israel: therefore will I play before the Lord. ." 2 Samuel 6: 20-22
SUGGESTED FURTHER READING: 1 Peter 3: 1-7

It is a happy thing when we are enabled to rejoice together in our family relationships; when husband and wife help each other on the path to heaven. There can be no happier position than that of the Christian man who finds, in every holy wish he has for God, a helper; who finds that often she outstrips him; that when he would do something, she suggests something more; when he would serve his Master there is a hint given that more yet might be done, and no obstacle put in the way, but every assistance rendered. Happy is that man and blessed is he. He has received a treasure from God, the like of which could not be bought for diamonds. That man is blessed of the Most High; he is heaven's favourite, and he may rejoice in the special favour of his God. But when it is the other way, and I know it is the case with some of you, then it is a sore trial indeed. Perhaps, though a careful, cautious, prudent, and excellent worldly woman, she cannot see with you in the things which you love in the kingdom of God, and when you have done something which in the excess of your zeal seems to be but little, she thinks it inordinate and extravagant. "Oh," says she, "do you go and mix with these people? Does King David go and wear a linen ephod like a peasant? Do you go and sit down with that rabble? You? You can stand up for your dignity—put 'esquire' after your name, and yet walk in the street with any beggar that likes to call himself a Christian. You," says she, "you that are so cautious in everything else, you seem to have lost your head when you think about your religion."

FOR MEDITATION: Those close to the Lord Jesus Christ, his friends and family, could not understand him (Mark 3: 21; John 7: 5) but God worked in their lives (Acts 1: 14; 1 Corinthians 9: 5). Don't despair of your loved ones who seem so far from God (1 Corinthians 7: 16).

SERMON NO. 321

The best of masters

"Peace I leave with you, my peace I give unto you: not as the world giveth, give I unto you." John 14: 27
SUGGESTED FURTHER READING: 1 Thessalonians 5: 23-28

It is the same with the world at this day. Everyone greets us in writing with a "Dear sir," or a "My dear sir," and concludes with "Yours very truly," and "Yours sincerely." We call all "friends," and if we meet but casually we express the utmost anxiety with regard to one another's health, and we carefully enquire after each other's families; when perhaps we shall no sooner have passed by the person than we shall forget his existence, and certainly shall entertain no anxious thoughts with regard to his welfare, nor any loving remembrance of him. The world gives very largely when it gives compliments. Oh, what blessings would descend upon all our heads, if the blessings uttered could be blessings bestowed. Even when the "Good bye" is given, which translated means, "God be with you"—if that could be but true, and if God could be with us, in answer to that prayer, so little understood, how rich might we be! But alas! the way of the world is, "Be ye warmed and filled;" but it has not that which should warm, nor that which should fill. It is a world of words; high-sounding, empty, all-deceiving words. Now this is not so with Christ. If he says "Peace be with you," his benediction is most true and full of sweet sincerity. He left his own peace in heaven, that he might give the peace which he enjoyed with his Father, to us in this world of sorrow, for thus he puts it, "My peace I give unto you." Christ, when he blesses, blesses not in word only, but in deed. The lips of truth cannot promise more than the hands of love will surely give. He gives not in compliment. Furthermore, even when the world's wishes of peace are sincere, what are they but mere wishes?

FOR MEDITATION: Greetings and best wishes from the lips of a Christian should be modelled on Christ, not the world. Do you go in for the "polite lie" or are your concerns for others genuine (Philippians 2: 20; 3 John 2)?

SERMON NO. 247

Providence

"But the very hairs of your head are all numbered." Matthew 10: 30
SUGGESTED FURTHER READING: Acts 16: 6-10

I shall always regard the fact of my being here today as a remarkable instance of providence. I should not have occupied this hall probably, and been blessed of God in preaching to multitudes if it had not been for what I considered an untoward accident. I should have been at this time studying in College, instead of preaching here, but for a singular circumstance which happened. I had agreed to go to College: the tutor had come to see me, and I went to see him at the house of a mutual friend; I was shown by the servant into one drawing-room in the house, he was shown into another. He sat and waited for me two hours; I sat and waited for him two hours. He could wait no longer, and went away thinking I had not treated him well; I went away and thought he had not treated me well. As I went away this text came into my mind, "Seekest thou great things for thyself? Seek them not." So I wrote to say that I must positively decline; I was happy enough amongst my own country people, and got on very well in preaching, and I did not care to go to College. I have now had four years of labour. But, speaking after the manner of men, those who have been saved during that time would not have been saved, by my instrumentality at any rate, if it had not been for the remarkable providence turning the whole tenor of my thoughts, and putting things into a new track. You have often had strange accidents like that. When you have resolved to do a thing, you could not do it anyhow; it was quite impossible. God turned you another way, and proved that providence is indeed the master of all human events.

FOR MEDITATION: God is never taken by surprise or inconvenienced by accidents. He puts his people in the right place at the right time (Esther 4: 14).

NOTE: Spurgeon commenced this sermon with an account of an event at Halifax the previous Wednesday (7 April) during a snow storm. He preached in a wooden structure to thousands in the afternoon and evening. With only a hundred people left to exit, some flooring collapsed, injuring a couple. Three hours later the whole building collapsed. Had it not been for a fast thaw, there could have been a catastrophe.

SERMON NO.187

Spiritual resurrection

"And you hath he quickened, who were dead in trespasses and sins."
Ephesians 2: 1
SUGGESTED FURTHER READING: Colossians 2: 9-14

Does it not seem a strange thing, that you, who have walked to this place this morning, shall be carried to your graves; that the eyes with which you now behold me shall soon be glazed in everlasting darkness; that the tongues, which just now moved in song, shall soon be silent lumps of clay; and that your strong and stalwart frame, now standing in this place, will soon be unable to move a muscle, and become a loathsome thing, the brother of the worm and the sister of corruption? You can scarcely get hold of the idea; death does such awful work with us, it is such a vandal with this mortal fabric, it so rends to pieces this fair thing that God has built up, that we can scarcely bear to contemplate his works of ruin. Now, endeavour, as well as you can, to get the idea of a dead corpse, and when you have done so, please to understand, that this is the metaphor employed in my text, to set forth the condition of your soul by nature. Just as the body is dead, incapable, unable, unfeeling, and soon about to become corrupt and putrid, so are we if we be unquickened by divine grace; dead in trespasses and sins, having within us death, which is capable of developing itself in worse and worse stages of sin and wickedness, until all of us here, left by God's grace, should become loathsome beings; loathsome through sin and wickedness, even as the corpse through natural decay. Understand, that the doctrine of the Holy Scripture is, that man by nature, since the fall, is dead; he is a corrupt and ruined thing; in a spiritual sense, utterly and entirely dead. And if any of us shall come to spiritual life, it must be by the quickening of God's Spirit, given to us sovereignly through the good will of God the Father, not for any merits of our own, but entirely of his own abounding and infinite grace.

FOR MEDITATION: Have you passed from death to life by faith in the Lord Jesus Christ (John 5: 24)? Better to be a nobody alive in Christ than a king dead in trespasses and sins (Ecclesiastes 9: 4).

SERMON NO. 127

A willing people and an immutable leader

"Thy people shall be willing in the day of thy power, in the beauties of holiness from the womb of the morning: thou hast the dew of thy youth." Psalm 110: 3
SUGGESTED FURTHER READING: 1 Kings 19: 9-18

Christ shall always have a people. In the darkest ages Christ has always had a church; and if darker times shall come, he will have his church still. Oh! Elijah, thy unbelief is foolish. Thou sayest, "I, only I, am left alone, and they seek my life." No, Elijah, in those caves of the earth God has his prophets, hidden by seventies. Thou too, poor unbelieving Christian, at times thou sayest, "I, even I, am left." Oh! If thou hadst eyes to see, if thou couldst travel a little, thy heart would be glad to find that God does not lack a people. It cheers my heart to find that God has a family everywhere. We do not go anywhere but we find really earnest hearts—men full of prayer. I bless God that I can say, concerning the church wherever I have been, though they are not many, there are a few, who sigh and groan over the sorrows of Israel. There are chosen bands in every church, thoroughly earnest men who are looking out for, and are ready to receive their Master, who cry to God that he would send them times of refreshing from the presence of the Lord. Do not be too sad; God has a people, and they are willing now; and when the day of God's power shall come, there is no fear about the people. Religion may be at a low ebb, but it never was at such a low ebb that God's ship was stranded. It may be ever so low, but the devil shall never be able to cross the river of Christ's church dry shod. He shall always find abundance of water running in the channel. God grant us grace to look out for his people, believing that there are some everywhere, for the promise is, "thy people shall be willing in the day of thy power."

FOR MEDITATION: Do you feel one of the few? God's people may be nearer and more numerous than you imagine (Acts 18: 9,10); even when we are very few, Christ is nearer than we sometimes imagine (Matthew 18: 20).

David's dying song

"Although my house be not so with God; yet he hath made with me an everlasting covenant, ordered in all things, and sure: for this is all my salvation, and all my desire, although he make it not to grow." 2 Samuel 23: 5
SUGGESTED FURTHER READING: Colossians 3: 1-4

If God were to put my salvation in my hands, I should be lost in ten minutes; but my salvation is not there—it is in Christ's hands. You have read of the celebrated dream of John Newton, which I will tell you to the best of my recollection. He thought he was out at sea, on board a vessel, when some bright angel flew down and presented him with a ring, saying, "As long as you wear this ring you shall be happy, and your soul shall be safe." He put the ring on his finger, and he felt happy to have it in his own possession. Then there came a spirit from the vast deep, and said to him; "The ring is nothing but folly;" and by deceit and flattery the spirit at last persuaded him to slip the ring from off his finger, and he dropped it in the sea. Then there came fierce things from the deep; the mountains bellowed, and hurled upward their volcanic lava: all the earth was on fire, and his soul in the greatest trouble. By and by a spirit came, and diving below, brought up the ring, and showing it to him, said, "Now thou art safe, for I have saved the ring." Now might John Newton have said, "Let me put it on my finger again." "No, no; you cannot take care of it yourself;" and up the angel flew, carrying the ring away with him, so that then he felt secure, since no deceit of hell could get it from him again, for it was up in heaven. My life is "hid with Christ in God."

FOR MEDITATION: Satan is unable to snatch anyone from the mighty hand of God (Job 1: 12; 2: 6; Luke 22: 31,32; John 10: 28,29). But he still has the unbeliever in his grasp.

The parable of the sower

"A sower went out to sow his seed: and as he sowed, some fell by the wayside; and it was trodden down, and the fowls of the air devoured it. And some fell upon a rock; and as soon as it was sprung up, it withered away, because it lacked moisture. And some fell among thorns; and the thorns sprang up with it, and choked it. And other fell on good ground, and sprang up, and bare fruit an hundredfold. And when he had said these things, he cried, He that hath ears to hear, let him hear." Luke 8: 5-8
SUGGESTED FURTHER READING: Colossians 1: 1-10

The ground was good; not that it was good by nature, but it had been made good by grace. God had ploughed it; he had stirred it up with the plough of conviction, and there it lay in ridge and furrow as it should be. And when the Gospel was preached, the heart received it, for the man said, "That's just the Christ I want. Mercy!" said he, "it's just what a needy sinner requires. A refuge! God help me to fly to it, for a refuge I sorely want." The preaching of the gospel was **the** vital thing which gave comfort to this disturbed and ploughed soil. Down fell the seed; it sprung up. In some cases it produced a fervency of love, a largeness of heart, a devotedness of purpose, like seed which produced a hundredfold. The man became a mighty servant for God, he spent himself and was spent. He took his place in the vanguard of Christ's army, stood in the hottest of the battle, and did deeds of daring which few could accomplish,—the seed produced a hundredfold. It fell in another heart of like character;—the man could not do the most, still he did much. He gave himself, just as he was, up to God, and in his business he had a word to say for the business of the world to come. In his daily walk, he quietly adorned the doctrine of God his Saviour,—he brought forth sixtyfold. Then it fell on another, whose abilities and talents were but small; he could not be a star, but he would be a glow-worm; he could not do as the greatest, but he was content to do something, even though it were the least. The seed had brought forth in him tenfold, perhaps twentyfold.

FOR MEDITATION: Quantity of fruit is desirable, but quality of fruit is essential—fruit that has gone mouldy is useless. The Lord Jesus Christ is looking for fruit in quantity and fruit which lasts (John 15: 5,16).

SERMON NO. 308

Christ—our substitute

"For he hath made him to be sin for us, who knew no sin; that we might be made the righteousness of God in him." 2 Corinthians 5: 21
SUGGESTED FURTHER READING: Isaiah 53: 10-12

In no sense is he ever a guilty man, but always is he an accepted and a holy one. What, then, is the meaning of that very forcible expression of my text? We must interpret Scriptural modes of expression by the words of the speakers. We know that our Master once said himself, "This cup is the new covenant in my blood;" he did not mean that the cup was the covenant. He said, "Take, eat, this is my body"—none of us conceives that the bread is the literal flesh and blood of Christ. We take that bread as if it were the body, and it actually represents it. Now, we are to read a passage like this, according to the analogy of faith. Jesus Christ was made by his Father sin for us, that is, he was treated as if he had himself been sin. He was not sin; he was not sinful; he was not guilty; but, he was treated by his Father, as if he had not only been sinful, but as if he had been sin itself. That is a strong expression used here. Not only has he made him to be the substitute for sin, but to be sin. God looked on Christ as if Christ had been sin; not as if he had taken up the sins of his people, or as if they were laid on him, though that were true, but as if he himself had positively been that noxious—that God-hating—that soul-damning thing, called sin. When the judge of all the earth said, "Where is sin?" Christ presented himself. He stood before his Father as if he had been the accumulation of all human guilt; as if he himself were that thing which God cannot endure, but which he must drive from his presence for ever.

FOR MEDITATION: God regarded Christ crucified just as if he were sin, not Son. The substitutionary atonement is the key which enables the Christian to make use of the description "Just as if I'd never sinned."

Little sins

"Is it not a little one?" Genesis 19: 20
SUGGESTED FURTHER READING: Romans 2: 1-11

There is a deep pit, and the soul is falling down,—oh how fast it is falling! There! The last ray of light at the top has disappeared, and it falls on and on and on, and so it goes on falling—on and on and on—for a thousand years! "Is it not getting near the bottom yet? No, you are no nearer the bottom yet: it is the "bottomless pit;" it is on and on and on, and so the soul goes on falling, perpetually, into a deeper depth still, falling for ever into the "bottomless pit" and on and on and on, into the pit that has no bottom! Woe without termination, without hope of coming to a conclusion. The same dreadful idea is contained in those words, "The wrath to come." Notice, hell is always "the wrath to come." If a man has been in hell a thousand years, it is still "to come." What you have suffered in the past is as nothing, in the dread account, for still the wrath is "to come." And when the world has grown grey with age, and the fires of the sun are quenched in darkness, it is still "the wrath to come." And when other worlds have sprung up, and have turned into their palsied age, it is still "the wrath to come." And when your soul, burnt through and through with anguish, sighs at last to be annihilated, even then this awful thunder shall be heard, "the wrath to come—to come—to come." Oh, what an idea! I know not how to utter it! And yet for little sins, remember you incur "the wrath to come."

FOR MEDITATION: This shocking description can give only a faint idea of the just punishment of our sins. Are you trusting in the Lord Jesus Christ to deliver you from the wrath to come? He is able to do it because he suffered the wrath of his loving heavenly Father on the cross (Romans 5: 9; 1 Thessalonians 1: 10).

"We may not know, we cannot tell, What pains He had to bear;
But we believe it was for us, He hung and suffered there."

Do you?

SERMON NO. 248

The Redeemer's prayer

"Father, I will that they also, whom thou hast given me, be with me where I am; that they may behold my glory, which thou hast given me: for thou lovedst me before the foundation of the world." John 17: 24
SUGGESTED FURTHER READING: Song of Solomon 5: 1-8

When we get a glimpse of Christ, many step in to interfere. We have our hours of contemplation, when we draw near to Jesus, but alas! how the world steps in and interrupts even our most quiet moments—the shop, the field, the child, the wife, the head, perhaps the very heart, all these are interlopers between ourselves and Jesus. Christ loves quiet; he will not talk to our souls in the busy market place, but he says, "Come, my love, into the vineyard, get thee away into the villages, there will I show thee my love." But when we go to the villages, behold the Philistine is there, the Canaanite has invaded the land. When we would be free from all thought except thought of Jesus, the wandering band of Bedouin thoughts come upon us, and they take away our treasures, and spoil our tents. We are like Abraham with his sacrifice; we lay out the pieces ready for the burning, but foul birds come to feast on the sacrifice which we desire to keep for our God and for him alone. We have to do as Abraham did; "When the birds came down upon the sacrifice, Abraham drove them away." But in heaven there shall be no interruption, no weeping eyes shall make us for a moment pause in our vision; no earthly joys, no sensual delights, shall create a discord in our melody; there shall we have no fields to till, no garment to spin, no wearied limb, no dark distress, no burning thirst, no pangs of hunger, no weepings of bereavement; we shall have nothing to do or think upon, but for ever to gaze upon that Sun of righteousness, with eyes that cannot be blinded, and with a heart that can never be weary.

FOR MEDITATION: We are never going to be free from outside distractions and wandering thoughts in this life, but we do need to seek to have some time each day when we can shut them out as far as possible and spend time alone with our heavenly Father (Matthew 6: 6).

SERMON NO.188

The uses of the law

"Wherefore then serveth the law?" Galatians 3: 19
SUGGESTED FURTHER READING: Proverbs 26: 12-16

I find that the proudest and most self-righteous people are those who do nothing at all, and have no shadow of pretence for any opinion of their own goodness. The old truth in the book of Job is true now. You know in the beginning of the book of Job it is said, "The oxen were ploughing, and the asses were feeding beside them." That is generally the way in this world. The oxen are ploughing in the church —we have some who are labouring hard for Christ—and the asses are feeding beside them, on the finest livings and the fattest of the land. These are the people who have so much to say about self-righteousness. What do they do? They do not do enough to earn a living, and yet they think they are going to earn heaven. They sit down and fold their hands, and yet they are so reverently righteous, because they sometimes dole out a little in charity. They do nothing, and yet boast of self-righteousness. And with Christian people it is the same. If God makes you laborious, and keeps you constantly engaged in his service, you are less likely to be proud of your self-righteousness than you are if you do nothing. But at all times there is a natural tendency to it. Therefore, God has written the law, that when we read it we may see our faults; that when we look into it, as into a looking-glass, we may see the impurities in our flesh, and have reason to abhor ourselves in sackcloth and ashes, and still cry to Jesus for mercy. Use the law in this fashion, and in no other.

FOR MEDITATION: The more we learn, the more we realise how little we know; the more we do, the more we realise how little we do; the holier we become, the more we realise how unholy we are. Being sluggish is most unsuitable for the Christian (Hebrews 6: 10-12).

Final perseverance

"For it is impossible for those who were once enlightened, and have tasted of the heavenly gift, and were made partakers of the Holy Ghost, And have tasted the good word of God, and the powers of the world to come, If they shall fall away, to renew them again unto repentance; seeing they crucify to themselves the Son of God afresh, and put him to an open shame." Hebrews 6: 4-6
SUGGESTED FURTHER READING: Hebrews 10: 26-39

God preserves his children from falling away; but he keeps them by the use of means; and one of these is, the terrors of the law, showing them what would happen if they were to fall away. There is a deep precipice: what is the best way to keep any one from going down there? Why, to tell him that if he did he would inevitably be dashed to pieces. In some old castle there is a deep cellar where there is a vast amount of stale air and gas which would kill anybody who went down. What does the guide say? "If you go down you will never come up alive." Who thinks of going down? The very fact of the guide telling us what the consequences would be, keeps us from it. Our friend puts away from us a cup of arsenic; he does not want us to drink it, but he says, "If you drink it, it will kill you." Does he suppose for a moment that we should drink it? No; he tells us the consequence, and he is sure we will not do it. So God says, "My child, if you fall over this precipice you will be dashed to pieces." What does the child do? He says, "Father, keep me; hold thou me up, and I shall be safe." It leads the believer to greater dependence on God, to a holy fear and caution, because he knows that if he were to fall away he could not be renewed, and he stands far away from that great gulf, because he knows that if he were to fall into it there would be no salvation for him. It is calculated to excite fear; and this holy fear keeps the Christian from falling.

FOR MEDITATION: God is the One who keeps us from falling (Jude 24), but he still tells us that we have some responsibility to keep ourselves in his love (Jude 21).

The carnal mind

"The carnal mind is enmity against God." Romans 8: 7
SUGGESTED FURTHER READING: Romans 5: 6-11

Let me suppose an impossible case for a moment. Let me imagine a man entering heaven without a change of heart. He comes within the gates. He hears a sonnet. He starts! It is to the praise of his enemy. He sees a throne, and on it sits one who is glorious; but it is his enemy. He walks streets of gold, but those streets belong to his enemy. He sees hosts of angels; but those are the servants of his enemy. He is in an enemy's house; for he is at enmity with God. He could not join the song, for he would not know the tune. There he would stand; silent, motionless; till Christ should say, with a voice louder than ten thousand thunders, "What doest thou here? Enemies at a marriage banquet? Enemies in the children's house? Enemies in heaven? Get thee gone! Depart ye cursed, into everlasting fire in hell!" Oh! sirs, if the unregenerate man could enter heaven, I mention once more the oft-repeated saying of Whitefield, he would be so unhappy in heaven, that he would ask God to let him run down into hell for shelter. There must be a change, if you consider the future state; for how can enemies to God ever sit down at the banquet of the Lamb? And to conclude, let me remind you—and it is in the text after all—that this change must be worked by a power beyond your own. An enemy may possibly make himself a friend, but **enmity** cannot. If it be but an adjunct of his nature to be an enemy he may change himself into a friend; but if it is the very essence of his existence to be enmity, positive enmity, enmity cannot change itself. No, there must be something done more than we can accomplish.

FOR MEDITATION: The Lord Jesus Christ has done for us much more than he commanded his disciples to do for their enemies (Luke 6: 27-28).

Full redemption

"There shall not an hoof be left behind." Exodus 10: 26
SUGGESTED FURTHER READING: Revelation 20: 1-10

A man once wrote a book to prove the devil a fool. Certainly, when all matters shall come to their destined consummation, Satan will prove to have been a magnificent fool. Folly, magnified to the highest degree by subtlety, shall be developed in Satan. Ah! Thou trailing serpent, what hast thou now after all? I saw thee but a few thousand years ago, twining around the tree of life, and hissing out thy deceptive words. Ah! how glorious was the serpent then—a winged creature, with his azure scales. Yes, and thou didst triumph over God. I heard thee as thou didst go hissing down to thy den. I heard thee say to thy brood,—vipers in the nest as they are,—"My children, I have stained the Almighty's works: I have turned aside his loyal subjects; I have injected my poison into the heart of Eve, and Adam hath fallen too; my children let us hold a jubilee, for I have defeated God." Oh, my enemy; I think I see thee now, with thy head all broken, and thy jaw-teeth smashed, and thy venom-bags all emptied, and thou thyself a weary length of agony, rolling miles afloat along a sea of fire, tortured, destroyed, overcome, tormented, ashamed, hacked, hewed, dashed in pieces, and made a hissing, and a scorn for children to laugh at, and made a scoff throughout eternity. Ah! well, brethren, the great Goliath hath gained nothing by his boasting: Christ and his people have really lost nothing by Satan. All they lost once, has been re-taken. The victory has not simply been a capture of that which was lost, but a gaining of something more. We are in Christ more than we were before we fell. "Not a hoof shall be left behind."

FOR MEDITATION: Victory over Satan will be celebrated with joy (Revelation 12: 10-12; Romans 16: 20) but for the moment we must remain on our guard against him (1 Corinthians 7: 5; 2 Corinthians 2: 11; Ephesians 4: 27; 6: 11; 1 Timothy 3: 6,7; 1 Peter 5: 8,9).

A divine challenge

"Thus saith the Lord, let my people go, that they may serve me." Exodus 8: 1
SUGGESTED FURTHER READING: James 3: 3-6

Moses goes to Pharaoh yet again, and says, "Thus saith the Lord, let my people go, that they may serve me." And at one time the haughty monarch says he will let some go; at another time he will let them all go, but they are to leave their cattle behind. He will hold on to something; if he cannot have the whole he will have a part. It is wonderful how content the devil is if he can but nibble at a man's heart. It does not matter about swallowing it whole; only let him nibble and he will be content. Let him but bite at the fag ends and be satisfied, for he is wise enough to know that if a serpent has but an inch of bare flesh to sting, he will poison the whole. When Satan cannot get a great sin in he will let a little one in, like the thief who goes and finds shutters all coated with iron and bolted inside. At last he sees a little window in a chamber. He cannot get in, so he puts a little boy in, that he may go round and open the back door. So the devil has always his little sins to carry about with him to go and open back doors for him, and we let one in and say, "O, it is only a little one." Yes, but how that little one becomes the ruin of the entire man! Let us take care that the devil does not get a foothold, for if he gets but a foothold, he will get his whole body in and we shall be overcome.

FOR MEDITATION: Beware of giving Satan a window of opportunity (Ephesians 4: 27), it is amazing how much damage can be caused by something apparently little (1 Corinthians 5: 6; Hebrews 12: 15).

A vision of the latter day glories

"And it shall come to pass in the last days, that the mountain of the Lord's house shall be established in the top of the mountains, and shall be exalted above the hills; and all nations shall flow unto it." Isaiah 2: 2 & Micah 4: 1
SUGGESTED FURTHER READING: 2 Thessalonians 2: 1-15

I am looking for the advent of Christ; it is this that cheers me in the battle of life—the battle and cause of Christ. I look for Christ to come, somewhat as John Bunyan described the battle of Captain Credence with Diabolus. The inhabitants of the town of Mansoul fought hard to protect their city from the prince of darkness, and at last a pitched battle was fought outside the walls. The captains and the brave men of arms fought all day till their swords were knitted to their hands with blood; many and many a weary hour did they seek to drive back the Diabolonians. The battle seemed to waver in the balance; sometimes victory was on the side of faith, and then, triumph seemed to hover over the crest of the prince of hell; but just as the sun was setting, trumpets were heard in the distance; Prince Emmanuel was coming, with trumpets sounding, and with banners flying; and while the men of Mansoul pressed onward sword in hand, Emmanuel attacked their foes in the rear, and getting the enemy between them both, they went on, driving their enemies at the sword's point, till at last, trampling over their dead bodies, they met, and hand to hand the victorious church saluted its victorious Lord. Even so must it be. We must fight on day by day and hour by hour; and when we think the battle is almost decided against us, we shall hear the trump of the archangel, and the voice of God, and he shall come, the Prince of the kings of the earth; at his name, with terror shall they melt, and like snow driven before the wind from the bare side of a mountain shall they fly away; and we, the church militant, trampling over them, shall salute our Lord, shouting, "Hallelujah, hallelujah, hallelujah, the Lord God omnipotent reigneth."

FOR MEDITATION: The Lord's second coming is an encouragement for us to hold fast to what we have (Revelation 2: 25; 3: 11). "Hold the fort, for I am coming!"

SERMON NO. 249

The cry of the heathen

"And a vision appeared to Paul in the night; There stood a man of Macedonia, and prayed him, saying, Come over unto Macedonia, and help us." Acts 16: 9
SUGGESTED FURTHER READING: 2 Corinthians 8: 1-15

There is no fear of any one becoming improvidently liberal. You need not be frightened that anyone here will give a thousand pounds this morning. We provide ample accommodation for those who feel inclined to do so. If anyone should be overtaken with such an enormous fit of generosity, we will register and remember it. But I fear there are no people like Barnabas now. Barnabas brought all he had, and put it into the treasury. "My dear friend, do not do that; do not be so rash." Ah! he will not do that; there is no necessity for you to advise him. But I do say again, if Christianity were truly in our hearts; if we were what we professed to be; the men of generosity whom we meet with now and hold up as very paragons and patterns would cease to be wonders, for they would be as plentiful as leaves upon the trees. We demand of no man that he should beggar himself; but we do demand of every man who makes a profession that he is a Christian, that he should give his fair proportion, and not be content with giving as much to the cause of God as his own servant. We must have it that the man who is rich must give richly. We know the widow's mite is precious, but the widow's mite has been an enormously great loss to us. That widow's mite has lost Jesus Christ many a thousand pounds. It is a very good thing in itself; but people with thousands a year talk of giving a widow's mite. What a wicked application of what never can apply to them. No; in our proportion we must serve our God.

FOR MEDITATION: We are instructed to give in proportion (2 Corinthians 8: 12), in pleasure (2 Corinthians 9: 7) and in privacy (Matthew 6: 2-4). How do you calculate how much you should be giving to God's work each week? In prayer?

SERMON NO. 189

David's dying prayer

"Let the whole earth be filled with his glory; Amen, and Amen." Psalm 72: 19
SUGGESTED FURTHER READING: Isaiah 6: 1-8

Is there not one among you that can win a laurel wreath? Have I not one true Christian heart here that is set for work and labour? Have I not one man that will devote himself for God and for his truth? Henry Martyn! Thou art dead; and is thy mantle buried with thee? Brainerd, thou sleepest with thy fathers; and is thy spirit dead too, and shall there never be another Brainerd? Knibb, thou hast ascended to thy God; and is there nowhere another Knibb? Williams, thy martyred blood still crieth from the ground; and is there nowhere another Williams? What! Not among this dense mass of young and burning spirits? Is there not one that can say in his heart, "Here am I, send me"? "This hour, being saved by God's grace, I give myself up to him, to go wherever he shall be pleased to send me, to testify his gospel in foreign lands"? What! Are there no Pauls now? Have we none who will be apostles for the Lord of hosts? I think I see one who, putting his lips together, makes this silent resolve—"By God's grace I this day devote myself to him; through trouble and through trial I will be his, if he will help me; for missionary work or for anything else I give up my all to God; and if I may die as Williams did, and wear the blood-red crown of martyrdom, I will be proud; and if I may live to serve my Master, like a Brainerd, and die at last worn out, here I am, do but have me, Master; give me the honour of leading the forlorn hope, of leading the vanguard of Christianity; here I am, send me."

FOR MEDITATION: The earth is going to be filled with the knowledge of the glory of God (Habakkuk 2: 14). Every believer has a contribution to make towards that goal, big or small. Are you playing your part?

Gospel missions

"And the word of the Lord was published throughout all the region."
Acts 13: 49
SUGGESTED FURTHER READING: Matthew 28: 16-20

The claim of authority ensures a degree of progress. How did Mohammed come to have so strong a religion in his time? He was all alone, and he went into the market-place and said, "I have received a revelation from heaven." He persuaded men to believe it. He said, "I have a revelation from heaven." People looked at his face; they saw that he looked upon them earnestly as believing what he said, and some five or six of them joined him. Did he prove what he said? Not he. "You must," he said, "believe what I say, or there is no Paradise for you." There is a power in that kind of thing, and wherever he went his statement was believed, not on the ground of reasoning, but on his authority, which he declared to be from Allah; and a century later, a thousand sabres had flashed from a thousand sheaths, and his word had been proclaimed through Africa, Turkey, Asia, and even in Spain. The man claimed authority—he claimed divinity; therefore he had power. Take again the increase of Mormonism. What has been its strength? Simply this—the assertion of power from heaven. That claim is made, and the people believe it, and now they have missionaries in almost every country of the habitable globe, and the book of Mormon is translated into many languages. Though there never could be a delusion more transparent, or a counterfeit less skilful, and more lying upon the very surface, yet this simple pretension to power has been the means of carrying power with it. Now, my brethren, we have power; we are God's ministers; we preach God's truth; the great Judge of heaven and earth has told us the truth.

FOR MEDITATION: Christ preached with authority which made men sit up and take notice (Luke 4: 31-37). His power has not weakened, but are we limiting him in any way (1 Corinthians 1: 17; 2: 4,5)?

SERMON NO. 76

The desolations of the Lord, the consolations of his saints.

"Come, behold the works of the Lord, what desolations he hath made in the earth. He maketh wars to cease unto the end of the earth; he breaketh the bow, and cutteth the spear in sunder; he burneth the chariot in the fire." Psalm 46: 8-9
SUGGESTED FURTHER READING: 1 Samuel 5: 1-7

Jehovah still standeth, "the same yesterday, to-day, and for ever." One generation of idols has passed away, and another comes, and the desolations stand—memorials of the might of God. Turn now your eyes to Assyria, that mighty empire. Did she not sit alone? She said she should see no sorrow. Remember Babylon, too, who boasted with her. But where are they, and where are now their gods? With ropes about their necks they have been dragged in triumph by our archaeologists; and now in the halls of our land, they stand as memorials of the ignorance of a race that is long since extinct. And then, turn to the fairer idolatries of Greece and Rome. Fine poetic conceptions were their gods! Theirs was a grand idolatry, one that never shall be forgotten. Despite all its vice and lust, there was such a high mixture of the purest poetry in it, that the mind of man, though it will ever recollect it with sorrow, will still think of it with respect. But where are their gods? Where are the names of their gods? Are not the stars the last memorials of Jupiter, Saturn, and Venus? As if God would make his universe the monument of his destroyed enemy! Where else are their names to be found? Where shall we find a worshipper who adores their false deity? They are past, they are gone! To the moles and to the bats are their images cast, while many an unroofed temple, many a dilapidated shrine, stand as memorials of that which was, but is not—and is passed away for ever. I suppose there is scarce a kingdom of the world where you do not see God's handiwork in crushing his enemies.

FOR MEDITATION: The gods created by man can be destroyed by man, but the Lord made the heavens (Psalm 96: 5; Isaiah 37: 15-20). The false religions of today become the museum pieces of tomorrow.

Christ's people—imitators of him

"Now when they saw the boldness of Peter and John, and perceived that they were unlearned and ignorant men, they marvelled; and they took knowledge of them, that they had been with Jesus." Acts 4: 13
SUGGESTED FURTHER READING: Ephesians 4: 11-16

I will ever maintain—that by grace we are saved, and not by ourselves; but equally must I testify, that where the grace of God is, it will produce fitting deeds. To these I am ever bound to exhort you, while you are ever expected to have good works for necessary purposes. Again, I do not, when I say that a believer should be a striking likeness of Jesus, suppose that any one Christian will perfectly exhibit all the features of our Lord and Saviour Jesus Christ; yet my brethren, the fact that perfection is beyond our reach, should not diminish the ardour of our desire after it. The artist, when he paints, knows right well that he shall not be able to excel Apelles; but that does not discourage him; he uses his brush with all the greater pains, that he may at least in some humble measure resemble the great master. So the sculptor; though persuaded that he will not rival Praxiteles, will hew out the marble still, and seek to be as near the model as possible. Just so the Christian man; though he feels he never can mount to the height of complete excellence, and perceives that he never can on earth become the exact image of Christ, still holds it up before him, and measures his own deficiencies by the distance between himself and Jesus. This will he do, forgetting all he has attained, he will press forward, crying, Excelsior! Going upwards still, desiring to be conformed more and more to the image of Christ Jesus.

FOR MEDITATION: Christians are fellow-pupils in the masterclass of the supreme Master (John 13: 12-15).

N.B: **Apelles** (4th century BC) Court painter to Alexander the Great.
Praxiteles (mid 4th century BC) Athenian sculptor. Regarded as one of the greatest Greek sculptors of his day.

The beginning, increase, and end of the divine life

"Though thy beginning was small, yet thy latter end should greatly increase." Job 8:7
SUGGESTED FURTHER READING: 2 Corinthians 13: 5-9

If thou art saved—though the date be erased—yet do thou rejoice and triumph evermore in the Lord thy God. True, there are some of us who can remember the precise spot where we first found the Saviour. The day will never be forgotten when these eyes looked to the cross of Christ and found their tears all wiped away. But thousands in the fold of Jesus know not when they were brought in; be it enough for them to know they are there. Let them feed upon the pasture, let them lie down beside the still waters, for whether they came by night or by day they did not come at a forbidden hour. Whether they came in youth or in old age, it matters not; all times are acceptable with God, "and whosoever cometh," come he when he may, "he will in no wise cast out." Does it not strike you as being very foolish reasoning if you should say in your heart, "I am not converted because I do not know when?" Nay, with such reasoning as that, I could prove that old Rome was never built, because the precise date of her building is unknown; nay, we might declare that the world was never made, for its exact age even the geologist cannot tell us. We might prove that Jesus Christ himself never died, for the precise date on which he expired on the tree is lost beyond recovery; nor doth it signify much to us. We know the world was made, we know that Christ did die, and so you—if you are now reconciled to God, if now your trembling arms are cast around that cross, you too are saved— though the beginning was so small that you cannot tell when it was. Indeed, in living things, it is hard to put the finger upon the beginning.

FOR MEDITATION: An ongoing Christ-experience in the present without a crisis experience in the past is far more valid than an isolated crisis experience in the past without the evidence of an ongoing Christ-experience in the present.

SERMON NO. 311

War! War! War!

"Fight the Lord's battles." 1 Samuel 18: 17
SUGGESTED FURTHER READING: James 3: 13-18

It is the Christian's duty always to have war with war. To have bitterness in our hearts against any man that lives is to serve Satan. We must speak very strongly and sternly against error, and against sin; but against men we have not a word to say, though it were the Pope himself. I have no enmity in my heart against him as a man, but as anti-Christ. With men the Christian is one. Are we not every man's brother? "God hath made of one flesh all people that dwell upon the face of the earth." The cause of Christ is the cause of humanity. We are friends to all, and are enemies to none. We do not speak evil, even of the false prophet himself, as a man; but, as a false prophet, we are his sworn opponents. Now, Christians, you have a difficult battle to fight, because you fight with all evil and hostility between man and man: you are to be peacemakers. Go wherever you may, if you see a quarrel you are to abate it. You are to pluck firebrands out of the fire, and strive to quench them in the waters of lovingkindness. It is your mission to bring the nations together, and weld them into one. It is yours to make man love man, to make him no more the devourer of his kind. This you can only do by being the friends of purity. Smite error, smite sin, and you have done your best to promote happiness and union among mankind. Oh, go, Christian, in the Spirit's strength, and smite your own anger—put that to the death; smite your own pride—level that; and then smite every other man's anger. Make peace wherever you can, scatter peace with both your hands.

FOR MEDITATION: "Blessed are the peacemakers." (Matthew 5: 9) Men need to hear of the Prince of Peace (Isaiah 9: 6) who alone can give them peace with God and, as a result, peace with man (Ephesians 2: 14-17).

Christ glorified as the builder of his church

"He shall build the temple of the Lord; and he shall bear the glory."
Zechariah 6: 13
SUGGESTED FURTHER READING: Revelation 19: 1-10

This glory is undivided glory. In the church of Christ in heaven, no one is glorified but Christ. He who is honoured on earth has some one to share the honour with him, some inferior helper who laboured with him in the work; but Christ has none. He is glorified, and it is all his own glory. Oh, when you get to heaven, you children of God, will you praise any but your Master? Calvinists, today you love John Calvin; will you praise him there? Lutherans, today you love the memory of that stern reformer; will you sing the song of Luther in heaven? Followers of Wesley, you revere that evangelist; will you in heaven have a note for John Wesley? None, none, none! Giving up all names and all honours of men, the strain shall rise in undivided and unjarring unison "Unto him that loved us, and washed us from our sins in his own blood, unto him be glory for ever and ever." But again; he shall have all the glory; all that can be conceived, all that can be desired, all that can be imagined shall come to him. Today, you praise him, but not as you can wish; in heaven you shall praise him to the summit of your desire. Today you see him magnified, but you see not all things put under him; in heaven all things shall acknowledge his dominion. There every knee shall bow before him, and every tongue confess that he is Lord. He shall have all the glory. But to conclude on this point; this glory is continual glory. It says he shall bear all the glory. When shall this dominion become exhausted? When shall this promise be so fulfilled that it is put away as a worn out garment? Never.

FOR MEDITATION: "Thine is the kingdom, and the power, and the glory, for ever." (Matthew 6: 13). Can you really say 'Amen' to this?

Regeneration

"Except a man be born again, he cannot see the kingdom of God." John 3: 3
SUGGESTED FURTHER READING: Luke 13: 22-30

"Angels, principalities, and powers, would you be willing that men who love not God, who believe not in Christ, who have not been born again, should dwell here?" I see them, as they look down upon us, and hear them answering, "No! Once we fought the dragon, and expelled him, because he tempted us to sin! We must not, and we will not, have the wicked here. These alabaster walls must not be soiled with black and lustful fingers; the white pavement of heaven must not be stained and rendered filthy by the unholy feet of ungodly men. No!" I see a thousand spears bristling, and the fiery faces of a myriad seraphs thrust over the walls of paradise. "No, while these arms have strength, and these wings have power, no sin shall ever enter here." I address myself moreover to the saints of heaven, redeemed by sovereign grace: "Children of God, are you willing that the wicked should enter heaven as they are, without being born again? You say you love men, but are you willing that they should be admitted as they are?" I see Lot rise up, and he cries, "Admit them into heaven! No! What! Must I be vexed by the conversation of Sodomites again, as once I was!" I see Abraham; and he comes forward, and he says, "No; I cannot have them here. I had enough of them whilst I was with them on earth—their jests and jeers, their silly talkings, their vain conversation, vexed and grieved us. We want them not here." And, heavenly though they be, and loving as their spirits are, yet there is not a saint in heaven who would not resent, with the utmost indignation, the approach of any one of you to the gates of paradise, if you are still unholy, and have not been born again.

FOR MEDITATION: Matthew 13: 41-43; Luke 16: 23-26 — at best the unsaved will have a distant view of heaven which will only add to their torment.

Divine sovereignty

"Is it not lawful for me to do what I will with mine own?" Matthew 20: 15
SUGGESTED FURTHER READING: Luke 19: 11-27

There is no attribute of God more comforting to his children than the doctrine of divine sovereignty. Under the most adverse circumstances, in the most severe troubles, they believe that sovereignty has ordained their afflictions, that sovereignty overrules them, and that sovereignty will sanctify them all. There is nothing for which the children of God should more earnestly contend than the dominion of their Master over all creation—the Kingship of God over all the works of his own hands—the throne of God, and his right to sit upon that throne. On the other hand, there is no doctrine more hated by unbelievers, no truth which they have kicked about so much, as the great, stupendous, but yet most certain doctrine of the sovereignty of the infinite Jehovah. Men will allow God to be everywhere except on his throne. They will allow him to be in his workshop to fashion worlds and to make stars. They will allow him to be in his treasury to dispense his alms and bestow his bounties. They will allow him to sustain the earth and bear up its pillars, or light the lamps of heaven, or rule the waves of the ever-moving ocean; but when God ascends his throne, his creatures then gnash their teeth; and when we proclaim an enthroned God, and his right to do as he wills with his own, to dispose of his creatures as he thinks well, without consulting them in the matter, then it is that we are ridiculed, and then it is that men turn a deaf ear to us, for God on his throne is not the God they love. They love him anywhere better than they do when he sits with his sceptre in his hand and his crown upon his head.

FOR MEDITATION: Do you have to think twice before addressing Jesus as Lord? Judas Iscariot could never bring himself to do it—the other disciples could say "Lord" (Matthew 26: 22); Judas could only say "Rabbi/Master/Teacher" (Matthew 26: 25,49).

SERMON NO. 77

The Sunday School teacher —a steward

"Give an account of thy stewardship." Luke 16: 2
SUGGESTED FURTHER READING: 2 Chronicles 34: 1-3

I see nothing in the Bible that should lead me to believe that the office of the preacher is more honourable than that of the teacher. It seems to me, that every Sunday School teacher has a right to put "Reverend" before his name as much as I have, or if not, if he discharges his trust he certainly is a "Right Honourable". He teaches his congregation and preaches to his class. I may preach to more, and he to less, but still he is doing the same work, though in a small sphere. I am sure I can sympathise with Mr Carey, when he said of his son Felix, who left the missionary work to become an ambassador, "Felix has drivelled into an ambassador;" meaning to say, that he was once a great person as a missionary, but that he had afterwards accepted a comparatively insignificant office. So I think we may say of the Sabbath-school teacher, if he gives up his work because he cannot attend to it, on account of his enlarged business, he drivels into a rich merchant. If he forsakes his teaching because he finds there is much else to do, he drivels into something less than he was before; with one exception, if he is obliged to give up to attend to his own family, and makes that family his Sabbath school class, there is no drivelling there; he stands in the same position as he did before. I say they who teach, they who seek to pluck souls as brands from the burning, are to be considered as honoured persons, second far to him from whom they received their commission; but still in some sweet sense lifted up to become fellows with him, for he calls them his brethren and his friends.

FOR MEDITATION: Never look down on children's work; it is a serious responsibility to teach them the things of God (James 3: 1-2). If it is your responsibility, thank God for the privilege and ask him to make you a faithful steward (1 Corinthians 4: 2).

SERMON NO. 192

Terrible convictions and gentle drawings

"When I kept silence, my bones waxed old through my roaring all the day long. For day and night thy hand was heavy upon me: my moisture is turned into the drought of summer." Psalm 32: 3,4
SUGGESTED FURTHER READING: Acts 16: 11-34

I have met with at least a score of persons who found Christ and then mourned their sins more afterwards than they did before. Their convictions have been more terrible after they have known their interest in Christ than they were at first. They have seen the evil after they have escaped from it; they had been plucked out of the miry clay, and their feet set on a rock, and then afterwards they have seen more fully the depth of that horrible pit out of which they have been snatched. It is not true that all who are saved suffer these convictions and terrors; there are a considerable number who are drawn by the cords of love and the bands of a man. There are some who, like Lydia, have their hearts opened not by the crowbar of conviction, but by the picklock of divine grace. Sweetly drawn, almost silently enchanted by the loveliness of Jesus, they say, "Draw me, and I will run after thee." And now you ask me the question—"Why has God brought me to himself in this gentle manner?" Again I say—there are some questions better unanswered than answered; God knows best the reason why he does not give you these terrors; leave that question with him. But I may tell you an anecdote. There was a man once who had never felt these terrors, and he thought within himself—"I never can believe I am a Christian unless I do." So he prayed to God that he might feel them, and he did feel them, and what do you think is his testimony? He says, "Never, never do that, for the result was fearful in the extreme." If he had but known what he was asking for, he would not have asked for anything so foolish.

FOR MEDITATION: The important thing is not **how** we are brought to Christ, but **that** we are brought to Christ. The wind sometimes blows fiercely; sometimes it blows gently (John 3: 8). But we should not presume upon God's kindness, forbearance and patience—they lead us to repentance (Romans 2: 4).

SERMON NO. 313

Peace at home, and prosperity abroad

"He maketh peace in thy borders, and filleth thee with the finest of the wheat. He sendeth forth his commandment upon earth: his word runneth very swiftly." Psalm 147: 14-15
SUGGESTED FURTHER READING: 1 Thessalonians 1

Suppose the pulpit in our land gives an uncertain sound. As a result God's people begin to forsake the assembling of themselves together; no crowds gather to hear the Word; places begin to get empty; prayer-meetings become more and more deserted; the efforts of the Church may be still carried on, but they are merely a matter of routine; there is no life, no heart in it. I am supposing a case you see, a case which I trust we never may see. Things get worse and worse; the doctrines of the gospel become expunged and unknown; they that fear the Lord no more speak one to another. Still for a little time the money continues to be brought into the Society, and foreign missions are sustained. Can you not imagine in the next report, "We have had no converts this year; our income is still maintained; but notwithstanding that, our brethren feel that they are labouring under the greatest possible disadvantages; in fact, some of them wish to return home and renounce the work." Another year—the missionary spirit has grown cold in the churches, its funds decrease. Another year, and yet another; it becomes a moot point among us as to whether missions are absolutely necessary or not. We have come at last to the more advanced point which some divines have already reached, and begin to question whether Mohammed and Confucius had not a revelation from God as well as Jesus Christ. And now we begin to say, "Is it needful that we should extend the gospel abroad at all? We have lost faith in it; we see it does nothing at home, shall we send that across the sea which is a drug on the market here, and distribute as a healing for the wounds of the daughters of Zidon and of Tyre that which has not healed the daughter of Jerusalem?"

FOR MEDITATION: A healthy church is the light of the world; an unhealthy church will be as much use to the world as the seven churches of Revelation are today (Matthew 5: 13-16).

SERMON NO. 314

The necessity of the Spirit's work

"And I will put my Spirit within you." Ezekiel 36: 27
SUGGESTED FURTHER READING: 1 Corinthians 12: 1-13

Talking one day with a countryman, he used this figure: "In the middle of winter I sometimes think how well I could mow; and in early spring I think, how I would like to reap; I feel just ready for it; but when mowing time comes, I find I have no strength to spare." So when you have no troubles, couldn't you mow them down at once? When you have no work to do, couldn't you do it? But when work and trouble come, you find how difficult it is. Many Christians are like the stag, who talked to itself, and said, "Why should I run away from the dogs? Look what a fine pair of horns I've got, and look what heels I've got too; I might do these hounds some mischief. Why not let me stand and show them what I can do with my antlers? I can keep off any quantity of dogs." No sooner did the dogs bark, than off the stag went. So with us. "Let sin arise," we say, "we will soon rip it up, and destroy it; let trouble come, we will soon get over it;" but when sin and trouble come, we then find what our weakness is. Then we have to cry for the help of the Spirit; and through him we can do all things, though without him we can do nothing at all. In all the acts of the Christian's life, whether it be the act of consecrating one's self to Christ, or the act of daily prayer, or the act of constant submission, or preaching the gospel, or ministering to the necessities of the poor, or comforting the desponding, in all these the Christian finds his weakness and his powerlessness, unless he is clothed about with the Spirit of God.

FOR MEDITATION: The Christian is dependant on the Holy Spirit for gifts, graces (Galatians 5: 22,23) and devotions (Romans 8: 26). Do you serve God in the strength which he supplies (1 Peter 4: 11) or are you content to struggle on uselessly in your own strength?

The world turned upside down

"These that have turned the world upside down are come hither also."
Acts 17: 6
SUGGESTED FURTHER READING: Matthew 5: 1-12

"Blessed are the merciful: for they shall obtain mercy." The merciful are not much respected in this world—at least if they are imprudently merciful; the man who forgives too much, or who is too generous, is not considered to be wise. But Christ declares that he who has been merciful—merciful to supply the wants of the poor, merciful to forgive his enemies and to pass by offences, shall obtain mercy. Here, again, is the world turned upside down. "Blessed are the pure in heart: for they shall see God." The world says, "Blessed is the man who indulges in a carefree life." If you ask the common run of mankind who is the happy man, they will tell you, "The happy man is he who has abundance of money, and spends it freely, and is freed from restraint—who leads a merry dance of life, who drinks deep of the cup of intoxication—who revels riotously, who, like the wild horse of the prairie, is not restrained by reason, but who dashes across the broad plains of sin, unharnessed, unguided, unrestrained." This is the man whom the world calls happy: the proud man, the mighty man, the Nimrod, the man who can do just as he wishes, and who spurns to keep the narrow way of holiness. Now, the Scripture says, not so, for "Blessed are the pure in heart, for they shall see God"

"Blest is the man who shuns the place Where sinners love to meet;
Who fears to tread their wicked ways, And hates the scoffer's seat...."

The man who cannot touch one thing because that would be lascivious, nor another because that would spoil his communion with his Master; a man who cannot frequent this place of amusement, because he could not pray there, and cannot go to another, because he could not hope to have his Master's sanction upon an hour so spent—that man is blessed!

FOR MEDITATION: The world was turned upside down through men who had been turned upside down (Mark 9: 34,35; 10: 42-44). Do we need to know a lot more of that in our churches and individual lives?

SERMON NO. 193

Salvation of the Lord

"Salvation is of the Lord." Jonah 2: 9
SUGGESTED FURTHER READING: Ephesians 2: 1-10

"Salvation is of the Lord," in the application of it. "No," says the Arminian, "it is not; salvation is of the Lord, inasmuch as he does all for man that he can do; but there is something that man must do, which if he does not do, he must perish." That is the Arminian way of salvation. I thought of this very theory of salvation when I stood by the side of that window of Carisbrooke Castle, out of which King Charles, of unhappy and unrighteous memory, attempted to escape. I read in the guide book that everything was provided for his escape; his followers had means at the bottom of the wall to enable him to fly across the country, and on the coast they had their boats lying ready to take him to another land; in fact, everything was ready for his escape. But here was the important circumstance; his friends had done all they could; he was to do the rest; but that doing the rest was just the point and brunt of the battle. It was to get out of the window, out of which he was not able to escape by any means, so that all his friends did for him went for nothing, so far as he was concerned. So with the sinner. If God had provided every means of escape, and only required him to get out of his dungeon, he would have remained there to all eternity. Why, is not the sinner by nature dead in sin? And if God requires him to make himself alive, and then afterwards he will do the rest for him, then verily, my friends, we are not so much obliged to God as we had thought; for if he requires so much as that of us, and we can do it, we can do the rest without his assistance.

FOR MEDITATION: The converted are alive and can open the door to the Saviour (Revelation 3: 20); but he had to open it himself the first time when they were still unbelieving and dead (Acts 16: 14).

The form of sound words

"Hold fast the form of sound words, which thou hast heard of me, in faith and love which is in Christ Jesus." 2 Timothy 1: 13
SUGGESTED FURTHER READING: Deuteronomy 6: 4-7, 20-25

Let me exhort you, as much as lies in you, to give your children sound instruction in the great doctrines of the gospel of Christ. I believe that what Irving once said is a great truth. He said, "In these modern times you boast and glory, and you think yourselves to be in a high and noble condition, because you have your Sabbath-schools and British-schools, and all kinds of schools for teaching youth. I tell you," he said, "that philanthropic and great as these are, they are the ensigns of your disgrace; they show that your land is not a land where parents teach children at home. They show you there is a want of parental instruction; and though they be blessed things, these Sabbath-schools, they are indications of something wrong, for if we all taught our children there would be no need of strangers to say to our children 'Know the Lord.'" I trust you will never give up that excellent puritanical habit of catechising your children at home. Any father or mother who entirely gives up a child to the teaching of another has made a mistake. There is no teacher who wishes to absolve a parent from what he ought to do himself. He is an assistant, but he was never intended to be a substitute. Teach your children; bring out your old catechisms again, for they are, after all, blessed means of instruction, and the next generation shall outstrip those that have gone before it; for the reason why many of you are weak in the faith is this, you did not receive instruction in your youth in the great things of the gospel of Christ. If you had, you would have been so grounded, and settled, and firm in the faith, that nothing could by any means have moved you.

FOR MEDITATION: Faithful teaching from his mother and grandmother had prepared Timothy for his further education from the apostle Paul (Acts 16: 1-3; 2 Timothy 1: 5, 3: 14-15).

A caution to the presumptuous

"Let him that thinketh he standeth take heed lest he fall."
1 Corinthians 10: 12
SUGGESTED FURTHER READING: Hebrews 10: 19-25

These strong men sometimes will not use the means of grace, and therefore they fall. There are some persons here, who rarely attend a place of worship; they do not profess to be religious; but I am sure they would be astonished if I were to tell them, that I know some professedly religious people who are accepted in some churches as being true children of God, who yet make it a habit of stopping away from the house of God, because they conceive they are so advanced that they do not want it. You smile at such a thing as that. They boast such deep experience within; they have a volume of sweet sermons at home, and they will stop and read them; they need not go to the house of God, for they are fat and flourishing. They conceit themselves that they have received food enough seven years ago to last them the next ten years. They imagine that old food will feed their souls now. These are your presumptuous men. They are not to be found at the Lord's table, eating the body and drinking the blood of Christ, in the holy emblems of bread and wine. You do not see them in their closets; you do not find them searching the Scriptures with holy curiosity. They think they stand—they shall never be moved; they fancy that means are intended for weaker Christians; and leaving those means, they fall. They will not have the shoe to put upon the foot, and therefore the flint cuts them; they will not put on the armour, and therefore the enemy wounds them—sometimes well-nigh unto death. In this deep quagmire of neglect of the means, many a proud professor has been smothered.

FOR MEDITATION: Thomas was absent to his cost (John 20: 24,25). Can you always give your "apologies for absence" to the Lord and to your fellow-members with a clear conscience?

Thoughts on the last battle

"The sting of death is sin; and the strength of sin is the law. But thanks be to God, which giveth us the victory through our Lord Jesus Christ."
1 Corinthians 15: 56,57
SUGGESTED FURTHER READING: Psalm 116

While the Bible is one of the most poetical of books, though its language is unutterably sublime, yet we must remark how constantly it is true to nature. There is no straining of a fact, no glossing over a truth. However dark may be the subject, while it lights it up with brilliance, yet it does not deny the gloom connected with it. If you will read this chapter of Paul's epistle, so justly celebrated as a masterpiece of language, you will find him speaking of that which is to come after death with such exaltation and glory, that you feel, "If this be to die, then it were well to depart at once." Who has not rejoiced, and whose heart has not been lifted up, or filled with a holy fire, while he has read such sentences as these: "In a moment, in the twinkling of an eye, at the last trump: for the trumpet shall sound, and the dead shall be raised incorruptible, and we shall be changed. For this corruptible must put on incorruption, and this mortal must put on immortality. So when this corruptible shall have put on incorruption, and this mortal shall have put on immortality, then shall be brought to pass the saying that is written, Death is swallowed up in victory. O Death, where is thy sting? O grave, where is thy victory?" Yet with all that majestic language, with all that bold flight of eloquence, he does not deny that death is a gloomy thing. Even his very figures imply it. He does not laugh at it; he does not say, "Oh, it is nothing to die;" he describes death as a monster; he speaks of it as having a sting; he tells us wherein the strength of that sting lies; and even in the exclamation of triumph he imputes that victory not to unaided flesh, but he says, "Thanks be to God which giveth us the victory through our Lord Jesus Christ."

FOR MEDITATION: Death is no laughing matter, but for the Christian it need not be a crying matter either (1 Thessalonians 4: 13,14).

The teaching of the Holy Spirit

"But the Comforter, which is the Holy Ghost, whom the Father will send in my name, he shall teach you all things, and bring all things to your remembrance, whatsoever I have said unto you." John 14: 26
SUGGESTED FURTHER READING: Galatians 1: 10-17

The Holy Spirit specially teaches to us Jesus Christ. It is the Holy Spirit who manifests the Saviour to us in the glory of his person; the complex character of his manhood and of his deity; it is he who tells us of the love of his heart, of the power of his arm, of the clearness of his eye, the preciousness of his blood, and of the prevalence of his plea. To know that Christ is my Redeemer, is to know more than Plato could have taught me. To know that I am a member of his body, of his flesh, and of his bones; that my name is on his breast, and engraved on the palms of his hands, is to know more than the Universities of Oxford or Cambridge could teach to all their scholars. Not at the feet of Gamaliel did Paul learn to say—"He loved me, and gave himself for me." Not in the midst of the rabbis, or at the feet of the members of the Sanhedrin, did Paul learn to cry—"What things were gain to me, those I counted loss for Christ." "God forbid that I should glory, save in the cross of our Lord Jesus Christ." No, this must have been taught as he himself confesses—not of flesh and blood, but of the Holy Spirit. I need only hint that it is also the Spirit who teaches us our adoption. Indeed, all the privileges of the new covenant, beginning from regeneration, running through redemption, justification, pardon, sanctification, adoption, preservation, continual safety, even unto an abundant entrance into the kingdom of our Lord and Saviour Jesus Christ—all is the teaching of the Holy Spirit.

FOR MEDITATION: The Holy Spirit exercises a perfect teaching ministry (1 John 2: 27); how good a pupil (disciple) are you?

Holy violence

"From the days of John the Baptist until now the kingdom of God suffereth violence, and the violent take it by force." Matthew 11: 12
SUGGESTED FURTHER READING: Genesis 32: 22-32

Frequently complaints are made and surprise expressed by individuals who have never found a blessing rest upon anything they have attempted to do in the service of God. "I have been a Sunday-school teacher for years," says one, "and I have never seen any of my girls or boys converted." No, and the reason most likely is, you have never been violent about it; you have never been compelled by the divine Spirit to make up your mind that converted they should be, and no stone shall be left unturned until they were. You have never been brought by the Spirit to such a passion, that you have said, "I cannot live unless God bless me; I cannot exist unless I see some of these children saved." Then, falling on your knees in agony of prayer, and putting forth afterwards your trust with the same intensity towards heaven, you would never have been disappointed, "for the violent take it by force." And you too, my brother in the gospel, you have marvelled and wondered why you have not seen souls regenerated. Did you ever expect it? Why, you preach like one who does not believe what he is saying. Those who believe in Christ, may say of you with kind partiality, "Our minister is a dear good man;" but the careless young men that attend your ministry say, "Does that man expect to make me believe that which he only utters as a dry story, and to convince me when I see him go through the service with all the dullness and monotony of dead routine?" Oh, my brethren, what we want today in the churches is violence; not violence against each other, but violence against death, and hell, against the hardness of other men's hearts, and against the sleepiness of our own.

FOR MEDITATION: Do you mean business with God or do you just go through the motions? It can make all the difference (2 Kings 4: 31-35; Mark 9: 28,29).

SERMON NO. 252

Human responsibility

"If I had not come and spoken unto them, they had not had sin: but now they have no cloke for their sin." John 15: 22
SUGGESTED FURTHER READING: Matthew 24: 29-31

The liar, the fornicator, and the drunkard shall have their portion with unbelievers. Hell was made first of all for men who despise Christ, because that is the A1 sin, the cardinal vice, and men are condemned for that. Other iniquities come following after them, but this one goes before them to judgement. Imagine for a moment that time has passed, and that the day of judgement is come. We are all gathered together, both living and dead. The trumpet-blast sounds exceeding loud and long. We are all attentive, expecting something marvellous. The exchange stands still in its business; the shop is deserted by the tradesman; the crowded streets are filled. All men stand still; they feel that the last great business-day is come, and that now they must settle their accounts for ever. A solemn stillness fills the air: no sound is heard. All, all is silent. Presently a great white cloud with solemn state sails through the sky, and then—hark! The twofold clamour of the startled earth. On that cloud there sits one like unto the Son of Man. Every eye looks, and at last there is heard a unanimous shout—"It is he! It is he!" and after that you hear on the one hand, shouts of "Hallelujah, Hallelujah, Hallelujah, Welcome, Welcome, Welcome Son of God." But mixed with that there is a deep bass, composed of the weeping and wailing of the men who have persecuted him, and who have rejected him. Listen! I think I can dissect the sonnet; I think I can hear the words as they come separately, each one of them, tolling like a death knell. What say they? They say, "Rocks hide us, mountains fall upon us, hide us from the face of him that sits upon the throne."

FOR MEDITATION: What we are going to say about Christ in eternity will be an amplified version of our attitudes towards him in time. In this life we have the opportunity to change our minds and trust Christ; in eternity we will never be able to change our tune (Matthew 25: 30,46).

SERMON NO. 194

Christ—the power and wisdom of God

"Christ the power of God, and the wisdom of God." 1 Corinthians 1: 24
SUGGESTED FURTHER READING: Acts 10: 34-43

Christ is the power of God, for he is the Creator of all things, and by Him all things exist. But when he came to earth, took upon himself the fashion of a man, tabernacled in the inn, and slept in the manger, he still gave proof that he was the Son of God; not so much so when, as an infant of a span long, the immortal was the mortal, and the infinite became a babe; not so much so in his youth, but afterwards when he began his public ministry, he gave abundant proofs of his power and godhead. The winds hushed by his finger uplifted, the waves calmed by his voice, so that they became solid as marble beneath his tread; the tempest, cowering at his feet, as before a conqueror whom it knew and obeyed; these things, these stormy elements, the wind, the tempest, and the water, gave full proof of his abundant power. The lame man leaping, the deaf man hearing, the dumb man singing, the dead rising, these, again, were proofs that he was the "power of God." When the voice of Jesus startled the shades of Hades, and rent the bonds of death, with "Lazarus come forth!" and when the carcase rotten in the tomb woke up to life, there was proof of his divine power and godhead. A thousand other proofs he afforded; but we need not stay to mention them to you who have Bibles in your houses, and who can read them every day. At last he yielded up his life, and was buried in the tomb. Not long, however, did he sleep; for he gave another proof of his divine power and godhead, when starting from his slumber, he affrighted the guards with the majesty of his grandeur, not being held by the bonds of death, they being like green twigs before our conquering Samson, who had meanwhile pulled up the gates of hell, and carried them on his shoulders far away.

FOR MEDITATION: This very same power of God is mighty to save believers through the gospel (Romans 1: 16), is at work within them (Ephesians 1: 19) and can enable them to fight the good fight of the faith against all evil powers (Ephesians 6: 10-13).

God alone the salvation of His people

"He only is my rock and my salvation." Psalm 62: 2
SUGGESTED FURTHER READING: Mark 9: 1-8

If God alone is our rock, and we know it, are we not bound to put all our trust **in** God, to give all our love **to** God, to set all our hope **upon** God, to spend all our life **for** God, and to devote our whole being **to** God? If God be all I have, sure, all I have shall be God's. If God alone is my hope, sure, I will put all my hope upon God; if the love of God is alone that which saves, sure, he shall have my love alone. Come, let me talk to thee, Christian, for a little while, I want to warn thee not to have two Gods, two Christs, two friends, two husbands, two great Fathers; not to have two fountains, two rivers, two suns, or two heavens, but to have only one. I want to bid thee now, as God hath put all salvation in himself, to bring all thyself unto God. Come, let me talk to thee! In the first place, Christian, never join anything with Christ. Wouldest thou stitch thy old rags into the new garment he giveth? Wouldest thou put new wine into old bottles? Wouldst thou put Christ and self together? Thou mightest as well yoke an elephant and an ant; they could never plough together. What! Wouldest thou put an archangel in the same harness with a worm, and hope that they would drag thee through the sky! How inconsistent! How foolish! What! Thyself and Christ? Sure, Christ would smile; nay, Christ would weep, to think of such a thing! Christ and man together? **Christ and Co?** No, it never shall be; he will have nothing of the sort; he must be all. Note how inconsistent it would be to put anything else with him.

FOR MEDITATION: What candidates for an equal share of the devotion due only to the Triune God do you face? Give them the same answer as Jesus gave Satan (Matthew 4: 10).

SERMON NO. 80

Forgiveness

"I, even I, am he that blotteth out thy transgressions for mine own sake, and will not remember thy sins." Isaiah 43: 25

SUGGESTED FURTHER READING: Acts 8: 26-40

There are some passages of scripture which have been more abundantly blessed to the conversion of souls than others. They may be called salvation texts. We may not be able to discover how it is, or why it is, but certainly it is the fact, that some chosen verses have been more used of God to bring men to the cross of Christ than any others in his Word. Certainly they are not more inspired, but I suppose they are more noticeable from their position, from their peculiar phraseology more adapted to catch the eye of the reader, and more suitable to a prevailing spiritual condition. All the stars in the heavens shine very brightly, but only a few attract the eye of the mariner, and direct his course; the reason is this, that those few stars from their peculiar grouping are more readily distinguished, and the eye easily fixes upon them. So I suppose it is with those passages of God's Word which especially attract attention, and direct the sinner to the cross of Christ. It so happens that this text is one of the chief of them. I have found it, in my experience, to be a most useful one; for out of the hundreds of persons who have come to me to narrate their conversion and experience, I have found a very large proportion who have traced the divine change which has been wrought in their hearts to the hearing of this precious declaration of sovereign mercy read, and the application of it with power to their souls: "I, even I, am he that blotteth out thy transgressions for mine own sake, and will not remember thy sins."

FOR MEDITATION: The texts often quoted by Spurgeon towards the end of his sermons—Mark 16: 16; 1 Timothy 1: 15. Has God used a particular text to bring you to himself?

The hope of future bliss

"As for me, I will behold thy face in righteousness: I shall be satisfied, when I awake, with thy likeness." Psalm 17: 15
SUGGESTED FURTHER READING: Revelation 7: 13-17

He will be satisfied, the Psalmist says, when he wakes up in God's likeness. Satisfaction! This is another joy for the Christian when he shall enter heaven. Here we are never thoroughly satisfied. True, the Christian is satisfied from himself; he has that within which is a well-spring of comfort, and he can enjoy solid satisfaction. But heaven is the home of true and real satisfaction. When the believer enters heaven I believe his imagination will be thoroughly satisfied. All he has ever thought of he will there see; every holy idea will be solidified; every mighty conception will become a reality; every glorious imagination will become a tangible thing that he can see. His imagination will not be able to think of anything better than heaven; and should he sit down through eternity, he would not be able to conceive of anything that should outshine the lustre of that glorious city. His imagination will be satisfied. Then his intellect will be satisfied.

"Then shall I see, and hear, and know, All I desired, or wished, below."

Who is satisfied with his knowledge here? Are there not secrets we want to know—depths of the secrets of nature that we have not entered? But in that glorious state we shall know as much as we want to know. The memory will be satisfied. We shall look back upon the vista of past years, and we shall be content with whatever we endured, or did, or suffered on earth.

"There, on a green and flowery mount, My wearied soul shall sit,
And with transporting joys recount, The labours of my feet."

Hope will be satisfied, if there be such a thing in heaven. We shall hope for a future eternity, and believe in it. But we shall be satisfied as to our hope continually.

FOR MEDITATION: The difference between now and then is beyond our finest imaginations (1 Corinthians 13: 12; 1 John 3: 2).

A sense of pardoned sin

"Thou hast cast all my sins behind thy back." Isaiah 38: 17
SUGGESTED FURTHER READING: Psalm 32

We are saved by faith, and not by feeling. "We walk by faith and not by sight." Yet there is as much connection between faith and hallowed feeling, as there is between the root and the flower. Faith is permanent, just as the root is ever in the ground; feeling is casual, and has its seasons. Just as the bulb does not always shoot up the green stem; far less is it always crowned with the many, many-coloured flower. Faith is the tree, the essential tree; our feelings are like the appearance of that tree during the different seasons of the year. Sometimes our soul is full of bloom and blossom, and the bees hum pleasantly, and gather honey within our hearts. It is then that our feelings bear witness to the life of our faith, just as the buds of spring bear witness to the life of the tree. Presently, our feelings gather still greater vigour, and we come to the summer of our delights. Again, perhaps, we begin to wither into the dry and yellow leaf of autumn; nay, sometimes the winter of our despondency and despair will strip away every leaf from the tree, and our poor faith stands like a blasted stem without a sign of greenness. And yet, my brethren, so long as the tree of faith is there we are saved. Whether faith blossom or not, whether it bring forth joyous fruit in our experience or not, so long as it be there in all its permanence we are saved. Yet we should have the gravest reason to distrust the life of our faith, if it did not sometimes blossom with joy, and often bring forth fruit unto holiness.

FOR MEDITATION: True joy cannot exist without saving faith (1 Peter 1: 8-9), but sometimes our salvation needs to have its joy restored (Psalm 51: 12).

A psalm of remembrance

"We have known and believed the love that God hath to us." 1 John 4: 16
SUGGESTED FURTHER READING: Habakkuk 3: 16-19

"Hast thou considered my servant Job?" "Ah," says Satan, "he serves thee now, but thou hast set a hedge about him and blessed him, let me but touch him." Now he has come down to you, and he has afflicted you in your estate, afflicted you in your family, and at last he has afflicted you in your body. Shall Satan be the conqueror? Shall grace give way? O my dear brother, stand up now and say once more, once for all, "I tell thee, Satan, the grace of God is more than a match for thee; he is with me, and in all this I will not utter one word against the Lord my God. He doeth all things well—well, even now, and I do rejoice in him." The Lord is always pleased with his children when they can stand up for him when circumstances seem to belie him. Here come the witnesses into court. The devil says, "Soul, God has forgotten thee, I will bring in my witness." First he summons your debts—a long bill of losses. "There," says he "would God suffer you to fall thus, if he loved you?" Then he brings in your children—either their death, or their disobedience, or something worse, and says, "Would the Lord suffer these things to come upon you, if he loved you?" At last he brings in your poor tottering body, and all your doubts and fears, and the hidings of Jehovah's face. "Ah," says the devil, "do you believe that God loves you now?" Oh, it is noble, if you are able to stand forth and say to all these witnesses, "I hear what you have to say, let God be true, and every man and everything be a liar. I believe none of you. You all say, God does not love me; but he does, and if the witnesses against his love were multiplied a hundredfold, yet still would I say, "I know whom I have believed."

FOR MEDITATION: The question is bound to be asked sooner or later (Psalm 42: 3,10). The apostle Paul gives the greatest answer (Romans 8: 35-39).

Looking unto Jesus

"They looked unto him, and were lightened: and their faces were not ashamed." Psalm 34: 5
SUGGESTED FURTHER READING: 1 Timothy 2: 1-7

See there he sits in heaven, he has led captivity captive, and now sits at the right hand of God, for ever making intercession for us. Can your faith picture him today? Like a great high priest of old, he stands with outstretched arms: there is majesty in his demeanour, for he is no mean cringing suppliant. He does not beat his breast, nor cast his eyes upon the ground, but with authority he pleads, enthroned in glory now. There on his head is the bright shining mitre of his priesthood, and look you, on his breast are glittering the precious stones whereon the names of his elect are everlastingly engraved; hear him as he pleads, hear you not what it is?—is that your prayer that he is mentioning before the throne? The prayer that this morning you offered before you came to the house of God, Christ is now offering before his Father's throne. The vow which just now you uttered when you said, "Have pity and have mercy,"—he is now uttering there. He is the Altar and the Priest, and with his own sacrifice he perfumes our prayers. And yet, mayhap, you have been at prayer many a day, and had no answer; poor weeping suppliant, you have sought the Lord and he has not heard you, or at least not answered you to your soul's delight; you have cried unto him, but the heavens have been as brass, and he has shut out your prayer, you are full of darkness and heaviness on account of this, "Look to him, and be lightened." If you do not succeed, he will; if your intercession be unnoticed, his cannot be passed away; if your prayers can be like water spilt on a rock which cannot be gathered up, yet his prayers are not like that, he is God's Son, he pleads and must prevail.

FOR MEDITATION: The prayers of the true seeker and of believers are not a waste of effort; they are not like letters lost in the post, but reach the throne of God (Acts 10: 4; Revelation 5: 8). But only praying in the name of the Lord Jesus Christ is accepted; prayers addressed to saints, to false gods or to the dead are always turned away—"not known here."

SERMON NO. 195

Heavenly rest

"There remaineth therefore a rest to the people of God." Hebrews 4: 9
SUGGESTED FURTHER READING: Revelation 14: 12-16

From Monday morning till Saturday night, many of you will not be able to lay aside your needle and your thread, except when, tired and weary, you fall back on your chair, and are lulled to sleep by your thoughts of labour! Oh! how seasonable will heaven's rest be to you! Oh! how glad will you be, when you get there, to find that there are no Monday mornings, no more toil for you, but rest, eternal rest! Others of you have had manual labour to perform; you have reason to thank God that you are strong enough to do it, and you are not ashamed of your work; for labour is an honour to a man. But still there are times when you say, "I wish I were not so dragged to death by the business of London life." We have but little rest in this huge city; our day is longer, and our work is harder than our friends in the country. You have sometimes sighed to go into the green fields for a breath of fresh air; you have longed to hear the song of the sweet birds that used to wake you when you were young; you have regretted the bright blue sky, the beauteous flowers, and the thousand charms of a country life. And, perhaps, you will never get beyond this smoky city; but remember, when you get up there, "sweet fields arrayed in living green," and "rivers of delight" shall be the place where you shall rest, you shall have all the joys you can conceive of in that home of happiness.

FOR MEDITATION: The Christian's rest in heaven will be enriched by the worth of his work for Christ on earth (1 Corinthians 3: 13-15). Spurgeon says:- "There, up in heaven, Luther has no more to face a thundering Vatican; Paul has no more to run from city to city, and continent to continent; there Baxter has no more to toil in his pulpit, to preach with a broken heart to hard hearted sinners; there no longer has Knox to "cry aloud and spare not" against the immoralities of the false church." What will you be missing?

SERMON NO. 133

The God of the aged

"Even to your old age I am he; and even to hoar hairs will I carry you: I have made, and I will bear; even I will carry, and will deliver you." Isaiah 46: 4
SUGGESTED FURTHER READING: Psalm 71: 1-18

Middle aged man! Listen to what David says, again, "I have been young, and now am old; yet have I not seen the righteous forsaken, nor his seed begging bread." Go on, then, unsheath your sword once more. "The battle is the Lord's;" leave your declining years to him, and give your present years to him. Live to him now, and he will never cast you away when you are old. Do not lay up for old age and keep back from the cause of God; but rather trust God for the future. Be "diligent in business;" but take care you do not hurt your spirit, by being too diligent, by being grasping and selfish. Remember you will

"Want but little here below, Nor want that little long."

And lastly, my dear venerable fathers in the faith, and mothers in Israel, take these words for your joy. Do not let the young people catch you indulging in melancholy, sitting in your chimney corner, grumbling and growling, but go about cheerful and happy, and they will think how blessed it is to be a Christian. If you are surly and fretful, they will think the Lord has forsaken you; but keep a smiling countenance, and they will think the promise is fulfilled. "And even to your old age I am he; and even to hoar hairs will I carry you: I have made, and I will bear; even I will carry, and will deliver you." Do, I beseech you, my venerable friends, try to be of a happy temperament and cheerful spirit, for a child will run away from a surly old man; but there is not a child in the world who does not love his grandfather if he is cheerful and happy. You can lead us to heaven if you have got heaven's sunlight on your face.

FOR MEDITATION: Elderly believers—the Bible tells us about their testimony (Psalm 92: 14,15; Proverbs 16: 31), their teaching (Titus 2: 2,3) and their treatment (1 Timothy 5: 1,2).

NOTE: This sermon was substantially repeated at Stambourne, Essex, two days later on the commemoration of the jubilee of Spurgeon's grandfather, Rev James Spurgeon.

SERMON NOS. 81-82

The two effects of the gospel

"For we are unto God a sweet savour of Christ, in them that are saved, and in them that perish; To the one we are the savour of death unto death; and to the other the savour of life unto life. And who is sufficient for these things?" 2 Corinthians 2: 15,16

SUGGESTED FURTHER READING: Acts 13: 42-52

The Gospel produces different effects. It must seem a strange thing, but it is strangely true, that there is scarcely ever a good thing in the world of which some little evil is not the consequence. Let the sun shine in brilliance—it shall moisten the wax, it shall harden clay; let it pour down floods of light on the tropics—it will cause vegetation to be extremely luxuriant, the richest and choicest fruits shall ripen, and the fairest of all flowers shall bloom, but who does not know, that there the worst of reptiles and the most venomous snakes are also brought forth? So it is with the gospel. Although it is the very sun of righteousness to the world, although it is God's best gift, although nothing can be in the least comparable to the vast amount of benefit which it bestows upon the human race, yet even of that we must confess, that sometimes it is the "savour of death unto death." But we are not to blame the gospel for this; it is not the fault of God's truth; it is the fault of those who do not receive it. It is the " savour of life unto life" to every one that listens to its sound with a heart that is open to its reception. It is only "death unto death" to the man who hates the truth, despises it, scoffs at it, and tries to oppose its progress.

FOR MEDITATION: There is hope for one in whom the law of God produces a sense of death (Romans 7: 10); it is a fearful thing when the life-giving Gospel is rejected and hardens the dead sinner.

The eternal name

"His name shall endure for ever." Psalm 72: 17
SUGGESTED FURTHER READING: Luke 23: 32-43

Do you see yonder thief hanging upon the cross? Behold the fiends at the foot thereof, with open mouths; charming themselves with the sweet thought, that another soul shall give them meat in hell. Behold the death-bird, fluttering his wings over the poor wretch's head; vengeance passes by and stamps him for her own; deep on his breast is written "a condemned sinner;" on his brow is the clammy sweat, expressed from him by agony and death. Look in his heart: it is filthy with the crust of years of sin; the smoke of lust is hanging within, in black festoons of darkness; his whole heart is hell condensed. Now, look at him. He is dying. One foot seems to be in hell; the other hangs tottering in life—only kept by a nail. There is a power in Jesus' eye. That thief looks: he whispers, "Lord, remember me." Turn your eye again there. Do you see that thief? Where is the clammy sweat? It is there. Where is that horrid anguish? Is it **not** there? Positively there is a smile upon his lips. The fiends of hell where are they? There are none; but a bright seraph is present, with his wings outspread, and his hands ready to snatch that soul, now a precious jewel, and bear it aloft to the palace of the great King. Look within his heart: it is white with purity. Look at his breast: it is not written "condemned," but "justified." Look in the book of life: his name is engraved there. Look on Jesus' heart: there on one of the precious stones he bears that poor thief's name. Yes, once more, look! Do you see that bright one amid the glorified, clearer than the sun, and fair as the moon? That is the thief! That is the power of Jesus; and that power shall endure for ever.

FOR MEDITATION: Jesus has the power to save to the uttermost all who seek God through him (Hebrews 7: 25); have you been "crucified with Christ" (Galatians 2: 20)?

Characteristics of faith

"Then said Jesus unto him, Except ye see signs and wonders, ye will not believe." John 4: 48
SUGGESTED FURTHER READING: Matthew 12: 38-42

Trust in the Lord; wait patiently for him; cast all thy confidence where he put all thy sins, namely, upon Christ Jesus alone, and thou shalt be saved, with or without any of these signs and wonders. I am afraid some Christians in London have fallen into the same error of wanting to see signs and wonders. They have been meeting together in special prayer-meetings to seek for a revival; and because people have not dropped down in a fainting fit, and have not screamed and made a noise, perhaps they have thought the revival has not come. Oh that we had eyes to see God's gifts in the way God chooses to give them! Where the Spirit works in the soul, we are always glad to see true conversion, and if he chooses to work in the church in London, we shall be glad to see it. If men's hearts are renewed, what matter it though they do not scream out. If their consciences are quickened, what matters it though they do not fall into a fit; if they do but find Christ, who is to regret that they do not lie for five or six weeks motionless and senseless. Take it without the signs and wonders. For my part I have no craving for them. Let me see God's work done in God's own way—a true and thorough revival, but the signs and wonders we can readily dispense with, for they are certainly not demanded by the faithful, and they will only be the laughing-stock of the faithless.

FOR MEDITATION: A demand for signs and wonders regularly meets with the same response in the New Testament—Matthew 12: 38-40; 16: 1-4; John 2: 18-22; 1 Corinthians 1: 22-24.

SERMON NO. 317

Justice satisfied

"Just, and the justifier of him which believeth in Jesus". Romans 3: 26
"Just to forgive us our sins, and to cleanse us from all unrighteousness."
1 John 1: 9
SUGGESTED FURTHER READING: Genesis 50: 15-21

I have heard of Mr John Wesley, that he was attended in most of his journeyings by one who loved him very much, and was willing, I believe, to have died for him. Still he was a man of a very stubborn and obstinate disposition, and Mr Wesley was not perhaps the very kindest man at all times. Upon one occasion he said to this man, "Joseph, take these letters to the post." "I will take them after preaching, sir." "Take them now, Joseph," said Mr Wesley. "I wish to hear you preach, sir; and there will be sufficient time for the post after service." "I insist upon your going now, Joseph." "I will not go at present." "You won't?" "No, sir." "Then you and I must part," said Mr Wesley. "Very good, sir." The good men slept over it. Both were early risers. At four o'clock the next morning, the refractory helper was accosted with, "Joseph, have you considered what I said—that we must part?" "Yes, sir." "And must we part?" "Please yourself, sir." "Will you ask my pardon, Joseph?" "No, sir." "You won't?" "No, sir." "Then I will ask **yours**, Joseph!" Poor Joseph was instantly melted, and they were at once reconciled. When once the grace of God has entered the heart, a man ought to be ready to seek forgiveness for an injury done to another. There is nothing wrong in a man confessing an offence against a fellow-man, and asking pardon for the wrong he has done him. If you have done aught, then, against any man, leave thy gift before the altar, and go and make peace with him, and then come and make peace with God. You are to make confession of your sin to God. Let that be humble and sincere. You cannot mention every offence, but do not hide one.

FOR MEDITATION: If we cannot bring ourselves to apologise to and to forgive those we have seen, we must know little about true confession to and the forgiveness of God whom we have not seen (Matthew 6: 14,15; 1 John 4: 20).

A present religion

"Beloved, now are we the sons of God." 1 John 3: 2
SUGGESTED FURTHER READING: Hebrews 13: 1-8

We need not talk of walking righteously, and soberly, in the world to come—

"There all is pure, and all is clear, There all is joy and love."

There will be no duty to discharge between the tradesmen and the customers, between the debtor and the creditor, between the father and the child, between the husband and the wife, in heaven, for all these relationships will have passed away. Religion must be intended for this life; the duties of it cannot be practised, unless they are practised here. But besides these, there are other duties devolving upon the Christian. Though it is every man's duty to be honest and sober, the Christian has another code of law. It is the Christian's duty to love his enemies, to be at peace with all men, to forgive as he hopes to be forgiven; it is his duty not to resist evil, when smitten on the one cheek to turn the other also; it is his duty to give to him that asketh of him, and from him that would borrow of him not to turn away—he is to be a liberal soul, devising liberal things. It is the Christian's duty to visit his Master's children when they are sick, so that it may be said to him at last, "I was sick, and naked, and in prison, and ye visited me, and ministered to my necessities." Now, if religion be not a thing for this world, I ask you how it is possible to perform its duties at all? There are no poor in heaven whom we can comfort and visit; there are no enemies in heaven whom we can graciously forgive; and there are not injuries inflicted, or wrongs endured, which we can bear with patience. Religion must have been intended in the very first place for this world, it must have been meant that now we should be the sons of God.

FOR MEDITATION: Faith in Christ is the qualification for a place in heaven; work for Christ is the qualification for rewards in heaven in addition to a place in heaven (Matthew 10: 40-42).

Elijah's appeal to the undecided

"How long halt ye between two opinions? If the Lord be God, follow him: if Baal, then follow him." 1 Kings 18: 21
SUGGESTED FURTHER READING: John 13: 12-19

I insist that it is your bounden duty, if you believe in God, simply because he is God, to serve him and obey him. I do not tell you it is for your advantage—it may be, I believe it is—but that I put aside from the question; I demand of you that you follow God, if you believe him to be God. If you do not think he is God; if you really think that the devil is God, then follow him; his pretended godhead shall be your plea, and you shall be consistent; but if God be God, if he made you, I demand that you serve him; if it is he who puts the breath into your nostrils, I demand that you obey him. If God be really worthy of worship, and you really think so, I demand that you either follow him, or else deny that he is God at all. Now, professor, if thou sayest that Christ's gospel is the only gospel, if thou believest in the divinity of the gospel, and puttest thy trust in Christ, I demand of thee to follow out the gospel, not merely because it will be to thy advantage, but because the gospel is divine. If thou makest a profession of being a child of God, if thou art a believer, and thinkest and believest religion is the best, the service of God most desirable, I do not come to plead with thee because of any advantage thou wouldst get by being holy; it is on this ground that I put it, that the Lord is God; and if he be God, it is thy business to serve him. If his gospel be true, and thou believest it to be true, it is thy duty to carry it out.

FOR MEDITATION: Four things God will not accept—hypocrisy (Luke 6: 46), half-heartedness (Luke 9: 59-62), double-mindedness (James 1: 6-8) and lukewarmness (Revelation 3: 15,16).

Indwelling sin

"Then Job answered the Lord, and said, Behold, I am vile." Job 40: 3,4
SUGGESTED FURTHER READING: Galatians 5: 13-24

When we believe in Jesus Christ all our sins are pardoned; yet the power of sin, although it is weakened and kept under by the dominion of the new-born nature which God infuses into our souls, does not cease, but still lingers in us, and will do so to our dying day. It is a doctrine held by all the orthodox, that there still dwells in the regenerate the lusts of the flesh, and that there still remains in the hearts of those who are converted by God's mercy, the evil of carnal nature. I have found it very difficult to distinguish, in experimental matters, concerning sin. It is usual with many writers, especially with hymn writers, to confound the two natures of a Christian. Now, I hold that there is in every Christian two natures, as distinct as were the two natures of the God-Man Christ Jesus. There is one nature which cannot sin, because it is born of God—a spiritual nature, coming directly from heaven, as pure and as perfect as God himself, who is the author of it; and there is also in man that ancient nature which, by the fall of Adam, has become altogether vile, corrupt, sinful, and devilish. There remains in the heart of the Christian a nature which cannot do that which is right, any more than it could before regeneration, and which is as evil as it was before the new birth—as sinful, as altogether hostile to God's laws, as ever it was—a nature which, as I said before, is curbed and kept under by the new nature in a great measure, but which is not removed and never will be until this tabernacle of our flesh is broken down, and we soar into that land into which there shall never enter anything that defiles.

FOR MEDITATION: Are there times when you cannot understand your own behaviour? You are in good company (Romans 7: 15-25). But the Christian, having received the new nature, need not and should not give in to the old nature as if he could do nothing about it.

SERMON NO. 83

The church of Christ

"And I will make them and the places round about my hill a blessing; and I will cause the shower to come down in his season; there shall be showers of blessing." Ezekiel 34: 26
SUGGESTED FURTHER READING: Psalm 67

The object of God in choosing a people before all worlds, was not only to save that people, but through them to confer essential benefits upon the whole human race. When he chose Abraham he did not elect him simply to be God's friend, and the recipient of peculiar privileges; but he chose him to make him, as it were, the conservator of truth. He was to be the ark in which the truth should be hidden. He was to be the keeper of the covenant on behalf of the whole world; and when God chooses any men by his sovereign electing grace, and makes them Christ's, he does it not only for their own sake, that they may be saved, but for the world's sake. For know ye not that "ye are the light of the world. A city that is set on an hill cannot be hid." "Ye are the salt of the earth;" and when God makes you salt, it is not only that you may have salt in yourselves, but that like salt you may preserve the whole mass. If he makes you leaven it is that like the little leaven you may leaven the whole lump. Salvation is not a selfish thing; God does not give it for us to keep to ourselves, but that we may thereby be made the means of blessing to others; and the great day shall declare that there is not a man living on the surface of the earth but has received a blessing in some way or the other through God's gift of the gospel. The very keeping of the wicked in life, and granting of the reprieve, was purchased with the death of Jesus and through his sufferings and death the temporal blessings which both we and they enjoy are bestowed on us. The gospel was sent that it might first bless those that embrace it, and then expand, so as to make them a blessing to the whole human race.

FOR MEDITATION: God kept his promise to Abraham (Genesis 12: 2,3). Has God blessed you? In what ways are you passing on the blessing to others?

SERMON NO. 28

High doctrine

"And all things are of God." 2 Corinthians 5: 18
SUGGESTED FURTHER READING: Ephesians 3: 7-13

There are some men who seem to think that God does his work bit by bit: altering and making additions as he goes on. They cannot believe that God had a plan; they believe that the most ordinary architect on earth has prefigured to himself some idea of what he means to build, though it were but a mud cottage, but the Most High God, who created the heavens and the earth, when he says, "Behold, I create new heavens and a new earth, wherein dwelleth righteousness," has no plan but what is left to the caprice of manhood; he is to have no decrees, no purposes, no determinations, but men are to do as they will, and so virtually man is to usurp the place of God, and God is to become the dependant of man. Nay, my brethren, in all the work of salvation, God is the sole and supreme designer. He planned the time when, and the manner how, each of his people should be brought to himself; he did not leave the number of his saved ones to chance, or to what was worse than chance—to the depraved will of man; he did not leave the choice of persons to mere accident, but on the stones of the eternal breastplate of the great High Priest he engraved the names of those he chose. He did not leave so much as one tent-pin, one single line or yard of canvas to be afterwards arranged; the whole of the tabernacle was given by pattern in the holy mount. In the building of the temple of grace, every stone was squared and chiselled in the eternal decree, its place ordained and settled, nor shall that stone be dug from its quarry till the hour ordained, nor shall it be placed in any other position than that which God, after the counsel of his own will has ordained.

FOR MEDITATION: Man has no idea what he is doing himself, but he is very good at questioning what God does (Luke 23: 34-39).

Constraining love

"Oh love the Lord, all ye his saints." Psalm 31: 23
SUGGESTED FURTHER READING: 1 John 4: 7-12

Christ's love to us we sometimes guess at, but, ah, it is so far beyond our thoughts, our reasonings, our praises, and our apprehension too, in the sweetest moments of our most spiritual ecstasy,—who can tell it? "Oh, how he loved us!" When Jesus wept at the grave of Lazarus, the Jews exclaimed with surprise—"Behold how he loved him." Verily, you might say the like with deeper emphasis. There was nothing in you to make him love you, but he left heaven's throne for you. As he came down the celestial hills, methinks the angels said "Oh, how he loved them." When he lay in the manger an infant, they gathered round and said, "Oh how he loves." But when they saw him sweating in the garden, when he was put into the crucible, and began to be melted in the furnace, then indeed, the spirits above began to know how much he loved us. Oh Jesus! When I see thee mocked and spat upon—when I see thy dear cheeks become a reservoir for all the filth and spittle of unholy mouths—when I see thy back rent with knotted whips—when I behold thy honour and thy life both trailing in the dust—when I see thee charged with madness, with treason, with blasphemy—when I behold thy hands and feet pierced, thy body stripped naked and exposed—when I see thee hanging on the cross between heaven and earth, in torments dire and excruciating—when I hear thee cry "I thirst," and see the vinegar thrust to thy lips—when I hear thy direful cry, "My God, my God, why hast thou forsaken me," my spirit is compelled to say, "Oh how he loves!"

FOR MEDITATION: How cold and hardhearted we must be to ever question the Lord's love towards us (Malachi 1: 2).

The believer's challenge

"Who is he that condemneth? It is Christ that died, yea rather, that is risen again, who is even at the right hand of God, who also maketh intercession for us." Romans 8: 34
SUGGESTED FURTHER READING: Romans 6: 1-11

Christ was in his death the hostage of the people of God. He was the representative of all the elect. When Christ was bound to the tree, I see my own sin bound there; when he died every believer virtually died in him; when he was buried we were buried in him, and when he was in the tomb, he was, as it were, God's hostage for all his church, for all that ever should believe on him. Now, as long as he was in prison, although there might be ground of hope, it was but as light sown for the righteous; but when the hostage came out, behold the first fruit of the harvest! When God said, "Let my Anointed go free, I am satisfied and content in him," then every elect vessel went free in him; then every child of God was released from imprisonment no more to die, not to know bondage or fetter for ever. I do see ground for hope when Christ is bound, for he is bound for me; I do see reason for rejoicing when he dies, for he dies for me, and in my room and stead; I do see a theme for solid satisfaction in his burial, for he is buried for me; but when he comes out of the grave, having swallowed up death in victory, my hope bursts into joyous song. He lives , and because he lives I shall live also. He is delivered and I am delivered too. Death has no more dominion over him and no more dominion over me; his deliverance is mine, his freedom mine for ever. Again, I repeat it, the believer should take strong draughts of consolation here. Christ is risen from the dead, how can we be condemned?

FOR MEDITATION: The reality of having been united with Christ in his death, burial and resurrection should be acted out in believer's baptism; but it should also be acted out in believer's daily living (1 Peter 3: 21-4: 2).

The report of the spies

"And they brought up an evil report of the land which they had searched unto the children of Israel, saying, The land, through which we have gone to search it, is a land that eateth up the inhabitants thereof; and all the people that we saw in it are men of a great stature."
Numbers 13: 32 and 14: 6-7
SUGGESTED FURTHER READING: Romans 2: 17-24

Every unguarded word you use, every inconsistent act, puts a slur on Christ. The world, you know, does not find fault with you—they lay it all to your Master. If you make a slip tomorrow, they will not say, "That is John Smith's human nature;" they will say, "That is John Smith's religion." They know better, but they will be sure to say it; they will be sure to put all the mischief at the door of Christ. Now, if you could bear the blame yourself you might bear it manfully; but do not allow Christ to bear the blame—do not suffer his reputation to be tarnished—do not permit his banner to be trampled in the dust. Then there is another consideration. You must remember, if you do wrong, the world will be quite sure to notice you. The world carries two bags: in the bag at the back they put all the Christian's virtues—in the bag in front they put all our mistakes and sins. They never think of looking at the virtues of holy men; all the courage of martyrs, all the fidelity of confessors, and all the holiness of saints, is nothing to them; but our iniquities are ever before them. Please do recollect, that wherever you are, as a Christian, the eyes of the world are upon you; the Argus eyes of an evil generation follow you everywhere. If a church is blind the world is not. It is a common proverb, "As sound asleep as a church," and a very true one, for most churches are sound asleep; but it would be a great falsehood if anyone were to say, "As sound asleep as the world," for the world is never asleep. Sleeping is left to the church. And remember, too, that the world always wears magnifying glasses to look at Christians' faults.

FOR MEDITATION: Like Mary our souls and words may magnify the Lord (Luke 1: 46), but does any area of our lives allow the unbelieving world to magnify our sins instead?

SERMON NO. 197

Presumptuous sins

"Keep back thy servant also from presumptuous sins." Psalm 19: 13
SUGGESTED FURTHER READING: 2 Samuel 11

This prayer was the prayer of a saint, the prayer of a holy man of God. Did David need to pray thus? Did the "man after God's own heart" need to cry, "Keep back thy servant"? Yes, he did. And note the beauty of the prayer. If I might translate it into more metaphorical style, it is like this: "Curb thy servant from presumptuous sins." "Keep him back, or he will wander to the edge of the precipice of sin. Hold him in, Lord; he is apt to run away; curb him; put the bridle on him; do not let him do it; let thine overpowering grace keep him holy; when he would do evil, then do thou draw him to good, and when his evil propensities would lead him astray, then do thou check him." "Keep back thy servant from presumptuous sins." What, then? Is it true that the best of men may sin presumptuously? Ah! It is true. It is a solemn thing to find the apostle Paul warning saints against the most loathsome of sins. He says, "Mortify therefore your members which are upon the earth, fornication, uncleanness, idolatry, inordinate affection," and such like. What! Do saints want warning against such sins as these? Yes, they do. The highest saints may sin the lowest sins, unless kept by divine grace. You old experienced Christians, boast not in your experience; you may yet trip up unless you cry, "Hold thou me up, and I shall be safe." You whose love is fervent, whose faith is constant, whose hopes are bright, say not, "I shall never sin," but rather cry out, "Lord, lead me not into temptation, and when there leave me not there; for unless thou hold me fast I feel I must, I shall decline, and prove an apostate after all."

FOR MEDITATION: Five ways to lay hold of the power of God against temptation:

Pray	(Luke 22: 40)
Obey	(Psalm 17: 5)
Watch	(1 Corinthians 16: 13)
Exhort	(Hebrews 3: 13)
Read	(Psalm 119: 11)

SERMON NO. 135

Salvation to the uttermost

"Wherefore he is able also to save them to the uttermost that come unto God by him, seeing he ever liveth to make intercession for them."
Hebrews 7: 25
SUGGESTED FURTHER READING: Romans 8: 31-34

It is pleasant to look back to Calvary's hill, and to behold that bleeding form expiring on the tree; it is sweet, amazingly sweet, to pry with eyes of love between those thick olives, and hear the groanings of the Man who sweat great drops of blood. Sinner, if you ask me how Christ can save you, I tell you this—he can save you, because he did not save himself; he can save you, because he took your guilt and endured your punishment. There is no way of salvation apart from the satisfaction of divine justice. Either the sinner must die, or else someone must die for him. Sinner, Christ can save you, because, if you come to God by him, then he died for you. God has a debt against us, and he never remits that debt; he will have it paid. Christ pays it, and then the poor sinner goes free. And we are told another reason why he is able to save: not only because he died, but because he lives to make intercession for us. That Man who once died on the cross is alive; that Jesus who was buried in the tomb is alive. If you ask me what he is doing, I bid you listen. Listen, if you have ears! Did you not hear him, poor penitent sinner? Did you not hear his voice, sweeter than harpers playing on their harps? Did you not hear a charming voice? Listen! What did it say? "O my Father! Forgive.......!" Why, he mentioned your own name! "O my Father, forgive him; he knew not what he did. It is true he sinned against light, and knowledge, and warnings; sinned willfully and woefully; but, Father, forgive him!" Penitent, if you can listen, you will hear him praying for you. And that is why he is able to save.

FOR MEDITATION: How often do you stop and think what Christ is doing for you right now, if you are a Christian (1 John 2: 1)?

A free salvation

"Yea, come, buy wine and milk without money and without price."
Isaiah 55: 1
SUGGESTED FURTHER READING: Romans 15: 13-16

He who is a happy Creator will be a happy Redeemer; and those who have tasted that the Lord is gracious, can bear witness that the ways of religion "are ways of pleasantness and all her paths are peace." And if this life were all, if death were the burial of all our life, and if the shroud were the winding-sheet of eternity, still to be a Christian would be a bright and happy thing, for it lights up this valley of tears, and fills the wells in the valley of Baca to the brim with streams of love and joy. The gospel, then, is like wine. It is like milk, too, for there is everything in the gospel that you want. Do you want something to bear you up in trouble? It is in the gospel—"a very present help in time of trouble." Do you need something to nerve you for duty? There is grace all-sufficient for everything that God calls you to undergo or to accomplish. Do you need something to light up the eye of your hope? Oh! There are joy-flashes in the gospel that may make your eye flash back again the immortal fires of bliss. Do you want something to make you stand steadfast in the midst of temptation? In the gospel there is that that can make you immovable, always abounding in the work of the Lord. There is no passion, no affection, no thought, no wish, no power which the gospel has not filled to the very brim. The gospel was obviously meant for manhood; it is adapted to it in its every part. There is knowledge for the head; there is love for the heart; there is guidance for the foot. There is milk and wine, in the gospel of our Lord Jesus Christ.

FOR MEDITATION: Do you limit the Gospel to being something only for the need of the unconverted? It also strengthens the believer (Romans 16:25).

SERMON NO. 199

Christ manifesting himself to his people

"Judas saith unto him, not Iscariot, Lord, how is it that thou wilt manifest thyself unto us, and not unto the world?" John 14: 22

SUGGESTED FURTHER READING: 2 Corinthians 12: 1-10

I was reading a short time ago of a Mr Tennant. He was about to preach one evening, and thought he would take a walk. As he was walking in a wood he felt so overpoweringly the presence of Christ, and such a manifestation of him, that he knelt down, and they could not discover him at the hour when he was to have preached. He continued there for hours, insensible as to whether he was in the body or out of the body; and when they waked him he looked like a man who had been with Jesus, and whose face shone. He never should forget, he said, to his dying day, that season of communion, when positively, though he could not see Christ, Christ was there, holding fellowship with him, heart against heart, in the sweetest manner. A wondrous display it must have been. You must know something of it, if not much; otherwise you have not gone far on your spiritual course. God teach you more, and lead you deeper! "Then shall ye know, when ye follow on to know the Lord." Then, what will be the natural effects of this spiritual manifestation? The first effect will be humility. If a man says, "I have had such and such spiritual communication, I am a great man;" he has never had any communications at all; for "God has respect unto the humble, but the proud he knoweth afar off." He does not want to come near them to know them, and will never give them any visits of love. It will give a man happiness; for he must be happy who lives near to God. Again: it will give a man holiness. A man who has not holiness has never had this manifestation. Some men profess a great deal; but do not believe any man unless you see that his deeds answer to what he says.

FOR MEDITATION: The above account may be a blessing or a temptation to you! If we seek experiences for their own sake, Satan will ensure that we get some; our business is to seek to know Christ more and more (Philippians 3: 10; 2 Peter 3: 18).

SERMON NO. 29

The heavenly race

"So run, that ye may obtain." 1 Corinthians 9: 24
SUGGESTED FURTHER READING: Hebrews 11: 39-12: 2

When zealous racers on yonder heath are flying across the plain, seeking to obtain the reward, the whole heath is covered with multitudes of persons, who are eagerly gazing upon them, and no doubt the noise of those who cheer them onward and the thousand eyes of those who look upon them, have a tendency to make them stretch every nerve, and press with vigour on. It was so in the games to which the apostle alludes. There the people sat on raised platforms, while the racers ran before them, and they cried to them, and the friends of the racers urged them forward, and the kindly voice would ever be heard bidding them go on. Now, Christian brethren, how many witnesses are looking down upon you. Down! Do I say? It is even so. From the battlements of heaven the angels look down upon you, and they seem to cry today to you with sweet, silvery voice, "Ye shall reap if ye faint not; ye shall be rewarded if ye continue steadfast in the work and faith of Christ." And the saints look down upon you—Abraham, Isaac, and Jacob; martyrs and confessors, and your own pious relatives who have ascended to heaven, look down upon you; and if I might so speak, I think sometimes you might hear the clapping of their hands when you have resisted temptation and overcome the enemy; and you might see their suspense when you are lagging in the course, and you might hear their friendly word of caution as they bid you gird up the loins of your mind, and lay aside every weight, and still speed forward; never resting to take your breath, never staying for a moment's ease till you have attained the flowery beds of heaven, where you may rest for ever.

FOR MEDITATION: Do Spurgeon's words, spoken on a Friday afternoon from the "Grand Stand, Epsom Race-course" strike you as over-fanciful? The pages of Scripture are full of lessons from the heroes of faith, still speaking to us down the centuries (Hebrews 11: 4). They witness to us from their own experience "It can be done; by God's grace we ran the race; by God's grace you can run it too" (2 Timothy 4: 7).

SERMON NO. 198

The scales of judgement

"Tekel; Thou art weighed in the balances, and art found wanting."
Daniel 5: 27.
SUGGESTED FURTHER READING: Psalm 62

Into those scales I must go. God will not take me on my profession. I may bring my witnesses with me; I may bring my minister and the deacons of the church to give me a character, which might be thought all-sufficient among men, but God will tolerate no subterfuge. Into the scales he will put me, do what I may; whatever the opinion of others may be of me, and whatever my own profession. And let me remember, too, that I must be altogether weighed in the scales. I cannot hope that God will weigh my head and pass over my heart—that because I have correct notions of doctrine, therefore he will forget that my heart is impure, or my hands guilty of iniquity. My all must be cast into the scales. Come, let me stretch my imagination, and picture myself about to be put into those scales. Shall I be able to walk boldly up and enter them, knowing whom I have believed, and being persuaded that the blood of Christ and his perfect righteousness shall bear me harmless through it all; or shall I be dragged with terror and dismay? Shall the angel come and say, "Thou must enter." Shall I bend my knee and cry, "Oh, it is all right," or shall I seek to escape? Now, thrust into the scale, do I see myself waiting for one solemn moment. My feet have touched the bottom of the scales, and there stand those everlasting weights, and now which way are they turned? Which way shall it be? Do I descend in the scale with joy and delight, being found through Jesus' righteousness to be full weight, and so accepted; or must I rise, light, frivolous, unsound in all my fancied hopes, and kick the beam?

FOR MEDITATION: We all ought to check our weight before God does (2 Corinthians 13: 5). The scales of God's judgement will show in our favour only if Jesus Christ, the Rock of Ages, is in us. Do you need to put on weight?

The wicked man's life, funeral, and epitaph

"And so I saw the wicked buried, who had come and gone from the place of the holy, and they were forgotten in the city where they had so done: this also is vanity." Ecclesiastes 8: 10
SUGGESTED FURTHER READING: Luke 16: 19-23

Go into Bunhill Fields, and stand by the memorial of John Bunyan, and you will say, "Ah! There lies the head that contained the brain which thought out that wondrous dream of the Pilgrim's Progress from the City of Destruction to the Better Land. There lies the finger that wrote those wondrous lines which depict the story of him who came at last to the land Beulah, and waded through the flood, and entered into the celestial city. And there are the eyelids which he once spoke of, when he said, "If I lie in prison until the moss grows on my eyelids, I will never make a promise to withhold from preaching." And there is that bold eye that penetrated the judge, when he said, "If you will let me out of prison today, I will preach again tomorrow, by the help of God." And there lies that loving hand that was ever ready to receive into communion all them that loved the Lord Jesus Christ: I love the hand that wrote the book, "Water Baptism no bar to Christian Communion." I love him for that sake alone, and if he had written nothing else but that, I would say, "John Bunyan, be honoured for ever." And there lies the foot that carried him up Snow Hill to go and make peace between a father and a son, in that cold day, which cost him his life. Peace to his ashes! Wait, O John Bunyan, till thy Master sends his angel to blow the trumpet; and methinks, when the archangel sounds it, he will almost think of thee, and this shall be a part of his joy, that honest John Bunyan, the greatest of all Englishmen, shall rise from his tomb at the blowing of that great trump. You cannot say so of the wicked.

FOR MEDITATION: In Heaven the saved are still known by name—Abraham, Lazarus; in hell the lost are at best known only by a description—Dives is just the Latin for "a rich man". See the contrast in Proverbs 10: 7. Are the names and burial-places of John Bunyan's enemies well known even on earth?

Israel in Egypt

"And they sing the song of Moses the servant of God, and the song of the Lamb, saying, Great and marvellous are thy works, Lord God Almighty; just and true are thy ways, thou King of saints." Revelation 15: 3
SUGGESTED FURTHER READING: Exodus 15: 1-18

One part of the song of Moses consisted in praising the ease with which God destroyed his enemies. "Thou didst blow with thy wind, the sea covered them; they sank as lead in the mighty waters." If we had gone to work to destroy the hosts of Pharaoh, what a multitude of engines of death should we have required. If the work had been committed to us, to cut off the hosts, what marvellous preparations, what thunder, what noise, what great activity there would have been. But mark the grandeur of the expression. God did not even lift himself from his throne to do it: he saw Pharaoh coming; he seemed to look upon him with a placid smile; he did just blow with his lips, and the sea covered them. You and I will marvel at the last how easy it has been to overthrow the enemies of the Lord. We have been tugging and toiling all our lifetime to be the means of overthrowing systems of error: it will astonish the church when her Master shall come to see how, as the ice dissolveth before the fire, all error and sin shall be utterly destroyed in the coming of the most High. We must have our societies and our machinery, our preachers and our gatherings, and rightly too; but God will not require them at the last. The destruction of his enemies shall be as easy to him as the making of a world. In passive silence unmoved he sat; and he did but break the silence with "Let there be light" and light was. So shall he at the last, when his enemies are raging furiously, blow with his winds, and they shall be scattered.

FOR MEDITATION: Creation took God a matter of a few days; the destruction of a great power will take him only a fraction of the time (Revelation 18: 8,10,17,19).

SERMON NO. 136

Omniscience

"Thou God seest me." Genesis 16: 13
SUGGESTED FURTHER READING: Psalm 94: 4-11

It were hard to suppose a God who could not see his own creatures; it were difficult in the extreme to imagine a divinity who could not behold the actions of the works of his hands. The word which the Greeks applied to God implied that he was a God who could see. They called him Theos; and they derived that word, if I read rightly, from the root *theisthai,* to see, because they regarded God as being the all-seeing one, whose eye took in the whole universe at a glance, and whose knowledge extended far beyond that of mortals. God Almighty, from his very essence and nature, must be an Omniscient God. Strike out the thought that he sees me, and you extinguish Deity by a single stroke. There would be no God if that God had no eyes, for a blind God is not God at all. We could not conceive such a one. Stupid as idolaters may be, it is very hard to think that even they had fashioned a blind god: even they have given eyes to their gods, though they see not. Juggernaut, or Jagannatha (a god worshipped in some areas of Hinduism), has eyes stained with blood; and the gods of the ancient Romans had eyes, and some of them were called far-seeing gods. Even the heathen can scarce conceive of a god that has no eyes to see, and certainly we are not so mad as to imagine for a single second that there can be a Deity without the knowledge of everything that is done by man beneath the sun. I say it is as impossible to conceive of a God who did not observe everything, as to conceive of a round square. When we say, "Thou God," we do, in fact, comprise in the word "God" the idea of a God who sees everything, "Thou God seest me."

FOR MEDITATION: The proofs of Jesus' deity in Mark 2: 5-8: He could see faith, forgive sins and perceive the thoughts of the heart. He still can!

Unimpeachable justice

"Against thee, thee only, have I sinned, and done this evil in thy sight: that thou mightest be justified when thou speakest, and be clear when thou judgest." Psalm 51: 4
SUGGESTED FURTHER READING: 1 Samuel 15: 1-31

We have heard of men who have confessed their guilt, and afterwards tried to extenuate their crime, and show some reasons why they were not so guilty as apparently they would seem to be; but when the Christian confesses his guilt, you never hear a word of extenuation or apology from him. He says, "Against thee, thee only, have I sinned, and done this evil in thy sight:" and in saying this, he makes God just when he condemns him, and clear when he sentences him for ever. Have you ever made such a confession? Have you ever thus bowed yourselves before God? Or have you tried to palliate your guilt, and call your sins by little names, and speak of your crimes as if they were but light offences? If you have, then you have not felt the sentence of death in yourselves, and you are still waiting till the solemn death-knell shall toll the hour of your doom, and you shall be dragged out, amidst the universal hiss of the execration of the world, to be condemned for ever to flames which shall never know abatement. Again: after the Christian confesses his sin, he offers no promise that he will of himself behave better. Some, when they make confessions to God, say, "Lord, if thou forgive me I will not sin again;" but God's penitents never say that. When they come before him they say, "Lord, once I promised, once I made resolves, but I dare not make them now, for they would be so soon broken, that they would increase my guilt; and my promises would be so soon violated, that they would sink my soul deeper in hell. I can only say, if thou wilt create in me a clean heart, I will be thankful for it, and will sing to thy praise for ever; but I cannot promise that I will live without sin, or work out a righteousness of my own. I dare not promise, my Father, that I shall never go astray again."

FOR MEDITATION: Does your confession of sin to God include the excuses of a King Saul or the acquiescence of a King David, the man after God's own heart (1 Samuel 13: 14)?

The power of the Holy Spirit

"The power of the Holy Ghost." Romans 15: 13
SUGGESTED FURTHER READING: Acts 2: 1-21

In a few more years—I know not when, I know not how—the Holy Spirit will be poured out in a far different style from the present. There are diversities of operations; and during the last few years it has been the case that the diversified operations have consisted in very little pouring out of the Spirit. Ministers have gone on in dull routine, continually preaching—preaching—preaching, and little good has been done. I do hope that perhaps a fresh era has dawned upon us, and that there is a better pouring out of the Spirit even now. For the hour is coming, and it may be even now is, when the Holy Spirit shall be poured out again in such a wonderful manner that many shall run to and fro, and knowledge shall be increased—the knowledge of the Lord shall cover the earth as the waters cover the surface of the great deep; when his kingdom shall come, and his will shall be done on earth even as it is in heaven. We are not going to be dragging on for ever like Pharaoh with the wheels off his chariot. My heart exults and my eyes flash with the thought that very likely I shall live to see the out-pouring of the Spirit; when "the sons and the daughters of God again shall prophecy, and the young men shall see visions, and the old men shall dream dreams." Perhaps there shall be no miraculous gifts—for they will not be required; but yet there shall be such a miraculous amount of holiness, such an extraordinary fervour of prayer, such a real communion with God and so much vital religion, and such a spread of the doctrines of the cross, that everyone will see that verily the Spirit is poured out like water, and the rains are descending from above. For that let us pray: let us continually labour for it, and seek it of God.

FOR MEDITATION: Spurgeon saw answers to his prayers in the 1859 revival. What are your visions for revival? Lots of excitement with extravagant claims that the Holy Spirit is involved? Or a genuine work of the Spirit which speaks for itself in real conversions, true fellowship and godly living (Acts 2: 37-47)?

SERMON NO. 30

Vile ingratitude

"Again the word of the Lord came unto me, saying, Son of man, cause Jerusalem to know her abominations." Ezekiel 16: 1,2
SUGGESTED FURTHER READING: 1 Corinthians 6: 12-20

God gives to his people riches, and they offer them before the shrine of their covetousness. He gives them talent, and they prostitute it to the service of their ambition. He gives them judgement, and they pander to their own advancement, and seek not the interest of his kingdom. He gives them influence; that influence they use for their own aggrandisement, and not for his honour. This is like taking his gold, and his jewels, and hanging them upon the neck of the god Ashtaroth. Ah! Let us take care when we think of our sins, that we set them in this light. It is taking God's mercies to lavish them upon his enemies. Now, if you were to make me a present of some token of your regard, I think it would be the meanest and most ungracious thing in the world I could do to take it over to your enemy, and say, "There, I come to pay my respects." To pay my respects to your foe with that which had been the token of your favour! There are two kings at enmity with one another—two powers that have been at battle, and one of them has a rebellious subject, who is caught in the very act of treason, and condemned to die. The king very graciously pardons him, and then munificently endows him. "There," says he, "I give you a thousand crown-pieces;" and that man takes the bounty, and devotes it to increasing the resources of the king's enemies. Now, that were a treason and baseness too vile to be committed by worldly men. Alas then! That is what you have done. You have bestowed on God's enemies what God gave to you as a love-token. Oh, men and brethren, let us bow ourselves in dust and ashes before God.

FOR MEDITATION: Is a readiness to use God's gifts selfishly the reason why he appears to say "No" to so many of your prayer-requests (James 4: 3-4)?

His name—the mighty God

"The mighty God." Isaiah 9: 6
SUGGESTED FURTHER READING: Hebrews 2: 10-18

Great is the mystery of godliness, for the passage from which the text is taken says, "Unto us a child is born." A child! What can a child do? It totters in its walk, it trembles in its steps—and it is a child newly born. Born! An infant hanging on its mother's breast, an infant deriving its nourishment from a woman? That! Can that work wonders? Yea, saith the prophet, "Unto us a child is born." But then it is added, "Unto us a Son is given." Christ was not only born, but given. As man he is a child born, as God he is the Son given. He comes down from on high; he is given by God to become our Redeemer. But here behold the wonder! "His name," this child's name, "shall be called Wonderful, Counsellor, the mighty God." Is this child, then, to us the mighty God? If so, O brethren, without controversy, great is the mystery of godliness indeed! And yet, just let us look through the history of the church, and discover whether we have not ample evidence to substantiate it. This child born, this Son given, came into the world to issue a challenge against sin. For thirty years and upwards he had to struggle and wrestle against temptations more numerous and more terrible than man had ever known before. Adam fell when a woman tempted him; Eve fell when a serpent offered fruit to her, but Christ, the second Adam, stood invulnerable against all the shafts of Satan, though tempted he was in all points like as we are. Not one arrow out of the quiver of hell was spared; the whole were shot against him. Every arrow was aimed against him with all the might of Satan's archers, and that is not little! And yet, without sin or taint of sin, more than conqueror he stood.

FOR MEDITATION: Here, on the morning of his 25th birthday, Spurgeon gloried in the birthday of his great elder brother, the Lord Jesus Christ— God born of a woman, given in the likeness of sinful flesh so that God could condemn our sin in his flesh (Galatians 4: 4; Romans 8: 3). What an appropriate birthday meditation, remembering how Christ identified with us so that we could be identified with him!

SERMON NO. 258

The outpouring of the Holy Spirit

"While Peter yet spake these words, the Holy Ghost fell on all them which heard the word." Acts 10: 44
SUGGESTED FURTHER READING: Micah 3: 5-8

There is a necessity that the preacher himself, if souls are to be saved, should be under the influence of the Spirit. I have constantly made it my prayer that I might be guided by the Spirit even in the smallest and least important parts of the service; for you cannot tell if the salvation of a soul may depend upon the reading of a hymn, or upon the selection of a chapter. Two persons have joined our church and made a profession of being converted simply through my reading a hymn—"Jesus, lover of my soul." They did not remember anything else in the hymn; but those words made such a deep impression upon their mind, that they could not help repeating them for days afterwards, and then the thought arose, "Do I love Jesus?" And then they considered what strange ingratitude it was that he should be the lover of their souls, and yet they should not love him. Now I believe the Holy Spirit led me to read that hymn. And many persons have been converted by some striking saying of the preacher. But why was it the preacher uttered that saying? Simply because he was led thereunto by the Holy Spirit. Rest assured, beloved, that when any part of the sermon is blessed to your heart, the minister said it because he was ordered to say it by his Master. I might preach today a sermon which I preached on Friday, and which was useful then, and there might be no good whatever come from it now, because it might not be the sermon which the Holy Spirit would have delivered today. But if with sincerity of heart I have sought God's guidance in selecting the topic, and he rests upon me in the preaching of the Word, there is no fear but that it shall be found adapted to your immediate wants. The Holy Spirit must rest upon your preachers.

FOR MEDITATION: The one who is filled with the Spirit (Ephesians 5: 18) is filled with the word of Christ (Colossians 3: 16); the mark of being filled with the Spirit is speaking the word of God (Luke 1: 41, 42, 67; Acts 2: 4; 4: 8,31; 7: 55,56; 13: 9-10). Do you pray this for your preachers? And for yourself?

SERMON NO. 201

Mercy, omnipotence, and justice

"The Lord is slow to anger, and great in power, and will not at all acquit the wicked." Nahum 1: 3
SUGGESTED FURTHER READING: Nehemiah 9: 9-31

Have you ever observed that scene in the garden of Eden at the time of the fall? God had threatened Adam, that if he sinned he should surely die. Adam sinned: did God make haste to sentence him? 'Tis sweetly said, "The Lord God walked in the garden in the cool of the day." Perhaps that fruit was plucked at early morn, maybe it was plucked at noon-tide; but God was in no haste to condemn; he waited till the sun was well nigh set, and in the cool of the day came, and as an old expositor has put it very beautifully, when he did come he did not come on wings of wrath, but he "walked in the garden in the cool of the day." He was in no haste to slay. I think I see him, as he was represented then to Adam, in those glorious days when God walked with man. Methinks I see the wonderful similitude in which the unseen did veil himself: I see it walking among the trees so slowly—if it is right to give such a picture—beating its breast, and shedding tears that it should have to condemn man. At last I hear its doleful voice: "Adam, where art thou? Where hast thou cast thyself, poor Adam? Thou hast cast thyself from my favour; thou hast cast thyself into nakedness and into fear; for thou art hiding thyself. Adam, where art thou? I pity thee. Thou thoughtest to be God. Before I condemn thee I will give thee one note of pity. Adam, where art thou?" Yes, the Lord was slow to anger, slow to write the sentence, even though the command had been broken, and the threatening was therefore of necessity brought into force.

FOR MEDITATION: There are good and bad ways of taking advantage of God's apparent slowness (2 Peter 3: 3,4,9).

SERMON NO. 137

The majestic voice

"The voice of the Lord is full of majesty." Psalm 29: 4
SUGGESTED FURTHER READING: Hebrews 1: 1-4

In some sense Jesus Christ may be called the voice of God, for you know he is called the Word of God frequently in Scripture; and I am sure this Word of God "is full of majesty." The voice and the word are very much the same thing. God speaks: it is his Son. His Son is the Word; the Word is his Son, and the voice is his Son. Truly the voice, the Word of God, "is full of majesty." Angels! Ye can tell what majesty sublime invested his blest person when he reigned at his Father's right hand; ye can tell what were the brightnesses which he laid aside to become incarnate; ye can tell how sparkling was that crown, how mighty was that sceptre, how glorious were those robes bedecked with stars. Spirits! Ye who saw him when he stripped himself of all his glories, ye can tell what was his majesty. And oh! Ye glorified, ye who saw him ascend up on high, leading captivity captive—ye beloved songsters, who bow before him, and unceasingly sing his love! Ye can tell how full of majesty he is. High above all principalities and powers ye see him sit; angels are but servants at his feet; and the mightiest monarchs like creeping worms beneath his throne. High there, where God alone reigns, beyond the sight of angels or the gaze of immortal spirits—there he sits, not majestic merely, but full of majesty. Christian! Adore your Saviour; adore the Son of God; reverence him, and remember at all seasons and times, how little so ever you may be, your Saviour, with whom you are allied, the Word of God, is essentially full of majesty.

FOR MEDITATION: The Lord Jesus Christ is full of grace and truth (John 1: 14); in him the fulness of God dwells bodily (Colossians 1: 19; 2: 9). It should be a staggering thought that every Christian has received from his fullness (John 1: 16; Ephesians 1: 22,23).

The plea of faith

"Do as thou hast said." 2 Samuel 7: 25
SUGGESTED FURTHER READING: Psalm 19: 7-11

Unless we know what God has said, it will be folly to say, "do as thou hast said." Perhaps there is no book more neglected in these days than the Bible. I do truly believe there are more mouldy Bibles in this world than there are of any sort of neglected books. We have stillborn books in abundance; we have innumerable books which never see any circulation, but we have no book that is so much bought, and then so speedily laid aside, and so little used, as the Bible. If we buy a newspaper, it is generally handed from one person to another, or we take care to peruse it pretty well; indeed some go so far as to read advertisements and all. If a person purchases a novel, it is well known how he will sit and read it all the way through, till the midnight candle is burnt out; the book must be finished in one day, because it is so admirable and interesting; but the Bible, of course, in the estimation of many, is not an interesting book; and the subjects it treats of are not of any very great importance. So most men think; they think it is a very good book to carry out on a Sunday, but never meant to be used as a book of pleasure, or a book to which one could turn with delight. Such is the opinion of many; but no opinion can be more apart from the truth; for what other book deals with truths half so important as those that concern the soul? What book can so well deserve my attention as that which is written by the greatest of all authors, God himself?

FOR MEDITATION: This book will become a hindrance to your soul if you allow it to become a substitute for your daily Bible reading. The correct use of these daily readings is found in Acts 17: 11.

The desire of the soul in spiritual darkness

"With my soul have I desired thee in the night." Isaiah 26: 9
SUGGESTED FURTHER READING: Psalm 42

There are times when all the saints can do is to desire. We have a vast number of evidences of piety: some are practical, some are experimental, some are doctrinal; and the more evidences a man has of his piety the better, of course. We like a number of signatures, to make a deed more valid, if possible. We like to invest property in a great number of trustees, in order that it may be all the safer; and so we love to have many evidences. Many witnesses will carry our case in the courts better than a few: and so it is well to have many witnesses to testify to our piety. But there are seasons when a Christian cannot get any. He can get scarcely one witness to come and attest his godliness. He asks for good works to come and speak for him. But there will be such a cloud of darkness about him, and his good works will appear so black that he will not dare to think of their evidences. He will say, "True, I hope this is the right fruit; I hope I have served God; but I dare not plead these works as evidences." He will have lost assurance, and with it his enjoyment of communion with God. "I have had that fellowship with him," perhaps he will say, and he will summon that communion to come and be in evidence. But he has forgotten it, and it does not come, and Satan whispers it is a fancy, and the poor evidence of communion has its mouth gagged, so that it cannot speak. But there is one witness that very seldom is gagged, and one that I trust the people of God can always apply, even in the night: and that is, "I have desired thee—I have desired thee in the night."

FOR MEDITATION: The light shines best in the darkness (John 1: 5); the people of God have proved it when all else has failed them (Psalm 73: 21-26; Jonah 2:1-7).

The sound in the mulberry trees

"When thou hearest the sound of a going in the tops of the mulberry trees, that then thou shalt bestir thyself: for then shall the Lord go out before thee, to smite the host of the Philistines." 2 Samuel 5: 24
SUGGESTED FURTHER READING: 2 Timothy 2: 14-19

If any of your acquaintance have been in the house of God, if you have induced them to go there, and you think there is some little good doing but you do not know, take care of that little. It may be God has used us as a foster mother to bring up his child, so that this little one may be brought up in the faith, and this newly converted soul may be strengthened and edified. But I'll tell you, many of you Christians do a deal of mischief, by what you say when going home. A man once said that when he was a lad he heard a certain sermon from a minister, and felt deeply impressed under it. Tears stole down his cheeks, and he thought within himself, "I will go home to pray." On the road home he fell into the company of two members of the church. One of them began saying, "Well, how did you enjoy the sermon?" The other said, "I do not think he was quite sound on such a point." "Well," said the other, "I thought he was rather off his guard," or something of that sort; and one pulled one part of the minister's sermon to pieces, and another the other, until, said the young man, before I had gone many yards with them, I had forgotten all about it; and all the good I thought I had received seemed swept away by those two men, who seemed afraid lest I should get any hope, for they were just pulling that sermon to pieces which would have brought me to my knees. How often have we done the same! People will say, "What did you think of that sermon?" I gently tell them nothing at all, and if there is any fault in it—and very likely there is, it is better not to speak of it, for some may get good from it.

FOR MEDITATION: If you must have the sermon for Sunday lunch, beware of devouring someone's faith along with it (Mark 4: 4,15).

A home mission sermon

"Whatsoever thy hand findeth to do, do it with thy might; for there is no work, nor device, nor knowledge, nor wisdom, in the grave, whither thou goest" Ecclesiastes 9: 10
SUGGESTED FURTHER READING: Luke 22: 24-27

George Washington, the commander-in-chief, was going around among his soldiers. They were hard at work, lifting a heavy piece of timber at some fortification. There stood the corporal of the regiment calling out to his men, "Heave there, heave ahoy!" and giving them all kinds of directions. As large as possible the good corporal was. So Washington, alighting from his horse, said to him, "What is the good of your calling out to those men, why don't you help them yourself and do part of the work." The corporal drew himself up and said, "Perhaps you are not aware to whom you are speaking, sir; I am a corporal." "I beg your pardon," said Washington; "you are a corporal are you; I am sorry I should have insulted you." So he took off his own coat and waistcoat and set to work to help the men build the fortification. When he had done he said, "Mr Corporal, I am sorry I insulted you, but when you have any more fortifications to get up, and your men won't help you, send for George Washington, the commander-in-chief, and I will come and help them." The corporal slunk away perfectly ashamed of himself. And so Christ Jesus might say to us, "Oh, you don't like teaching the poor; it is beneath your dignity; then let your commander-in-chief do it; he can teach the poor, he can wash the feet of the saints, he can visit the sick and afflicted—he came down from heaven to do this, and he will set you the example." Surely we should each be ashamed of ourselves, and declare from this time forward whatever it is, be it great or little, if it comes to our hand, and if God will but give us help and give us grace, we will do it with all our might.

FOR MEDITATION: Our Master knew how to be humble (Philippians 2: 6-9); he also knows how to deal with people who are proud or humble (1 Peter 5: 5-6).

The conversion of Saul of Tarsus

"And when we were all fallen to the earth, I heard a voice speaking unto me, and saying in the Hebrew tongue, Saul, Saul, why persecutest thou me? it is hard for thee to kick against the pricks." Acts 26: 14

SUGGESTED FURTHER READING: John 15: 16-25

When you were first pricked in the heart, how personal the preacher was. I remember it well. It seemed to me that I was the only person in the whole place, as if a black wall were round about me, and I were shut in with the preacher, something like the prisoners at the penitentiary, who each sit in their cell and can see no one but the chaplain. I thought all he said was meant for me; I felt persuaded that some one knew my character, and had written to him and told him all, and that he had personally picked me out. Why, I thought he fixed his eyes on me; and I have reason to believe he did, but still he said he knew nothing about my case. Oh, that men would hear the word preached, and that God would so bless them in their hearing, that they might feel it to have a personal application to their own hearts. But note again—the apostle received some information as to the persecuted one. If you had asked Saul who it was he persecuted, he would have said, "Some poor fishermen, that had been setting up an impostor; I am determined to put them down." "Why, who are they? They are the poorest of the world, the very scum and dregs of society; if they were princes and kings we perhaps might let them have their opinion; but these poor miserable ignorant fellows, I do not see why they are allowed to carry out their infatuation, and I shall persecute them. Moreover, most of them are women I have been persecuting—poor, ignorant creatures. What right have they to set their judgement up above the priests? They have no right to have an opinion of their own, and therefore it is quite right for me to make them turn away from their foolish errors." But see in what a different light Jesus Christ puts it. He does not say, "Saul, Saul, why didst thou persecute Stephen?" or "Why art thou about to drag the people of Damascus to prison;" No—"Saul, Saul, why persecutest thou me?"

FOR MEDITATION: What a personal Saviour the Lord Jesus Christ is! He personally calls his people to himself (Luke 19: 5) and he takes it personally when they are persecuted (Luke 10: 16).

SERMON NO. 202

Prayer—the forerunner of mercy

"Thus saith the Lord God; I will yet for this be enquired of by the house of Israel, to do it for them; I will increase them with men like a flock."
Ezekiel 36: 37
SUGGESTED FURTHER READING: 1 Samuel 22: 9-23: 5

First, I enquire what the promise is. I turn to my Bible, and I seek to find the promise whereby the thing which I desire to seek is certified to me as being a thing which God is willing to give. Having enquired so far as that, I take that promise, and on my bended knees I enquire of God whether he will fulfil his own promise. I take to him his own word of covenant, and I say to him, "O Lord, wilt thou not fulfil it, and wilt thou not fulfil it now?" So that there, again, prayer is enquiry. After prayer I look out for the answer; I expect to be heard; and if I am not answered I pray again, and my repeated prayers are but fresh enquiries. I expect the blessing to arrive; I go and enquire whether there is any tidings of its coming. I ask; and thus I say, "Wilt thou answer me, O Lord? Wilt thou keep thy promise. Or wilt thou shut up thine ear, because I misunderstand my own wants and mistake thy promise?" Brethren, we must use enquiry in prayer, and regard prayer as being, first, an enquiry for the promise, and then on the strength of that promise an enquiry for the fulfilment. We expect something to come as a present from a friend: we first have the note, whereby we are informed it is upon the road. We enquire as to what the present is by the reading of the note; and then, if it arrive not, we call at the accustomed place where the parcel ought to have been left, and we ask or enquire for such and such a thing. We have enquired about the promise, and then we go and enquire again, until we get an answer that the promised gift has arrived and is ours. So with prayer.

FOR MEDITATION: Asking comes in two shapes—questions and requests. God is able to give us all the answers we need (Luke 11: 9,10).

SERMON NO. 138

Hatred without cause

"They hated me without a cause." John 15: 25
SUGGESTED FURTHER READING: 1 Peter 4: 12-19

Take care, if the world does hate you, that it hates you without a cause. If the world is to oppose you, it is of no use making the world oppose you. This world is bitter enough, without my putting vinegar in it. Some people seem to fancy the world will persecute them; therefore, they put themselves into a fighting posture, as if they invited persecutions. Now, I do not see any good in doing that. Do not try and make other people dislike you. Really, the opposition some people meet with is not for righteousness' sake, but for their own sin's sake, or their own nasty temper's sake. Many a Christian lives in a house—a Christian servant girl perhaps; she says she is persecuted for righteousness' sake. But she is of a bad disposition; she sometimes speaks sharp, and then her mistress reproves her. That is not being persecuted for righteousness' sake. There is another, a merchant in the city, perhaps; he is not looked upon with much esteem. He says he is persecuted for righteousness' sake; whereas, it is because he did not keep a bargain some time ago. Another man says he is persecuted for righteousness' sake; but he goes about assuming authority over everybody, and now and then persons turn round and reproach him. Look to it, Christian people, that if you are persecuted, it is for righteousness' sake; for if you get any perse-cution yourself you must keep it yourself. The persecutions you bring on yourself for your own sins, Christ has nothing to do with them; they are chastisements on you. They hated Christ without a cause; then fear not to be hated. They hated Christ without a cause; then court not to be hated, and give the world no cause for it.

FOR MEDITATION: The apostle Paul knew what suffering for Christ's sake really means (2 Corinthians 11: 23-27). It was something he avoided when he could appeal to the law, (Acts 22: 25-29) and he did not pretend to be persecuted when he brought trouble upon himself (Acts 23: 1-5).

Men chosen—fallen angels rejected

"Verily he took not on him the nature of angels; but he took on him the seed of Abraham." Hebrews 2: 16

SUGGESTED FURTHER READING: 2 Peter 2: 4-9

Adam broke the covenant of works; he touched the accursed fruit, and in that day he fell. Ah! What a fall was there! Then you, and I, and all of us fell down, while cursed sin triumphed over us; there were no men that stood; there were some angels that stood, but no men, for the fall of Adam was the fall of our entire race. After one portion of the angels had fallen, it pleased God to stamp their doom, and make it fast and firm; but when man fell, it did not so please God; he had threatened to punish him, but in his infinite mercy he made some the object of his special affection, for whom he provided a precious remedy, and secured it by the blood of his everlasting Son. These are the persons whom we call the elect; and those whom he has left to perish, perish on account of their own sins, most justly, to the praise of his glorious justice. Now, here you notice divine sovereignty; sovereignty, that God chose to put both men and angels on the footing of their free-will, sovereignty, in that he chose to punish all the fallen angels with utter destruction; sovereignty, in that he chose to reprieve, and grant an eternal pardon to a number, whom no man can number, selected out of men, who shall infallibly be found before his right hand above. My text mentions this great fact, for when properly translated it reads thus:- "He took not up angels, but he took on him the seed of Abraham."

FOR MEDITATION: The Lord Jesus Christ witnessed Satan's expulsion from Heaven, and as surely guarantees the believer's entrance into Heaven (Luke 10: 18,20).

The necessity of increased faith

"And the apostles said unto the Lord, Increase our faith." Luke 17: 5
SUGGESTED FURTHER READING: Romans 4: 13-25

The apostles said to the Lord, "Increase our faith!" They went to the right person. They did not say to themselves, "I will increase my faith;" they did not cry to the minister, "Preach a comforting sermon, and increase my faith;" they did not say, "I will read such-and-such a book, and that will increase my faith." No, they said to the Lord, "Increase our faith." Faith's author can alone increase it. I could inflate your faith till it turned into presumption, but I could not make it grow. It is God's work to feed faith, as well as to give it life at first; and if any of you desire to have a growing faith, go and take your burden this morning to God's throne, crying, "Lord, increase our faith!" If you feel that your troubles have been increased, go to the Lord, and say, "Increase our faith!" If your money is accumulating, go to the Lord, and say, "Increase our faith;" for you will want more faith as you get more prosperity. If your property is diminishing, go to him, and say, "Increase our faith," so that what you lose in one scale you may gain in the other. Are you sickly and full of pain this morning? Go to your Master, and say, "Increase our faith, so that I may not be impatient, but be able to bear it well." Are you tired and weary? Go and supplicate, "Increase our faith!" Have you little faith? Take it to God, and he will turn it into great faith. There is no hot-house for growing tender plants in like a house that is within the curtains—the tabernacle of God, where his glory dwells.

FOR MEDITATION: The Christian has no need to undertake pilgrimages and to seek out so-called holy men to increase his faith. The expert in increasing faith is the very one in whom we have faith, who lives in us by his Spirit (Hebrews 12: 2).

SERMON NO. 32

Personal service

"O Lord, truly I am thy servant; I am thy servant, and the son of thine handmaid: thou hast loosed my bonds." Psalm 116: 16
SUGGESTED FURTHER READING: Romans 6: 15-23

A liberty to be holy is a grander liberty than a licence to be sinful. A liberty to be conscientious; a liberty to know forgiven sin; a liberty to trample upon conquered lusts, this is an infinitely wider liberty than that which would permit me to be the comfortable slave of sin, and yet indulge the elusive hope that I may one day enter the kingdom of heaven. The largest expressions that can ever be used by the boldest minister of free grace, cannot here be exaggerations. Luther may exhaust his thunders, and Calvin may spend his logic, but after all the grand things that have been spoken about the liberty wherewith Christ has made us free, we are freer than those men knew. Free as the very air he breathes is the Christian, if he lives up to his privileges. If he is in bondage at all, it is because he has not as yet yielded his spirit fully to the redeeming and emancipating influence of the gospel of the Lord Jesus Christ. In the fullest and widest sense therefore, the believer may cry, "Thou has loosed my bonds." Nor is this liberty merely consistent with the profoundest and most reverent service, but the service is, indeed, a main characteristic of the exalted freedom. "Truly I am thy servant; I am thy servant and the son of thine handmaid." This does not conflict with the sentence that follows it,—"Thou hast loosed my bonds." This fact of my being God's servant is to me a proof and evidence, and a delightful fruit and effect of my having had my bonds loosed by the great emancipator, the Lord Jesus Christ. Service then, as well as liberty!

FOR MEDITATION: The Christian has been freed from being a slave of sin in order to become a servant of God. Does your lifestyle illustrate this (Galatians 5: 13)?

An earnest invitation

"Kiss the Son, lest he be angry, and ye perish from the way, when his wrath is kindled but a little. Blessed are all they that put their trust in him."
Psalm 2: 12
SUGGESTED FURTHER READING: Psalm 1

Those that trust in him are blessed; and I would observe, first, that they are **really** blessed. It is no fiction, no imaginary blessing; it is a real blessedness which belongs to those who trust in God: a blessedness that will stand the test of consideration, the test of life, and the trial of death; a blessedness into which we cannot plunge too deeply, for none of it is a dream, but all a reality. Again, those that trust in him have not only a real blessedness, but they oftentimes have a **conscious** blessedness. They know what it is to be blest in their troubles, for they are in their trials comforted, and they are blest in their joys, for their joys are sanctified. They are blest and they know it, they sing about it and they rejoice in it. It is their joy to know that God's blessing is come to them not in word only but in very deed. They are blessed men and blessed women.

"They would not change their blest estate
For all the world calls good and great."

Then, further, they are not only really blessed, and consciously blessed, but they are **increasingly** blessed. Their blessedness grows. They do not go downhill, as the wicked do, from bright hope to black despair. They do not diminish in their delights, the river deepens as they wade into it. They are blessed when the first ray of heavenly light streams on their eyeballs; they are blessed when their eyes are opened wider still, to see more of the love of Christ; they are blessed the more their experience widens, and their knowledge deepens, and their love increases. They are blessed in the hour of death, and, best of all, their blessedness increases to eternal blessedness,— the perfection of the saints at the right hand of God. "Blessed are all they that put their trust in him."

FOR MEDITATION: How often do you take time to count your blessings in Christ?

SERMON NO. 260

The sympathy of the two worlds

"There is joy in the presence of the angels of God over one sinner that repenteth." Luke 15: 10
SUGGESTED FURTHER READING: Luke 1: 5-23

Our text tells us that the angels of God rejoice over repenting sinners. How is that? They are always as happy as they can be; how can they be any happier? The text does not say that they are any happier; but perhaps that they show their happiness more. A man may have a Sabbath every day, as he ought to if he is a Christian; and yet on the first day of the week he will let his Sabbatarianism come out plainly; for then the world shall see that he rests. "A merry heart hath a continual feast;" but then even the merry heart has some special days on which it feasts well. To the glorified, every day is a Sabbath, but of some it can be said, "and that Sabbath was an high day." There are days when the angels sing more loudly than usual; they are always harping God's praise, but sometimes the gathering hosts who have been flitting far through the universe, come home to their centre; and round the throne of God, standing in close ranks, marshalled not for battle but for music, on certain set and appointed days they chant the praises of the Son of God, "who loved us and gave himself for us." And do you ask me when those days occur? I tell you, the birthday of every Christian is a sonnet day in heaven. There are Christmas days in paradise, where Christ's high mass is kept, and Christ is glorified not because he was born in a manger, but because he is born in a broken heart. There are days—good days in heaven; days of poetry, red letter days, of overflowing adoration. And these are days when the shepherd brings home the lost sheep upon his shoulder, when the church has swept her house and found the lost piece of money.

FOR MEDITATION: The Lord Jesus Christ keeps his angels informed about us (Luke 12: 8,9). Have they received good news about you?

Christ lifted up

"And I, if I be lifted up from the earth, will draw all men unto me." John
12: 32
SUGGESTED FURTHER READING: 1 Corinthians 2: 1-5

Christ preached his own truth, and the common people heard him gladly,
and the multitude flocked to listen to him. My good ministering brother,
have you got an empty church? Do you want to fill it? I will give you a good
recipe, and if you will follow it, you will, in all probability, have your chapel
full to the doors. Burn all your manuscripts, that is number one. Give up
your notes, that is number two. Read your Bible and preach it as you find it in
the simplicity of its language. And give up all your latinized English. Begin
to tell the people what you have felt in your own heart, and beseech the Holy
Spirit to make your heart as hot as a furnace for zeal. Then go out and talk to
the people. Speak to them like their brother. Be a man amongst men. Tell
them what you have felt and what you know, and tell them heartily with a
good, bold face; and, my dear friend, I do not care who you are, you will get
a congregation. But if you say, "Now, to get a congregation, I must buy an
organ." That will not serve you a bit. "But we must have a good choir." I
would not care to have a congregation that comes through a good choir.
"No," says another, "but really I must alter my style of preaching a little."
My dear friend, it is not the style of preaching, it is the style of feeling.
People sometimes begin to mimic other preachers, because they are
successful. Why, the worst preachers are those who mimic others, whom
they look upon as standards. Preach naturally. Preach out of your hearts just
what you feel to be true, and the old soul-stirring words of the gospel will
soon draw a congregation.

FOR MEDITATION: Are we brave enough to do it? We ought not to expect the
world to be attracted to Christ when we obscure him by our reliance on
gimmicks and by being second-rate mimics of things they can find done
better elsewhere. But the unbeliever cannot find the true Gospel and a
crucified Christ anywhere else!

SERMON NO. 139

Christ exalted

"This man, after he had offered one sacrifice for sins for ever, sat down on the right hand of God; From henceforth expecting till his enemies be made his footstool." Hebrews 10: 12,13
SUGGESTED FURTHER READING: Revelation 22: 12-21

Many of us are expecting that Christ will come; we cannot tell you when, we believe it to be folly to pretend to guess the time, but we are expecting that even in our life the Son of God will appear, and we know that when he shall appear he will tread his foes beneath his feet, and reign from pole to pole, and from the river even to the ends of the earth. Not long shall antichrist sit on her seven hills; not long shall the false prophet delude his millions; not long shall idol gods mock their worshippers with eyes that cannot see, and hands that cannot handle, and ears that cannot hear—"Lo! He comes, with clouds descending;" In the winds I see his chariot wheels; I know that he approaches, and when he approaches he "breaks the bow and cuts the spear in sunder, and burns the chariot in the fire;" and Christ Jesus shall then be king over the whole world. He is king now, virtually; but he is to have another kingdom; I cannot see how it is to be a spiritual one, for that is come already; he is as much king spiritually now as he ever will be in his Church, although his kingdom will assuredly be very extensive; but the kingdom that is to come, I take it, will be something even greater than the spiritual kingdom; it will be a visible kingdom of Christ on earth. Then kings must bow their necks before his feet; then at his throne the tribes of earth shall bend; then the rich and mighty, the merchants of Tyre, and the travellers where gold is found, shall bring their spices and myrrh before him, and lay their gold and gems at his feet;

"Jesus shall reign where'er the sun
Does his successive journeys run;
His kingdom stretch from shore to shore,
Till moons shall wax and wane no more."

FOR MEDITATION: You may, or may not, agree with some of the detail of Spurgeon's understanding of the Second Coming. But do you share his spirit of enthusiasm and readiness, or are you too much in love with the present world (2 Timothy 4: 8-10)?

SERMON NO. 91

Profit and loss

"What shall it profit a man, if he shall gain the whole world, and lose his own soul?" Mark 8: 36
SUGGESTED FURTHER READING: Luke 12: 15-21

Spiritually man is a great trader—he is trading for his own welfare; he is trading for time and for eternity; he keeps two shops: one shop is kept by an apprentice of his, a rough unseemly hand, of clayey mould, called the body; the other business, which is an infinitely more vast concern, is kept by one that is called "the soul" a spiritual being, who does not traffic upon little things, but who deals with hell or heaven, and trades with the mighty realities of eternity. Now, a merchant would be very unwise who should pay all attention to some small off-hand shop of his, and take no account whatever of a large establishment. And he would, indeed, be negligent, who should very carefully jot down every trifle of the expenditure of his own household, but should never think of reckoning the expenses of some vast concern that may be hanging on his hands. But the most of men are just as foolish—they estimate the profits (as they conceive them to be) which are gained in that small corner shop called the body, but they too seldom reckon up the awful loss which is brought about by a negligence of the soul's concerns in the great matters of eternity. Let me beseech you, my brethren, while you are not careless of the body, as, indeed, you ought not to be, seeing that it is, in the case of believers, the temple of the Holy Spirit, to take more especial care of your souls. Decorate the tenement, but do not suffer the inhabitant to die of starvation; do not paint the ship while you are letting the crew perish for want of stores on board. Look to your soul, as well as to your body; to the life, as well as to that by which you live.

FOR MEDITATION: We can be so bodily minded that we are no heavenly use (1 Timothy 4: 8 gives the right balance).

A wise desire

"He shall choose our inheritance for us." Psalm 47: 4
SUGGESTED FURTHER READING: Genesis 45: 4-11

If you turn to the pages of inspiration, and read the lives of some of the most eminent saints, I think you will be obliged to see the marks of God's providence in their histories too plainly to be mistaken. Take, for instance, the life of Joseph. There is a young man who from early life serves God. Read that life till its latest period when he gave commandment concerning his bones, and you cannot help marvelling at the wondrous dealings of providence. Did Joseph choose to be hated of his brethren? But, yet, was not their envy a material circumstance in his destiny? Did he choose to be put into the pit? But was not the putting into the pit as necessary to his being made a king in Egypt as Pharaoh's dream? Did Joseph desire to be tempted of his mistress? He chose to reject the temptation, but did he choose the trial? No; God sent it. Did he choose to be put into the dungeon? No. And had he anything to do with the baker's dream, or with Pharaoh's either? Can you not see, all the way through, from first to last, even in the forgetfulness of the butler, who forgot to speak of Joseph till the appointed time came, when Pharaoh should want an interpreter, that there was truly the hand of God? Joseph's brethren did just as they liked when they put him into the pit. Potiphar's wife followed the dictates of her own abandoned lust in tempting him. And yet, notwithstanding all the freedom of their will, it was ordained of God, and worked according together for one great end; to place Joseph on the throne; for as he said himself, "Ye meant it for evil, but God intended it for good, that he might save your souls alive!"

FOR MEDITATION: You may find yourself in undesirable circumstances, but God can take these bad things and work them together for your good and his glory if you are his child (Romans 8: 28). The all-knowing God knows what is best for us and can direct us clearly by our circumstances (Isaiah 48: 17).

Contentment

"For I have learned, in whatsoever state I am, therewith to be content."
Philippians 4: 11
SUGGESTED FURTHER READING: 1 Timothy 6: 6-11

The apostle Paul was a very learned man, but not the least among his manifold acquisitions in knowledge was this—he had learned to be content. Such learning is far better than much that is acquired in the schools. Their learning may look studiously back on the past, but too often those who cull the relics of antiquity with enthusiasm, are thoughtless about the present, and neglect the practical duties of daily life. Their learning may open up dead languages to those who will never derive any living benefit from them. Far better the learning of the apostle. It was a thing of ever-present utility, and alike serviceable for all generations; one of the rarest, but one of the most desirable accomplishments. I put the senior wrangler and the most learned of our Cambridge men, in the lowest form compared with this learned apostle; for this surely is the highest degree in humanities to which a man can possibly attain, to have learned in whatsoever state he is, to be content. You will see at once from reading the text, upon the very surface, that contentment in all states is not a natural propensity of man. Ill weeds grow apace; covetousness, discontent, and murmuring, are as natural to man as thorns are to the soil. You have no need to sow thistles and brambles; they come up naturally enough, because they are indigenous to earth, upon which rests the curse; so you have no need to teach men to complain, they complain fast enough without any education. But the precious things of the earth must be cultivated. If we would have wheat, we must plough and sow; if we want flowers, there must be the garden, and all the gardener's care. Now, contentment is one of the flowers of heaven, and if we would have it, it must be cultivated.

FOR MEDITATION: Proverbs 30: 7-9: the balanced prayer of Agur, an observant and humble man. Covetousness is the enemy of contentment.

The call of Abraham

"By faith Abraham when he was called to go out into a place which he should after receive for an inheritance, obeyed; and he went out, not knowing whither he went." Hebrews 11: 8
SUGGESTED FURTHER READING: John 10: 1-6

Follow the guide of divine providence and precept, lead it wherever it may. Let us follow the Shepherd, with a ready mind, because he has a perfect right to lead us wherever he pleases. We are not our own, we are bought with a price. If we were our own, we might be discontented with our circumstances, but since we are not, let this be our cry, "Do what thou wilt, O Lord, and though thou slay me, yet will I trust in thee;" we are not true to our profession of being Christians, if we pick and choose for ourselves. Picking and choosing are great enemies to submission. In fact, they are not at all consistent with it. If we are really Christ's Christians, let us say, "It is the Lord, let him do what seemeth him good." And then in the next place we ought to submit because wherever he may lead us, if we do not know where we go, we do know one thing, we know with whom we go; we do not know the road, but we do know the guide. We may feel that the journey is long, but we are quite sure that the everlasting arms that carry us are strong enough, even if the journey is very long. We do not know what may be the inhabitants of the land into which we may come, Canaanites or not; but we do know that the Lord our God is with us, and he shall surely deliver them into our hands. Another reason why we should follow with simplicity and faith all the commands of God, is this, because we may be quite sure they shall all end well. They may not be well apparently while they are going on, but they will end well at last.

FOR MEDITATION: God is well able to guide his children in the right way (Isaiah 30: 21); we know the one who is the Way himself (John 14: 4-6).

SERMON NO. 261

The mission of the Son of man

"For the Son of man is come to seek and to save that which was lost."
Luke 19: 10
SUGGESTED FURTHER READING: Luke 15: 1-7

It is strange what unusual places Christ finds some of his people in! I knew one of Christ's sheep who was found out by his Master while committing robbery. I knew another who was found out by Christ, while he was spiting his old mother by reading the Sunday newspaper and making fun of her. Many have been found by Jesus Christ, even in the midst of sin and vanity. I knew a preacher of the gospel who was converted in a theatre. He was listening to a play, an old-fashioned piece, that ended with a sailor drinking a glass of gin before he was hung, and he said, "Here's to the prosperity of the British nation, and the salvation of my immortal soul;" and down went the curtain; and down went my friend too, for he ran home with all his might. Those words, "The salvation of my immortal soul," had struck him to the quick; and he sought the Lord Jesus in his chamber. Many a day he sought him, and at last he found him to his joy and confidence. But for the most part Christ finds his people in his own house; but he finds them often in the worst of tempers, in the most hardened conditions; and he softens their hearts, awakens their consciences, subdues their pride, and takes them to himself; but they would never come to him unless he came to them. Sheep go astray, but they do not come back again by themselves. Ask the shepherd whether his sheep come back, and he will tell you, "No, sir; they will wander, but they never return." When you find a sheep that ever came back by himself, then you may hope to find a sinner that will come to Christ by himself. No; it must be sovereign grace that must seek the sinner and bring him home.

FOR MEDITATION: We all like sheep have gone astray; we have all gone our own way (Isaiah 53: 6); we have all ended up like sheep without a shepherd (Matthew 9: 36). The Lord Jesus Christ is the great shepherd (Hebrews 13: 20), the good shepherd (John 10: 11,14) and the giving shepherd who gave his life for his sheep (John 10: 11) and who gives eternal life to his sheep (John 10: 28). Have you been found by him and returned to him (1 Peter 2: 25)?

SERMON NO. 204

A simple sermon for seeking souls

"Whosoever shall call upon the name of the Lord shall be saved."
Romans 10: 13
SUGGESTED FURTHER READING: Ecclesiastes 5: 1-7

"I thought," said somebody addressing me one day, "I thought when I was in the garden, surely Christ could take my sins away, just as easily as he could move the clouds. Do you know, sir, in a moment or two the cloud was all gone, and the sun was shining. Thought I to myself, the Lord is blotting out my sin." Such a ridiculous thought as that, you say, cannot occur often. I tell you, it does, very frequently indeed. People suppose that the greatest nonsense in all the earth is a manifestation of divine grace in their hearts. Now, the only feeling I ever want to have is just this,—I want to feel that I am a sinner and that Christ is my Saviour. You may keep your visions, and ecstasies, and raptures, and dances to yourselves; the only feeling that I desire to have is deep repentance and humble faith; and if, poor sinner, you have got that, you are saved. Why, some of you believe that before you can be saved there must be a kind of electric shock, some very wonderful thing that is to go all through you from head to foot. Now hear this, "The word is nigh thee, even in thy mouth, and in thy heart: ...That if thou shalt confess with thy mouth the Lord Jesus, and shalt believe in thine heart.... Thou shalt be saved." What do you want with all this nonsense of dreams and supernatural thoughts? All that is wanted is, that as a guilty sinner, I should come and cast myself on Christ. That done, the soul is safe, and all the visions in the universe could not make it safer.

FOR MEDITATION: "God be merciful to me a sinner" was Christ's description of a man calling upon God and being justified (Luke 18: 13,14). Any insistence on special experiences and strange happenings is an evidence of having departed from Christ, the head of the church (Colossians 2: 18,19).

SERMON NO. 140

An exposition of 1 John 3: 1-10

"Whosoever abideth in him sinneth not: whosoever sinneth hath not seen him, neither known him." 1 John 3: 6
SUGGESTED FURTHER READING: Romans 7: 15-25

This plain, simple verse has been twisted by some who believe in the doctrine of perfection, and they have made it declare that it is possible for some to abide in Christ, and therefore not to sin. But you will remark that it does not say, that some that abide in Christ do not sin; but it says that none who abide in Christ sin. "Whosoever abideth in him sinneth not." Therefore this passage is not to be applied to a few who attain to what is called by our Arminian friends the fourth degree—perfection; but it appertains to all believers; and of every soul in Christ it may be said, that he sinneth not. In reading the Bible, we read it simply as we would read another book. We ought not to read it as a preacher his text, with the intention of making something out of every word; but we should read it as we find it written: "Whosoever abideth in Christ sinneth not." Now we are sure that cannot mean that he does not sin at all, but it means that he sins not habitually, he sins not designedly, he sins not finally, so as to perish. The Bible often calls a man righteous; but that does not mean that he is perfectly righteous. It calls a man a sinner, but it does not imply that he may not have done some good deeds in his life; it means that that is the man's general character. So with the man who abides in Christ: his general character is not that he is a sinner, but that he is a saint—he sinneth not openly, wilfully, before men. In his own heart, he has much to confess, but his life before his fellow creatures is such a one that it can be said of him "Whosoever abideth in him sinneth not."

FOR MEDITATION: If Christians enjoy sinless perfection in this life, why do the epistles of the New Testament contain so much about practical Christian living? John does not deny the existence of sin in the believer (1 John 1: 8-10), but writes to discourage the believer from sinning (1 John 2: 1).

An exposition of 1 Corinthians 15

"And that he was buried, and that he rose again the third day according to the scriptures: And that he was seen of Cephas, then of the twelve: After that he was seen of above five hundred brethren at once; ... After that he was seen of James; then of all the apostles. And last of all he was seen of me also, as of one born out of due time." 1 Corinthians 15: 4-8
SUGGESTED FURTHER READING: Matthew 28: 11-15

The resurrection of Jesus Christ from the dead is one of the best attested facts on record. There were so many witnesses to behold it, that if we do in the least degree receive the credibility of men's testimonies, we cannot and we dare not doubt that Jesus rose from the dead. It is all very easy for infidels to say that these persons were deceived, but it is equally foolish, for these persons could not every one of them have been so positively deceived as to say that they had seen this man, whom they knew to have been dead, afterwards alive; they could not all, surely, have agreed together to help on this imposture; if they did, it is the most marvellous thing we have on record, that not one of them ever broke faith with the others, but that the whole mass of them remained firm. We believe it to be quite impossible that so many rogues should have agreed for ever. They were men who had nothing to gain by it; they subjected themselves to persecution by affirming this very fact; they were ready to die for it, and did die for it. Five hundred or a thousand persons who had seen him at different times, declared that they did see him, and that he rose from the dead; the fact of his death having been attested beforehand. How, then, dare any man say that the Christian religion is not true, when we know for a certainty that Christ died and rose again from the dead? And knowing that, who shall deny the divinity of the Saviour? Who shall say that he is not mighty to save? Our faith has a solid basis, for it has all these witnesses on which to rest, and the more sure witness of the Holy Spirit witnessing in our hearts.

FOR MEDITATION: The task of inventing myths in connection with the resurrection has always been left to the enemies of Christ. His followers had the more straightforward role of simply passing on what they had seen and heard (Acts 4: 20).

The New Park Street tracts, 1856

SUGGESTED READING: Acts 9: 17-22

The Infidel's Sermon to the Pirates
(Arranger's summary of tract—A rich unbeliever sailed in ignorance with pirates, who spared his life after mistaking him for a priest. Later when pressed to preach to them, he was given words which melted their hearts and converted him.)

How marvellous the providence of God, and the sovereignty of his grace! Who is he that has stepped beyond the range of Almighty love? Or has sinned too much to be forgiven? Reader! Are you an infidel? What would you do in a similar situation? What other doctrine than that of Scripture would benefit pirates? Certainly not your own. What would you like to teach your own children? Certainly not your own sentiments. You feel that you would not wish your own offspring blaspheming God. Moreover, forgive us, if we declare our opinion that you know that there is a God, though with your lips you deny him. Think, we implore you, of your Maker, and of his Son, the Saviour; and may eternal love bring even you to the Redeemer.

The Actress
(Arranger's summary of tract: A converted actress renounced her profession. Persuaded to give one final performance, she was unable to sing her entrance song and could only substitute the hymn that had first proclaimed God's mercy to her. The audience ridiculed her, but some considered their ways. She later married a gospel minister.)
Perhaps, dear reader, you are a great transgressor, then you fear there is no forgiveness for you; let this remove your fears. You may be the vilest creature out of hell, and yet grace can make you as pure as the angels in heaven. God would be just should he damn you, but he can be just and yet save you. Do you feel that the Lord has a right over you to do as he pleases? Do you feel that you have no claim upon him? Then, rejoice, for Jesus Christ has borne your guilt, and carried your sorrows, and you shall assuredly be saved. You are a sinner in the true sense of that word, then remember Jesus came to save sinners, and you among the rest, if you know yourself to be a sinner.

FOR MEDITATION: God often saves the very people we would write off!

PART OF NOS. 81-82

The ceremony of laying the first stone of the New Tabernacle, 16 August 1859

SUGGESTED READING: 3 John: 5-11

We believe in what are called the five great points commonly known as Calvinistic; but we do not regard those five points as being barbed shafts which we are to push into the bowels of Christendom. We look upon them as being five great lamps which help to illuminate the cross, or rather five bright emanations springing from the glorious covenant of our Triune God, and illustrating the great doctrine of Jesus crucified. Against all comers, especially against all lovers of Arminianism, we defend and maintain pure gospel truth. At the same time I can make this public declaration, that I am no Antinomian. I do not belong to the sect of those who are afraid to invite the sinner to Christ. I warn him, I invite him, I exhort him. Hence, then, I have reproach on either hand. Inconsistency is urged by some, as if anything that God commanded could be inconsistent. I will glory in such inconsistency even to the end. I bind myself precisely to no form of doctrine. I love those five points as being the angles of the gospel, but then I love the centre between the angles better still. Moreover, we are Baptists, and we cannot swerve from this matter of discipline, nor can we make our church half-and-half in that matter. The witness of our church must be one and indivisible. We must have one Lord, one faith, and one baptism. And yet dear to our hearts is that great article of the Nicene Creed, the "Communion of Saints." I do not believe in the communion of Episcopalians. I do not believe in the communion of Baptists. I dare not sit with them exclusively. I think I should be almost strict communicant enough not to sit with them at all, because I should say, "This is not the communion of saints, it is the communion of Baptists." Whosoever loves the Lord Jesus Christ in verity and truth has a hearty welcome, and is not only permitted, but invited to communion with the Church of Christ.

FOR MEDITATION: What binds you to others in fellowship? Oneness in the great fundamentals of the Gospel? Or a man-made grouping? The first would make you like Spurgeon, the second can easily lead to the extremes of unequal ecumenism or schism.

PART OF NOS. 268-70

The story of God's mighty acts

"We have heard with our ears, O God, our fathers have told us, what work thou didst in their days, in the times of old." Psalm 44: 1
SUGGESTED FURTHER READING: 2 Chronicles 29: 31-36

The old stagers in our churches believe that things must grow, gently, by degrees; we must go step by step onwards. Concentrated action and continued labour, they say, will ultimately bring success. But the marvel is, all God's works have been sudden. When Peter stood up to preach, it did not take six weeks to convert the three thousand. They were converted at once and baptised that very day; they were that hour turned to God, and became as truly disciples of Christ as they could have been if their conversion had taken seventy years. So was it in the day of Martin Luther: it did not take Luther centuries to break through the thick darkness of Rome. God lit the candle and the candle burned, and there was the light in an instant—God works suddenly. If any one could have stood in Wurtemburg, and have said, "Can popery be made to quail, can the Vatican be made to shake?" The answer would have been:—"No; it will take at least a thousand years to do it. Popery, the great serpent, has so twisted itself about the nations, and bound them so fast in its coil, that they cannot be delivered except by a long process." However, God said, "Not so." He smote the dragon sorely, and the nations went free; he cut the gates of brass, and broke in sunder the bars of iron, and the people were delivered in an hour. Freedom came not in the course of years, but in an instant. The people that walked in darkness saw a great light, and upon them that dwelt in the land of the shadow of death, did the light shine. So was it in Whitefield's day. The rebuking of a slumbering church was not the work of ages; it was done at once. Have you never heard of the great revival under Whitefield?

FOR MEDITATION: We tend to label God "slow", but he is only "slow to anger" (2 Peter 3: 9). He was a very quick Creator and we should take encouragement from the fact that he has brought revival out of the blue before and can do it again (Isaiah 66: 8; Acts 2: 2).

A lecture for little-faith

"We are bound to thank God always for you, brethren, as it is meet,
because that your faith groweth exceedingly, and the charity of every one
of you all toward each other aboundeth." 2 Thessalonians 1: 3
SUGGESTED FURTHER READING: Matthew 17: 14-21

When faith commences in the soul it is simply looking unto Jesus, and
perhaps even then there are so many clouds of doubts, and so much dimness
of the eye, that we have need for the light of the Spirit to shine upon the cross
before we are able even so much as to see it. When faith grows a little, it rises
from looking to Christ to coming to Christ. He who stood afar off and
looked to the cross, by-and-by plucks up courage, and getting heart to
himself, he runneth up to the cross; or perhaps he doth not run, but hath to
be drawn before he can so much as creep thither, and even then it is with a
limping gait that he draweth nigh to Christ the Saviour. But that done, faith
goeth a little farther: it layeth hold on Christ; it begins to see him in his
excellency, and appropriates him in some degree, conceives him to be a real
Christ and a real Saviour, and is convinced of his suitability. And when it
hath done as much as that, it goeth further; it leaneth on Christ; it leaneth on
its Beloved; casteth all the burden of its cares, sorrows, and griefs upon that
blessed shoulder, and permitteth all its sins to be swallowed up in the great
red sea of the Saviour's blood. And faith can then go further still; for having
seen and run towards him, and laid hold upon him, and having leaned upon
him, faith in the next place puts in a humble, but a sure and certain claim to
all that Christ is and all that he has wrought; and then, trusting alone in this,
appropriating all this to itself, faith mounteth to full assurance; and out of
heaven there is no state more rapturous and blessed.

FOR MEDITATION: How would you describe the state of your faith? Do you
want to grow in faith (Luke 17: 5)?

Substitution

"For he hath made him to be sin for us, who knew no sin; that we might be made the righteousness of God in him." 2 Corinthians 5: 21
SUGGESTED FURTHER READING: 1 Peter 2: 18-25

Of this God in Christ, our text says that he knew no sin. It does not say that he did not sin; that we know: but it says more than that; he did not know sin; he knew not what sin was. He saw it in others, but he did not know it by experience. He was a perfect stranger to it. It is not barely said, that he did not take sin into his heart, but he did not know it. It was no acquantance of his. He was the acquaintance of grief; but he was not the acquaintance of sin. He knew no sin of any kind,—no sin of thought, no sin of birth, no original, no actual transgression; no sin of lip, or of hand, did ever Christ commit. He was pure, perfect, spotless; like his own divinity, without spot or blemish, or any such thing. This gracious person, is he who is spoken of in the text. He was a person utterly incapable of committing anything that was wrong. It has been asserted lately, by some ill-judged one, that Christ was capable of sin. I think it was Irving who started some such idea, that if Christ was not capable of sinning, he could not have been capable of virtue. "For," say they, "if a man must necessarily be good, there is no virtue in his goodness." Away with their ridiculous nonsense! Is not God necessarily good? And who dares deny that God is virtuous? Are not the glorified spirits in heaven necessarily pure? And yet are they not holy because of that very necessity? Are not the angels, now that they are confirmed, necessarily faultless? And shall any one dare to deny angelic virtue! The thing is not true; it needs no freedom in order to create virtue. Freedom and virtue generally go together; but necessity and virtue are as much brother and sister as freedom and virtue. Jesus Christ was not capable of sin.

FOR MEDITATION: It would have been awful for the sinless Christ to suffer just for one sin of one man. But for him to suffer for all the sins of a countless multitude past, present and future must have been appalling beyond all imagination. How God must hate sin! How he must love poor sinners! Did Christ die for you (Galatians 2: 20)?

Continental tour ★1

SUGGESTED READING: Mark 9: 38-41

In Brussels I heard a good sermon in a Romish church. The church was crowded with people, many of them standing, though you might have a seat for a halfpenny or a farthing. But I stood too. And that good man—for I believe he is a good man—preached the Lord Jesus with all his might. He spoke of the love of Christ, so that I, a very poor hand at the French language, could fully understand him, and my heart kept beating within me as he spoke of the beauties of Christ and the preciousness of his blood, and of his power to save the chief of sinners. He did not say justification by faith, but he did say, "Efficacy of the blood," which comes to very much the same thing. He did not tell us we were saved by grace and not by our works, but he did say that all the works of men were less than nothing when they were brought into competition with the blood of Christ, and that that blood was in itself enough. True there were objectionable sentences, as naturally there must be, but I could have gone to that man and could have said, "Brother, you have spoken the truth;" and if I had been handling the text myself, I must have done it in the same way, if I could have done it as well. I was pleased to find my own opinion verified in that case, that there are some, even in the apostate church, who cleave unto the Lord; some sparks of heavenly fire that tremble amidst the rubbish of old superstition, some lights that are not blown out, even by the strong wind of popery, but still cast a feeble gleam across the waters sufficient to guide the soul to the rock Christ Jesus.

FOR MEDITATION: We may find it impossible to understand or agree with their position, but the true believing saints of God can sometimes be found in the most unexpected places (1 Kings 18: 3-4; Philippians 4: 22. NB: The Caesar in question was Nero!)

Continental tour ★2

SUGGESTED READING: Philippians 2: 12-16

At Zurich I saw in the great fair what I also saw at Baden-Baden, a sight which gave me pleasure, namely, the little star of truth shining amid the darkness. Opposite the house at Baden, where Satan was winning souls at the gaming table, there was a little stall at which an agent of the Bible Society was selling Bibles and Testaments. I went up and bought a Testament from him, and felt quite cheered to see the little battery erected right before the fortifications of Satan, for I felt in my soul it was mighty through God to the pulling down of the stronghold. There in the midst of the fair at Zurich where they were selling all manner of things, like John Bunyan's Vanity Fair, there stood a humble looking man with his stall, upon which there were Bibles, Testaments, and Mr Ryle's Tracts. It is always a great comfort to me to see my sermons in French and other languages sold at the same shops as those of that excellent man of God. There is the simple gospel in his tracts, and they are to my knowledge singularly owned of God. How sweet it is to see these dear brethren in other churches, loving our Lord, and honoured by him. At Lucerne we stopped and spent our third Sabbath day and of all days in the year, Sabbath days on the Continent are most wretched, so far as the means of grace are concerned. This, however, was spent in quiet worship in our own chamber. Our first Sabbath was a dead waste, for the service at church was lifeless, spiritless, graceless, powerless. Even the grand old prayers were so badly read, that it was impossible to be devout while hearing them, and the sermon upon "The justice of God in destroying the Canaanites," was as much adapted to convert a sinner, or to edify a saint, as Burke's Peerage, or Walker's dictionary.

FOR MEDITATION: In what ways do you think Spurgeon would have applied the title of the sermon which so disappointed him, so that it could be beneficial to saint and sinner alike?

PART OF NOS. 331-332

Continental tour ★3

SUGGESTED READING: 1 Corinthians 9: 19-23

I was allowed to stand in the pulpit of John Calvin. I am not superstitious, but the first time I saw this medal bearing the venerated effigy of John Calvin I kissed it, imagining that no one saw the action. I was very greatly surprised when I received this magnificent present, which shall be passed round for your inspection. On the one side is John Calvin with his visage worn by disease and deep thought, and on the other side is a verse fully applicable to that man of God. "He endured, as seeing him who is invisible." That is the very character of the man. That glorious man, Calvin! I preached in the cathedral. I do not think half the people understood me in the Cathedral of St. Peter's; but they were very glad to see and join in heart with the worship in which they could not join with understanding. I did not feel very happy when I came out in full clergyman's dress, but the request was put to me in such a beautiful way that I could have worn the Pope's tiara, if by so doing I could preach the gospel more freely. They said,—"Our dear brother comes to us from another country. Now, when an ambassador comes from another country, he has a right to wear his own costume at Court; but, as a mark of very great esteem, he sometimes condescends to the manners of the country which he visits, and wears the Court dress." "Well," I said—"yes, that I will, certainly, if you do not require it, but merely ask it as a token of my Christian love. I shall feel like running in a sack, but it will be your fault." But it was John Calvin's cloak, and that reconciled it to me very much. I do love that man of God, suffering all his life long, enduring not only persecutions from without but a complication of disorders from within; and yet serving his Master with all his heart.

FOR MEDITATION: The advice "When in Rome do as the Romans do" may lead the believer into unhealthy compromise. When in Geneva Spurgeon willingly became as a Genevan for the sake of the gospel. Does the same thought motivate us to be adaptable, without compromise, in order to win all sorts and conditions of men?

Continental tour ★4

SUGGESTED READING: Job 38: 22-30

We went up the Mer de Glace on mules. I had the great satisfaction of
hearing three or four avalanches come rolling down like thunder. In
descending, I was alone and in front, I sat down and mused, but I soon
sprang up, for I thought the avalanche was coming right on me, there was
such a tremendous noise and rushing. We crossed many places where the
snow, in rushing down from the top, had swept away every tree and every
stone, and left nothing but the stumps of the trees, and a kind of slide from
the top of the mountain to the very valley. What extraordinary works of
God there are to be seen here! We have no idea of what God is. As I went
among these valleys, I felt like a little creeping insect, wondering what the
world could be, but having no idea of its greatness. I sank lower and lower,
and growing smaller and smaller, while my soul kept crying out "Great
God, how infinite art thou! What worthless worms are we!"

FOR MEDITATION (Spurgeon): If you cannot travel, remember this sweet
verse:-

"But in his looks a glory stands,
The noblest labour of thine hands;"

Get a view of Christ, and you have seen more than mountains, cascades, and
valleys, and seas can ever show you. Thunders may bring their sublimest
uproar, and lightnings their awful glory; earth may give its beauty, and stars
their brightness; but all these put together can never rival HIM;

"God in the person of his Son,
Has all his mightiest works outdone."

PART OF NOS. 331-332

How saints may help the devil

"That thou mayest bear thine own shame, and mayest be confounded in all that thou hast done, in that thou art a comfort unto them." Ezekiel 16: 54
SUGGESTED FURTHER READING: Nehemiah 5: 1-9

The church of Christ appears to be as worldly as the world itself, and professors of religion have become as sharp in trade and as ungenerous in their dealing as those that have never professed to serve him. And now what does the world say? It throws this in our teeth. If it is accused of loving the things of time and sense, it answers, "And so do you." If we tell the world that it has set its hopes upon a shadow, it replies, "But we have set our hope upon the selfsame thing in which you are trusting; you are as worldly, as grasping, as covetous as we are; your protest has lost its force; you are no longer witnesses against us—we are accusers of you." Another point in which the sinner often excuses himself is the manifest worldliness of many Christians. You will see Christian men and women as fond of dress, and as pleased with the frivolities of the age, as any other persons possible could be; just as anxious to adorn their outward person, so as to be seen of men; just as ambitious to win the praise which fools accord to fine dressing, as the most silly fop or the most gaudy among worldly women. What saith the world, when we turn round to it, and accuse it of being a mere butterfly, and finding all its pleasures in gaudy toys? "Oh! Yes," it says, "we know your cant, but it is just the same with you. Do you not stand up and sing,

'Jewels to thee are gaudy toys,
 And gold is sordid dust'

And yet you are just as fond of glittering as we are; your doctors of divinity pride themselves just as much in their D.D. as any of us in other titles."

FOR MEDITATION: Do your deeds give the world reasons to glorify God (Matthew 5: 16) or excuses to blaspheme God (Romans 2: 24)?

Everybody's sermon

"I have multiplied visions, and used similitudes." Hosea 12: 10
SUGGESTED FURTHER READING: Matthew 13: 36-43

If you have an opportunity to journey into the country during the next three weeks, you will, if your heart is rightly attuned, find a marvellous mass of wisdom couched in a cornfield. Why, I could not attempt for a moment to open the mighty mines of golden treasure which are hidden there. Think, beloved, of the joy of the harvest. How does it tell us of the joy of the redeemed, if we, being saved, shall at last be carried like shocks of corn fully ripe into the granary. Look at the ear of corn when it is fully ripe, and see how it bends toward the earth! It held its head erect before, but in getting ripe how humble does it become! And how does God speak to the sinner, and tell him, that if he would be fit for the great harvest he must drop his head and cry, "Lord have mercy upon me a sinner." And when we see the weeds spring up amongst wheat, have we not our Master's parable over again of the tares among the wheat; and are we not reminded of the great day of division, when he shall say to the reaper, "Gather first the tares and bind them in bundles, to burn them, but gather the wheat into my barn." O yellow field of corn, thou preachest well to me, for thou sayest to me, the minister, "Behold, the fields are ripe already to the harvest. Work thou thyself, and pray thou the Lord of the harvest to send forth more labourers into the harvest." And it preaches well to thee, thou man of years, it tells thee that the sickle of death is sharp, and that thou must soon fall, but it cheers and comforts thee, for it tells thee that the wheat shall be safely housed, and it bids thee hope that thou shalt be carried to thy Master's home to be his joy and his delight for ever. Hark, then, to the rustling eloquence of the yellow harvest.

FOR MEDITATION: Some Scriptures on summer and harvest: (Genesis 8: 22; Proverbs 6: 8; 10: 5; 26: 1; Jeremiah 8: 20).

A preacher from the dead

"And he said unto him, If they hear not Moses and the prophets, neither will they be persuaded, though one rose from the dead." Luke 16: 31
SUGGESTED FURTHER READING: 1 Samuel 28: 3-19

Spirit that hath returned from another world, tell me, how are men judged? Why are they condemned? Why are they saved? I hear him say, "Men are condemned because of sin. Read the ten commandments of Moses, and you will find the ten great condemnations whereby men are for ever cut off." I knew that before, bright Spirit; thou hast told me nothing! "No," says he, "and nothing can I tell." "Because I was hungry, and ye gave me no meat; I was thirsty, and ye gave me no drink; I was sick, and ye visited me not; I was in prison, and ye came not unto me; therefore, inasmuch as ye did it not unto one of the least of these my brethren, ye did it not to me. Depart, ye cursed!" "Why, Spirit, was that the word of the king?" "It was" says he. "I have read that too; thou hast told me no more." If you do not know the difference between right and wrong from reading the Scripture, you would not know it if a spirit should tell you; if you do not know the road to hell and the road to heaven from the Bible itself, you would never know it at all. No book could be more clear, no revelation more distinct, no testimony more plain. And since without the agency of the Spirit, these testimonies are insufficient for salvation, it follows that no further declaration would avail. Salvation is ascribed wholly to God, and man's ruin only to man. What more could a spirit tell us, than a distinct declaration of these two great truths.—"O Israel, thou hast destroyed thyself; but in me is thine help found!" Beloved, we do solemnly say again, that Holy Scripture is so perfect, so complete, that it cannot want the supplement of any declaration concerning a future state. All that you ought to know concerning the future you may know from Holy Scripture.

FOR MEDITATION: The rich man in the account (not called a parable) given by Jesus was full of false doctrine—praying to a saint, seeking some kind of second chance after death, rejecting the sufficiency of Scripture (Luke 16: 24,30). Note the place from which these doctrines come (1 Timothy 4: 1; James 3 :15).

SERMON NO. 143

The Father of lights

"Every good gift and every perfect gift is from above, and cometh down from the Father of lights, with whom is no variableness, neither shadow of turning." James 1: 17

SUGGESTED FURTHER READING: Revelation 21: 22-22: 5

The apostle, having thus introduced the sun as a figure to represent the Father of lights, finding that it did not bear the full resemblance of the invisible God, seems constrained to amend it by a remark that, unlike the sun, our Father has no turning or variableness. The sun has its daily variation; it rises at a different time each day, and it sets at various hours in the course of the year. It moves into other parts of the heavens. It is clouded at times, and eclipsed at times. It also has tropic; or, turning. It turns its chariot to the South, until, at the solstice, God bids it reverse its rein, and then it visits us once more. But God is superior to all figures or emblems. He is immutable. The sun changes, mountains crumble, the ocean shall be dried up, the stars shall wither from the vault of night; but God, and God alone, remains ever the same. Were I to enter into a full discourse on the subject of immutability, my time, if multiplied by a high number, would fail me. But reminding you that there is no change in His power, justice, knowledge, oath, threatening, or decree, I will confine myself to the fact that His love to us knows no variation. How often it is called unchangeable, everlasting love! He loves me now as much as he did when first he inscribed my name in his eternal book of election. He has not repented of his choice. He has not blotted out one of his chosen; there are no erasures in that book; all whose names are written in it are safe for ever.

FOR MEDITATION: As part of creation the sun speaks of the character of God (Romans 1: 20) but even at its brightest can only give a glimpse of his glory. Praise God for the Lord Jesus Christ, the true light (John 1: 9) whose face, when transfigured, shone like the sun (Matthew 17: 2); God the Son has made God the Father of light known to us (John 1: 18).

1ST SERMON AT NEW PARK ST.

The faultless assembly

"They are without fault before the throne of God." *Revelation 14: 5*
SUGGESTED FURTHER READING: 1 Corinthians 11: 17-22

We need not go far without seeing that there is, among Christians, a want of love to one another. There is not too much love in our churches; certainly, we have none to give away. We have heard that:

"Whatever brawls disturb the street,
There should be peace at home."

But it is not always as it should be. We have known churches where the members can scarcely sit down at the Lord's table without some disagreement. There are people who are always finding fault with the minister, and there are ministers finding fault with the people; there is among them "a spirit that lusteth to envy," and "where envying and strife is, there is confusion and every evil work." We have met with people among whom it would be misery to place ourselves, because we do not love war; we love peace and charity. Alas! How continually do we hear accounts of disputings and variance in churches! O beloved, there is too little love in the churches! If Jesus were to come amongst us, might He not say to us, "This is My commandment, that ye love one another; but how have you kept it when you have been always finding fault with one another? And how ready you have been to turn your sword against your brother!" But, beloved, "they are without fault before the throne of God." Those who on earth could not agree, are sure to agree when they get to heaven. There are some who have crossed swords on earth, but who have held the faith, and have been numbered amongst the saints in glory everlasting. There is no fighting amongst them now; "they are without fault before the throne of God."

FOR MEDITATION: The very best of Christians may have fallen out with one another (Acts 15: 39), but the Bible entreats disputants to agree in the Lord (Philippians 4: 2). It is beautiful when brothers dwell in unity (Psalm 133: 1), but perplexing when they wrong each other (Acts 7: 26). May God help us to do "on earth as it is in Heaven."

2ND SERMON AT NEW PARK ST.

Everywhere and yet forgotten

"Who knoweth not in all these that the hand of the Lord hath wrought this? In whose hand is the soul of every living thing, and the breath of all mankind." Job 12: 9,10
SUGGESTED FURTHER READING: Deuteronomy 8: 11-20

This forgetfulness of God is growing upon this perverse generation. Time was, in the old puritanic days, when every shower of rain was seen to come from heaven, when every ray of sunshine was blessed, and God was thanked for having given fair weather to ingather the fruits of the harvest. Then, men talked of God as doing everything. But in our days where is our God? We have the laws of matter. Alas! Alas! That names with little meaning should have destroyed our memory of the Eternal One. We talk now of phenomena, and of the chain of events, as if all things happened by machinery; as if the world were a huge clock which had been wound up in eternity, and continued to work without a present God. Nay, not only our philosophers, but even our poets rant in the same way. They sing of the works of nature. But who is that fair goddess, Nature? Is she a heathen deity, or what? Do we not act as if we were ashamed of our God, or as if his name had become obsolete? Go abroad wherever you may, you hear little said concerning him who made the heavens, and who formed the earth and the sea; but everything is nature, and the laws of motion and of matter. And do not Christians often use words which would lead you to suppose that they believed in the old goddess, Luck, or rested in that equally false deity, Fortune, or trembled before the demon of Misfortune? Oh for the day when God shall be seen, and little else beside! Better, my brethren, that philosophical discoveries were lost, than that God should be concealed behind them. Better that our poets had ceased to write, and that all their flaming words were buried with their ashes, than that they should serve as a cloud before the face of the eternal Creator.

FOR MEDITATION: When men replace Father God by mother nature, God leaves them to behave in ways which are unnatural and opposed to their false new deity (Romans 1: 21-27).

SERMON NO. 326

Sin slain

"And, behold, as Barak pursued Sisera, Jael came out to meet him, and said unto him, Come, and I will shew thee the man whom thou seekest. And when he came into her tent, behold, Sisera lay dead, and the nail was in his temples." Judges 4: 22
SUGGESTED FURTHER READING: Hebrews 12: 1-4

Rest not content till the blood of your enemy stains the ground, until he is crushed, and dead, and slain. Oh, sinner, I beseech you, never be content until grace reign in your heart, and sin is altogether subdued. Indeed, this is what every renewed soul longs for, and must long for, nor will it rest satisfied until all this shall be accomplished. There was a time when some of us thought we would slay our sins. We wanted to put them to death, and we thought we would drown them in floods of penitence. There was a time, too, when we thought we would starve our sins; we thought we would keep out of temptation, and not go and pander to our lusts, and then they would die; and some of us can recollect when we gagged our lusts, when we pinioned their arms, and put their feet in the stocks, and then thought that would deliver us. But brethren, all our ways of putting sin to death were not sufficient; we found the monster still alive, insatiate for his prey. We might rout his hired ruffians, but the monster was still our conqueror. We might put to flight our habits, but the nature of sin was still in us, and we could not overcome it. Yet did we groan and cry daily, "Oh wretched man that I am, who shall deliver me from the body of this death?" It is a cry to which we are accustomed even at this day, and which we shall never cease to utter, till we can say of our sins, "They are gone," and of the very nature of sin, that it has been extinguished, and that we are pure and holy even as when the first Adam came from his Maker's hands.

FOR MEDITATION: We should never underestimate the power of sin, but we can never overestimate the power of the Lord Jesus Christ to conquer sin. Sin may remain, but it need not reign (Romans 6: 12).

The meek and lowly One

"Come unto me, all ye that labour and are heavy laden, and I will give you rest. Take my yoke upon you, and learn of me; for I am meek, and lowly in heart; and ye shall find rest unto your souls. For my yoke is easy, and my burden is light." Matthew 11: 28-30
SUGGESTED FURTHER READING: Matthew 21: 1-17

Christ on earth was a king; but there was nothing about him of the exclusive pomp of kings, which excludes the common people from their society. Look at the eastern king Ahasuerus, sitting on his throne. He is considered by his people as a superior being. None may come in unto the king, unless he is called for. Should he venture to pass the circle, the guards will slay him, unless the king stretches out the golden sceptre. Even Esther, his beloved wife, is afraid to draw near, and must put her life in her hand, if she comes into the presence of the king uncalled. Christ is a king; but where is his pomp? Where the janitor that keeps his door, and thrusts away the poor? Where the soldiers that ride on either side of his chariot to screen the monarch from the sight of poverty? See thy King, O Sion! He comes, he comes in royal pomp! Behold, Judah, behold thy King cometh! But how cometh he? "Meek and lowly, riding upon an ass, and upon a colt, the foal of an ass." And who are his attendants? See, the young children, boys and girls! They cry, "Hosannah! Hosannah! Hosannah!" And who are they that wait upon him? His poor disciples. They pull the branches from the trees; they cast their garments in the street, and there he rides on—Judah's royal king. His courtiers are the poor; his pomp is that tribute which grateful hearts delight to offer. O sinners, will you not come to Christ? There is nothing in him to keep you back. You need not say, like Esther did of old, "I will go in unto the king, and if I perish, I perish." Come and welcome! Come and welcome! Christ is more ready to receive you than you are to come to him. Come to the King!

FOR MEDITATION: The character of the King should be reflected in the character of his subjects (Matthew 5: 3,5,10). 3 John 9,10 describes exactly what is not called for!

SERMON NO. 265

Sovereign grace and man's responsibility

"But Esaias is very bold, and saith, I was found of them that sought me not; I was made manifest unto them that asked not after me. But to Israel he saith, All day long I have stretched forth my hands unto a disobedient and gainsaying people." Romans 10: 20,21
SUGGESTED FURTHER READING: Matthew 26: 20-25

I see in one place, God presiding over all in providence; and yet I see, and I cannot help seeing, that man acts as he pleases, and that God has left his actions to his own will, in a great measure. Now, if I were to declare that man was so free to act, that there was no control of God over his actions, I should be driven very near to atheism; and if, on the other hand, I declare that God so overrules all things, as that man is not free enough to be responsible, I am driven at once into Antinomianism or fatalism. That God predestines, and that man is responsible, are two things that few can see. They are believed to be inconsistent and contradictory; but they are not. It is just the fault of our weak judgment. Two truths cannot be contradictory to each other. If, then, I find taught in one place that everything is foreordained, that is true; and if I find in another place that man is responsible for all his actions, that is true; and it is my folly that leads me to imagine that two truths can ever contradict each other. These two truths, I do not believe, can ever be welded into one upon any human anvil, but one they shall be in eternity: they are two lines that are so nearly parallel, that the mind that shall pursue them farthest, will never discover that they converge; but they do converge, and they will meet somewhere in eternity, close to the throne of God, whence all truth springs.

FOR MEDITATION: The Bible does not tell us everything; nor does it give a full explanation of what it does tell us. But it tells us more than enough to give us a sound foundation for our faith and obedience (Deuteronomy 29: 29; John 20: 30,31).

Waiting only upon God

"My soul, wait thou only upon God." Psalm 62: 5
SUGGESTED FURTHER READING: Proverbs 3: 1-8

We must mark God's providence leading us; and then let us go. But he that goes before providence will be very glad to run back again. Take your trouble, whatever it is, to the throne of the most High and on your knees put up the prayer, "Lord, direct me." You will not go wrong. But do not do as some do. Many a person comes to me and says, "I want your advice, sir; as my minister, perhaps you could tell me what I ought to do." Sometimes it is about their getting married. Why, they have made up their minds before they ask me, they know that; and then they come to ask my advice. "Do you think that such and such a thing would be prudent, sir? Do you think I should change my position in life?" And so on. Now, first of all, I like to know, "Have you made your mind up?" In most cases they have—and I fear you serve God the same. We make up our mind what we are going to do, and then we go down on our knees, and say, "Lord, show me what I ought to do;" and then we follow out our intention and say, "I asked God's direction." My dear friend, you did ask it, but you did not follow it; you followed your own. You liked God's direction so long as it pointed the way you wish to go; but if God's direction led the contrary to what you considered your own interest, it might have been a very long while before you had carried it out. But if we in truth seek God's guidance for us, we shall not go wrong, I know.

FOR MEDITATION: We sometimes get it into our heads that God should do whatever we want, rather than the opposite. If we call him our Master, we should seek to play the part of his followers (Mark 10: 35-40).

God in the covenant

"I will be their God." Jeremiah 31: 33
SUGGESTED FURTHER READING: 2 Samuel 22: 1-7

Child of God, let me urge thee to make use of thy God. Make use of him in prayer; I beseech thee, go to him often, because he is thy God. If he were another man's God, thou mightest weary him; but he is thy God. If he were my God and not thine, thou wouldst have no right to approach him; but he is thy God; he has made himself over to thee, if we may use such an expression, (and I think we may) he has become the positive property of all his children, so that all he has, and all he is, is theirs. O child, wilt thou let thy treasury lie idle, when thou wantest it? No; go and draw from it by prayer.

"To him in every trouble flee,
Thy best, thy only friend."

Fly to him, tell him all thy wants. Use him constantly by faith, at all times. Oh! I beseech thee, if some dark providence has come over thee, use thy God as a sun, for he is a sun. If some strong enemy has come out against thee, use thy God for a shield, for he is a shield to protect thee. If thou hast lost thy way in the mazes of life, use him for a guide, for the great Jehovah will direct thee. If thou art in storms, use him, for he is the God who stilleth the raging of the sea, and saith unto the waves, "Be still." If thou art a poor thing, knowing not which way to turn, use him for a shepherd, for the Lord is thy Shepherd, and thou shalt not want. Whate'er thou art, where'er thou art, remember God is just what thou wantest, and he is just where thou wantest. I beseech thee, then, make use of thy God.

FOR MEDITATION: The false gods of the Greeks and Romans were given specific individual roles; the one true God is a glorious all-rounder—omnipotent, omniscient, omnipresent—the complete opposite of the false god (1 Kings 18: 27,37).

False professors solemnly warned

"For many walk, of whom I have told you often, and now tell you even weeping, that they are the enemies of the cross of Christ: Whose end is destruction, whose God is their belly, and whose glory is in their shame, who mind earthly things." Philippians 3: 18,19
SUGGESTED FURTHER READING: Acts 20: 18-35

The apostle was a very honest pastor—when he marked anything amiss in his people, he did not blush to tell them; he was not like your modern minister, whose pride is that he never was personal in his life, and who thus glories in his shame, for had he been honest, he would have been personal, for he would have dealt out the truth of God without deceitfulness, and would have reproved men sharply, that they might be sound in the faith. "I tell you," says Paul, "because it concerns you." Paul was very honest; he did not flinch from telling the whole truth, and telling it often too, though some might think that once from the lip of Paul would be of more effect than a hundred times from any one else. "I have told you often," says he, "and I tell you yet again that there are some who are the enemies of the cross of Christ." And while faithful, you will notice that the apostle was, as every true minister should be, extremely affectionate. He could not bear to think that any members of the churches under his care should swerve from the truth, he wept while he denounced them; he did not know how to wield the thunderbolt with a tearless eye; he did not know how to pronounce the threatening of God with a dry and husky voice. No; while he spoke terrible things the tear was in his eye, and when he reproved sharply, his heart beat was so high with love, that those who heard him denounce so solemnly, were yet convinced that his harshest words were dictated by affection. "I have told you often, and I tell you, even weeping, that they are the enemies of the cross of Christ."

FOR MEDITATION: What effect do you have upon your pastor (Hebrews 13: 17)?

Preach the gospel

"For though I preach the gospel, I have nothing to glory of: for necessity is laid upon me; yea, woe is unto me, if I preach not the gospel!"
1 *Corinthians* 9: 16
SUGGESTED FURTHER READING: Philippians 1: 12-18

There was a young woman under great distress of soul; she came to a very pious Christian man, who said "My dear girl, you must go home and pray." Well I thought within myself, that is not the Bible way at all. It never says, "Go home and pray." The poor girl went home; she did pray, and she still continued in distress. Then he said, "You must wait, you must read the Scriptures and study them." That is not the Bible way; that is not exalting Christ. I find a great many preachers are preaching that kind of doctrine. They tell a poor convinced sinner, "You must go home and pray, and read the Scriptures; you must attend the ministry;" and so on. Works, works, works—instead of "By grace are ye saved through faith." If a penitent should come and ask me, "What must I do to be saved?" I would say, "Christ must save you—believe on the name of the Lord Jesus Christ." I would neither direct to prayer, nor reading of the Scriptures, nor attending God's house; but simply direct to faith, naked faith in God's gospel. Not that I despise prayer—that must come after faith. Not that I speak a word against the searching of the Scriptures—that is an infallible mark of God's children. Not that I find fault with attendance on God's word—God forbid! I love to see people there. But none of these things are the way of salvation. It is nowhere written—"He that attendeth chapel shall be saved;" or, "He that readeth the Bible shall be saved." Nor do I read—"He that prayeth and is baptised shall be saved;" but, "He that believeth,"—he that has a naked faith in the "Man Christ Jesus,"—in his Godhead, in his manhood, is delivered from sin. To preach that faith alone saves is to preach God's truth.

FOR MEDITATION: The good news of the Gospel is not to be confused with our not-so-good advice. To think we are giving good news is not good enough (2 Samuel 4: 10).

SERMON NO. 34

Vessels of mercy—a sermon of self-examination

"And that he might make known the riches of his glory on the vessels of mercy, which he had afore prepared unto glory, Even us, whom he hath called, not of the Jews only, but also of the Gentiles?" Romans 9: 23,24
SUGGESTED FURTHER READING: Jeremiah 18: 1-6

Like every potter he first of all makes the outlines in the clay. You may have seen a man at work executing designs in glass. Perhaps at the very first moment you may form a rough guess of what the whole thing is to be, though the ornament and elaboration which constitute the main part of the beauty you cannot yet discover. Certain it is, that the moment a man begins to be prepared for heaven by the grace of God in his soul, you may see the outlines of what he is to be, although it is but the bare outlines. Shall I tell you what those outlines are? There is first of all in him—faith in Christ; a simple, child-like trust in him that did hang upon the tree. There is next in him another mark of the potter's hand—that is love to Christ—a love that is strong as death, though sometimes it seems to be feeble as a worm. There is in him also a hope that makes not ashamed, and a joy which makes glad his countenance. It is but the bare outline, as I have said, for the glory which excels is not there. The vase is only in its embryo, but yet sufficiently developed to give prophecy of its finished form; as for the pictures that shall be inlaid, as for all the many colours that shall be used on it, you cannot guess as yet, nor could you, unless you could climb to the potter's seat and see the plan upon which he looks as the clay revolves upon the wheel. Dear brothers and sisters, have you anything in you as yet of the great outlines? Can you say in truth, "I believe on the Lord Jesus?" Fear not then, my hearer, you are a vessel of mercy.

FOR MEDITATION: We have no right to talk rebelliously against our Maker (Isaiah 45: 9), but the Christian has the right to pray to "Our Father and Potter in Heaven" (Isaiah 64: 8).

The blind beggar

"And as he went out of Jericho.... blind Bartimaeus.... sat by the highway side begging." Mark 10: 46
SUGGESTED FURTHER READING: John 9: 39-41

To be both blind and poor, these were a combination of the sternest evils. One thinks it is scarcely possible to resist the cry of a beggar whom we meet in the street if he is blind. We pity the blind man when he is surrounded with luxury, but when we see a blind man in want, and following the beggar's trade in the busy streets, we can hardly forbear stopping to assist him. This case of Bartimaeus, however, is but a picture of our own. We are all by nature blind and poor. It is true we account ourselves able enough to see; but this is just one phase of our blindness. Our blindness is of such a kind that it makes us think our vision perfect; whereas, when we are enlightened by the Holy Spirit, we discover our previous sight to have been blindness indeed. Spiritually, we are blind; we are unable to discern our lost estate; unable to conceive the blackness of sin, or the terrors of the wrath to come. The unrenewed mind is so blind, that it perceives not the all-attractive beauty of Christ; the Sun of righteousness may arise with healing beneath his wings, but this is all in vain for those who cannot see his shining. Christ may do many mighty works in their presence, but they do not recognise his glory; we are blind until he has opened our eyes. But besides being blind we are also by nature poor. Our father Adam spent our birthright, lost our estates. Paradise, the homestead of our race, has become dilapidated, and we are left in the depths of beggary without anything with which we may buy bread for our hungry souls, or clothing for our naked spirits; blindness and beggary are the lot of all men after a spiritual fashion, till Jesus visits them in love.

FOR MEDITATION: Spiritually the unconverted are very often exactly the opposite of what they think they are. It can also be true of Christians, for better or worse (Revelation 2: 9; 3: 1,8,17,18).

SERMON NO. 266

Righteous hatred

"Ye that love the Lord, hate evil." Psalm 97: 10
SUGGESTED FURTHER READING: Genesis 39

With regard to some sins, if thou wouldst avoid them, take one piece of advice—run away from them. Sins of lust especially are never to be fought with, except after Joseph's way; and you know what Joseph did—he ran away. A French philosopher said, "Fly, fly, Telemaque; there remains no way of conquest but by flight." The true soldiers of Christ's cross will stand foot to foot with any sin in the world except this; but here they turn their backs and fly, and then they become conquerors. "Flee fornication," said one of old, and there was wisdom in the counsel; there is no way of overcoming it but by flight. If the temptation attack thee, shut thine eye and stop thy ear, and away, away from it; for thou art only safe when thou art beyond sight and earshot. "Ye that love the Lord, hate evil;" and endeavour with all your might to resist and overcome it in yourselves. Once again, ye that love the Lord, if ye would keep from sin, seek always to have a fresh anointing of the Holy Spirit, never trust yourselves a single day without having a fresh renewal of your piety before you go forth to the day's duties. We are never safe unless we are in the Lord's hands. No Christian, be he who he may, or what he may, though he be renowned for his piety and prayerfulness, can exist a day without falling into great sin unless the Holy Spirit shall be his protector. Old master Dyer says, "Lock up your hearts by prayer every morning, and give God the key, so that nothing can get in; and then when thou unlockest thy heart at night, there will be a sweet fragrance and perfume of love, joy, and holiness."

FOR MEDITATION: There are two sides to victory over temptation—resisting the flesh and yielding to the Spirit (Galatians 5: 16). Sometimes the emphasis will be to flee, sometimes to follow, sometimes to fight (1 Timothy 6: 11-12), but neither side will be effective without the other.

Love thy neighbour

"Thou shalt love thy neighbour as thyself." Matthew 19: 19
SUGGESTED FURTHER READING: Romans 12: 6-13

Remember that man's good requires that you should be kind to your fellow creatures. The best way for you to make the world better is to be kind yourself. Are you a preacher? Preach in a surly way, and in a surly tone to your church; a pretty church you will make of it before long! Are you a Sunday-school teacher? Teach your children with a frown on your face; a fine lot they will learn! Are you a master? Do you hold family prayer? Get in a passion with your servants, and say, "Let us pray." A vast amount of devotion you will develop in such a manner as that. Are you a warder of a gaol, and have prisoners under you? Abuse them and ill-treat them, and then send the chaplain to them. A fine preparation for the reception of the word of God! You have poor around you; you wish to see them elevated, you say. You are always grumbling about the poverty of their dwellings, and the meanness of their tastes. Go and make a great stir at them all—a fine way that would be to improve them! Now, just wash your face of that black frown, and buy a little of the essence of summer somewhere, and put it on your face; and have a smile on your lip, and say, "I love you. I am no cant, but I love you, and as far as I can I will prove my love to you. What can I do for you? Can I help you over a stile? Can I give you any assistance, or speak a kind word to you? Perhaps I could look after your little daughter. Can I fetch the doctor to your wife now she is ill?" All these kind things would be making the world a little better.

FOR MEDITATION: The effectiveness of what we say and do can depend to a large extent on how we say and do it (1 Corinthians 13: 1-3). Faith, virtue, knowledge, temperance, patience and godliness are to be supplemented by brotherly kindness and love (2 Peter 1: 5-7).

The day of atonement

"This shall be an everlasting statute unto you, to make an atonement for the children of Israel for all their sins once a year." Leviticus 16: 34
SUGGESTED FURTHER READING: Hebrews 9: 6-14

Jesus Christ "died, the just for the unjust, to bring us to God." That day of atonement happened only once a year, to teach us that only once should Jesus Christ die; and that though he would come a second time, yet it would be without a sin offering unto salvation. The lambs were perpetually slaughtered; morning and evening they offered sacrifice to God, to remind the people that they always needed a sacrifice; but the day of atonement being the type of the one great propitiation, it was but once a year that the high priest entered within the veil with blood as the atonement for the sins of the people. And this was at a certain set and appointed time; it was not left to the choice of Moses, or to the convenience of Aaron, or to any other circumstance which might affect the date; it was appointed to be on a peculiar set day, as you find at the 29th verse: "In the seventh month, on the tenth day of the month;" and at no other time was the day of atonement to be, to show us that God's great day of atonement was appointed and predestined by himself. Christ's expiation occurred but once, and then not by any chance; God had settled it from before the foundation of the world; and at that hour when God had predestined, on that very day that God had decreed that Christ should die, he was led like a lamb to the slaughter, and as a sheep before her shearers, he was dumb. It was but once a year, because the sacrifice should be once; it was at an appointed time in the year, because in the fulness of time Jesus Christ should come into the world to die for us.

FOR MEDITATION: Daily and annual sacrifices of animals could never bring salvation from sin—that required only the single sacrifice of Christ on a single day (Zechariah 3: 9; 12: 10; 13: 1; Hebrews 9: 25,26; 10: 11,12).

The Christian—a debtor

"Therefore, brethren, we are debtors." Romans 8: 12
SUGGESTED FURTHER READING: Luke 7: 36-50

Christian, stop and ponder for a moment! What a debtor thou art to divine **sovereignty!** Thou art not as some, who say, that thou didst choose thyself to be saved; but thou believest that God could have destroyed thee, if he had pleased, and that it is entirely of his own good pleasure that thou art made one of his, while others are suffered to perish. Consider, then, how much thou owest to his sovereignty! If he had willed it, thou wouldst have been among the damned; if he had not willed thy salvation, all thou couldst do would have been utterly powerless to deliver thee from perdition. Remember how much thou owest to his disinterested **love,** which rent his own Son from his bosom that he might die for thee! Let the cross and bloody sweat remind thee of thine obligation. Consider how much thou owest to his forgiving **grace,** that after ten thousand affronts he loves thee as infinitely as ever; and after a myriad sins, his Spirit still resides within thee. Consider what thou owest to his **power;** how he has raised thee from thy death in sin; how he has preserved thy spiritual life, how he has kept thee from falling, and how, though a thousand enemies have beset thy path, thou hast been able to hold on thy way! Consider what thou owest to his **immutability.** Though thou hast changed a thousand times, he has not changed once; though thou hast shifted thy intentions, and thy will, yet has he not once swerved from his eternal purpose, but still has held thee fast. Consider thou art as deep in debt as thou canst be to every attribute of God. To God thou owest thyself, and all thou hast. "Brethren, we are debtors."

FOR MEDITATION: The reasonable response to forgiven debt is love to God and to one another, but we will always be in debt (Romans 13: 8).

God's people in the furnace

"I have chosen thee in the furnace of affliction." Isaiah 48: 10
SUGGESTED FURTHER READING: Isaiah 43: 1-7

Beloved, the first thing I will give you is the comfort of the text itself—election. Comfort yourself with this thought: God says, "I have chosen thee in the furnace of affliction." "The fire is hot, but he has chosen me; the furnace burns, but he has chosen me; these coals are hot, I do not love the place, but he has chosen me." Ah! It comes like a soft gale assuaging the fury of the flame. It is like some gentle wind fanning the cheeks; yes, this one thought arrays us in fireproof armour, against which the heat has no power. "Let affliction come—God has chosen me. Poverty, you may come in at the door—God is in the house already, and he has chosen me. Sickness, you may come, but I will have this by my side for a balsam—God has chosen me. Whatever it is, I know that he has chosen me." The next comfort is that you have the Son of man with you in the furnace. In that silent bedchamber of yours, there sits by your side one whom you have not seen, but whom you love; and often when you know it not, he makes your bed in your affliction, and smooths your pillow for you. You are in poverty; but in that lonely house of yours that has nothing to cover its bare walls, where you sleep on a miserable straw mattress, you know that the Lord of life and glory is a frequent visitor; he often treads those bare floors, and putting his hands upon those walls he consecrates them! If you were in a palace he might not come there. He loves to come into these desolate places that he may visit you. The Son of man is with you, Christian.

FOR MEDITATION: There are some things that can only be proved in times of trouble (Daniel 3: 17,25,28,29; James 1: 12; 1 Peter 1: 6,7).

True prayer—true power

"Therefore I say unto you, What things soever ye desire, when ye pray, believe that ye receive them, and ye shall have them." Mark 11: 24

SUGGESTED FURTHER READING: Matthew 6: 5-13

Allow me to quote what an old preacher said upon the subject of prayer, and give it to you as a little word of advice—"Remember, the Lord will not hear thee, because of the arithmetic of thy prayers; he does not count their numbers. He will not hear thee because of the rhetoric of thy prayers; he does not care for the eloquent language in which they are conveyed. He will not listen to thee because of the geometry of thy prayers; he does not compute them by their length, or by their breadth. He will not regard thee because of the music of thy prayers; he doth not care for sweet voices, nor for harmonious periods. Neither will he look at thee because of the logic of thy prayers, or because they are well arranged. But he will hear thee, and he will measure the amount of the blessing he will give thee, according to the divinity of thy prayers. If thou canst plead the person of Christ, and if the Holy Ghost inspire thee with zeal and earnestness, the blessings which thou shalt ask, shall surely come unto thee." Brethren, I would like to burn the whole stock of old prayers that we have been using this fifty years. That "oil that goes from vessel to vessel,"—that "horse that rushes into the battle,"—that misquoted mangled text, "where two or three are met together, thou wilt be in the midst of them, and that to bless them," and all those other quotations which we have been manufacturing, and dislocating, and copying from man to man. I would that we came to speak to God, just out of our own hearts. It would be a grand thing for our prayer meetings.

FOR MEDITATION: There is a world of difference between performing prayers and real praying (Luke 18: 10-13).

The tabernacle of the Most High

"In whom ye also are builded together for an habitation of God through the Spirit." Ephesians 2: 22
SUGGESTED FURTHER READING: Colossians 1: 15-27

At last they come to these stones. But how rough, how hard, how unhewn. Yes, but these are the stones ordained of old in the decree, and these must be the stones, and none other. There must be a change effected. These must be brought in and shaped and cut and polished, and put into their places. I see the workmen at their labour. The great saw of the law cuts through the stone, and then comes the polishing chisel of the gospel. I see the stones lying in their places, and the church is rising. The ministers, like wise master-builders, are there running along the wall, putting each spiritual stone in its place; each stone is leaning on that massive corner stone, and every stone depending on the blood, and finding its security and its strength in Jesus Christ, the corner stone, elect, and precious. Do you see the building rise as each one of God's chosen is brought in, called by grace and quickened? Do you mark the living stones as in sacred love and holy brotherhood they are knit together? Have you ever entered the building, and seen how these stones lean upon one another bearing each other's burden, so fulfilling the law of Christ? Do you mark how the church loves Christ, and how the members love each other? How first the church is joined to the corner stone, and then each stone bound to the next, and the next to the next, till the whole building becomes one? Lo! The structure rises, and it is complete, and at last it is built. And now open wide your eyes, and see what a glorious building this is—the church of God. Men talk of the splendour of their architecture—this is architecture indeed.

FOR MEDITATION: Here, two days before the laying of the first stone of the Metropolitan Tabernacle, Spurgeon gave a timely reminder that the word "church" is a description of Christian people, not of any building in which they gather. Are you a living stone, built into the spiritual household of God (Ephesians 2: 19-22; 1 Peter 2: 4,5)?

SERMON NO. 267

The way of salvation

"Neither is there salvation in any other: for there is none other name under heaven given among men, whereby we must be saved." Acts 4: 12
SUGGESTED FURTHER READING: Isaiah 12

What a great word that word 'salvation' is! It includes the cleansing of our conscience from all past guilt, the delivery of our soul from all those propensities to evil which now so strongly predominate in us; it takes in, in fact, the undoing of all that Adam did. Salvation is the total restoration of man from his fallen estate; and yet it is something more than that, for God's salvation fixes our standing more secure than it was before we fell. It finds us broken in pieces by the sin of our first parent, defiled, stained, accursed: it first heals our wounds, it removes our diseases, it takes away our curse, it puts our feet upon the rock Christ Jesus, and having thus done, at last it lifts our heads far above all principalities and powers, to be crowned for ever with Jesus Christ, the King of heaven. Some people, when they use the word 'salvation,' understand nothing more by it than deliverance from hell and admittance into heaven. Now, that is not salvation: those two things are the effects of salvation. We are redeemed from hell because we are saved, and we enter heaven because we have been saved beforehand. Our everlasting state is the effect of salvation in this life. Salvation, it is true, includes all that, because salvation is the mother of it, and carries it within its bowels; but still it would be wrong for us to imagine that is the whole meaning of the word. Salvation begins with us as wandering sheep, it follows us through all our confused wanderings; it puts us on the shoulders of the shepherd; it carries us into the fold; it calls together the friends and the neighbours; it rejoices over us; it preserves us in that fold through life; and then at last it brings us to the green pastures of heaven, beside the still waters of bliss, where we lie down for ever, in the presence of the Chief Shepherd, never more to be disturbed.

FOR MEDITATION: Past salvation from sin's penalty (justification): present salvation from sin's power (sanctification): prospective salvation from sin's presence (glorification)—what a great salvation (Hebrews 2: 3). Don't miss it.

SERMON NO. 209

The good man's life and death

"For to me to live is Christ, and to die is gain." Philippians 1: 21
SUGGESTED FURTHER READING: 1 Thessalonians 4: 13-18

Not the greatest master-minds of earth understand the millionth part of the mighty meanings which have been discovered by souls emancipated from clay. Yes, brethren, "To die is gain." Take away, take away that hearse, remove that shroud; come, put white plumes upon the horses' heads, and let gilded trappings hang around them. There, take away that fife, that shrill sounding music of the death march. Lend me the trumpet and the drum. O hallelujah, hallelujah, hallelujah; why do we weep the saints to heaven; why need we lament? They are not dead, they are gone before. Stop, stop that mourning, refrain your tears, clap your hands, clap your hands.

"They are supremely blest,
Have done with sin, and care, and woe,
And with their Saviour rest."

What! Weep for heads that are crowned with garlands of heaven? Weep for hands that grasp the harps of gold? What, weep for eyes that see the Redeemer? What, weep for hearts that are washed from sin, and are throbbing with eternal bliss? What, weep for men that are in the Saviour's bosom? No; weep for yourselves that you are here. Weep that the mandate has not come which bids you to die. Weep that you must tarry. But weep not for them. I see them turning back on you with loving wonder, and they exclaim "Why weepest thou?" What, weep for poverty that it is clothed in riches? What, weep for sickness, that it has inherited eternal health? What, weep for shame, that it is glorified; and weep for sinful mortality, that it has become immaculate? Oh, weep not, but rejoice. "If you knew what it was that I have said unto you, and where I have gone, you would rejoice with a joy that no man should take from you." "To die is gain."

FOR MEDITATION: There is probably at least one Christian whom you miss terribly. The temporary loss and sorrow may be very hard for you (Philippians 2: 27), but the dead in Christ enjoy eternal blessedness (Revelation 14: 13).

SERMON NO. 146

Pride and humility

"Before destruction the heart of man is haughty, and before honour is humility." Proverbs 18: 12
SUGGESTED FURTHER READING: Romans 12: 3-6

What is humility? The best definition I have ever met with is, "to think rightly of ourselves." Humility is to make a right estimate of one's self. It is no humility for a man to think less of himself than he ought, though it might rather puzzle him to do that. Some persons, when they know they can do a thing, tell you they cannot; but you do not call that humility. A man is asked to take part in some meeting. "No," he says, "I have no ability"; yet if you were to say so yourself, he would be offended at you. It is not humility for a man to stand up and depreciate himself and say he cannot do this, that, or the other, when he knows that he is lying. If God gives a man a talent, do you think the man does not know it? If a man has ten talents he has no right to be dishonest to his Maker, and to say, "Lord, thou hast only given me five." It is not humility to underrate yourself. Humility is to think of yourself, if you can, as God thinks of you. It is to feel that if we have talents, God has given them to us, and let it be seen that, like freight in a vessel, they tend to sink us low. The more we have, the lower we ought to lie. Humility is not to say, "I have not this gift," but it is to say, "I have the gift, and I must use it for my Master's glory. I must never seek any honour for myself, for what have I that I have not received?"

FOR MEDITATION: Pride can lead us to misuse God's gifts for selfish ends. A false humility can lead to laziness and disobedience which causes someone else to have to do what we should be doing ourselves. The right balance is to serve the Lord with all humility as the apostle Paul could truthfully claim to have done (Acts 20: 19).

Making light of Christ

"But they made light of it, and went their ways, one to his farm, another to his merchandise." Matthew 22: 5
SUGGESTED FURTHER READING: Matthew 13: 9-17

It is making light of the gospel and of the whole of God's glorious things, when men go to hear and yet do not pay attention. How many who frequent churches and chapels to indulge in a comfortable nap! Think what a fearful insult that is to the King of heaven. Would they enter into Her Majesty's palace, ask an audience, and then go to sleep before her face? And yet the sin of sleeping in Her Majesty's presence, would not be so great, even though against her laws, as the sin of wilfully slumbering in God's sanctuary. How many go to our houses of worship who do not sleep, but who sit with vacant stare, listening as they would to a man who could not play a lively tune upon a good instrument. What goes in at one ear goes out at the other. Whatever enters the brain goes out without affecting the heart. Ah, my hearers, you are guilty of making light of God's gospel, when you sit under a sermon without paying attention to it! Oh! What would lost souls give to hear another sermon! What would yonder dying wretch who is just now nearing the grave, give for another Sabbath! And what will you give, one of these days, when you shall be close to Jordan's brink, that you might have one more warning, and listen once more to the wooing voice of God's minister! We make light of the gospel when we hear it, without solemn and awful attention to it.

FOR MEDITATION: Hear—listen—remember—obey (James 1: 25). A sleeping congregation is no more use than a sleeping preacher.

SERMON NO. 98

What are the clouds?

"The clouds are the dust of his feet." Nahum 1: 3
SUGGESTED FURTHER READING: Isaiah 40: 12-26

Great things with us are little things with God. What great things clouds are to us! There we see them sweeping along the skies! Then they rapidly increase till the entire sky becomes black and a dark shadow is cast upon the world; we foresee the coming storm, and we tremble at the mountains of cloud, for they are great. Great things are they? No, they are only the dust of God's feet. The greatest cloud that ever swept the face of the skies, was but one single particle of dust starting from the feet of the Almighty Jehovah. When clouds roll over clouds, and the storm is very terrible, it is only the chariot of God, as it speeds along the heavens, raising a little dust around him! "The clouds are the dust of his feet." Oh! Could you grasp this idea my friends, or had I words in which to put it into your souls, I am sure you would sit down in solemn awe of that great God who is our Father, or who will be our Judge. Consider, that the greatest things with man are little things with God. We call the mountains great, but what are they? They are but "the small dust of the balance." We call the nations great, and we speak of mighty empires; but the nations before him are but as "a drop of a bucket." We call the islands great and talk of ours boastingly—"He taketh up the isles as a very little thing." We speak of great men and of mighty—"The inhabitants [of the earth] in his sight are as grasshoppers." We talk of ponderous orbs moving millions of miles from us—in God's sight they are but little atoms dancing up and down in the sunbeam of existence. Compared with God there is nothing great.

FOR MEDITATION: Are you experiencing great distress or great success? Try to look at both kinds of circumstances from the viewpoint of God (Zechariah 4: 6-7).

SERMON NO. 36

Christ's first and last subject

"From that time Jesus began to preach, and to say, Repent: for the
kingdom of heaven is at hand." Matthew 4: 17. "And that repentance and
remission of sins should be preached in his name among all nations,
beginning at Jerusalem." Luke 24: 47
SUGGESTED FURTHER READING: Philippians 3: 1-14

If you are renewed by grace, and were to meet your old self, I am sure you
would be very anxious to get out of his company. "No," say you, "No, sir, I
cannot accompany you." "Why, you used to swear!" "I cannot now." "Well,
but," says he, "You and I are very near companions." "Yes, I know we are,
and I wish we were not. You are a deal of trouble to me every day. I wish I
could be rid of you for ever." "But," says Old Self, "you used to drink very
well." "Yes, I know it. I know you did, indeed, Old Self. You could sing a
song as merrily as any one. You were ringleader in all sorts of vice, but I am
no relation of yours now. You are of the old Adam, and I of the new Adam.
You are of your old father, the devil; but I have another—my Father, who is
in heaven." I tell you, brethren, there is no man in the world you will hate so
much as your old self, and there will be nothing you will so much long to get
rid of as that old man who once was dragging you down to hell, and who
will try his hand at it over and over again every day you live, and who will
accomplish it yet, unless that divine grace which has made you a new man
shall keep you a new man even to the end. Good Rowland Hill, in his
"Village Dialogues," gives the Christian, whom he describes in the first part
of the book, the name of Thomas Newman. Every man who goes to heaven
must have the name of new-man. We must not expect to enter there unless
we are created anew in Christ Jesus.

FOR MEDITATION: In our testimonies we should own up to what we used to be,
but in such a way that we also disown the people we used to be. Don't be like the
biography of a Christian which seems to glory in the sin of the past—reserve
all the glory for your Saviour (1 Corinthians 15: 9,10; 1 Timothy 1: 13-17).

Faith illustrated

*"For the which cause I also suffer these things: nevertheless I am not
ashamed: for I know whom I have believed, and am persuaded that he is
able to keep that which I have committed unto him against that day."*
2 *Timothy* 1: 12
SUGGESTED FURTHER READING: Hebrews 6: 13-20

Joab, when he fled from the sword of Solomon, laid hold on the horns of the
altar, thinking that surely when he had laid hold on the altar he was safe. His
was vain confidence, for he was dragged from the horns of the altar and
slain. But if you can lay hold on the horns of the altar of God, even Christ,
you are most surely safe, and no sword of vengeance can ever reach you. I
saw the other day a remarkable picture, which I shall use as an illustration of
the way of salvation by faith in Jesus. An offender had committed a crime
for which he must die, but it was in the olden time when churches were
considered to be sanctuaries in which criminals might hide themselves and
so escape. See the transgressor—he rushes towards the church, the guards
pursue him with their drawn swords, all athirst for his blood, they pursue
him even to the church door. He rushes up the steps, and just as they are
about to overtake him and hew him in pieces on the threshhold of the
church, out comes the Bishop, and holding up the crucifix he cries, "Back,
back! Stain not the precincts of God's house with blood! Stand back!" and
the guards at once respect the emblem and stand back, while the poor
fugitive hides himself behind the robes of the priest. It is even so with Christ.
The guilty sinner flies to the cross—flies straight away to Jesus, and though
Justice pursues him, Christ lifts up his wounded hands and cries to Justice,
"Stand back! Stand back! I shelter this sinner; in the secret place of my
tabernacle do I hide him; I will not suffer him to perish, for he puts his trust
in me."

FOR MEDITATION: We should never be ashamed to be seen hiding behind
Jesus (Mark 8: 38).

SERMON NO. 271

As thy days, so shall thy strength be

"As thy days, so shall thy strength be." Deuteronomy 33: 25
SUGGESTED FURTHER READING: Psalm 91

What a varying promise it is! I do not mean that the promise varies, but adapts itself to all our changes. "As thy days, so shall thy strength be." Here is a fine sunshiny morning; all the world is laughing; everything looks glad; the birds are singing, the trees seem to be all alive with music. "My strength shall be as my day is," says the pilgrim. Ah! Pilgrim, there is a little black cloud gathering. Soon it increases; the flash of lightning wounds the heaven, and it begins to bleed in showers. Pilgrim, "As thy days, so shall thy strength be." The birds have done singing, and the world has done laughing; but "as thy days, so shall thy strength be." Now the dark night comes on, and another day approaches—a day of tempest, and whirlwind, and storm. Dost thou tremble, pilgrim?—"As thy days, so shall thy strength be." "But there are robbers in the wood."—"As thy days so shall thy strength be." "But there are lions which devour me" "As thy days, so shall thy strength be." "But there are rivers; how shall I swim them?" Here is a boat to carry thee over; "As thy days, so shall thy strength be." "But there are fires: how shall I pass through them?" Here is the garment that will protect thee: "As thy days, so shall thy strength be." "But there are arrows that fly by day." Here is thy shield: "As thy days, so shall thy strength be." "But there is the pestilence that walketh in darkness." Here is thy antidote: "As thy days, so shall thy strength be." Wherever you may be, and whatever trouble awaits you, "As thy days, so shall thy strength be." Children of God, cannot you say that this has been true hitherto? I can.

FOR MEDITATION: We often spoil our lives by trying to live tomorrow today. God does not promise to provide for the needs of his people before they have them (Matthew 6: 34; 1 Corinthians 10: 13).

SERMON NO. 210

Five fears

"Yet surely I know that it shall be well with them that fear God, which fear before him." Ecclesiastes 8: 12
SUGGESTED FURTHER READING: Luke 12: 4-12

Fear may be yoked into the service of God. True fear, not fearing, but believing, saves the soul; not doubt, but confidence, is the strength and the deliverance of the Christian. Still, fear, as being one of those powers which God has given us, is not in itself sinful. Fear may be used for the most sinful purposes; at the same time it may be so ennobled by grace, and so used for the service of God, that it may become the very grandest part of man. In fact, Scripture has honoured fear, for the whole of piety is comprehended in these words, "Fear God"; "the fear of the Lord"; "them that fear him." These phrases are employed to express true piety, and the men who possess it. Fear, I have said, may ruin the soul. Alas! It has ruined multitudes. O Fear, you are the rock upon which many a ship has been wrecked. Many a soul has suffered spiritual destruction through you, but then it has been not the fear of God, but the fear of man. Many have rushed against the thick bosses of the Almighty's shield, and defied God, in order to escape the wrath of feeble man. Many through fear of worldly loss have brought great guilt into their consciences; some through fear of ridicule and laughter have not had the boldness to follow the right, and so have gone astray and been ruined. Yea, and where fear does not work utter destruction it is capable of doing much damage to the spirit. Fear has paralysed the arm of the most gigantic Christian, stopped him in his race, and impeded him in his labours. Faith can do anything, but fear, sinful fear, can do just nothing at all, except prevent faith from performing its labours.

FOR MEDITATION: The one you seek to please is the one you fear (Galatians 1: 10; 1 Thessalonians 2: 4).

The comer's conflict with Satan

"And as he was yet a coming, the devil threw him down, and tare him. And Jesus rebuked the unclean spirit, and healed the child, and delivered him again to his father." Luke 9: 42
SUGGESTED FURTHER READING: I John 5: 13-21

"There is a sin unto death; I do not say that he shall pray for it." "There," says the devil, "the apostle did not say he could even pray for the man who has committed certain sins." Then he reads that "sin against the Holy Ghost shall never be forgiven." "There," he says, "is your character: you have committed sin against the Holy Ghost, and you will never be pardoned." Then he brings another passage: "Let him alone; Ephraim is joined unto idols." "There," says Satan, "you have had no liberty in prayer lately; God has let you alone; you are given unto idols; you are entirely destroyed;" and the cruel fiend howls his song of joy, and makes a merry dance over the thought that the poor soul is to be lost. But do not believe him, my dear friends. No man has committed the sin against the Holy Ghost as long as he has grace to repent; it is certain that no man can have committed that sin if he flies to Christ and believes on him. No believing soul can commit it; no penitent sinner ever has committed it. If a man be careless and thoughtless—if he can hear a terrible sermon and laugh it off, and put away his convictions—if he never feels any strivings of conscience, there is a fear that he may have committed that sin. But as long as you have any desires for Christ, you have no more committed that sin than you have flown up to the stars and swept cobwebs from the skies. As long as you have any sense of your guilt, any desire to be redeemed, you cannot have fallen into that sin; as a penitent you may still be saved, for if you had committed it, you could not be penitent.

FOR MEDITATION: The devil is the father of lies, a murderer and sinner from the beginning (John 8: 44; I John 3: 8). His attempts to be a Bible expositor are never to be trusted (Luke 4: 9,10).

Tomorrow

"Boast not thyself of tomorrow; for thou knowest not what a day may bring forth." Proverbs 27: 1
SUGGESTED FURTHER READING: Proverbs 31: 10-25

On one occasion I pleaded for a friendly society, and not knowing a more appropriate text, I selected this, "Take no thought for the morrow, for tomorrow shall take thought for the things of itself." Some of my hearers, when I announced my text, feared the principle of it was altogether hostile to anything like an insurance, or providing for the future, but I just showed them that it was not, as I looked upon it. It is a positive command that we are to take no anxious thought concerning tomorrow. Now, how can I do that? How can I put myself into such a position that I can carry out this commandment of taking no thought for the morrow? If I were a man struggling in life, and had it in my power to insure for something which would take care of wife and family in after days, if I did not do it, you might preach to me for all eternity about not taking thought for the morrow; but I could not help doing it, when I saw those I loved around me unprovided for. Let it be in God's word, I could not practise it; I should still be at some time or other taking thought for the morrow. But let me go to one of the many excellent institutions which exist, and let me see that all is provided for, I come home and say, "Now, I know how to practise Christ's command of taking no thought for the morrow; I pay the policy-money once a year, and I take no further thought about it, for I have no occasion to do so now, and have obeyed the very spirit and letter of Christ's command." Our Lord meant that we were to get rid of cares.

FOR MEDITATION: Are you playing your part to provide practically for the members of your family? (1 Timothy 3: 4-5, 12; 5: 4,16). If not, perhaps you should start getting anxious (1 Timothy 5: 8).

Law and grace

"Moreover the law entered, that the offence might abound. But where sin abounded, grace did much more abound." Romans 5: 20
SUGGESTED FURTHER READING: 2 Peter 3: 10-14

There has always been the salt of grace in the world to counteract the power of sin. The clouds have never been so universal as to hide the day. But the time is fast approaching when grace shall extend all over our poor world and be universal. According to the Bible testimony, we look for the great day when the dark cloud which has swathed this world in darkness shall be removed, and it shall shine once more like all its sister planets. It has been for many a long year clouded and veiled by sin and corruption; but the last fire shall consume its rags and sackcloth. After that fire, the world in righteousness shall shine. The huge molten mass now slumbering in the bowels of our common mother shall furnish the means of purity. Palaces, and crowns, and peoples, and empires, are all to be melted down; and after, like a plague-house, the present creation has been burned up entirely, God will breathe upon the heated mass, and it will cool down again. He will smile on it as he did when he first created it, and the rivers will run down the new made hills, the oceans will float in new-made channels; and the world will be again the abode of the righteous for ever and for ever. This fallen world will be restored to its orbit; that gem which was lost from the sceptre of God shall be set again, yea, he shall wear it as a signet about his arm. Christ died for the world; and what he died for, he will have. He died for the whole world, and the whole world he will have, when he has purified and cleansed it, and fitted it for himself. "Where sin abounded, grace did much more abound;" for grace shall be universal, whereas sin will be destroyed.

FOR MEDITATION: The believer's sure and certain hope of being freed completely from the presence of sin then, is a strong motive for seeking to be as free as possible from it now (1 John 3: 2,3).

Reigning grace

"That as sin hath reigned unto death, even so might grace reign through righteousness unto eternal life by Jesus Christ our Lord." Romans 5: 21
SUGGESTED FURTHER READING: Romans 5: 12-17

An awful contemplation is that of the reign of sin. Permitted to come into this world as a usurper—having mounted its throne upon the heart of man by flattering blandishments, and crafty pleasantries, it was not long before it fully developed itself. Its first act was to smite Eden with blast and mildew by its breath; its next act was to slay the second child of man and that by the hand of the eldest born. Since then, its reign has been scarlet with blood, black with iniquity, and fraught with everything that can make the heart of man sad and wretched. Oh sin, thou tyrant monster, all the demons that ever sat upon the throne of Rome, were never such as thou art; and all the men, who from the wild north, have come forth as the scourges of man, the destroying angels of our race, though they have waded up to their knees in the blood of mortals, have never been so terrible as thou art. Thou hast reigned unto death, and that a death eternal—a death from which there shall be no resurrection—a death which casts souls into an eternal grave—a grave of fire. Our apostle now changes the subject, and represents man under the gracious state, as rejoicing in another government, ruled by another king. Just as sin has reigned, and with despotic and irresistible power has ground his subjects in the very dust, and then cast them into the flames, so does grace with irresistible goodness, constrain the chosen multitude to yield obedience, and thus prepares them for eternal bliss. See, it lifts up the beggar from the dunghill, and makes him to sit among princes. Mark its shining course, and behold it blessing the sons of man wherever it stretches out its silver sceptre, chasing away the misery of night, and giving the joy of gospel day.

FOR MEDITATION: Refugees from the dominion of darkness are accepted as citizens of the kingdom of God's beloved Son (Colossians 1: 13) and they will never be sent back to their former home.

Limiting God

"They... limited the Holy One of Israel." Psalm 78: 41
SUGGESTED FURTHER READING: Daniel 3: 13-28

He is not limited to means—to any means, much less to one of thy choosing.
If he deliver thee not by calming the tempest, he has a better way in store; he
will send from above and deliver thee; he will snatch thee out of the deep
waters lest the floods overflow thee. What might Shadrach, Meshach and
Abed-nego have said? Suppose they had got it into their heads that God
would deliver them in some particular way. They did have some such idea,
but they said, as if to prove that they trusted not really to their thought
about the deliverance—"Nevertheless, be it known unto thee, O king, we
will not worship thy gods, nor bow before the image which thou hast set
up." They were prepared to let God have his will, even though he used no
means of deliverance. But suppose, I say, they had conferred with flesh and
blood, and Shadrach had said, "God will strike Nebuchadnezzar dead; just
at the moment when the men are about to put us into the furnace the king
will turn pale and die, and so we shall escape." O my friends, they would
have trembled indeed when they went into the furnace if they had chosen
their own means of deliverance, and the king had remained alive. But
instead of this, they gave themselves up to God, even if he did not deliver
them. And, though he did not prevent their going into the furnace, yet he
kept them alive in it, so that not so much as the smell of fire had passed upon
them. It shall be even so with you. Repose in God. When thou seest him not,
believe him; when everything seems to contradict thy faith, still stagger not
at the promise. If HE hath said it, he can find ways and means to do it.

FOR MEDITATION: Our ways are not God's ways (Isaiah 55: 8-9). Where our
ways can multiply complications, his ways can humble us by their straightforward simplicity (Numbers 11: 21-23,31; 2 Kings 5: 10-14; Luke 9: 12-17).
How are you limiting God?

The voice of the blood of Christ

"The blood of sprinkling, that speaketh better things than that of Abel."
Hebrews 12: 24
SUGGESTED FURTHER READING: Genesis 4: 1-16

There is a cry heard in heaven; the angels are astonished; they rise up from their golden seats, and they enquire, "What is that cry?" God looks upon them, and he says, "It is the cry of blood; a man has been slain by his fellow; a brother by him who came from the bowels of the self-same mother has been murdered in cold blood, through malice. One of my saints has been murdered, and here he comes." And Abel entered into heaven, blood-red, the first of God's elect who had entered Paradise, and the first of God's children who had worn the blood-red crown of martyrdom. And then the cry was heard, loud and clear and strong; and thus it spoke: "Revenge! Revenge! Revenge!" And God himself, upstarting from his throne, summoned the culprit to his presence; questioned him, condemned him out of his own mouth, and made him henceforth a fugitive and a vagabond, to wander over the surface of the earth, which was to be sterile henceforth to his plough. And now, beloved, just contrast the blood of Christ with this. There is Jesus Christ, the incarnate Son of God; he hangs upon a tree; he is murdered—murdered by his own brethren. "He came unto his own, and his own received him not", but his own led him out to death. He bleeds; he dies; and then is heard a cry in heaven. The astonished angels again start from their seats, and they say, "What is this? What is this cry that we hear?" And the mighty Maker answers yet again, "It is the cry of blood; it is the cry of the blood of my only-begotten and well-beloved Son!" And God, uprising from his throne, looks down from heaven and listens to the cry. And what is the cry? It is not revenge; but the voice cries "Mercy! Mercy! Mercy!" Did you not hear it? It said, "Father, forgive them, for they know not what they do."

FOR MEDITATION: Abel died, but through his faith he still speaks to us (Hebrews 11: 4). Christ died and is alive for evermore (Revelation 1: 18); He is always speaking for us, if we come to God through him (Hebrews 7: 25).

SERMON NO. 211

Independence of Christianity

"Not by might, nor by power, but by my Spirit, saith the Lord of Hosts."
Zechariah 4: 6
SUGGESTED FURTHER READING: 2 Corinthians 3: 17-4: 7

The grand thing the church wants in this time, is God's Holy Spirit. You all get up plans and say, "Now, if the church were altered a little bit, it would go better." You think if there were different ministers, or different church order, or something different, then all would be well. No, dear friends, it is not there the mistake lies; it is that we want more of the Spirit. It is as if you saw a locomotive engine upon a railway, and it would not go, and they put up a driver, and they said, "Now, that driver will just do." They try another and another. One proposes that such-and-such a wheel should be altered, but still it will not go. Some one then bursts in amongst those who are conversing and says, "No, friends; but the reason why it will not move, is because there is no steam. You have no fire, you have no water in the boiler: that's why it will not go. There may be some faults about it; it may want a bit of paint here and there, but it will go well enough with all those faults if you do but get the steam up." But now people are saying, "This must be altered, and that must be altered;" but it would go no better unless God the Spirit should come to bless us. You may have the same ministers, and they shall be a thousand times more useful for God, if God is pleased to bless them. You shall have the same deacons, they shall be a thousand times more influential than they are now, when the Spirit is poured down upon them from on high. That is the church's great want, and until that want be supplied, we may reform, and reform, and still be just the same. We want the Holy Spirit.

FOR MEDITATION: God doesn't come to us in the most spectacular ways possible (1 Kings 19: 11-12). For his idea of power-evangelism see 1 Corinthians 1: 17,18,23,24; 2: 1-5, also Romans 1: 16.

Christ in the covenant

"I will give thee for a covenant of the people." Isaiah 49: 8
SUGGESTED FURTHER READING: 1 Corinthians 3: 16-23

When tempted to sin, reply, "I cannot do this great wickedness. I cannot, for I am one of Christ's." When wealth is before you to be won by sin, touch it not; say that you are Christ's else you would take it; but now you cannot. Tell Satan that you would not gain the world if you had to love Christ less. Are you exposed in the world to difficulties and dangers? Stand fast in the evil day, remembering that you are one of Christ's. Are you in a field where much is to be done, and others are sitting down idly and lazily, doing nothing? Go at your work, and when the sweat stands upon your brow and you are bidden to stay, say, "No, I cannot stop; I am one of Christ's. He had a baptism to be baptised with, and so have I, and I am in bondage until it is accomplished. I am one of Christ's. If I were not one of his, and purchased by blood, I might be like Issachar, crouching between two burdens; but I am one of Christ's." When the siren song of pleasure would tempt you from the path of right, reply, "Hush your strains, O temptress; I am one of Christ's. Your music cannot affect me; I am not my own, I am bought with a price." When the cause of God needs you, give yourself to it, for you are Christ's. When the poor need you, give yourself away, for you are one of Christ's. When, at any time there is anything to be done for his church and for his cross, do it, remembering that you are one of Christ's. I beseech you, never belie your profession. Go not where others could say, "He cannot be Christ's."

FOR MEDITATION: The Christian is doubly Christ's one—by his choice to bear fruit (John 15: 16) and by his purchase to glorify God in the body (1 Corinthians 6: 19,20). Are you giving him at present everything he paid for?

SERMON NO. 103

Election

"But we are bound to give thanks alway to God for you, brethren beloved of the Lord, because God hath from the beginning chosen you to salvation through sanctification of the Spirit and belief of the truth: Whereunto he called you by our gospel, to the obtaining of the glory of our Lord Jesus Christ." 2 Thessalonians 2: 13,14

SUGGESTED FURTHER READING: Psalm 33: 1-12

Revelation points us to a period long before this world was fashioned, to the days when the morning stars were formed; when, like drops of dew, from the fingers of the morning, stars and constellations fell trickling from the hand of God; when, by his own lips, he launched forth ponderous orbs; when with his own hand he sent comets, like thunderbolts, wandering through the sky, to find one day their proper sphere. We go back to years gone by, when worlds were made and systems fashioned, but we have not even approached the beginning yet. Until we go to the time when all the universe slept in the mind of God as yet unborn, until we enter the eternity where God the Creator lived alone, everything sleeping within him, all creation resting in his mighty gigantic thought, we have not guessed the beginning. We may go back, back, back, ages upon ages. We may go back, if we might use such strange words, whole eternities, and yet never arrive at the beginning. Our wing might be tired, our imagination would die away; if it could outstrip the lightnings flashing in majesty, power, and rapidity, it would soon weary itself before it could get to the beginning. But God from the beginning chose his people. When the unnavigated heavens were yet unfanned by the wing of a single angel; when space was shoreless, or else unborn when universal silence reigned; when neither a voice or whisper shocked the solemnity of silence; when there was no being and no motion, no time, and nothing but God himself alone in his eternity; when without the song of an angel, without the attendance of even the cherubim, long before the living creatures were born, or the wheels of the chariot of Jehovah were fashioned, even then, "in the beginning was the Word," and in the beginning God's people were one with the Word, and "in the beginning he chose them into eternal life." Our election then is eternal.

FOR MEDITATION: God's love is from everlasting to everlasting (Psalm 103: 17).

SERMON NOS. 41-42

Three homilies from one text

"And Jesus went about all Galilee, ... healing all manner of sickness and all manner of disease among the people. And his fame went throughout all Syria: and they brought unto him all sick people that were taken with divers diseases and torments, ...and he healed them. " Matthew 4: 23-25
SUGGESTED FURTHER READING: 2 Kings 6: 11-23

Take care that you bring your relatives to Christ on the arms of your faith. Faith is that which puts strength into prayer. The reason why we do not receive the answer to our supplications is, because we do not believe we shall be heard. You remember my sermon the other sabbath morning from the text, "Whatsoever things ye shall desire when ye pray, believe that ye receive them and ye shall have them." (*See August 13*) If you can exercise faith for a dead soul, that dead soul shall be quickened and receive faith itself. If you can look to Christ with the eye of faith for a blind soul, that blind soul shall have sight given it and it shall see. There is a wonderful power in vicarious faith—faith for another. Not that any one of you can be saved without faith yourself; but that when another believes for you and on your account, and quotes the promise before God for you, you may be unconscious of it, but God hears and answers that faith, and breathes on your soul, and gives you faith to believe in the Lord Jesus Christ. I do not think Christians exercise enough of this power. They are so busy with faith about their troubles, faith about their sins, faith about their personal experience, that they have not time to exercise that faith for another. Oh but surely that gift was never bestowed upon us for our own use merely, but for other people. Try it, Christian man; try it, Christian woman; see whether God is not as good as your faith when your faith is exercised concerning the soul of your poor neighbour, of your poor drunken kinsman, or of some poor soul who thus far has defied every effort to reclaim him from the error of his ways.

FOR MEDITATION: Sometimes Jesus healed the sick as the result of the faith of others (Matthew 8: 10,13; 15: 28; Mark 2: 5; 9: 23,24; Luke 8: 50; John 4: 50). Are you praying like this for the conversion of some who at present can't and won't pray for themselves?

SERMON NO. 333

Heaven and hell

"And I say unto you, That many shall come from the east and west, and shall sit down with Abraham, and Isaac, and Jacob, in the kingdom of heaven. But the children of the kingdom shall be cast out into outer darkness: there shall be weeping and gnashing of teeth." Matthew 8: 11-12
SUGGESTED FURTHER READING: Isaiah 46: 8-13

"I will," says man, and he never performs; "I shall," says he, and he breaks his promise. But it is never so with God's "shalls." If he says, "shall," it shall be; when he says, "will," it will be. Now he has said here, "many shall come." The devil says, "they shall not come;" but "they shall come." Their sins say, "you can't come;" God says, you "shall come." You, yourselves, say, "we won't come;" God says, "you shall come." Yes! There are some who are laughing at salvation, who scoff at Christ, and mock at the gospel; but I tell you some of you shall come yet. "What!" you say, "can God make me become a Christian?" I tell you yes, from here rests the power of the gospel. It does not ask your consent; but it gets it. It does not say, will you have it, but it makes you willing in the day of God's power. Not against your will, but it makes you willing. It shows you its value, and then you fall in love with it, and immediately you run after it and have it. Many people have said, "we will not have anything to do with religion," yet they have been converted. I have heard of a man who once went to chapel to hear the singing, and as soon as the minister began to preach, he put his fingers in his ears and would not listen. But by and by some tiny insect settled on his face, so that he was obliged to take one finger out of his ear to brush it away. Just then the minister said, "he that hath ears to hear, let him hear." The man listened; and God met with him at that moment to his soul's conversion.

FOR MEDITATION: When God speaks he means it—every single word (Psalm 119: 160; Proverbs 30: 5). Does this fact strike you when you read or hear his word?

Christ triumphant

"And having spoiled principalities and powers, he made a shew of them openly, triumphing over them in it." Colossians 2: 15
SUGGESTED FURTHER READING: Isaiah 63: 1-6

I might describe the mighty pictures at the end of the procession; for in the old Roman triumph, the deeds of the conqueror were all depicted in paintings. The towns he had taken, the rivers he had passed, the provinces he had subdued, the battles he had fought, were represented in pictures and exposed to the view of the people, who with great festivity and rejoicing, accompanied him in throngs, or beheld from the windows of their houses, and filled the air with their acclamations and applauses. I might present to you first of all the picture of hell's dungeons blown to atoms. Satan had prepared deep in the depths of darkness a prison-house for God's elect; but Christ has not left one stone upon another. On the picture I see the chains broken in pieces, the prison doors burnt with fire, and all the depths shaken to their foundations. On another picture I see heaven open to all believers; I see the gates that were fast shut heaved open by the golden lever of Christ's atonement. I see another picture, the grave despoiled; I behold Jesus in it, slumbering for awhile, and then rolling away the stone and rising to immortality and glory. But we cannot stay to describe these mighty pictures of the victories of his love. We know that the time shall come when the triumphant procession shall cease, when the last of his redeemed shall have entered into the city of happiness and of joy, and when with the shout of a trumpet heard for the last time, he shall ascend to heaven, and take his people up to reign with God, even our Father, for ever and ever, world without end.

FOR MEDITATION: The victory and triumph (or victory parade) are Christ's alone; if you are a Christian, your part in his victory procession is to be found in 2 Corinthians 2: 14.

The new heart

"A new heart also will I give you, and a new spirit will I put within you: and I will take away the stony heart out of your flesh, and I will give you an heart of flesh." Ezekiel 36: 26
SUGGESTED FURTHER READING: Matthew 9: 10-17

The promise is that he will give us new hearts and right spirits. Human nature is too far gone ever to be mended. It is not a house that is a little out of repair, with here and there a slate blown from the roof, and here and there a piece of plaster broken down from the ceiling. No, it is rotten throughout, the very foundations have been eroded; there is not a single timber in it which has not been eaten by the worm, from its uppermost roof to its lowest foundation; there is no soundness in it; it is all rottenness and ready to fall. God does not attempt to mend; he does not shore up the walls, and repaint the door; he does not garnish and beautify, but he determines that the old house shall be entirely swept away, and that he will build a new one. It is too far gone, I say, to be mended. If it were only a little out of repair, it might be mended. If only a wheel or two of that great thing called "manhood" were out of repair, then he who made man might put the whole to rights; he might put a new cog where it had been broken off, and another wheel where it had gone to ruin and the machine might work anew. But no, the whole of it is out of repair; there is not one lever which is not broken; not one axle which is not disturbed; not one of the wheels which act upon the others. The whole head is sick, and the whole heart is faint. From the sole of the foot, to the crown of the head, it is all wounds and bruises and putrefying sores. The Lord, therefore, does not attempt the repairing of this thing.

FOR MEDITATION: The only cure for man's sinful condition is a heart transplant carried out by the Great Physician (Romans 2: 28,29).

England's ills and sorrows

"Oh that my head were waters, and mine eyes a fountain of tears, that I might weep day and night for the slain of the daughter of my people!"
Jeremiah 9: 1
SUGGESTED FURTHER READING: Luke 19: 37-44

As ye stand on any of the hills around, and behold this monstrous city lying in the valley, say, "O London, London! how great thy guilt. Oh! that the Master would gather thee under his wing, and make thee his city, the joy of the whole earth! O London, London! Full of privileges, and full of sin; exalted to heaven by the gospel, thou shalt be cast down to hell by thy rejection of it!" And then, when ye have wept over London, go and weep over the street in which you live, as you see the sabbath broken, and God's laws trampled upon, and men's bodies profaned—go and weep! Weep, for the court in which you live in your humble property; weep for the square in which you live in your magnificent wealth; weep for your neighbours and your friends, lest any of them, having lived godless, may die godless! Then go to your house, weep for your family, for your servants, for your husband, for your wife, for your children. Weep, weep; cease not weeping, till God has renewed them by his Spirit. And if you have any friends with whom you sinned in your past life, be earnest for their salvation. George Whitefield said there were many young men with whom he played at cards, and spent hours wasting his time when he should have been about other business. When he was converted, his first thought was, "I must by God's grace have these converted too." And he never rested, till he could say, that he did not know of one of them, a companion of his guilt, who was not now a companion with him in the tribulation of the gospel. Oh, let it be so with you!

FOR MEDITATION: "Jesus wept" for others; "How he loved" (John 11: 35,36). What message do your tears or lack of tears convey about you?

Lovest thou me?

"So when they had dined, Jesus saith to Simon Peter, Simon, son of Jonas, lovest thou me more than these? He saith unto him, Yea, Lord; thou knowest that I love thee. He saith unto him, Feed my lambs. He saith to him again the second time, Simon, son of Jonas, lovest thou me? He saith unto him, Yea, Lord; thou knowest that I love thee. He saith unto him, Feed my sheep. He saith unto him the third time, Simon, son of Jonas, lovest thou me? Peter was grieved because he said unto him the third time, Lovest thou me? And he said unto him, Lord, thou knowest all things; thou knowest that I love thee. Jesus saith unto him, Feed my sheep. John 21: 15-17
SUGGESTED FURTHER READING: 1 Corinthians 13

He did not say, "Simon, son of Jonas, fearest thou me." He did not say, "Dost thou admire me? Dost thou adore me?" Nor was it even a question concerning his faith. He did not say, "Simon, son of Jonas, believest thou in me?" but he asked him another question, "Lovest thou me?" I take it, that is because love is the very best evidence of godliness. Love is the brightest of all the graces; and hence it becomes the best evidence. I do not believe love to be superior to faith; I believe faith to be the groundwork of our salvation; I think faith to be the mother grace, and love springs from it; faith I believe to be the root grace, and love grows from it. But then, faith is not an evidence for brightness equal to love. Faith, if we have it, is a sure and certain sign that we are God's children; and so is every other grace a sure and certain one, but many of them cannot be seen by others. Love is a more sparkling one than any other. If I have a true fear of God in my heart, then I am God's child; but since fear is a grace that is more dim and has not that halo of glory over it that love has, love becomes one of the very best evidences and one of the easiest signs of discerning whether we are alive to the Saviour. He that lacks love, must lack also every other grace in the proportion in which he lacks love. If love be little, I believe it is a sign that faith is little; for he that believes much loves much. If love be little, fear will be little, and courage for God will be little.

FOR MEDITATION: The commandments of God can be headed and summarised by one word—love (Matthew 22: 36-40; Romans 13: 8-10).

SERMON NO. 117

The question of fear and the answer of faith

"Will he plead against me with his great power? No; but he would put strength in me." Job 23: 6
SUGGESTED FURTHER READING: 2 Corinthians 2: 14-3: 5

Didst thou ever stand and take a view of heaven? Hast thou discerned the hills which lie between your soul and paradise? Hast thou counted the lions thou hast to fight, the giants to be slain, and the rivers to be crossed? Didst thou ever notice the many temptations with which thou art beset, the trials thou hast to endure, the difficulties thou hast to overcome, the dangers thou hast to avoid? Didst thou ever take a bird's eye view of heaven, and all the dangers which are strewn thickly along the path thither? And didst thou ever ask thyself this question, "How shall I, a poor feeble worm, ever get there?" Didst thou ever say within thyself, "I am not a match for all my foes, how shall I arrive at paradise?" If thou hast ever asked this question, I will tell thee what is the only answer for it: thou must be girded with almighty strength, or else thou wilt never gain the victory. Easy thy path may be, but it is too hard for thy infantile strength, without the almighty power. Thy path may be one of little temptation, and of shallow trial; but thou wilt be drowned in the floods yet, unless almighty power preserve thee. Mark me! However smooth thy way, there is nothing short of the bare arm of deity that can land any one of you in heaven. We must have divine strength, or else we shall never get there. And there is an illustration of these words: "No, but he will put his strength in me." "And shall I hold on to the end?" says the believer. Yes, thou wilt, for God's strength in is thee. "Shall I be able to bear such-and-such a trial?" Yes, thou wilt. Cannot omnipotence stem the torrent? And omnipotence is in thee; for, like Ignatius of old, thou art a God-bearer; thou bearest God about with thee. Thy heart is a temple of the Holy Spirit, and thou shalt yet overcome.

For meditation: Without Christ we can do nothing (John 15: 5)—we have no reason for self-confidence. In Christ we can do all things (Philippians 4: 13)—there is no need for despair. Do you regard yourself as self-sufficient or as Christ-sufficient? See 2 Corinthians 12: 9.

The death of the Christian

"Thou shalt come to thy grave in a full age, like as a shock of corn cometh in his season." Job 5: 26
SUGGESTED FURTHER READING: 2 Corinthians 5: 1-8

Wait a little, beloved. In a few more years you and I shall be carried through the heavens on the wings of angels. When I die, the angels approach. I am on the wings of cherubs. Oh, how they bear me up—how swiftly and yet how softly. I have left mortality with all its pains. Oh, how rapid is my flight! Just now I passed the morning star. Far behind me now the planets shine. Oh, how swiftly do I fly, and how sweetly! Cherubs! What sweet flight is yours, and what kind arms are these I lean upon. And on my way you kiss me with the kisses of love and affection. You call me brother. Cherubs; am I your brother? I who just now was captive in a tenement of clay—am I your brother? "Yes!" they say. Oh, hark, I hear music strangely harmonious! What sweet sounds come to my ears! I am nearing Paradise. Do not spirits approach with songs of joy? "Yes!" they say. And before they can answer, behold they come—a glorious convoy! I catch a sight of them as they are holding a great review at the gates of Paradise. And there is the golden gate. I enter in; and I see my blessed Lord. I can tell you no more. All else were things unlawful for flesh to utter. My Lord! I am with thee—plunged into thee—lost in thee just as a drop is swallowed in the ocean—as one single tint is lost in the glorious rainbow! Am I lost in thee, thou glorious Jesus? And is my bliss consummated? Is the wedding-day come at last? Have I really put on the marriage garments? And am I thine? Yes! I am.

FOR MEDITATION: Are you looking forward to this time (Philippians 1: 23)? You can if you are a Christian. The unbeliever has another prospect ahead (Hebrews 10: 27). See the contrast in Luke 16: 22,23.

Man's weakness, and God's anointing

"I am this day weak, though anointed king; and these men the sons of Zeruiah be too hard for me." 2 Samuel 3: 39
SUGGESTED FURTHER READING: 1 Kings 3: 3-9

David had been an adventurer in the cave, so long that he had grown used to it, and you never find him saying when he hid himself in Engedi, "I am this day weak." No; after the first season of bitterness I believe he came to love Adullam's dreary shelter; and the bleak mountains were dear to him. Now he has come into a new place, nations are at his feet, men bow before him. It is a new position, and he says "I am this day weak, though anointed king." Whenever you make a change in life; whenever God calls you to another set of duties, you will surely find out what perhaps you do not now believe—that you are weak, though anointed king. Here, too, David had come into new temptations. The arrows had been shot at him before, from one direction alone, now the storm ceases on one side, and begins on the other. If men knew that the storm would always come to one side of the house they would repair and strengthen it, and then they would not fear the blast; but if suddenly it whirled round and took the other corner, how would they be prepared for that? Take care, Christian men and women, how you change your position; for often it is a change for the worse. The arrows may not fly on the right, but they will meet you on the left, and perhaps that may be your weakest side, and there you will be smitten in the tenderest part. David had now no more the temptations which beset a venturer, but those which cluster thick around the throne; for where there is the honey of royalty, there will surely be the wasps of temptations. High places and God's praise do seldom agree; a full cup is not easily carried without spilling, and he that stands on a pinnacle needs a clear head and much grace.

FOR MEDITATION: Change may be what we desired or totally did not want; new circumstances may make us feel humble or proud. Always remember your weakness and God's strength, which is the answer to the honest "I am" of man (Exodus 4: 10-12; Judges 6: 14-16; Jeremiah 1: 6-8; Romans 7: 24,25; 1 Corinthians 15: 9,10; 2 Corinthians 12: 9,10).

SERMON NO. 334

Paul's desire to depart

"Having a desire to depart, and to be with Christ, which is far better."
Philippians 1: 23
SUGGESTED FURTHER READING: Romans 8: 14-30

Here we are like Israel in the wilderness, who had but one cluster from Eschol. There we shall be in the vineyard. Here we have the manna falling small, like coriander seed, but there shall we eat the bread of heaven and the old corn of the kingdom. We have sometimes on earth, lusts, ungratified desires, that lack satisfaction; but there the lust shall be slain and the desire shall be satisfied. There shall be nothing we can want; every power shall find the sweetest employment in that eternal world of joy. There will be a full and lasting fruition of Christ, and last of all upon this point there shall be a sharing with Christ in his glory, and that for ever. "We shall see him," yes, and let us have the next sentence, and "shall be like him when we shall see him as he is." Oh Christian, anticipate heaven for within a very short time thou shalt be rid of all thy trials and thy troubles; thine aching head shall be encircled with a crown of glory; thy poor panting heart shall find its rest and shall be satisfied with fulness as it beats upon the breast of Christ. Thy hands that now toil shall know no harder labour than harp-strings can afford. Thine eyes now filled with tears shall weep no longer. Thou shalt gaze in ineffable rapture upon the splendour of him who sits upon the throne. Nay, more, upon his throne shalt thou sit. He is King of kings, but thou shalt reign with him. He is a priest after the order of Melchisedec, but thou shalt be a priest with him. Oh rejoice! The triumph of his glory shall be shared by thee; his crown, his joy, his paradise, these shall be thine, and thou shalt be co-heir with him who is the heir of all things.

FOR MEDITATION: Being with Christ must be far better, because we will then be with Christ who is far better. God has prepared something far better for the believer (Hebrews 11: 40).

SERMON NO. 274

The fatherhood of God

"Our Father which art in heaven." Matthew 6: 9
SUGGESTED FURTHER READING: Luke 11: 1-13

A child, even though he is erring, always expects his father will hear what he has to say. "Lord, if I call thee King thou wilt say, "Thou art a rebellious subject; get thee gone." If I call thee Judge thou wilt say, "Be still, or out of thine own mouth will I condemn thee." If I call thee Creator thou wilt say unto me, "It repenteth me that I made man upon the earth." If I call thee my Preserver thou wilt say unto me, "I have preserved thee, but thou hast rebelled against me." But if I call thee Father, all my sinfulness doth not invalidate my claim. If thou be my Father, then thou lovest me; if I be thy child, then thou wilt regard me, and poor though my language be, thou wilt not despise it." If a child were called upon to speak in the presence of a number of persons, how very much alarmed he would be lest he should not use right language. I may sometimes feel concerned when I have to address a mighty audience, lest I should not select choice words, full well knowing that if I were to preach as I never shall, like the mightiest of orators, I should always have enough of carping critics to rail at me. But if I had my Father here, and if you could all stand in the relationship of father to me, I should not be very particular what language I used. When I talk to my Father I am not afraid he will misunderstand me; if I put my words a little out of place he understands my meaning somehow. When we are little children we only prattle; still our father understands us.

FOR MEDITATION: The Father always heard the Lord Jesus Christ (John 11: 41,42); by the working of the Holy Spirit he can understand us even when we cannot understand ourselves (Romans 8: 26,27). Never be afraid to go to him in prayer because words fail you.

SERMON NO. 213

The condescension of Christ

"For ye know the grace of our Lord Jesus Christ, that, though he was rich, yet for your sakes he became poor, that ye through his poverty might be rich." 2 Corinthians 8: 9
SUGGESTED FURTHER READING: Mark 15: 16-39

Our Lord Jesus might have said in all his sorrows, "I have known better days than these." When he was tempted of the devil in the wilderness, it must have been hard for him to have restrained himself from dashing the devil into pieces. If I had been the Son of God, feeling as I do now, if that devil had tempted me I should have dashed him into the nethermost hell, in the twinkling of an eye! And then conceive the patience our Lord must have had, standing on the pinnacle of the temple, when the devil said, "Fall down and worship me." He would not touch him, the vile deceiver, but let him do what he pleased. Oh! What might of misery and love there must have been in the Saviour's heart when he was spat upon by the men he had created; when the eyes he himself had filled with vision, looked on him with scorn, and when the tongues, to which he himself had given utterance, hissed and blasphemed him! Oh, my friends, if the Saviour had felt as we do, and I doubt not he did feel in some measure as we do—only by great patience he curbed himself—he might have swept them all away; and, as they said, he might have come down from the cross, and delivered himself, and destroyed them utterly. It was mighty patience that could bear to tread this world beneath his feet, and not to crush it, when it so ill-treated its Redeemer. You marvel at the patience which restrained him; you marvel also at the poverty he must have felt, the poverty of spirit, when they rebuked him and he reviled them not again; when they scoffed at him, and yet he said, "Father, forgive them, for they know not what they do." He had seen brighter days; that made his misery more bitter, and his poverty more poor.

FOR MEDITATION: In the garden Jesus could have used his power to call twelve legions of angels to his rescue (Matthew 26: 53), but instead he employed it to heal the ear of one of his enemies (Luke 22: 51). On the cross he could have used his power to save himself, but instead he continued to employ it to save others—his enemies, including us (Romans 5: 10).

SERMON NO. 151

An appeal to sinners

"This man receiveth sinners." Luke 15: 2
SUGGESTED FURTHER READING: Ephesians 1: 3-8

Allow us just to amplify that word: "this man **receiveth** sinners." Now, by that we understand that he receives sinners to all the benefits which he has purchased for them. If there be a fountain, he receives sinners to wash them in it; if there be medicine for the soul, he receives sinners to heal their diseases; if there be a house for the sick, an hospital, a home for the dying, he receives such into that retreat of mercy. All that he has of love, all that he has of mercy, all that he has of atonement, all that he has of sanctification, all that he has of righteousness—to all these he receives the sinner. Yea, more; not content with taking him to his house, he receives him to his heart. He takes the black and filthy sinner, and having washed him—"There," he says, "thou art my beloved; my desire is towards thee." And to consummate the whole, at last he receives the saints to heaven. Saints, I said, but I meant those who were sinners, for none can be saints truly, but those who once were sinners, and have been washed in the blood of Christ, and made white through the sacrifice of the lamb. Observe it then, beloved, that in receiving sinners we mean the whole of salvation; and this word in my text, "Christ **receiveth** sinners," grasps in the whole of the covenant. He receives them to the joys of paradise, to the bliss of the beatified, to the songs of the glorified, to an eternity of happiness for ever. "This man receiveth sinners;" and I dwell with special emphasis on this point,—he receives none else. He will have none else to be saved but those who know themselves to be sinners.

FOR MEDITATION: Contrast whom Christ receives with all that they receive in him in return (Luke 15: 20-24). Are you one of them?

Adoption

"Having predestinated us unto the adoption of children by Jesus Christ to himself, according to the good pleasure of his will." Ephesians 1: 5
SUGGESTED FURTHER READING: Romans 9: 10-24

It is at once a doctrine of Scripture and of common sense, that whatever God does in time he predestined to do in eternity. Some men find fault with divine predestination, and challenge the justice of eternal decrees. Now, if they will please remember that predestination is the counterpart of history, as an architectural plan, the carrying out of which we read in the facts that happen, they may perhaps obtain a slight clue to the unreasonableness of their hostility. I never heard any one among professors wantonly and wilfully find fault with God's dealings, yet I have heard some who would even dare to call in question the equity of his counsels. If the thing itself be right, it must be right that God intended to do the thing; if you find no fault with facts, as you see them in providence, you have no grounds to complain of decrees, as you find them in predestination, for the decrees and the facts are just the counterpart one of the other. Have you any reason to find fault with God, that he has been pleased to save you, and save me? Then why should you find fault because Scripture says he pre-determined that he would save us? I cannot see, if the fact itself is agreeable, why the decree should be objectionable. I can see no reason why you should find fault with God's foreordination, if you do not find fault with what does actually happen as the effect of it. Let a man but agree to acknowledge an act of providence, and I want to know how he can, except he runs in the very teeth of providence, find any fault with the predestination or intention that God made concerning that providence.

FOR MEDITATION: Some talk as if the doctrine of predestination is the enemy of the Christian. Scripture lists it as one of the "all things" that work together for good to them that love God and which prove that God is for us (Romans 8: 28-31).

Storming the battlements

"Go ye up upon her walls, and destroy; but make not a full end; take away her battlements; for they are not the Lord's." Jeremiah 5: 10
SUGGESTED FURTHER READING: Galatians 5: 25-6: 5

We sometimes trust too much in evidences and good works. Ralph Erskine did not say amiss when he remarked, "I have got more hurt by my good works than my bad ones." That seems something like Antinomianism, but it is true; we find it so by experience. "My bad works," said Erskine, "Always drove me to the Saviour for mercy; my good works often kept me from him, and I began to trust in myself." Is it not so with us? We often get a pleasing opinion of ourselves; we are preaching so many times a week; we attend so many prayer meetings; we are doing good in the Sabbath-school; we are valuable deacons; important members of the church; we are giving away so much in charity; and we say, "Surely I am a child of God—I must be. I am an heir of heaven. Look at me! See what robes I wear. Have I not indeed a right-eousness about me that proves me to be a child of God?" Then we begin to trust in ourselves, and say, "Surely I cannot be moved; my mountain stands firm and fast." Do you know what is the usual rule of heaven when we boast? Why the command is given to the foe—"Go up against him; take away his battlements; for they are not the Lord's." And what is the consequence? Why, perhaps God suffers us to fall into sin, and down goes self-sufficiency. Many a Christian owes his falls to a presumptuous confidence in his graces. I conceive that outward sin is not more abhorred by our God than this most wicked sin of reliance on ourselves. May none of you ever learn your own weakness by reading a black book of your own backslidings.

FOR MEDITATION: If pride and boasting are listed as sins of the unbeliever (Romans 1: 30; 2 Timothy 3: 2), they are just as much sins when the believer falls into them. Our good works should lead others to glorify God (Matthew 5: 16) and should surely have the same effect upon us.

A single eye and simple faith

"The light of the body is the eye: if therefore thine eye be single, thy whole body shall be full of light. But if thine eye be evil, thy whole body shall be full of darkness." Matthew 6: 22,23
SUGGESTED FURTHER READING: Philippians 3: 17-21

God will say to thee, "Take no thought for the morrow, be careful for nothing;" Mammon will say to thee, "Look ahead, be careful for everything;" and when God says to thee, "Give of thy substance to the poor;" Mammon will say, "Hold it tight, it is that giving that spoils everything;" and when God will say unto thee, "Set not thy affections on the things of earth;" Mammon will say, "Get money, get money, get it anyhow;" and when God saith, "Be upright;" Mammon will say, "Cheat thy own father if thou canst win by it." Mammon and God are at such extreme ends of the earth and so desperately opposed, that I trust, Christian, thou art not such a fool, as to attempt to serve them both. If thou dost thou hast the worldling's eye, and thou art a worldling thyself. Remember, too, if thou triest to do this we may suspect thee of having the hypocrite's eye. As Matthew Henry says, "The hypocrite is like the waterman; he pulls this way, but he looks that. He pretends to look to heaven, but he pulls towards his own interest. He says, 'he looks to Christ,' but he is always pulling towards his own private advantage. The true Christian, however, is like a traveller; he looks to the goal and then he walks straight on to it; he goes the way he is looking." Be then not like the hypocrite, who hath this double eye, looking one way and going the other. An old Puritan said, "A hypocrite is like the hawk; the hawk flies upward, but he always keeps his eye down on the prey; let him get up as high as he will, he is always looking on the ground. Whereas, the Christian is like the lark, he turns his eye up to heaven, and as he mounts and sings he looks upward and he mounts upward."

FOR MEDITATION: Not looking where you ought to be going can have disastrous consequences (Luke 6: 39-42).

SERMON NO. 335

Who can tell?

"Who can tell if God will turn and repent, and turn away from his fierce anger, that we perish not?" Jonah 3: 9
SUGGESTED FURTHER READING: Psalm 39

I remember many who have passed from the land of the living and have gone to another world—and some how suddenly, how rapidly! I have been startled at it often myself. I have seen some here on the Sabbath, and by the Tuesday or by the Thursday the message has come, "On what day can you bury such and such a one?" "Bury her!" "Yes, sir, bury her, she is gone;" and I have said, "How strange it seems that she should be dead who so lately was living in our midst!" Forty days is a long lease compared with that which you have any reason to conclude that God has bestowed on you. But what if it were forty years, how short a time even then. If you will but look with the eye of wisdom, how rapidly our years revolve. Are you not startled even now to see the withered leaf in your path? It was but yesterday that the fresh green buds were seen. It seems but a month ago since first we saw the wheat starting up from the ground, and now the harvest is over and gone and many of the birds have disappeared and the tints of autumn are succeeding the verdure of summer. Years seem but months now and months but days, and days pass so rapidly that they flit like shadows before us. O! men and women, if we could but measure life it is but a span, and in a time how short, how brief, every one of us must appear before his God. The shortness of time should help to arouse us.

FOR MEDITATION: Time seems to speed up the older we get! In contrast the unbeliever will discover in eternity that time has ground to a terrible halt.

SERMON NO. 275

His name—Wonderful

"His name shall be called Wonderful." Isaiah 9: 6
SUGGESTED FURTHER READING: Luke 1: 26-35

It is just the simple name that he deserves. They that know him best will say that the word does not overstrain his merits, but rather falls infinitely short of his glorious deserving. His name is called Wonderful. And mark, it does not merely say, that God has given him the name of Wonderful—though that is implied; but "his name shall be **called**" so. It **shall** be; it is at this time called Wonderful by all his believing people, and it shall be. As long as the moon endures, there shall be found men, and angels, and glorified spirits, who shall always call him by his right name. "His name shall be called Wonderful." I find that this name may bear two or three interpretations. The word is sometimes in Scripture translated "marvellous." Jesus Christ may be called marvellous; and a learned German interpreter says, that without doubt, the meaning of miraculous is also wrapt up in it. Christ is the marvel of marvels, the miracle of miracles. "His name shall be called Miraculous," for he is more than a man, he is God's highest miracle. "Great is the mystery of godliness; God was manifest in the flesh." It may also mean separated, or distinguished. And Jesus Christ may well be called this; for as Saul was distinguished from all men, being head and shoulders taller than they, so is Christ distinguished above all men; he is anointed with the oil of gladness above his fellows, and in his character, and in his acts, he is infinitely separated from all comparison with any of the sons of men. "Thou art fairer than the children of men; grace is poured into thy lips." He is "the chief among ten thousand and altogether lovely." "His name shall be called the Separated One," the distinguished one, the noble one, set apart from the common race of mankind.

FOR MEDITATION: It is not possible to exaggerate when we speak of the Lord Jesus Christ—the one who is to be called Saviour, Son and Sinless (Luke 1: 31-35)—no less than "God with us" (Matthew 1: 21-23).

Things that accompany salvation

"Things that accompany salvation." Hebrews 6: 9
SUGGESTED FURTHER READING: 1 Thessalonians 5: 8-11

The "things that accompany salvation" make a glorious march in the forefront of it— from election down to these precious opening buds of virtue in the sinner's heart. What a godly array! Sure the angels do sometimes fly along in admiration, and see this long array that heralds salvation to the heart. And now comes the precious casket set with gems and jewels. It is of God-like workmanship; no hammer was ever lifted on it; it was smitten out and fashioned upon the anvil of eternal might, and cast in the mould of everlasting wisdom; but no human hand hath ever defiled it, and it is set with jewels so unutterably precious, that if heaven and earth were sold they could never buy another salvation! And who are those that are close around it? There are three sweet sisters that always have the custody of the treasure—you know them; their names are common in Scripture—Faith, Hope, and Love, the three divine sisters; these have salvation in their hearts and do carry it about with them in their loins. **Faith,** who lays hold on Christ, and trusts all in him; that ventures everything upon his blood and sacrifice, and has no other trust. **Hope,** that with beaming eye looks up to Jesus Christ in glory, and expects him soon to come: looks downward, and when she sees grim death in her way, expects that she shall pass through with victory. And thou sweet **Love,** the sweetest of the three; she, whose words are music and whose eyes are stars; Love, also looks to Christ and is enamoured by him; loves him in all his offices, adores his presence, reverences his words; and is prepared to bind her body to the stake and die for him, who bound his body to the cross to die for her.

FOR MEDITATION: Faith, Hope and Love are close companions of one another and of salvation (1 Corinthians 13:13; 1 Thessalonians 1:3; Hebrews 6: 9-12). How well are you acquainted with them?

Comfort proclaimed

"Comfort ye, comfort ye my people, saith your God." Isaiah 40: 1
SUGGESTED FURTHER READING: Acts 12: 6-11

To angels, first of all, I believe this command is addressed: "Comfort ye,
comfort ye my people." You often talk about the insinuations of the devil; I
frequently hear you bemoaning yourselves because you have been attacked
by Apollyon, and have had a hard struggle with Beelzebub; you have found it
hard to resist his desperate thrusts which he made against you; and you are
always talking about him. Allow me to remind you that there is another side
of that question, for if evil spirits assault us, doubtless good spirits guard us;
and if Satan can cast us down, doubtless it is true God gives his angels
charge over us, to keep us in all our ways, and they shall bear us up in their
hands lest at any time we dash our feet against a stone. It is my firm belief
that angels are often employed by God to throw into the hearts of his people
comforting thoughts. There are many sweet thoughts which we have by the
way, when we sit down, and when we rise up, which we scarcely dare
attribute immediately to the Holy Spirit, but which are still beautiful and
calm, lovely, and fair, and consoling; and we attribute them to the ministry
of angels. Angels came and ministered unto Jesus, and I doubt not that they
minister unto us. Few of us have enough belief in the existence of spirits. I
like that saying of Milton's, "Millions of spiritual creatures walk this earth,
both when we sleep and when we wake." And if our minds were opened, if
our ears were attentive, we might hold fellowship with spirits that flit
through the air every moment. Around the death-bed of saints, angels
hover; by the side of every struggling warrior for Christ the angels stand.

FOR MEDITATION: The verses Spurgeon goes on to quote—Psalm 34: 7 and
Hebrews 1: 14.
Do you ever thank God for the ministry of his angels?

SERMON NO. 221

Repentance unto life

"Then hath God also to the Gentiles granted repentance unto life."
Acts 11: 18
SUGGESTED FURTHER READING: Luke 3: 1-14

Can they be sincerely penitent, and then go and transgress again immediately, in the same way as they did before? How can we believe you if you transgress again and again, and do not forsake your sin? We know a tree by its fruit; and you who are penitent will bring forth works of repentance. I have often thought it was a very beautiful instance, showing the power of penitence which a pious minister once related. He had been preaching on penitence, and had in the course of his sermon spoken of the sin of stealing. On his way home a labourer came alongside of him, and the minister observed that he had something under his smock-frock. He told him he need not accompany him farther; but the man persisted. At last he said, "I have a spade under my arm which I stole up at that farm; I heard you preaching about the sin of stealing, and I must go and put it there again." That was sincere penitence which caused him to go back and replace the stolen article. It was like those South Sea Islanders, of whom we read, who stole the missionaries' articles of apparel and furniture, and everything out of their houses; but when they were savingly converted they brought them all back. But many of you say you repent, yet nothing comes of it; it is not worth the snap of the finger. People sincerely repent, they say, that they should have committed a robbery, or that they have kept a gambling-house; but they are very careful that all the proceeds shall be laid out to their hearts' best comfort. True repentance will yield "works meet for repentance;" it will be practical repentance. Yet farther. You may know whether your repentance is practical by this test. Does it last or does it not?

FOR MEDITATION: As with faith, repentance without works is dead. Jesus could tell that the repentance of Zacchaeus was practical and real (Luke 19: 8-9).

Struggles of conscience

"How many are mine iniquities and sins? Make me to know my transgression and my sin." Job 13: 23
SUGGESTED FURTHER READING: John 8: 21-47

"Tell me how I can feel the need of my Saviour." The first advice I give you is this: Particularise your sins. Do not say "I am a sinner;" it means nothing; everybody says that. But say this, "Am I a liar? Am I a thief? Am I a drunkard? Have I had impure thoughts? Have I committed unclean acts? Have I in my soul often rebelled against God? Am I often angry without a cause? Have I a bad temper? Am I covetous? Do I love this world better than the world to come? Do I neglect prayer? Do I neglect the great salvation?" Put these questions and you will soon convict yourself much more readily as being a sinner. I have heard of a hypocritical old monk who used to whine out, while he whipped his back as softly as he could, "Lord, I am a great sinner, as big a sinner as Judas;" and when someone said, "Yes that you are—you are like Judas, a vile old hypocrite," then he would say, "No I am not." Then he would go on again, "I am a great sinner." Some one would say, "You are a great sinner, you broke the first commandment;" and then he would say, "No I have not." Then when he would go on and say, "I am a great sinner," some one would say, "Yes, you have broken the second commandment," and he would say, "No I have not;" and the same with the third and the fourth, and so on right through. So it came to pass he had kept the whole ten according to his own account, and yet he went on crying he was a great sinner. The man was a hypocrite, for if he had not broken the commandments, how could he be a sinner at all? You will find it better not to dwell on your sins as a whole, but to pen them, count them over, and look at them individually, one by one.

FOR MEDITATION: Christ did not die for a theoretical concept of sin, but for actual sins committed by practising sinners (Matthew 1: 21; 26: 28; 1 Corinthians 15: 3; Galatians1: 4; Hebrews 1: 3; 9: 28; 1 Peter 2: 24; 1 John 2: 2; Revelation 1: 5).

SERMON NO. 336

The duty of remembering the poor

"Only they would that we should remember the poor; the same which I also was forward to do." Galatians 2: 10
SUGGESTED FURTHER READING: James 2: 1-17

If you do not help the one that you see has the greatest need, I am afraid the love of God dwelleth not in you. It is a duty we owe to the poor of the Lord's flock, and we reap many advantages we should not have if we had not to remember the poor. Now, allow me to press home this obligation: why should we remember the poor? I shall not urge it upon the ground of common philanthropy and charity; that were a too mean and low way of addressing Christian men, although even they perhaps might be benefited by it. I shall urge it in another way. "Remember the poor," because they are your Lord's brethren. What! Do you not feel, like David, that you would do anything for Jonathan's sake? And if he hath some poor sick son, some Mephibosheth, lame in his feet, wilt thou not seat him at thy table, or give him a maintenance, if thou canst, seeing that Jonathan's blood is in his veins? Remember, beloved, the blood of Jesus runs in the veins of poor saints; they are his relatives, they are his friends; and if that move thee not, remember, they are thy friends too. They are thy brethren if thou art a child of God; they are allied to thee; if they are sons of God, so art thou, and they are brethren of thine. What! Let thy brother starve? If thou canst, wilt thou not relieve thy brother's necessity, not shield him from the cold, not ward off hunger, not provide for his needs? Oh! I know thou lovest Jesus; I know thou lovest the friends of Jesus, and I know thou lovest thine own family; and, therefore, thou wilt love thy poor brethren, wilt thou not? I know thou wilt; thou wilt relieve them.

FOR MEDITATION: Do you discriminate against some of your brothers and sisters in Christ? Your heavenly Father doesn't (Galatians 3: 28; Ephesians 6: 9).

A divided heart

"Their heart is divided; now shall they be found faulty." Hosea 10: 2
SUGGESTED FURTHER READING: 1 Corinthians 1: 4-12

If we would provoke the anger of the Most High and bring down trying providences on the churches, we have nothing to do but to be divided in our hearts and all will be accomplished. If we wish that every vial may empty out its ill, and that every vessel may withhold its oil, we have but to cherish our bickerings till they become animosities; we have but to nurse our animosities till they become hatreds, and all the work will be fully completed. And if this be the case in the church at large, it is peculiarly true in those various sections of it which we now call Apostolic Churches. Oh, my brethren, the smallest church in the world is potent for good when it has but one heart and one soul; when pastor, elders, deacons, and members, are bound together by a threefold cord that cannot be broken. Then are they mighty against every attack. But however great their numbers, however enormous their wealth, however splendid may be the talents with which they are gifted, they are powerless for good the moment they become divided amongst themselves. Union is strength. Blessed is the army of the living God, in that day when it goes forth to battle with one mind, and when its soldiers as with the tramp of one man, in undivided march, go onwards towards the attack. But a curse awaits that church which runs to and fro and which, divided in itself, has lost the main stay of its strength with which it should batter against the enemy. Division cuts our bowstrings, snaps our spears, houghs our horses, and burns our chariots in the fire. We are undone the moment the link of love is snapped. Let this perfect bond be once cut in twain and we fall down, and our strength is departed. By union we live, and by disunion we expire.

FOR MEDITATION: Believers are not to try to create "unity" with those who preach another gospel, but we are urged to maintain the unity that already exists between true believers (Ephesians 4: 3; Philippians 1: 27). What would somebody have to report about your church (and your own contribution in it)?

His name—the Counsellor

"For unto us a child is born, unto us a son is given; and the government shall be upon his shoulder: and his name shall be called Wonderful, Counsellor." Isaiah 9: 6
SUGGESTED FURTHER READING: Proverbs 8 (which was read earlier in the same service)

Tried child of God, your daughter is sick; your gold has melted in the fire; you are sick yourself, and your heart is sad. Christ counsels you, and he says, "Cast thy burden upon the Lord, he will sustain thee; he will never suffer the righteous to be moved." Young man, you that are seeking to be great in this world, Christ counsels you this morning. "Seekest thou great things for thyself? Seek them not." I shall never forget my early years. I was ambitious; I was seeking to go to college, to leave my poor people in the wilderness that I might become something great; and as I was walking that text came with power to my heart; "Seekest thou great things for thyself? Seek them not." I suppose about forty pounds a year was the sum total of my income, and I was thinking how I should make both ends meet, and whether it would not be a great deal better for me to resign my charge and seek something for the bettering of myself, and so forth. But this text ran in my ears, "Seekest thou great things for thyself? Seek them not." "Lord," said I, "I will follow thy counsel and not my own devices;" and I have never had cause to regret it. Always take the Lord for your guide, and you shall never go amiss. Backslider! You that have a name to live, and are dead, or nearly dead, Christ gives you counsel. "I counsel thee to buy of me, gold tried in the fire and white raiment, that thou mayest be clothed." And sinner! You that are far from God, Christ gives you counsel. "Come unto me, all ye that are weary and heavy laden, and I will give you rest." Depend on it, it is loving counsel. Take it.

FOR MEDITATION: God has promised to guide his children and to keep an eye on them (Psalm 32: 8). His guidance has a sure foundation and a great advantage over the thoughts and intentions of men (Psalm 33: 10,11). We can seek his guidance right where we are; isn't it strange that we can so often go to him last of all?

The mysteries of the brazen serpent

"And as Moses lifted up the serpent in the wilderness, even so must the Son of man be lifted up: That whosoever believeth in him should not perish, but have eternal life." John 3: 14,15
SUGGESTED FURTHER READING: John 12: 20-36

Let each of us who are called to the solemn work of the ministry remember, that we are not called to lift up doctrine, or church governments, or particular denominations; our business is to lift up Christ Jesus and to preach him fully. There may be times when church government is to be discussed, and peculiar doctrines are to be vindicated. God forbid that we should silence any part of truth: but the main work of the ministry—its every day work—is just exhibiting Christ, and crying out to sinners, "Believe, believe, believe on him who is the Lamb of God that taketh away the sins of the world." And let it be remembered, that if the minister preaches Christ plainly, that is all he has to do; if with affection and prayer he preaches Christ fully, if there were never a soul saved—which I believe would be impossible—he would have done his work, and his Master would say, "Well done." I have gone away from this hall, after preaching upon various doctrines, and though many have complimented me, foolishly, I have said to myself, "I can but groan that I had such a subject at all." And at another time, when I have been faltering in my delivery, and committed a thousand blunders in my speech, I have gone away as happy as a prince, because I have said, "I did preach Christ." There was enough for sinners to be saved by; and if all the papers in the world should abuse me, and all the men in the world should say 'cry him down'; he will still live and still breathe as long as he feels in himself, "I have preached to sinners, and Christ has been preached to them, so as they could understand and lay hold on him and be saved."

FOR MEDITATION: "We would see Jesus" (John 12: 21) is not just something to say to the preacher, but something to pray for the preacher (Colossians 4: 3,4).

SERMON NO. 153

The great Supreme

"Ascribe ye greatness unto our God." Deuteronomy 32: 3
SUGGESTED FURTHER READING: 1 Corinthians 3: 1-9

In Protestant countries there is a very strong tendency to priestcraft still. Though we do not bow down and worship images, and do not professedly put our souls into the hands of priests, yet, I am sorry to say it, there is scarce a congregation that is free from that error of ascribing greatness to their minister. If souls are converted, how very prone we are to think there is something marvellous in the man; and if saints are fed and satisfied with marrow and fatness, how prone we are to suppose that the preacher has something about him by which these wondrous things are done; and if a revival takes place in any part of the vineyard, it matters not in what denomination, there is an aptness in the human mind to ascribe some part of the glory and the praise to the mere human agency. Oh, beloved, I am sure that every right-minded minister will scorn the thought. We are but your servants for Christ's sake. We speak to you, as God helps us, what we believe to be God's truth; but ascribe not to us any honour or any glory. If a soul is saved, God from first to last has done it. If your souls are fed, thank the Master; be respectful and grateful to the servant as you will be, but most of all thank him who puts the word into the mouths of his servants, and who applies it to your heart. "Oh, down with priestcraft!" even I myself must down with it. "Down with it!" I cry. If I myself like Samson fall beneath its roof, let me fall myself and be crushed, well content in having pulled down or contributed to remove one solitary brick in that colossal house of Satan. Take care, friends, that you put no honour upon any man that you ought to have ascribed unto his Sovereign. "Ascribe ye greatness unto our God."

FOR MEDITATION: Why are you using these daily readings? We should thank God for Spurgeon, but many go too far and venerate Spurgeon himself. He reminds us that he too was a man (Acts 10: 26) and that the glory belongs not to him but to his and our God (Psalm 115: 1).

SERMON NO. 367

Declension from first love

"Nevertheless I have somewhat against thee, because thou hast left thy first love." Revelation 2: 4
SUGGESTED FURTHER READING: John 15: 9-14

There are some people who always live upon what they have been. I speak very plainly now. There is a brother in this church who may take it to himself; I hope he will. It is not very many years ago since he said to me, when I asked him why he did not do something—"Well, I have done my share; I used to do this, and I have done the other; I have done so and so." Oh, may the Lord deliver him, and all of us, from living on "has beens!" It will never do to say we have done a thing. Suppose, for a solitary moment, the world should say, "I have turned round; I will stand still." Let the sea say, "I have been ebbing and flowing these many years; I will ebb and flow no more." Let the sun say, "I have been shining, and I have been rising and setting for many days; I have done this enough to earn me a goodly name; I will stand still;" and let the moon wrap herself up in veils of darkness, and say, "I have illuminated many a night, and I have lighted many a weary traveller across the moors; I will shut up my lamp and be dark for ever." Brethren, when you and I cease to labour, let us cease to live. God has no intention to let us live a useless life. But mark this; when we leave our first works, there is no question about our having lost our first love; that is sure. If there be strength remaining, if there be still power mentally and physically, if we cease from our office, if we abstain from our labours, there is no solution of this question which an honest conscience will accept, except this, "Thou hast lost thy first love, and, therefore, thou hast neglected thy first works."

FOR MEDITATION: Past love is no substitute for present expressions of it (Philemon: 5-7,20). Present work is no guarantee that love cannot be lost in the future (Philemon: 24; 2 Timothy 4: 10).

Love to Jesus

"O thou whom my soul loveth." Solomon's Song 1: 7
SUGGESTED FURTHER READING: Psalm 103

The Christian, if he had no Christ to love, must die, for his heart has become Christ's. And so if Christ were gone, love could not be; then his heart would be gone too, and a man without a heart is dead. The heart, is it not the vital principle of the body? And love, is it not the vital principle of the soul? Yet there are some who profess to love the Master, but only walk with him by fits, and then go abroad like Dinah into the tents of the Shechemites. Oh, take heed, ye professors, who seek to have two husbands; my Master will never be a part-husband. He is not such a one as to have half of your heart. My Master, though he be full of compassion and very tender, hath too noble a spirit to allow himself to be half-proprietor of any kingdom. Canute, the Danish king, might divide England with Edmund the Ironside, because he could not win the whole country, but my Lord will have every inch of thee, or none. He will reign in thee from one end of the isle of man to the other, or else he will not put a foot upon the soil of thy heart. He was never part-proprietor in a heart, and he will not stoop to such a thing now. What saith the old Puritan? "A heart is so little a thing, that it is scarce enough for a sparrow's breakfast, and ye say it be too great a thing for Christ to have it all." No, give him the whole. It is but little when thou weighest his merit, and very small when measured with his loveliness. Give him all. Let thy united heart, thy undivided affection be constantly, every hour, given up to him.

FOR MEDITATION: The members of the Godhead are the only joint-owners of the Christian. May God teach us his way—that our hearts may be united and wholly for him (Psalm 86: 11-12).

SERMON NO. 338

The remembrance of Christ

"This do in remembrance of me." 1 Corinthians 11: 24
SUGGESTED FURTHER READING: Luke 22: 14-20

Our Saviour was wiser than all our teachers, and his remembrancers are true and real aids to memory. His love tokens have an unmistakable language, and they sweetly win our attention. Behold the whole mystery of the Lord's table. It is bread and wine which are lively emblems of the body and blood of Jesus. The power to excite remembrance consists in the appeal thus made to the senses. Here the eye, the hand, the mouth find joyful work. The bread is tasted, and entering within, works upon the sense of taste, which is one of the most powerful. The wine is sipped—the act is palpable; we know that we are drinking, and thus the senses, which are usually clogs to the soul, become wings to lift the mind in contemplation. Again, much of the influence of this ordinance is found in its simplicity. How beautifully simple the ceremony is—bread broken and wine poured out. There is no calling that thing a chalice, that thing a paten, and that a host. Here is nothing to burden the memory—here is the simple bread and wine. He must have no memory at all who cannot remember that he has eaten bread, and that he has been drinking wine. Note again, the deep relevance of these signs—how full they are of meaning. Bread broken—so was your Saviour broken. Bread to be eaten—so his flesh is meat indeed. Wine poured out, the pressed juice of the grape—so was your Saviour crushed under the foot of divine justice: his blood is your sweetest wine. Wine to cheer your heart—so does the blood of Jesus. Wine to strengthen and invigorate you—so does the blood of the mighty sacrifice.

FOR MEDITATION: We forget him when we absent ourselves from his table without good cause; we forget him when we attend the Communion Service as an optional add-on. "Remember Jesus Christ" (2 Timothy 2: 8).

The blood of the everlasting covenant

"The blood of the everlasting covenant." Hebrews 13: 20
SUGGESTED FURTHER READING: Hebrews 9: 15-26

With regard to Christ, his precious blood shed in Gethsemane, in Gabbatha and Golgotha, is the fulfilment of the covenant. By this blood sin is cancelled; by Jesus' agonies justice is satisfied; by his death the law is honoured; and by that precious blood in all its mediatorial efficacy, and in all its cleansing power, Christ fulfils all that he stipulated to do on behalf of his people towards God. Oh, believer, look to the blood of Christ, and remember that there is Christ's part of the covenant carried out. And now, there remains nothing to be fulfilled but God's part, there is nothing for thee to do; Jesus has done it all; there is nothing for free will to supply; Christ has done everything that God can demand. The blood is the fulfilment of the debtor's side of the covenant, and now God becomes bound by his own solemn oath to show grace and mercy to all whom Christ has redeemed by his blood. With regard to the blood in another respect, it is to God the Father the bond of the covenant. When I see Christ dying on the cross, I see the everlasting God from that time, if I may use the term of him who ever must be free, bound by his own oath and covenant to carry out every stipulation. Does the covenant say, "A new heart will I give you, and a right spirit will I put within you?" It must be done, for Jesus died, and Jesus' death is the seal of the covenant. Does it say, "I will sprinkle pure water upon you and you shall be clean; from all your iniquities will I cleanse you?" Then it must be done, for Christ has fulfilled his part.

FOR MEDITATION: The very character of God doubles the reliability of his purposes and promises (Hebrews 6: 13-18).

SERMON NO. 277

Confession and absolution

"And the publican, standing afar off, would not lift up so much as his eyes unto heaven, but smote upon his breast, saying, God be merciful to me a sinner." Luke 18: 13
SUGGESTED FURTHER READING: 1 John 1: 5-2: 2

The Greek explains more to us than the English does; and the original word here might be translated—"God be propitiated to me a sinner." There is in the Greek word a distinct reference to the doctrine of atonement. It is not the Unitarian's prayer—"God be merciful to me;" it is more than that—it is the Christian's prayer, "God be propitiated towards me, a sinner." There is, I repeat it, a distinct appeal to the atonement and the mercy-seat in this short prayer. Friends, if we would come before God with our confessions we must take care that we plead the blood of Christ. There is no hope for a poor sinner apart from the cross of Jesus. We may cry, "God be merciful to me," but the prayer can never be answered apart from the victim offered, the Lamb slain from before the foundation of the world. When thou hast thine eye upon the mercy-seat, take care to have thine eye upon the cross too. Remember that the cross is, after all, the mercy-seat; that mercy never was enthroned, until she hung upon the cross crowned with thorns. If thou wouldst find pardon, go to dark Gethsemane, and see thy Redeemer sweating blood in deep anguish. If thou wouldst have peace of conscience, go to Gabbatha, the pavement, and see thy Saviour's back flooded with a stream of blood. If thou wouldst have the last best rest to thy conscience, go to Golgotha; see the murdered victim as he hangs upon the cross, with hands and feet and side all pierced, as every wound is gaping wide with misery extreme. There can be no hope for mercy apart from the victim offered—even Jesus Christ the Son of God. Oh, come; let us one and all approach the mercy-seat, and plead the blood.

FOR MEDITATION: Confession of sins is a totally useless practice unless we go straight to God, the only one who can forgive us, pleading Christ crucified, the only valid reason for us to be forgiven. But when we come in God's way, we can come to him confidently (Hebrews 10: 19-22).

SERMON NO. 216

Fear not

"Fear not, thou worm Jacob, and ye men of Israel; I will help thee, saith the Lord, and thy redeemer, the Holy One of Israel." Isaiah 41: 14

SUGGESTED FURTHER READING: Psalm 8

Behold the heavens, the work of God's fingers; behold the sun guided in his daily march; go ye forth at midnight, and behold the heavens, consider the stars and the moon; look upon these works of God's hands, and if ye be men of sense and your souls are attuned to the high music of the spheres, ye will say, "What is man that thou art mindful of him, and the son of man that thou visitest him?" My God! When I survey the boundless fields of heaven, and see those ponderous orbs rolling therein—when I consider how vast are thy dominions—so wide that an angel's wing might flap to all eternity and never reach a boundary—I marvel that thou shouldst look on insects so obscure as man. I have taken the microscope and seen the insect upon the leaf, and I have called him small. I will not call him so again; compared with me he is great, if I put myself into comparison with God. I am so little, that I shrink into nothingness when I behold the almightiness of Jehovah—so little, that the difference between the microscopic creature and man dwindles into nothing, when compared with the infinite chasm between God and man. Let the mind rove upon the great doctrines of the Godhead; consider the existence of God from before the foundations of the world; behold him who is, and was, and is to come, the Almighty; let the soul comprehend as much as it can of the Infinite, and grasp as much as possible of the Eternal, and I am sure if you have minds at all, they will shrink with awe. The tall archangel bows himself before his Master's throne, and we shall cast ourselves into the lowest dust when we feel what base nothings, what insignificant specks we are, when compared with our all-adorable Creator.

FOR MEDITATION: Nothing is too big for God (Proverbs 30: 4); nothing is too small for God (Proverbs 30: 24-28). What is man? Both weak and wicked (Proverbs 30: 2,3,32). But God still cares (Proverbs 30: 5).

SERMON NO. 156

Thy Redeemer

"And thy redeemer, the Holy One of Israel." Isaiah 41: 14
SUGGESTED FURTHER READING: Psalm 118: 5-14

Hear Jehovah, the everlasting Father, saying, "I will help thee." "Mine are the ages: before the ages began, when there were no worlds, when nothing had been created, from everlasting I am thy God. I am the God of election, the God of the decree, the God of the covenant; by my strength I did set fast the mountains; by my skill I laid the pillars of the earth, and the beams of the firmament of heaven; I spread out the skies as a curtain, and as a tent for man to dwell in; I the Lord made all these things. I will help thee." Then comes Jehovah the Son. "And I also, am thy Redeemer, I am eternal; my name is wisdom. I was with God, when there were no depths, before he had digged the rivers, I was there as one brought up with him. I am Jesus, the God of ages; I am Jesus, the man of sorrows: 'I am he that liveth and was dead, I am alive for evermore.' I am the High Priest of thy profession, the Intercessor before the throne, the Representative of my people. I have power with God. I will help thee." Poor worm, thy Redeemer vows to help thee; by his bleeding hands he covenants to give thee aid. And then in comes the Holy Spirit. "And I," saith the Spirit, "am also God—not an influence, but a person—I, eternal and everlasting co-existent with the Father and the Son—I, who did brood over chaos, when as yet the world was not brought into form and fashion, and did sow the earth with the seeds of life when I did brood over it,—I, that brought again from the dead your Lord Jesus Christ, the Shepherd of the sheep, I who am the Eternal Spirit, by whose power the Lord Jesus did arise from the bondage of his tomb—I, by whom souls are quickened, by whom the elect are called out of darkness into light—I, who have power to maintain my children and preserve them to the end—I will help thee."

FOR MEDITATION: 2 Corinthians 13: 14: what a mighty benediction!

SERMON NO. 157

Fast-day service

"Hear ye the rod, and who hath appointed it." Micah 6: 9
SUGGESTED FURTHER READING: Nehemiah 1

This world is not the place of punishment for sin; not **the** place; it may sometimes be a place, but not usually. It is very customary among religious people, to talk of every accident which happens to men in the indulgence of sin, as if it were a judgment. The upsetting of a boat upon a river on a Sunday is assuredly understood to be a judgment for the sin of Sabbath-breaking. In the accidental fall of a house, in which persons were engaged in any unlawful occupation, the inference is at once drawn that the house fell because they were wicked. Now, however some religionists may hope to impress the people by such childish stories as those; I, for one, renounce them all. I believe what my Master says is true, when he declared, concerning the men upon whom the tower of Siloam fell, that they were not sinners above all the sinners that were upon the face of the earth. They were sinners; there is no doubt about it; but the falling of the wall was not occasioned by their sin, nor was their premature death the consequence of their excessive wickedness. Let me, however, guard this declaration, for there are many who carry this doctrine to an extreme. Because God does not usually visit each particular offence in this life upon the transgressor, men are apt to deny altogether the doctrine of judgments. But here they are mistaken. I feel persuaded that there are such things as national judgments, national chastisements for national sins—great blows from the rod of God, which every wise man must acknowledge to be, either a punishment of sin committed, or a premonition to warn us to a sense of the consequences of sins, leading us by God's grace to humble ourselves, and repent of our sin.

FOR MEDITATION: Reflect and pray over the state of the nation and its standing before God (Proverbs 14: 34).

Conversion

"Brethren, if any of you do err from the truth, and one convert him; Let him know, that he which converteth the sinner from the error of his way shall save a soul from death, and shall hide a multitude of sins." James 5: 19: 20
SUGGESTED FURTHER READING: 2 Corinthians 2: 5-11

The poor backslider is often the most forgotten. A member of the church has disgraced his profession; the church excommunicated him, and he was accounted "a heathen man and a publican." I know of men of good standing in the gospel ministry, who, ten years ago, fell into sin; and that is thrown in our teeth to this very day. When you speak of them you are at once informed, "Why, ten years ago they did so-and-so." Brethren, Christian men ought to be ashamed of themselves for taking notice of such things so long afterwards. True, we may use more caution in our dealings; but to reproach a fallen brother for what he did so long ago, is contrary to the spirit of John, who went after Peter, three days after he had denied his Master with oaths and curses. Nowadays it is the fashion, if a man falls, to have nothing to do with him. Men say, "he is a bad fellow; we will not go after him." Beloved, suppose he is the worst; is not that the reason why you should go most after him? Suppose he never was a child of God—suppose he never knew the truth, is not that the greater reason why you should go after him? I do not understand your excessive pride, that won't let you go after the chief of sinners. The worse the case, the more is the reason why we should go. But suppose the man is a child of God, and you have cast him off—remember, he is your brother; he is one with Christ as much as you are; he is justified, he has the same righteousness that you have; and if, when he has sinned, you despise him, in that you despise him you despise his Master. Take heed! You also may be tempted, and may one day fall.

FOR MEDITATION: Discipline should not be lax or non-existent (1 Corinthians 5: 1-2). But it is possible to go to the other extreme and overdo it.

The sons of God

"The Spirit itself beareth witness with our spirit, that we are the children of God; And if children, then heirs; heirs of God, and joint heirs with Christ; if so be that we suffer with him, that we may also be glorified together." Romans 8: 16,17
SUGGESTED FURTHER READING: Ephesians 1: 11-23

The believer is to be the heir, I say, not merely of God's works, not simply of God's gifts, but of God himself. Do we not talk of his omnipotence?—his almightiness is ours. Do we not speak of his omniscience?—all his wisdom is engaged in our behalf. Do we not say that he is love?—that love belongs to us. Can we not glory in that he is full of immutability, and changes not?— that eternal unchangeablenesss is engaged for the defence of the people of God. All the attributes of divinity are the property of God's children—their inheritance is built upon them. He himself is ours. Oh what riches! If we could say this morning, that all the stars belong to us; if we could turn the telescope to the most remote of the fixed stars, and then could say with the pride of possession, so natural to man, "That star, a thousand times bigger than the sun, is mine. I am the king of that inheritance." If we could then sweep the telescope along the milky way, and see the millions upon millions of stars that lie clustered together, and cry, "All these are mine," yet these possessions were but a speck compared with that which is in the text. Heir of God! He to whom all these things are but as nothing, gives himself up to be the inheritance of his people. Note yet a little further concerning the special privilege of heirship,—we are joint heirs with Christ. That is, whatever Christ possesses, as heir of all things, belongs to us. Splendid must be the inheritance of Jesus Christ. Is he not very God of very God, Jehovah's only begotten Son, most high and glorious?

FOR MEDITATION: The prayers of our glorious joint heir regarding our glorious joint inheritance (John 17: 9,10,24).

Grieving the Holy Spirit

"And grieve not the holy Spirit of God, whereby ye are sealed unto the day of redemption." Ephesians 4: 30
SUGGESTED FURTHER READING: Isaiah 63: 7-19

The Spirit of God is in your heart, and it is very, very easy indeed to grieve him. Sin is as easy as it is wicked. You may grieve him by impure thoughts. He cannot bear sin. If you indulge in lascivious expressions, or even if you allow imagination to dote upon any lascivious act, or if your heart goes after covetousness, if you set your heart upon anything that is evil, the Spirit of God will be grieved, for thus I hear him speaking of himself. "I love this man, I want to have his heart, and yet he is entertaining these filthy lusts. His thoughts, instead of running after me, and after Christ, and after the Father, are running after the temptations that are in the world through lust." And then his Spirit is grieved. He sorrows in his soul because he knows what sorrow these things must bring to our souls. We grieve him yet more if we indulge in outward acts of sin. Then is he sometimes so grieved that he takes his flight for a season, for the dove will not dwell in our hearts if we take loathsome carrion in there. A cleanly being is the dove, and we must not strew the place which the dove frequents with filth and mire; if we do he will fly elsewhere. If we commit sin, if we openly bring disgrace upon our religion, if we tempt others to go into iniquity by our evil example, it is not long before the Holy Spirit will be grieved. Again, if we neglect prayer; if our closet door is cobwebbed; if we forget to read the Scriptures; if the leaves of our Bible are almost stuck together by neglect; if we never seek to do any good in the world; if we live merely for ourselves and not for Christ, then the Holy Spirit will be grieved.

FOR MEDITATION: If we are grieving the Spirit, it is absolutely impossible for us to obey the command to "be filled with the Spirit" (Ephesians 5: 18).

Self-examination

*"Examine yourselves, whether ye be in the faith; prove your own selves.
Know ye not your own selves, how that Jesus Christ is in you, except ye be
reprobates?"* 2 Corinthians 13: 5
SUGGESTED FURTHER READING: 1 Corinthians 11: 23-32

"Examine:" that is a **scholastic idea.** A boy has been to school a certain time,
and his master puts him through his paces—questions him, to see whether
he has made any progress,—whether he knows anything. Christian,
catechise your heart; question it, to see whether it has been growing in grace;
question it, to see if it knows anything of vital godliness or not. Examine it:
pass your heart through a stern examination as to what it does know and
what it does not know, by the teaching of the Holy Spirit. Again: it is a
military idea. "Examine yourselves," or renew yourselves. Go through the
rank and file of your actions, and examine all your motives. Just as the
captain on review-day is not content with merely surveying the men from a
distance, but must look at all their equipment, so look well to yourselves;
examine yourselves with the most scrupulous care. And once again, this is a
legal idea. "Examine yourselves." You have seen the witness in the box,
when the lawyer has been examining him, or, as we have it, cross-examining
him. Now, mark: never was there a rogue less trustworthy or more deceitful
than your own heart, and as when you are cross-examining a dishonest
person—you set traps for him to try and find him out in a lie, so do with your
own heart. Question it backward and forward, this way and that way; for if
there be a loophole for escape, if there be any pretence for self-deception,
rest assured your treacherous heart will be ready enough to avail itself of it.
And yet once more: this is a **traveller's idea.** I find in the original Greek, it has
this meaning: "Go right through yourselves."

FOR MEDITATION: Is self-examination a foreign concept to you? It should be
done as least as regularly as we observe the Lord's Supper (1 Corinthians 11: 28);
God is able to assist us in our self-examination (Psalm 26: 2; 139: 23,24).

Instability

"Unstable as water, thou shalt not excel." Genesis 49: 4
Suggested further reading; 2 Peter 3: 14-18

Who are these unstable ones? When they were boys they could never complete a game; they must always be having something fresh; and now they are just as childish as when they were children. Look at them in doctrine: you never know where to find them. You meet them one day, and they are very full of some super doctrine; they have been to some strong Calvinist place, and nothing will suit them except the very highest doctrine, and that must be spiced with a little of the gall of bitterness, or they cannot think it is the genuine thing. Very likely next week they will be Arminians; they will give up all idea of a fixed fate, and talk of free-will, and man's responsibility like the most earnest Primitive Methodist. Then they steer another way. "Nothing is right but the Church of England. Is it not established by law? Ought not every Christian to go to his parish church?" Let them alone; they will be at the most schismatical shop in the metropolis before long. Or if they do not change their denomination they are always changing their minister. A new minister starts up; there is no one, since the apostles, like him; they take a seat and join the church; he is everything to them. In three months they have done with him; another minister rises up some distance off, and these people are not particular how far they walk; so they go to hear him. He is the great man of the age; he will see every man's candle out, and his will burn on. But a little trouble comes on the church, and they leave him. They have no attachment to anything; they are merely feathers in the wind, or corks on the wave.

FOR MEDITATION: Do you recognise yourself here? If not, guard your own stability carefully. But if you do, realise that we are not supposed to remain babes in Christ, but are to grow up (Ephesians 4: 14,15). Perhaps you are not sure whether Spurgeon is describing you; one question may help you decide—who has the rule over you? (Hebrews 13: 7,17).

Special thanksgiving to the Father

"Giving thanks unto the Father, which hath made us meet to be partakers of the inheritance of the saints in light: Who hath delivered us from the power of darkness, and hath translated us into the kingdom of his dear son." Colossians 1: 12,13
SUGGESTED FURTHER READING: Luke 11: 14-22

What an achievement was that, when, with their flocks and their herds, the whole host of Israel went out of Egypt, crossed the Jordan, and came into Canaan! My dear brethren, the whole of it was not equal to the achievement of God's powerful grace, when he brings one poor sinner out of the region of sin into the kingdom of holiness and peace. It was easier for God to bring Israel out of Egypt, to split the Red Sea, to make a highway through the pathless wilderness, to drop manna from heaven, to send the whirlwind to drive out the kings; it was easier for Omnipotence to do all this, than to translate a man from the power of darkness into the kingdom of his dear Son. This is the grandest achievement of Omnipotence. The sustenance of the whole universe, I do believe, is even less than this—the changing of a bad heart, the subduing of an iron will. But thanks be unto the Father, he has done all that for you and for me. He has brought us out of darkness; he has translated us, taken up the old tree that has struck its roots ever so deep— taken it up, blessed be God, roots and all, and planted it in a goodly soil. He had to cut the top off, it is true—the high branches of our pride; but the tree has grown better in the new soil than it ever did before. Who ever heard of moving so huge a plant as a man who has grown fifty years old in sin? Oh! What wonders hath our Father done for us!

FOR MEDITATION: "Our Father…Thy kingdom come" (Luke 11: 2). Pray for the spoiling of Satan, the salvation of sinners, the sanctification of saints, the second coming of the Sovereign.

SERMON NO. 319

Jacob and Esau

"Jacob have I loved, but Esau have I hated." Romans 9: 13
SUGGESTED FURTHER READING: Ezekiel 33: 11-20

My soul revolts at the idea of a doctrine that lays the blood of man's soul at God's door. I cannot conceive how any human mind, at least any Christian mind, can hold any such blasphemy as that. I delight to preach this blessed truth—salvation of God, from first to last—the Alpha and the Omega; but when I come to preach damnation, I say, damnation is of man, not of God; and if you perish, at your own hands must your blood be required. There is another passage. At the last great day, when all the world shall come before Jesus to be judged, have you noticed, when the righteous go on the right side, Jesus says, "Come, ye blessed of my Father,"—("of my Father," mark,)—"inherit the kingdom prepared"—(mark the next word)—"for **you**, from before the foundation of the world." What does he say to those on the left? "Depart, ye cursed." He does not say, "ye cursed of my Father," but, "ye cursed." And what else does he say? "into everlasting fire, prepared"—(not for **you**, but)—"for the devil and his angels." Do you see how it is guarded. Here is the salvation side of the question. It is all of God. "Come, ye blessed of my Father." It is a kingdom prepared for them. There you have election, free grace in all its length and breadth. But, on the other hand, you have nothing said about the Father—nothing about that at all. "Depart, ye cursed." Even the flames are said not to be prepared for sinners, but for the devil and his angels. There is no language that I can possibly conceive that could more forcibly express this idea, supposing it to be the mind of the Holy Spirit, that the glory should be to God, and that the blame should be laid at man's door.

FOR MEDITATION: The love of God towards a sinful Jacob should surprise us more than the hatred of God towards a sinful Esau.

The glorious habitation

"Lord, thou hast been our dwelling place in all generations." Psalm 90: 1
SUGGESTED FURTHER READING: 1 John 4: 13-16

Will you take my master's house on a lease for all eternity, with nothing to pay for it, nothing but the ground rent of loving and serving him for ever? Will you take Jesus, and dwell in him throughout eternity, or will you be content to be a houseless soul? Come inside, sir; see, it is furnished from top to bottom with all you want. It has cellars filled with gold, more than you will spend as long as you live; it has a parlour where you can entertain yourself with Christ, and feast on his love; it has tables well stored with food for you to live on for ever; it has a drawing-room of brotherly love where you can receive your friends. You will find a resting room up there where you can rest with Jesus; and on the top there is a look-out, whence you can see heaven itself. Will you have the house, or will you not? Ah, if you are houseless, you will say, "I should like to have the house; but may I have it?" Yes; there is the key. The key is, "Come to Jesus." But you say "I am too shabby for such a house." Never mind; there are garments inside. As Rowland Hill once said:

"Come naked, come filthy, come ragged, come poor,
Come wretched, come dirty, come just as you are."

If you feel guilty and condemned, come, and though the house is too good for you, Christ will make you good enough for the house. He will wash you, and cleanse you, and you will yet be able to sing with Moses, with the same unfaltering voice, "Lord, thou hast been my dwelling place throughout all generations."

FOR MEDITATION: The Christian has two addresses—a temporary earthly address and an eternal heavenly address, "in Christ" (Philippians 1: 1; Colossians 1: 2).

Magnificat

"Awake, awake, Deborah; awake, awake, utter a song; arise, Barak, and lead thy captivity captive, thou son of Abinoam." Judges 5: 12
SUGGESTED FURTHER READING: Psalm 108: 1-5

Wake up, my **love**, for thou must strike the key-note and lead the strain. Awake and sing unto thy beloved a song touching thy well-beloved. Give unto him choice canticles, for he is the fairest among ten thousand, and the altogether lovely. Come forth then with thy richest music, and praise the name which is as ointment poured forth. Wake up, my **hope**, and join hands with thy sister—love; and sing of blessings yet to come. Sing of my dying hour, when he shall be with me on my couch. Sing of the rising morning, when my body shall leap from its tomb into its Saviour's arms! Sing of the expected advent, for which thou lookest with delight! And, O my soul, sing of that heaven which he has gone before to prepare for thee, "that where he is, there may his people be." Awake my love—awake my hope—and thou my **faith**, awake also! Love has the sweetest voice, hope can thrill forth the higher notes of the sacred scale; but thou, O faith—with thy deep resounding bass melody—thou must complete the song. Sing of the promise sure and certain. Rehearse the glories of the covenant ordered in all things, and sure. Rejoice in the sure mercies of David! Sing of the goodness which shall be known to thee in all thy trials yet to come. Sing of that blood which has sealed and ratified every word of God. Glory in that eternal faithfulness which cannot lie, and of that truth which cannot fail. And thou, my **patience**, utter thy gentle but most gladsome hymn. Sing today of how he helped thee to endure in sorrows' bitterest hour. Sing of the weary way along which he has borne thy feet, and brought thee at last to lie down in green pastures, beside the still waters.

FOR MEDITATION: The songs of the Christian should arise from a thankful heart (Colossians 3: 16) stirred up by the word of Christ.

SERMON NO. 340

Come and welcome

"And the Spirit and the bride say, Come. And let him that heareth say, Come. And let him that is athirst come. And whosoever will, let him take the water of life freely." Revelation 22: 17
SUGGESTED FURTHER READING: John 6: 35-40

How wide is this invitation! There are some ministers who are afraid to invite sinners, then why are they ministers? They are afraid to perform the most important part of the sacred office. There was a time I must confess when I somewhat faltered when about to give a free invitation. My doctrinal sentiments did at that time somewhat hamper me. I boldly confess that I am unchanged as to the doctrines I have preached; I preach Calvinism as high, as stern, and as sound as ever; but I do feel, and always did feel an anxiety to invite sinners to Christ. And I do feel also, that not only is such a course consistent with the soundest doctrines, but that the other course is after all the unsound one, and has no title whatever to plead Scripture on its behalf. There has grown up in many churches an idea that none are to be called to Christ but what they call sensible sinners. I sometimes rebut that by remarking, that I call stupid sinners to Christ as well as sensible sinners, and that stupid sinners make by far the greatest proportion of the ungodly. But I glory in the confession that I preach Christ even to insensible sinners—that I would say even to the dry bones of the valley, as Ezekiel did, "Ye dry bones live!" doing it as an act of faith; not faith in the power of those that hear to obey the command, but faith in the power of God who gives the command to give strength also to those addressed, that they may be constrained to obey it. But now listen to my text; for here, at least, there is no limitation. But sensible or insensible, all that the text saith is, "Whosoever will, let him come and take the water of life freely." The one question I have to ask this morning is, art thou willing?

FOR MEDITATION: Jesus gladly received children and their carers; he rebuked his own disciples, some of God's children, who tried to get in the way (Mark 10: 13-16). Are we helping or hindering others who need to come to Christ?

SERMON NO. 279

The Comforter

"But the Comforter, which is the Holy Ghost, whom the Father will send in my name, he shall teach you all things, and bring all things to your remembrance, whatsoever I have said unto you." John 14: 26
SUGGESTED FURTHER READING: 1 Peter 1: 10-12, 22-25

I have heard many fanatical persons say that the Holy Spirit revealed this and that to them. Now that is very generally revealed nonsense. The Holy Spirit does not reveal anything fresh now. He brings old things to our remembrance. "He shall teach you all things, and bring all things to your remembrance whatsoever I have told you." The canon of revelation is closed; there is no more to be added. God does not give a fresh revelation, but he rivets the old one. When it has been forgotten, and laid in the dusty chamber of our memory, he brings it out and cleans the picture, but does not paint a new one. There are no new doctrines, but the old ones are often revived. It is not, I say, by any new revelation that the Spirit comforts. He does so by telling us old things over again; he brings a fresh lamp to manifest the treasures hidden in Scripture; he unlocks the strong chests in which the truth has long lain, and he points to secret chambers filled with untold riches; but he creates no more, for enough is done. Believer! There is enough in the Bible for thee to live upon for ever. If thou shouldst outnumber the years of Methuselah, there would be no need for a fresh revelation; if thou shouldst live till Christ should come upon the earth, there would be no necessity for the addition of a single word; if thou shouldst go down as deep as Jonah, or even descend as David envisaged into the belly of hell, still there would be enough in the Bible to comfort thee without a supplementary sentence. But Christ says, "He shall take of mine and shall show it unto you."

FOR MEDITATION: The Spirit of truth who guides into all the truth (John 16: 13) does not work independently of Jesus the truth (John 14: 6), the only true God (John 17: 3) and the word of truth (John 17: 17). Otherwise "What is truth?" (John 18: 38).

The true Christian's blessedness

"We know that all things work together for good to them that love God, to them who are the called according to his purpose." Romans 8: 28
SUGGESTED FURTHER READING: Philemon 4-20

All things work together for the Christian's eternal and spiritual good. And yet I must say here, that sometimes all things work together for the Christian's temporal good. You know the story of old Jacob. "Joseph is not, and Simeon is not, and ye will take Benjamin away; all these things are against me," said the old patriarch. But if he could have read God's secrets, he might have found that Simeon was not lost, for he was retained as a hostage—that Joseph was not lost, but gone before to smooth the passage of his grey hairs into the grave, and that even Benjamin was to be taken away by Joseph in love to his brother. So that what seemed to be against him, even in temporal matters, was for him. You may have heard also the story of that eminent martyr who was wont always to say, "All things work together for good." When he was seized by the officers of Queen Mary, to be taken to the stake to be burned, he was treated so roughly on the road that he broke his leg; and they jeeringly said, "All things work together for good, do they? How will your broken leg work for your good?" "I don't know," he said, "but for my good I know it will work, and you shall see it so." Strange to say, it proved true that it was for his good; for being delayed a day or so on the road through his lameness, he just arrived in London in time enough to hear that Elizabeth was proclaimed queen, and so he escaped the stake by his broken leg. He turned round upon the men who carried him, as they thought, to his death, and said to them, "Now will you believe that all things work together for good?"

FOR MEDITATION: We are called upon to rejoice in our sufferings, not for their own sake, but because of the outcome (Romans 5: 3,4; James 1: 2-4). If we, like God, knew the end from the beginning, we would laugh in the midst of our trials, as we shall later (Luke 6: 21).

Memento mori

"Oh that they were wise, that they understood this, that they would consider their latter end." Deuteronomy 32: 29
SUGGESTED FURTHER READING: Ecclesiastes 12: 1-7

I know not when, nor where, nor how I shall breathe out my life. Into that sacred ark I cannot look—that ark of the secrets of God. I cannot pry between the folded leaves of that book which is chained to the throne of God, wherein is written the whole history of man. When I walk by the way I may fall dead in the streets; an apoplexy may usher me into the presence of my Judge. Riding along the road, I may be carried as swiftly to my tomb. While I am thinking of the multitudes of miles over which the fiery wheels are running, I may be in a minute, without a moment's warning, sent down to the shades of death. In my own house I am not safe. There are a thousand gates to death, and the roads from earth to Hades are innumerable. From this spot in which I stand there is a straight path to the grave; and where you sit there is an entrance into eternity. Oh, let us consider then, how uncertain life is. Talk we of a hair; it is something massive when compared with the thread of life. Speak we of a spider's web; it is ponderous compared with the web of life. We are but as a bubble; nay, less substantial. As a moment's foam upon the breaker, such are we. As an instant spray—nay, the drops of spray are enduring as the orbs of heaven compared with the moments of our life. Oh, let us, then, prepare to meet our God, because when and how we shall appear before him is quite unknown to us. We may never go out of this hall alive. Some of us may be carried hence on young men's shoulders, as Ananias and Sapphira of old. We may not live to see our homes again.

FOR MEDITATION: The New Park Street Pulpit contains no sermons from October 1856. On the 19th a congregation of some 7,000 assembled for the first time at the Royal Surrey Gardens Music Hall. As Spurgeon prayed some troublemakers cried out "Fire" and in the ensuing panic seven people were trampled to death. Spurgeon never forgot it. "Memento mori"—"Remember you must die."

SERMON NO. 304

Christ's estimate of his people

"How fair is thy love, my sister, my spouse! how much better is thy love than wine! and the smell of thine ointments than all spices! Thy lips, O my spouse, drop as the honeycomb; honey and milk are under thy tongue; and the smell of thy garments is like the smell of Lebanon."
Solomon's Song 4: 10,11
SUGGESTED FURTHER READING: I Thessalonians 4: 1-12

When he comes and begins to praise you, and tells you, "That your lips drop as the honeycomb, that all your actions smell of myrrh, and that your love is better than wine, and that the thoughts under your tongue are better to him than wine and milk," what will you say? "Oh, Lord, I cannot say thou art mistaken, for thou art infallible; but if I dared so think thou art mistaken, I should say, "Thou art mistaken in me;" but Lord I cannot think thou art mistaken, it must be true. Still, Lord, I do not deserve it; I am conscious I do not and I never can deserve it; still if thou wilt help me, I will strive to be worthy of thy praise in some feeble measure. I will seek to live up to those high praises which thou hast passed upon me. If thou sayest, "My love is better than wine;" Lord, I will seek to love thee better, that the wine may be richer and stronger. If thou sayest, "My graces are like the smell of ointment," Lord, I will try to increase them, so as to have many great pots filled with them; and if my words drop as the honeycomb, Lord, there shall be more of them, and I will try to make them better, so that thou mayest think more of such honey; and if thou declarest that the thoughts under my tongue are to thee like honey and milk, then, Lord, I will seek to have more of those divine thoughts; and if my daily actions are to thee as the smell of Lebanon, Lord, I will seek to be more holy, to live nearer to thee; I will ask for grace, that my actions may be really what thou sayest they are."

FOR MEDITATION: Do you serve God because you feel you ought to, out of a sense of duty? Or because you want to, out of a sense of his love and acceptance of you in Christ? God's grace should motivate us to obey him even more than God's law does (Romans 6: 15).

Christ's prayer for his people

"I pray not that thou shouldest take them out of the world, but that thou shouldest keep them from the evil." John 17: 15
SUGGESTED FURTHER READING: Philippians 1: 19-26

We never have any encouragement to ask God to let us die. Christians are always wanting to die when they have any trouble or trial. You ask them why? "Because we would be with the Lord." O yes, they want to be with the Lord, when troubles and temptations come upon them. But it is not because they are yearning to be with the Lord, it is because they desire to get rid of their troubles. They want to get home, not so much for the Saviour's company, as to get out of the little hard work. They did not wish to go away when they were in quiet and prosperity. Like lazy fellows, as most of us are, when we get into a little labour we beg to go home. It is quite right sometimes that you should desire to depart, because you would not prove yourself to be a true Israelite if you did not want to go to Jerusalem. You may pray to be taken home out of the world, but Christ will not take up the petition. When your prayers come to the Lord, this little one may try to get amongst them, but Christ will say, "I do not know anything about you, 'I pray not that thou shouldest take them out of the world.'" You may wish it sincerely, and really desire it, but you will not at present get your Master to pray with you. Instead, then, of crying, or wishing to be away from the battle, brace yourself up in the name of the Lord. Every wish to escape the fight is but a desertion of your Master.

FOR MEDITATION: Elijah prayed it while he was afraid for his life (1 Kings 19: 3,4)! But God had a different departure planned for him (2 Kings 2: 11). Jonah prayed it twice when he was angry (Jonah 4: 3,9) soon after begging God to deliver him from drowning (Jonah 2: 2,7). What a good thing God rejects our foolish requests when we or they are outside his will. Paul had the mind of Christ on this matter.

The High Priest standing between the dead and the living

"And Aaron took as Moses commanded, and ran into the midst of the congregation; and behold, the plague was begun among the people: and he put on incense, and made an atonement for the people. And he stood between the dead and the living; and the plague was stayed." Numbers 16: 47, 48
SUGGESTED FURTHER READING: Hebrews 4: 14-5: 10

Jesus, the propitiator, is to be looked upon as the ordained one—called of God as was Aaron. Settled in eternity as being the predestined propitiation for sin, he came into the world as an ordained priest of God; receiving his ordination not from man, neither by man; but like Melchisedec, the priest of the most high God, without father, without mother, without descent, having neither beginning of days nor end of life, he is a priest for ever after the order of Melchisedec. Stand back, sons of Korah, all of you who call yourselves priests. I can scarce imagine that any man in this world who takes to himself the title of a priest, unless he takes it in the sense in which all God's people are priests,—I cannot imagine that a priest can enter heaven. I would not say a thing too stern or too severe; but I do most thoroughly believe that an assumption of the office of priest is so base an assumption of the priestly office of Christ, that I could as well conceive of a man being saved who called himself God, as conceive of a man being saved who called himself a priest; if he really means what he says, he has so trampled upon the priestly prerogative of Christ, that it seems to me he has touched the very crown jewels, and is guilty of a blasphemy, which, unless it be repented of, shall surely bring damnation on his head. Shake your garments, you ministers of Christ, from all priestly assumption; come out from among them; touch not the unclean thing. There are no priests now specially to minister among men. Jesus Christ and he only is the priest of his Church. He has made all of us priests and kings unto our God.

FOR MEDITATION: Because the Christian has a Father in heaven, he is not to call any man his spiritual father on earth (Matthew 23: 9); because the Christian has a great High Priest in heaven (1 Timothy 2: 5), he is not to regard any man as his priest on earth. We are no longer living in Old Testament times!

SERMON NO. 341

The chaff driven away

"The ungodly are not so: but are like the chaff which the wind driveth away." Psalm 1: 4
SUGGESTED FURTHER READING: 1 Peter 2: 11-17

Christian habits are the best business habits, if men would but believe it. When a man mixes his religion with his business and allows every act of his life to be guided by it, he stands the best chance in this world, if I may be allowed such a secular expression, for "Honesty is the best policy" after all, and Christianity is the best honesty. The sharp cutting competition of the times may be called honesty—it is only called so on earth, it is not called so by God, for there is a good deal of cheating in it. Honesty in the highest sense—Christian honesty—will be found after all to be the best policy in everything, and there will ordinarily be a prosperity, even worldly prosperity, attending a good man in the patient industrious pursuit of his calling. But if he does not have that success he craves, still there is one thing he knows, he would have it if it were best for him. I often know Christian men talk in this fashion; "Well I do but very little business," says one, "but I have enough coming in to live upon comfortably and happy. I never cared much for push and competition; I never felt that I was fit for it, and I sometimes thank God that I never thrust myself out into the rough stream, but that I was content to keep along shore." And I have marked this one thing, and as a matter of fact I know it cannot be disproved, that many such humble-minded men are the very best of Christians, they live the happiest lives, and whatsoever they do certainly does prosper, for they get what they expected though they did not expect much, and they get what they want though their wants are not very large.

FOR MEDITATION: Honesty honours God, and God honours those who honour him (1 Samuel 2: 30). Dishonesty in the early church was strikingly exposed (Acts 5: 1-11).

Grace reviving Israel

"I will be as the dew unto Israel: he shall grow as the lily, and cast forth his roots as Lebanon. His branches shall spread, and his beauty shall be as the olive tree, and his smell as Lebanon. They that dwell under his shadow shall return; they shall revive as the corn, and grow as the vine: the scent thereof shall be as the wine of Lebanon." Hosea 14: 5-7
SUGGESTED FURTHER READING: Colossians 3: 16-4: 1

The most beautiful tree in a garden is the one that bears the most fruit: and there is a promise given to a Christian that after his branches have spread, his beauty shall be as the olive tree; that is, he shall grow and be laden with fruit. The olive tree is evergreen; and so is the beauty of the Christian. Alas for the beautiful Christians we have in some of our places of worship on Sunday! Glorious Christians! If they could be packed up and sent to heaven just as they are, provided their appearances were true indications of their state, what a blessed thing it would be! But alas! On the Monday they have not the same sort of dress they had on Sunday, and therefore they have not the same kind of actions. Dear friends, there is so much Sunday religion in these days! Now, I like a Monday religion, and a Tuesday religion, and a Wednesday religion, and a Thursday religion, and a Friday religion, and a Saturday religion. I do not think the religion of the pulpit, or the religion of the pen, is to be relied upon. I think it is the religion of a draper's shop, the religion of a corn exchange, religion in a house, religion in the street, and the religion of a fireside, that proves us to be God's children. But how would some of you come off if you were weighed in these balances? Fine fellows, on Sunday; but poor creatures on Monday! You are not well arrayed then; but ah! If you were Christians, you would always be well arrayed: yes, you would always be as beautiful as the olive tree.

FOR MEDITATION: God wants us to live the Christian life, not to live the Christian meeting! True worship involves practice as well as praise (Romans 12: 1; James 1: 26-27).

Light at evening time

"It shall come to pass, that at evening time it shall be light." Zechariah 14:7
SUGGESTED FURTHER READING: Luke 24: 13-21, 28-35

God very frequently acts in grace in such a manner that we can find a parallel in nature. For instance, God says, "… as the rain cometh down and the snow from heaven, and returneth not thither, … so shall my word be, …it shall not return unto me void, but it shall accomplish that which I please, and it shall prosper in the thing whereto I sent it." We find him speaking concerning the coming of Christ, "He shall come down like rain upon the mown grass: as showers that water the earth." We find him likening the covenant of grace to the covenant which he made with Noah concerning the seasons, and with man concerning the different revolutions of the year—"Seed-time and harvest, and cold and heat, and summer and winter, and day and night shall not cease." We find that the works of creation are very frequently the mirror of the works of grace, and that we can draw figures from the world of nature to illustrate the great acts of God in the world of his grace towards his people. But sometimes God oversteps nature. In nature after evening comes night. The sun has had its hours of journeying; the fiery steeds are weary; they must rest. Lo, they descend the azure steeps and plunge their burning fetlocks in the western sea, while night in her dark chariot follows at their heels. God, however, oversteps the rule of nature. He is pleased to send to his people times when the eye of reason expects to see no more day, but fears that the glorious landscape of God's mercies will be shrouded in the darkness of his forgetfulness. But instead, God overleaps nature, and declares that at evening time, instead of darkness there shall be light.

FOR MEDITATION: The text has only ever been true on one occasion in a physical sense (Joshua 10: 12-14), but God, to whom even the darkness is light (Psalm 139: 12), is always repeating the event spiritually in the lives of his people.

The wounds of Jesus

"He showed them his hands and his feet." Luke 24: 40
SUGGESTED FURTHER READING: Isaiah 25: 6-9

There are three things in Christ that death never met with before, all of which are fatal to it. There was in Christ, innocence. Now, as long as man was innocent, he could not die. Adam lived as long as he was innocent. Now, Christ was about to die; but death sucked in innocent blood; he sucked in his own poison and he died. Again, blessedness is that which takes away the sting of death. Now Christ, even when he was dying, was "God over all, blessed for ever." All that death had ever killed before was under the curse; but this man was never by nature under the curse, because for our sakes he was not born into this world a cursed man. He was the seed of woman it is true, but still not of carnal generation. He did come under the curse when he took upon himself our sins, but not for his own sins. He was in himself blessed. Death sucked in blessed blood; he had never done that before—all others have been under the curse—and that slew death. Yet another thing. Death had never met before with any man who had life in himself. But when death drank Christ's blood it drank life. For his blood is the life of the soul, and is the seed of life eternal. Wherever it goes, does it not give life to the dead? And death, finding that it had drunk into its own veins life in the form of Jesus' blood, gave up the ghost; and death itself is dead, for Christ has destroyed it, by the sacrifice of himself; he has put it away; he has said, "Oh death, where is thy sting? Oh grave, where is thy victory?"

FOR MEDITATION: On the cross Jesus was making the arrangements for death's own funeral (1 Corinthians 15: 26; Revelation 20: 14).

None but Jesus

"He that believeth on him is not condemned." John 3: 18
SUGGESTED FURTHER READING: Hebrews 12: 5-11

You are never liable as a believer to punishment for your sins. You will be chastised on account of them, as a father chastises his child; that is part of the gospel dispensation; but you will not be smitten for your sins as the lawgiver smites the criminal. Your Father may often punish you as he punished the wicked, but never for the same reason. The ungodly stand on the ground of their own demerits; their sufferings are awarded as their due deserts. But your sorrows do not come to you as a matter of desert; they come to you as a matter of love. God knows that in one sense your sorrows are such a privilege that you may account of them as a boon you do not deserve. I have often thought of that when I have had a sore trouble. I know some people say, "You deserved the trouble." Yes, my dear brethren, but there is not enough merit in all the Christians put together, to deserve such a good thing as the loving rebuke of our heavenly Father. Perhaps you cannot see that; you cannot think that a trouble can come to you as a real blessing in the covenant. But I know that the rod of the covenant is as much the gift of grace as the blood of the covenant. It is not a matter of merit; it is given to us because we need it. But I question whether we were ever so good as to deserve it. We were never able to get up to so high a standard as to deserve so rich, so gracious a providence as this covenant blessing—the rod of our chastening God.

FOR MEDITATION: When disciplined by his heavenly Father, the Christian is experiencing a beatitude (Job 5: 17; Psalm 94: 12)!

Chastisement

"And ye have forgotten the exhortation which speaketh unto you as unto children, My son, despise not thou the chastening of the Lord, nor faint when thou art rebuked of him." Hebrews 12: 5
SUGGESTED FURTHER READING: Deuteronomy 8: 1-6

What son is there whom the Father chasteneth not? You ministers of God who preach the gospel, is there amongst your ranks one son whom his Father chastens not? Unanimously they reply, "We all have been chastened." You holy prophets who testified God's word with the Holy Ghost from heaven, is there one amongst your number whom God chastened not? Abraham, Daniel, Jeremiah, Isaiah, Malachi, answer; and unanimously cry, "There is not one among us whom the Father chasteneth not." You kings, you chosen ones, you Davids and you Solomons, is there one in your high and lofty ranks who has escaped chastisement? Answer David! Were you not obliged to cross the brook Kedron in the darkness? Answer Hezekiah! Did you not spread the letter before the Lord? Answer Jehoshaphat! Did you not have the cross when the ships were broken that were sent to Tarshish for gold? Oh starry host above, translated out of the reach of the trials of this world, is there one amongst you whom the Father chastened not? Not one; there is not one in heaven whose back was unscarred by the chastening rod, if he attained to the age when he needed it. The infant alone escapes, flying at once from his mother's breast to heaven. There is one whom I will ask, the Son of God, the Son par excellence, the chief of all the family. Son of God Incarnate, did you escape the rod? Son without sin, were you a Son without punishment? Were you chastised? Hark! The hosts of earth and heaven reply—the church militant and triumphant answer: "The chastisement of our peace was even upon him; he suffered; he bore the cross; he endured the curse as well as any of us; yea, more, he endured ten thousand-fold more chastisement than any of us can by any possibility endure."

FOR MEDITATION: Christians have different gifts and different callings, but this is something shared by all. How do you react when God disciplines you? Does the experience leave you dismissive, discouraged or (as God intends) disciplined?

A basket of summer fruit

"Thus hath the Lord God shewed unto me: and behold a basket of summer fruit. And he said, Amos, what seest thou? And I said, A basket of summer fruit. Then said the Lord unto me, The end is come upon my people of Israel; I will not again pass by them any more." Amos 8: 1,2
SUGGESTED FURTHER READING: 2 Peter 3: 1-10

For thousands of years the Lord came not, although sin was rampant and the darkness dense, nothing could excite the Lord to an unwise haste. Nor on the other hand did he stay beyond the proper hour; for when the fulness of time was come, God sent forth his Son, born of a woman, made under the law. In heaven we shall probably discover that Christ came to die for our sins precisely at the only fitting moment, that in fact redemption's work could not have been so wisely accomplished at the gates of the garden of Eden as on Calvary; and that the reign of Herod and the Roman Caesar afforded the most fitting era for the sacrifice of the Cross. And so shall it be with regard to the second advent of our blessed Lord and Master. We are apt to say, "Why are his chariots so long in coming? Do not the virgins sleep because the bridegroom tarries, the wise as well as the foolish, have they not all slumbered and slept?" And many are the servants who say in their heart, "My Lord delayeth his coming," and are ready therefore to beat their fellow-servants, to drink and to be drunken; but cheer your hearts, you who look for his appearing. He will not come too hastily, for why should the sun arise until darkness has had its hour? Nor will he delay his appearing one moment beyond the proper time, for should not the sun beam forth in the morning? We know and are persuaded that when he shall stand a second time upon the earth, it shall be as much the fulness of time for him to come, as it was the fulness of time when he came at first.

FOR MEDITATION: We know that Christ was born at the right time (Galatians 4: 4) and that he died for us at the right time (Romans 5: 6). We cannot tell when he will come again, but it will be at the right time (Acts 17: 31). The right time to trust in him is now (2 Corinthians 6: 2).

SERMON NO. 343

The Saviour's many crowns

"On his head were many crowns." Revelation 19: 12
SUGGESTED FURTHER READING: Revelation 4

All the mighty doers in Christ's church ascribe their crown to him. What a glorious crown is that which Elijah will wear—the man who went to Ahab, and when Ahab said, "Hast thou found me, O mine enemy?" reproved him to his very face—the man who took the prophets of Baal, and let not one of them escape, but hewed them in pieces and made them a sacrifice to God. What a crown will he wear who ascended into heaven in a chariot of fire! What a crown, again, belongs to Daniel, saved from the lion's den—Daniel, the earnest prophet of God. What a crown will be that which shall glitter on the head of the weeping Jeremiah, and the eloquent Isaiah! What crowns are those which shall cover the heads of the apostles! What a weighty diadem is that which Paul shall receive for his many years of service! And then, my friends, how shall the crown of Luther glitter, and the crown of Calvin; and what a noble diadem shall that be which Whitefield shall wear, and all those men who have so valiantly served God, and who by his might have put to flight the armies of the Aliens, and have maintained the gospel banner erect in troubled times! No, but let me point to you a scene. Elijah enters heaven, and where goes he with that crown which is instantly put upon his head? See, he flies to the throne, and stooping there, he uncrowns himself, "Not unto me, not unto me, but unto thy name be all the glory!" See the prophets as they stream in one by one; without exception, they put their crowns upon the head of Christ. And mark the apostles, and all the mighty teachers of the church: they all bow there and cast their crowns at his feet, who, by his grace, enabled them to win them.

FOR MEDITATION: Will you receive any of the crowns mentioned in the New Testament?—The crown of rejoicing—for faithful evangelism out of love for the lost. The crown of righteousness—for faithful expectation out of love for the Lord's presence. The crown of resurrection life—for faithful endurance out of love for the Lord's person. The crown of renown—for faithful examples out of love for the Lord's people (1 Thessalonians 2: 19; 2 Timothy 4: 8; James 1: 12; 1 Peter 5: 2-4).

SERMON NO. 281

The Shulamite's choice prayer

"Set me as a seal upon thine heart, as a seal upon thine arm; for love is strong as death; jealousy is cruel as the grave; the coals thereof are coals of fire, which hath a most vehement flame. Many waters cannot quench love, neither can the floods drown it." Solomon's Song 8: 6-7
SUGGESTED FURTHER READING: Ephesians 3: 14-21

"Set me as a seal upon thine heart, as a seal upon thine arm. Love me, Lord. Help me, Lord. Let thy heart move towards me; let thine arm move for me too. Think of me, Lord; set me on thy heart. Work for me, Lord, set me on thine arm. Lord, I long to have thy love, for I hear it is as strong as death, and thou knowest I am chained by Satan, and am his bond-slave. Come and deliver me: thou art more than a match for my cruel tyrant. Come with thy strong love and set me free. I hear that thy love is as firm as hell itself. Lord, that is such a love as I want. Though I know I shall vex thee and wander from thee, come and love me with a love that is firm and everlasting. O Lord, I feel there is nothing in me that can make thee love me. Come and love me, then, with that love which finds its own fuel. Love me with those coals of fire which have a 'vehement flame.' And since many waters cannot quench thy love, prove that in me; for there are many waters of sin in me, but Lord, help me to believe that thy love is not quenched by them; there are many corruptions in me, but Lord, love me with that love which my corruptions cannot quench. Here, Lord, I give myself away; take me; make me what thou wouldst have me to be, and keep and preserve me even to the end." May the Lord help you to pray that prayer, and then may he answer it for his mercy's sake.

FOR MEDITATION: Omnipotent God loves his people with an omnipotent, all-conquering love (Romans 8: 35-39) which surpasses all knowledge and imagination. Can you say with assurance that he "so" loves you (John 3: 16; 1 John 4: 11)?

SERMON NO. 364

The security of the Church

"As the mountains are round about Jerusalem, so the Lord is round about his people from henceforth even for ever." Psalm 125: 2
SUGGESTED FURTHER READING: Jude 17-25

As the Church always has been preserved, the text assures us she always will be, henceforth even for ever. There is a nervous old woman here. Last Saturday night she read the newspaper, and she saw something about five or six clergymen going over to Rome: she laid down her spectacles, and she began crying, "Oh! The Church is in danger, the Church is in danger." Ah! Put your spectacles on; that is all right; never mind about the loss of those fellows. Better gone; we did not want them; do not cry if fifty more follow them; do not be at all alarmed. Some church may be in danger, but God's church is not. That is safe enough; that shall stand secure, even to the end. I remember with what alarm some of my friends received the tidings of the geological discoveries of modern times, which did not quite agree with their interpretation of the Mosaic history of the creation. They thought it an awful thing that science should discover something which seemed to contradict the Scriptures. Well, we lived over the geological difficulty, after all. And since then there have been different sets of philosophic infidels, who have risen up and made wonderful discoveries; and poor timid Christians have thought, "What a terrible thing! This surely will be the end of all true religion; when science can bring facts against us, how shall we be able to stand?" They just waited about another week, and suddenly found that science was not their enemy, but their friend, for the Truth, though tried in a furnace, like silver seven times, is ever a gainer by the trial. To those that hate the church, she shall ever be a thorn in your side! Oh! you that would batter her walls to pieces, know this, that she is impregnable.

FOR MEDITATION: The enemies of the church build on an unsteady foundation of deliberately ignoring facts (2 Peter 3: 5). The church is built on the immovable rock Christ Jesus (Matthew 16: 18) and she shall not be moved (Psalm 46: 5).

SERMON NO. 161

The exaltation of Christ

"Wherefore God also hath highly exalted him, and given him a name which is above every name: That at the name of Jesus every knee should bow, of things in heaven, and things in earth, and things under the earth; And that every tongue should confess that Jesus Christ is Lord, to the glory of God the Father." Philippians 2: 9-11
SUGGESTED FURTHER READING: John 17: 1-5

Look at him! Can your imagination picture him? Behold his transcendent glory! The majesty of kings is swallowed up; the pomp of empires dissolves like the white mist of the morning before the sun; the brightness of assembled armies is eclipsed. He in himself is brighter than the sun, more terrible than armies with banners. See him! See him! Oh! Hide your heads, you monarchs; put away your gaudy pageantry, you lords of this poor narrow earth! His kingdom knows no bounds; without a limit his vast empire stretches out itself. Above him all is his; beneath him many a step are angels, and they are his; and they cast their crowns before his feet. With them stand his elect and ransomed, and their crowns too are his. And here upon this lower earth stand his saints, and they are his, and they adore him; and under the earth, among the infernals, where devils growl their malice, even there is trembling and adoration; and where lost spirits, with wailing and gnashing of teeth for ever lament their being, even there, there is the acknowledgement of his Godhead, even though the confession helps to make the fire of their torments. In heaven, in earth, in hell, all knees bend before him, and every tongue confesses that he is God. If not now, yet in the time that is to come this shall be carried out, that every creature of God's making shall acknowledge his Son to be "God over all, blessed for ever. Amen." Oh! My soul anticipates that blessed day, when this whole earth shall bend its knee before its God willingly! I do believe there is a happy era coming, when there shall not be one knee unbent before my Lord and Master.

FOR MEDITATION: Those who refuse to acknowledge the Lord Jesus Christ in this life (2 John 7) will be forced to acknowledge him in the next—but it will be too late to do them any good. Those who trust in him now will enjoy praising him for ever.

SERMON NO. 101

The God of peace

"Now the God of peace be with you all. Amen." Romans 15: 33
SUGGESTED FURTHER READING: Philippians 4: 1-9

Let me briefly show you the appropriateness of this prayer. We indeed ought to have peace amongst ourselves. Joseph said to his brethren when they were going home to his father's house, "See that ye fall not out by the way." There was something extremely beautiful in that exhortation. You have all one father, you are of one family. Let men of two nations disagree; but you are of the seed of Israel; you are of one tribe and nation; your home is in one heaven. "See that ye fall not out by the way." The way is rough; there are enemies to stop you. See that if you fall out when you get home, you do not fall out by the way. Keep together; stand by one another, defend each other's character; manifest continual affection. The world hates you because you are not of the world. Oh! You must take care that you love one another. You are all going to the same house. You may disagree here, and not speak to one another, and be almost ashamed to sit at the same table, even at the sacrament; but you will all have to sit together in heaven. Therefore do not fall out by the way. Consider, again, the great mercies you have all shared together. You are all pardoned, you are all accepted, elected, justified, sanctified, and adopted. See that you fall not out when you have so many mercies. Joseph has filled your sacks, but if he has put some extra thing into Benjamin's sack, do not quarrel with Benjamin about that, but rather rejoice because your sacks are full. You have all got enough, you are all secure, you have all been dismissed with a blessing.

FOR MEDITATION: The God of love and peace will be seen to be present when his people live in peace with one another (2 Corinthians 13: 11)

Tender words of terrible apprehension

"The wicked shall be turned into hell, and all the nations that forget God."
Psalm 9: 17
SUGGESTED FURTHER READING: Ezekiel 8: 5-18

How often do you forget his presence too! In the midst of a crowd, you are conscious every one of you of the presence of man, but perhaps this very moment you are ignoring the fact that God is here. In your shop on the morrow how carefully you will take heed that your conduct is circumspect if the eye of your fellow-man is observing you. But before the presence of God, with the Eternal eye upon you, you can presume to practice the paltry tricks of trade or to do that which you would not have revealed to mortals for all the world; careful to shut the door, and draw the curtain, and hide yourselves in secret from men; strangely forgetting that when the curtain is drawn and the door is shut, God is there still. No walls can shut him out; no darkness can conceal the deed from his eye; he is everywhere and sees us in all things. Why, my hearers, we are all guilty in this respect in a measure; we forget the actual presence and the overlooking eye of God. We talk as we dare not talk if we were thinking that he heard us. We act as we would not act if we were conscious that God was there. We indulge in thoughts which we should cast out if we could but bear in perpetual remembrance the abiding presence of God, the Judge of the whole earth. Forgetting God is so common a sin, that the believer himself needs to repent of it, and ask to have it forgiven, while the unbeliever may solemnly confess this to be his crying sin, a piece of guilt to which he dare not profess innocence.

FOR MEDITATION: The Christian should make a positive effort to do everything to the satisfaction of his unseen but seeing Lord (Ephesians 6: 5-7). This was the principle that Joseph adopted (Genesis 39: 9).

Fast-day service: An exposition of Daniel 9:1-19

Taken from brief exposition of Daniel 9: 1-19 (This comment is on vv 10-15)
SUGGESTED FURTHER READING: Psalm 85

The prophet in his prayer pleads what God has done for them, as the reason why he should bare his arm; he tells how God delivered Israel out of Egypt; and he therefore prays that God would deliver them from their present trouble. And, my brethren, not Israel itself could boast a nobler history than we, measuring it by God's bounties. We have not yet forgotten an armada scattered before the breath of heaven, scattered upon the angry deep as a trophy of what God can do to protect his favoured isle. We have not yet forgotten a fifth of November, wherein God discovered many plots that were formed against our religion and our commonwealth. We have not yet lost the old men, whose tales of even the victories in war are still a frequent story. We remember how God swept before our armies the man who thought to make the world his dominion, who designed to cast his shoe over Britain, and make it a dependency of his kingdom. God fought for us; he fought with us; and he will continue to do so. He has not left his people, and he will not leave us, but he will be with us even to the end. Cradle of liberty! Refuge of distress! Storms may rage around you, but not upon you, nor shall all the wrath and fury of men destroy you, for God has pitched his tabernacle in your midst, and his saints are the salt in your midst.

FOR MEDITATION: These stirring words, spoken at the time of the Indian mutiny, are equally true of God's faithfulness during the worldwide conflicts of the twentieth century. But do Spurgeon's words "We have not yet forgotten" retain any ring of truth in a nation which appears intent on moving further away from God by the day? While we may "Remember, remember the fifth of November," few could probably explain why we do so!

N.B. Read again the text for yesterday's reading—pray that a forgetful nation will remember and turn back to its Creator and Judge.

Let us pray

"But it is good for me to draw near to God." Psalm 73: 28
SUGGESTED FURTHER READING: James 4: 1-8

Draw near to God with living, loving prayer; present the promise, and you shall obtain the fulfilment. Many things I might say of prayer; our old divines are full of high praise concerning it. The early fathers speak of it as if they were writing sonnets. Chrysostom preached of it as if he saw it incarnate in some heavenly form. And the choicest metaphors were gathered together to describe in rapturous phrase the power, nay, the omnipotence of prayer. Would to God we loved prayer as our fathers did of old. It is said of James the Less, that he was so much in prayer that his knees had become hard like those of a camel. It was doubtless but a legend, but legends are often based on truths. And certain it is that Hugh Latimer, that blessed saint and martyr of our God, was accustomed to pray so earnestly in his old age, when he was in his cell, that he would often pray until he had no strength left to rise, and the prison attendants had need to lift him from his knees. Where are the men like these? Oh angel of the covenant, where can you find them? When the Son of Man comes shall he find prayer on the earth? Ours are not worthy of the name of supplication. Oh that we had learned that sacred art, that would draw near to God, and plead his promise. Cowper has put several things together in one hymn.

Prayer clears the sky;	"Prayer makes the darkened cloud withdraw."
Prayer is a heaven-climber;	"Prayer climbs the ladder Jacob saw."
Prayer makes even Satan quake;	"For Satan trembles when he sees, The weakest saint upon his knees."

FOR MEDITATION: Do you regard your prayer-life as a dead, boring routine? May God teach us to draw near to him and enjoy the relationship in a living and meaningful way (Luke 11: 1-4).

SERMON NO. 288

The Christian's heaviness and rejoicing

"Wherein ye greatly rejoice, though now for a season, if need be, ye are in heaviness through manifold temptations." 1 Peter 1: 6
SUGGESTED FURTHER READING: Philippians 2: 25-30

"Though now for a season, if need be, ye are in heaviness." It does not say, "Though now for a season you are suffering pain, though now for a season you are poor"; but "you are in heaviness;" your spirits are taken away from you; you are made to weep; you cannot bear the pain; you are brought to the very dust of death, and wish that you might die. Your faith itself seems as if it would fail you. That is the thing for which there is a 'need be'. That is what my text declares, that there is an absolute 'need be' that sometimes the Christian should not endure his sufferings with a gallant and a joyous heart; there is a 'need be' that sometimes his spirits should sink within him, and that he should become even as a little child, smitten beneath the hand of God. Ah! Beloved, we sometimes talk about the rod, but it is one thing to see the rod, and it is another thing to feel it; and many a time have we said within ourselves, "If I did not feel so low spirited as I now do, I should not mind this affliction;" and what is that but saying, "If I did not feel the rod I should not mind it?" It is that breaking down of the spirit, that pulling down of the strong man, that is the very festering of the soreness of God's scourging—the blueness of the wound, whereby the soul is made better.

FOR MEDITATION: Whenever you are overwhelmed by such distress, remember that your Saviour also experienced it on your behalf (Mark 14: 33-34). He knows what it is like and can help you (Hebrews 2: 18; 4: 15-16).

The first and great commandment

"Thou shalt love the Lord thy God with all thy heart, and with all thy soul, and with all thy mind, and with all thy strength: this is the first commandment." Mark 12: 30
SUGGESTED FURTHER READING: 2 John 1-6

We are bound to love God with all our heart, soul, mind, and strength. Thus, we deduce that we are to love God supremely. Thou art to love thy wife, O husband. Thou canst not love her too much except in one case, if thou shouldst love her before God, and prefer her pleasure to the pleasure of the Most High. Then wouldst thou be an idolater. Child! Thou art to love thy parents; thou canst not love him too much who begat thee, nor her too much who brought thee forth; but remember, there is one law that doth override that. Thou art to love thy God more than thy father or thy mother. He demands thy first and thy highest affection: thou art to love him "with all thy heart." We are allowed to love our relatives: we are taught to do so. He that does not love his own family is worse than a heathen man and a publican. But we are not to love the dearest object of our hearts so much as we love God. You may erect little thrones for those whom you rightly love; but God's throne must be a glorious high throne; you may set them upon the steps, but God must sit on the very seat itself. He is to be enthroned, the royal One within your heart, the king of your affections. Have you kept this commandment? I know I have not; I must plead guilty before God; I must cast myself before him, and acknowledge my transgression. But nevertheless, there standeth the commandment—"Thou shalt love God with all thy heart" that is, thou shalt love him supremely.

FOR MEDITATION: The Lord Jesus Christ preached what he practised (Matthew 10: 37,38). His Heavenly Father's house came first, but he was obedient in his earthly parents' house (Luke 2: 48-51); his Heavenly Father's will came first (Matthew 26: 39), but even while he was carrying it out, his earthly mother's wellbeing was upon his heart (John 19: 26-27). We love our families, our fellow-believers and the lost ones best, when we love and obey God first.

SERMON NO. 162

One antidote for many ills

"Turn us again, O Lord God of hosts, cause thy face to shine; and we shall be saved." Psalm 80: 19
SUGGESTED FURTHER READING: Revelation 3: 1-6

We want a revival, if we would promote the glory of God. The proper object of a Christian's life is God's glory. The church was made on purpose to glorify God; but it is only a revived church that brings glory to his name. Do all the churches honour God? I tell you no; there are some that dishonour him—not because of their erroneous doctrines, nor perhaps because of any defect in their formalities, but because of the want of life in their religion. There is a meeting for prayer; six people assemble beside the minister. Does that proclaim your homage to God? Does that do honour to Christianity? Go to the homes of these people; see what is their conversation when they are alone; mark how they walk before God. Go to their sanctuaries and hear their hymns; there is the beauty of music, but where is the life of the people? Listen to the sermon; it is elaborate, polished, complete, a masterpiece of oratory. But ask yourselves, "Could a soul be saved under it, except by a miracle? Was there anything in it adapted to stir men up to goodness? It pleased their ears; it instructed them in some degree, perhaps, but what was there in it to teach their hearts?" God knows there are many such preachers. Notwithstanding their learning and their wealth, they do not preach the gospel in its simplicity, and they do not draw near to God our Father. If we would honour God by the church, we must have a warm church, a burning church, loving the truths it holds, and carrying them out in the life. Oh that God would give us life from on high, lest we should be like that church of old of whom it was said, "Thou hast a name to live, and art dead."

FOR MEDITATION: Is the revival of God's church and the glory of his name in this land a great concern to you (Psalm 85: 6-9)?

A call to the unconverted

"For as many as are of the works of the law are under the curse: for it is written, Cursed is every one that continueth not in all things which are written in the book of the law to do them." Galatians 3: 10
SUGGESTED FURTHER READING: Matthew 25: 31-46

Suddenly a voice is heard, and shrieks from some, and songs from others—he comes—he comes—he comes; and every eye must see him. There he is; the throne is set upon a cloud, which is white as alabaster. There he sits. It is He, the Man that died on Calvary—I see his pierced hands—but ah, how changed! No thorn crown now. He stood at Pilate's bar, but now the whole earth must stand at his bar. But listen! The trumpet sounds again: the Judge opens the book, there is silence in heaven, a solemn silence: the universe is still. "Gather mine elect together, and my redeemed from the four winds of heaven." Swiftly they are gathered. As with a lightning flash, the angel's wing divides the crowd. Here are the righteous all in-gathered; and sinner, there are you, on the left hand, left out, left to abide the burning sentence of eternal wrath. Listen! The harps of heaven play sweet melodies; but to you they bring no joy, though the angels are repeating the Saviour's welcome to his saints. "Come, ye blessed of my Father, inherit the kingdom prepared for you from the foundation of the world." You have had that moment's respite, and now his face is gathering clouds of wrath, the thunder is on his brow; he looks on you that have despised him, you that scoffed his grace, that scorned his mercy, you that broke his Sabbath, you that mocked his cross, you that would not have him to reign over you; and with a voice louder than ten thousand thunders, he cries, "Depart, ye cursed." And then—No, I will not follow you. I will not tell of quenchless flames: I will not talk of miseries for the body, and tortures for the spirit. But hell is terrible; damnation is doleful. Oh, escape! escape!

FOR MEDITATION: Any one of your sins would send you to hell (James 2: 10). No one but Jesus can divert you to heaven (Acts 4: 12). Make sure you are trusting in him alone for your salvation.

Healing for the wounded

"He healeth the broken in heart, and bindeth up their wounds." Psalm 147: 3
SUGGESTED FURTHER READING: Isaiah 57: 15-21

Poor sinner, breathe thy wish to him, let thy sigh come before him, for "he healeth the broken in heart." There thou liest wounded on the plain. "Is there no physician?" thou criest; "Is there none?" Around thee lie thy fellow-sufferers, but they are as helpless as thyself. Thy mournful cry cometh back without an answer, and space alone hears thy groan. Ah! The battle-field of sin has one kind visitor; it is not abandoned to the vultures of remorse and despair. I hear footsteps approaching; they are the gentle footsteps of Jehovah. With a heart full of mercy, he is hasting to his repenting child. In his hands there are no thunders, in his eyes no anger, on his lips no threatening. See how he bows himself over the mangled heart! Hear how he speaks! "Come, now, and let us reason together, saith the Lord; though your sins be as scarlet, they shall be as white as snow; though they be red like crimson, they shall be as wool." And if the patient dreads to look in the face of the mighty being who addresses him, the same loving mouth whispers, "I, even I, am he that blotteth out thy transgressions for my name's sake." See how he washes every wound with sacred water from the side of Jesus; mark how he spreads the ointment of forgiving grace, and binds around each wound the fair white linen, which is the righteousness of saints. Does the mourner faint under the operation? He puts medicine to his lips, exclaiming, "I have loved thee with an everlasting love." Yes, it is true—most true—neither dream nor fiction, "He healeth the broken in heart, and bindeth up their wounds." How condescending is the Lord of heaven, thus to visit poor forsaken man.

FOR MEDITATION: Physical health is desirable, but short-lived; spiritual health is far more to be desired and will last for ever (3 John 2). We can live for a while with physical illness, but the unbeliever will die eternally with spiritual disease.

Self-sufficiency slain

"Without me ye can do nothing." John 15: 5
SUGGESTED FURTHER READING: 2 Chronicles 32: 20-31

You are not capable of performing the lowest act of the divine life, except as you receive strength from God the Holy Spirit. And surely, my brethren, it is generally in these little things that we find out most of all our weakness. Peter can walk the waves of the sea, but he cannot bear the derision of a little maid. Job can endure the loss of all things, but the upbraiding words of his false friends, though they be but words, and break no bones—make him speak far more bitterly than all the sore boils which were in his very skin. Jonah said he did well to be angry, even unto death, about a gourd. Have you not often heard that mighty men who have outlived hundreds of battles have been slain at last by the most trivial accident? And has it not been so with professed Christians? They stood uprightly in the midst of the greatest trials; they have outlived the most arduous struggles, and yet in an evil hour, trusting to themselves, their foot has slipped under some slight temptation, or because of some small difficulty. John Newton says: "The grace of God is as necessary to create a right temper in Christians on the breaking of a china plate as on the death of an only son." These little leaks need the most careful stopping. The plague of flies is no more easy to be stayed than that of the destroying angel. In little as well as in great things the just must live by faith. In trifles as well as in nobler exercises the believer should be conscious of his own inability,—should never say of any act, "Now I am strong enough to perform this; I need not go to God in prayer about this; this is so little a thing."

FOR MEDITATION: We need to bring everything to God in prayer, not only the things which worry us (Philippians 4: 6); the apostle Paul had learned how to face all situations and how to do all things in Christ who strengthened him (Philippians 4: 13).

The sweet uses of adversity

"Shew me wherefore thou contendest with me." Job 10: 2
SUGGESTED FURTHER READING: Psalm 119: 65-72

There was a fair ship which belonged to the great Master of the seas; it was about to sail from the port of grace to the haven of glory. Before it left the shore the great Master said, "Mariners, be brave! Captain, be bold! For not a hair of your head shall perish; I will bring you safely to your desired haven. The angel of the winds is commissioned to take care of you on your way." The ship sailed confidently with its streamers flying in the air. It floated along at a swift rate with a fair wind for many days. But suddenly there came a hurricane which drove them from the course, strained their mast until it bent as if it could snap in two. The sail was torn to ribbons; the sailors were alarmed and the captain himself trembled. They had lost their course. They were off the right track, and they mourned exceedingly. When the day dawned the waves were quiet, and the angel of the winds appeared; and they spoke unto him, and said, "Oh angel, were you not asked to take charge of us, and preserve us on our journey?" He answered, "It was even so, and I have done it. You were steering on confidently, and you knew not that a little ahead of your vessel lay a quicksand upon which she would be wrecked and swallowed up quick. I saw that there was no way for your escape but to drive you from your course. See, I have done as it was commanded me: go on your way." This is a parable of our Lord's dealings with us. He often drives us from our smooth course which we thought was the right track to heaven. But there is a secret reason for it; there is a quicksand ahead that is not marked in the chart. We know nothing about it; but God sees it, and he will not permit this fair vessel, which he has himself insured, to be stranded anywhere; he will bring it safely to its desired haven.

FOR MEDITATION: If an ass can inconvenience a false prophet to deliver him from imminent danger (Numbers 22: 21-34), God is able to obstruct his people in one way or another when they are heading for trouble. We can only see the benefits later (Hebrews 12: 11).

The evil and its remedy

"The iniquity of the house of Israel and Judah is exceeding great."
Ezekiel 9: 9 "The blood of Jesus Christ his Son cleanseth us from all sin."
1 John 1: 7
SUGGESTED FURTHER READING: Mark 3: 22-30

There are some sins that show a diabolical extent of degraded ingenuity—some sins of which it is a shame to speak, or of which it is disgraceful to think. But note here: "The blood of Jesus Christ cleanseth from all sin." There may be some sins of which a man cannot speak, but there is no sin which the blood of Christ cannot wash away. Blasphemy, however profane; lust, however bestial; covetousness, however far it may have gone into theft and plundering; breach of the commandments of God, however much of riot it may have run, all this may be pardoned and washed away through the blood of Jesus Christ. In all the long list of human sins, though that be long as time, there stands but one sin that is unpardonable, (Matthew 12: 31) and that one no sinner has committed if he feels within himself a longing for mercy, for that sin once committed, the soul becomes hardened, dead, and seared, and never desires afterwards to find peace with God. I therefore declare to thee, O trembling sinner, that however great thine iniquity may be, whatever sin thou mayest have committed in all the list of guilt, however far thou mayest have exceeded all thy fellow-creatures, though thou mayest have distanced the Pauls and Magdalens and every one of the most heinous culprits in the black race of sin, yet the blood of Christ is able now to wash thy sin away. Mark! I speak not lightly of thy sin, it is exceedingly great; but I speak still more loftily of the blood of Christ. Great as thy sins are, the blood of Christ is greater still. Thy sins are like great mountains, but the blood of Christ is like Noah's flood; twenty cubits upwards shall this blood prevail, and the top of the mountains of thy sin shall be covered.

FOR MEDITATION: The price of life is far too costly for man to achieve his redemption (Psalm 49: 7-9), but the Prince of life has achieved it (Psalm 49: 15) by his own death (Acts 3: 15).

Awake! Awake!

"Therefore let us not sleep as do others; but let us watch and be sober."
1 Thessalonians 5: 6
SUGGESTED FURTHER READING: Titus 1: 7- 2: 8

"Let us watch." There are many that never watch. They never watch against sin; they never watch against the temptations of the enemy; they do not watch against themselves, nor against "the lusts of the flesh, the lusts of the eye, and the pride of life." They do not watch for opportunities to do good, they do not watch for opportunities to instruct the ignorant, to confirm the weak, to comfort the afflicted, to succour them that are in need; they do not watch for opportunities of glorifying Jesus, or for times of communion; they do not watch for the promises; they do not watch for answers to their prayers; they do not watch for the second coming of our Lord Jesus. These are the refuse of the world: they watch not, because they are asleep. But let us watch: so shall we prove that we are not slumberers. Again: let us "be sober." Albert Barnes says, this most of all refers to abstinence, or temperance in eating and drinking. Calvin says, not so: this refers more especially to the spirit of moderation in the things of the world. Both are right: it refers to both. There be many that are not sober; they sleep, because they are not so; for insobriety leadeth to sleep. They are not sober—they are drunkards, they are gluttons. They are not sober—they cannot be content to do a little business—they want to do a great deal. They are not sober—they cannot carry on a trade that is sure—they must speculate. They are not sober—if they lose their property, their spirit is cast down within them, and they are like men that are drunken with wormwood. If on the other hand, they get rich, they are not sober: they so set their affections upon things on earth that they become intoxicated with pride.

FOR MEDITATION: The Christian in the pew should aim at the same standards as those which he expects to see in the Christian in the pulpit (1 Corinthians 11: 1).

SERMON NO. 163

God's barriers against man's sin

"Fear ye not me? saith the Lord: will ye not tremble at my presence, which have placed the sand for the bound of the sea by a perpetual decree, that it cannot pass it: and though the waves thereof toss themselves, yet can they not prevail; though they roar, yet can they not pass over it? But this people hath a revolting and rebellious heart; they are revolted and gone."
Jeremiah 5: 22-23
SUGGESTED FURTHER READING: Isaiah 1: 1-4

God here contrasts the obedience of the strong, the mighty, the untamed sea, with the rebellious character of his own people. "The sea," saith he, "obeys me; it never breaks its boundary; it never leaps from its channel; it obeys me in all its movements. But man, poor puny man, the little creature whom I could crush as the moth, will not be obedient to me. The sea obeys me from shore to shore, without reluctance, and its ebbing floods, as they retire from its bed, each of them says to me, in the voices of the pebbles, 'O Lord, we are obedient to thee, for thou art our master.' But my people", says God, "are a revolting and a rebellious people; they go astray from me." And is it not, my brethren, a marvellous thing, that the whole earth is obedient to God, save man? Even the mighty leviathan, who maketh the deep to be hoary, sinneth not against God, but his course is ordered according to his Almighty Master's decree. Stars, those wondrous masses of light, are easily directed by the very wish of God; clouds, though they seem erratic in their movement, have God for their pilot; "he maketh the clouds his chariot;" and the winds, though they seem restive beyond control, yet do they blow, or cease to blow just as God wills. In heaven, on earth, even in the lower regions, we could scarcely find such a disobedience as that which is practised by man; at least, in heaven, there is a cheerful obedience; and in hell there is constrained submission to God, while on earth man makes the base exception, he is continually revolting and rebelling against his Maker.

FOR MEDITATION: Jonah, a great wind, a great fish, a plant, a worm, an east wind (Jonah 1: 3,4,17; 2: 10; 4: 6-8)—which is the odd one out? Answer: God's servant Jonah—the rest obeyed God at once. This should humble us!

SERMON NO. 220

The work of the Holy Spirit

"Are ye so foolish? having begun in the Spirit, are ye now made perfect by the flesh?" Galatians 3: 3
SUGGESTED FURTHER READING: John 3: 1-8

It is simple enough for a man that hath the Spirit in him to believe, when he hath the written Word before him and the witness of the Spirit in him; that is easy enough. But for the poor, tried sinner, who cannot see anything in the Word of God but thunder and threatening—for him to believe—ah, my brethren, it is not such a little matter as some make it to be. It needs the fulness of the power of God's Spirit to bring any man to such a faith as that. Well, when the sinner has thus believed, then the Holy Spirit brings all the precious things to him. There is the blood of Jesus; that can never save my soul, unless God the Spirit takes that blood, and sprinkles it upon my conscience. There is the perfect spotless righteousness of Jesus; it is a robe that will fit me and adorn me from head to foot, but it is no use to me till I have put it on; and I cannot put it on myself; God the Holy Spirit must put the robe of Jesus' righteousness on me. There is the covenant of adoption, whereby God gives me the privileges of a son; but I cannot rejoice in my adoption until I receive the spirit of adoption whereby I may be able to cry, "Abba, Father." So, beloved, you see that every point that is brought out in the experience of the new-born Christian, every point in that part of salvation which we call its beginning in the soul, has to do with God the Holy Spirit. There is no step that can be taken without him, there is nothing which can be accomplished aright without him.

FOR MEDITATION: It is impossible to begin in the flesh and end up with the Spirit (John 6: 63-64; Romans 8: 9).

The Holy Spirit—the great Teacher

"Howbeit when he, the Spirit of truth, is come, he will guide you into all truth: for he shall not speak of himself; but whatsoever he shall hear, that shall he speak: and he will shew you things to come." John 16: 13
SUGGESTED FURTHER READING: Psalm 25: 4-14

If I give myself to the Holy Spirit and ask his guidance, there is no fear of my wandering. Again, we rejoice in this Spirit because he is ever-present. We fall into a difficulty sometimes; we say, "Oh, if I could take this to my minister, he would explain it; but I live so far off, and am not able to see him." That perplexes us, and we turn the text round and round and cannot make anything out of it. We look at the commentators. We take down pious Thomas Scott, and, as usual, he says nothing about it if it be a dark passage. Then we go to holy Matthew Henry, and if it is an easy Scripture, he is sure to explain it; but if it is a text hard to be understood, it is likely enough, of course, left in his own gloom. And even Dr Gill himself, the most consistent of commentators, when he comes to a hard passage, manifestly avoids it in some degree. But when we have no commentator or minister, we have still the Holy Spirit. And let me tell you a little secret: whenever you cannot understand a text, open your Bible, bend your knee, and pray over that text; and if it does not split into atoms and open itself, try again. If prayer does not explain it, it is one of the things God did not intend you to know, and you may be content to be ignorant of it. Prayer is the key that openeth the cabinets of mystery. Prayer and faith are sacred keys that can open secrets, and obtain great treasures. There is no college for holy education like that of the blessed Spirit, for he is an ever-present tutor, to whom we have only to bend the knee, and he is at our side, the great expositor of truth.

FOR MEDITATION: We sometimes hold up our own spiritual education by failing to believe and obey what we have already been taught (1 Corinthians 3: 1-3; Hebrews 5: 11-14). Are you a difficult pupil?

All-sufficiency magnified

"I can do all things through Christ which strengtheneth me."
Philippians 4: 13
SUGGESTED FURTHER READING: Acts 22: 6-16

Christians, beware lest that village in which you have found a quiet retreat from the cares of business, should rise up in judgment against you, to condemn you, because, having means and opportunity, you use the village for rest, but never seek to do any good in it. Take care, masters and mistresses, lest your servant's souls be required of you at the last great day. "I worked for my master;" they say, "he paid me my wages, but had no respect to his greater Master, and never spoke to me, though he heard me swear, and saw me going on in my sins." If I could I would thrust a thorn into the seat where you are now sitting, and make you spring up for a moment to the dignity of a thought of your responsibilities. Why, sirs, what has God made you for? What has he sent you here for? Did he make stars that should not shine, and suns that should give no light, and moons that should not cheer the darkness? Has he made rivers that shall not be filled with water, and mountains that shall not stay the clouds? Has he made even the forests which shall not give a habitation to the birds; or has he made the prairie which shall not feed the wild flocks? And has he made thee for nothing? Why, man, the nettle in the corner of the churchyard has its uses, and the spider on the wall serves her Maker; and you, a man in the image of God, a blood-bought man, a man who is in the path and track to heaven, a man regenerated, twice created, are you made for nothing at all but to buy and to sell, to eat and to drink, to wake and to sleep, to laugh and to weep, to live to yourself?

FOR MEDITATION: The Christian—chosen to do (John 15: 16), created to do (Ephesians 2: 10), commanded to do (1 Corinthians 10: 31), continue to do (Galatians 6: 9,10). What?

Man's ruin and God's remedy

"And the Lord said unto Moses, Make thee a fiery serpent, and set it upon a pole: and it shall come to pass, that every one that is bitten, when he looketh upon it, shall live." Numbers 21: 8
SUGGESTED FURTHER READING: Luke 23: 1-5

Christ's redemption was so plenteous, that had God willed it, if all the stars of heaven had been peopled with sinners, Christ need not have suffered another pang to redeem them all—there was a boundless value in his precious blood. And, sinner, if there were so much as this, surely there is enough for thee. And then again, if thou art not satisfied with Christ's sin-offering, just think a moment; God is satisfied, God the Father is content, and must not thou be? The Judge saith, "I am satisfied; let the sinner go free, for I have punished the Surety in his stead;" and if the Judge is satisfied, surely the criminal may be. Oh! Come, poor sinner, come and see; if there is enough to appease the wrath of God there must be enough to answer all the requirements of man. "Nay, nay," saith one, "but my sin is such a terrible one that I cannot see in the substitution of Christ that which is like to meet it." What is thy sin? "Blasphemy." Why, Christ died for blasphemy: this was the very charge which man imputed to him, and therefore you may be quite sure that God laid it on him if men did. "Nay, nay," saith one, "but I have been worse than that; I have been a liar." It is just what men said of him. They declared that he lied when he said, "If this temple be destroyed I will build it in three days." See in Christ a liar's Saviour as well as a blasphemer's Saviour. "But," says one, "I have been in league with Beelzebub." Just what they said of Christ. They said that he cast out devils through Beelzebub. So man laid that sin on him, and man did unwittingly what God would have him do. I tell thee, even that sin was laid on Christ.

FOR MEDITATION: Christ was truly a sign spoken against (Luke 2: 34). Men called him many names which God had never given him—Beelzebub (Matthew 10: 25), glutton and drunkard (Matthew 11: 19), impostor (Matthew 27: 63), liar (John 8: 13), sinner (John 9: 24), demon-possessed and mad (John 10: 20), and blasphemer (John 10: 33). On the cross God treated his Son as if he was everything that man had accused him of, and every other sin besides.

SERMON NO. 285

Samson conquered

"And she said, The Philistines be upon thee, Samson. And he awoke out of his sleep, and said, I will go out as at other times before, and shake myself. And he wist not that the Lord was departed from him. But the Philistines took him, and put out his eyes, and brought him down to Gaza, and bound him with fetters of brass; and he did grind in the prison house."
Judges 16: 20,21
SUGGESTED FURTHER READING: Colossians 2: 1-8

Do any of you wish to be backsliders? Do you wish to betray the holy profession of your religion? My brethren, is there one among you who this day makes a profession of love to Christ, who desires to be an apostate? Is there one of you who desires like Samson to have his eyes put out, and to be made to grind in the mill? Would you, like David, commit a great sin, and go with broken bones to the grave? Would you, like Lot, be drunken, and fall into lust? No, I know what you say, "Lord, let my path be like the eagle's flight; let me fly upwards to the sun, and never stay and never turn aside. Oh, give me grace that I may serve thee, like Caleb, with a perfect heart, and that from the beginning even to the end of my days, my course may be as the shining light, which shineth more and more unto the perfect day." I know what is your desire. How, then, shall it be accomplished? Look well to your consecration; see that it is sincere; see that you mean it, and then look up to the Holy Spirit, after you have looked to your consecration, and beg of him to give you daily grace; for as day by day the manna fell, so must you receive daily food from on high. And, remember, it is not by any grace you have in you, but by the grace that is in Christ, and that must be given to you hour by hour, that you are to stand, and having done all, to be crowned at last as a faithful one, who has endured unto the end.

FOR MEDITATION: The best way to guard against backsliding is not to keep still, but to grow in the grace and knowledge of the Lord Jesus Christ (2 Peter 3: 17,18).

The loved ones chastened

"As many as I love, I rebuke and chasten: be zealous therefore, and repent."
Revelation 3: 19
SUGGESTED FURTHER READING: Job 12: 1-6

See how the righteous are cast down. How often is virtue dressed in the rags of poverty! How frequently is the most pious spirit made to suffer from hunger, and thirst, and nakedness! We have sometimes heard the Christian say, when he has contemplated these things, "Surely, I have served God in vain; it is for nothing that I have chastened myself every morning and vexed my soul with fasting; for lo, God hath cast me down, and he lifteth up the sinner. How can this be?" The wise of the heathen could not answer this question, and they therefore adopted the expedient of cutting the intricate knot. "We cannot tell how it is," they might have said; therefore they flew at the fact itself, and denied it. "The man that prospers is favoured of the gods; the man who is unsuccessful is obnoxious to the Most High." So said the heathen, and they knew no better. Those more enlightened people who talked with Job in the days of his affliction, did not get much further; for they believed that all who served God would have a hedge about them; God would multiply their wealth and increase their happiness; while they saw in Job's affliction, as they conceived, a certain sign that he was a hypocrite, and, therefore God had quenched his candle and put out his light in darkness. And alas! Even Christians have fallen into the same error. They have been apt to think that if God lifts a man up, there must be some excellence in him; and if he chastens and afflicts, they are generally led to think that it must be an exhibition of wrath. Now hear the text, and the riddle is all made clear; listen to the words of Jesus, speaking to his servant John, and the mystery is solved. "As many as I love, I rebuke and chasten: be zealous therefore, and repent."

FOR MEDITATION: God is good to his children, both providing for them and disciplining them (Deuteronomy 8: 1-5). Teachings such as the "Prosperity Gospel" and "Healing being in the Atonement" miss the point that such blessings are guaranteed to the believer only in the Glory (Revelation 21: 3-7).

SERMON NO. 164

Love's commendation

"But God commendeth his love toward us, in that, while we were yet sinners, Christ died for us." Romans 5: 8
SUGGESTED FURTHER READING: Hebrews 2: 5-9

I could almost conceive a parliament in heaven. The angels are assembled; the question is proposed to them: "Cherubim and seraphim, cohorts of the glorified, ye spirits that like flames of fire, at my bidding fly, ye happy beings, whom I have created for my honour! Here is a question which I condescend to offer for your consideration: Man has sinned; there is no way for his pardon but by someone suffering and paying blood for blood. Who shall it be?" I can conceive that there was silence throughout the great assembly. Gabriel spoke not: he would have stretched his wings and flapped the heavens in a moment, if the deed had been possible; but he felt that he could never bear the guilt of a world upon his shoulders, and, therefore, still he sat. And there the mightiest of the mighty, those who could shake a world if God should will it, sat still, because they felt all powerless to accomplish redemption. I do not conceive that one of them would have ventured to hope that God himself would assume flesh and die. I do not think it could have entered even into angelic thought to conceive that the mighty Maker of the skies should bow his awful head and sink into a grave. I cannot imagine that the brightest and most seraphic of these glorified ones would for an instant have suffered such a thought to abide with him. And when the Son of God, rising from his throne, spoke to them and said, "Principalities and powers! I will become flesh, I will veil this Godhead of mine in robes of mortal clay, I will die!" I think I see the angels for once astonished.

FOR MEDITATION: Man had sinned; man must suffer. Only a real, yet sinless man could take his place; God the Son alone qualified for the task (Romans 8: 3).

The character of Christ's people

"They are not of the world, even as I am not of the world." John 17: 16
SUGGESTED FURTHER READING: Leviticus 19: 35-37

Look at Jesus' character; how different from every other man's—pure, perfect, spotless, even such should be the life of the believer. I plead not for the possibility of sinless conduct in Christians, but I must hold that grace makes men to differ, and that God's people will be very different from other kinds of people. A servant of God will be God's man everywhere. As a chemist, he could not indulge in any tricks that such men might play with their drugs; as a grocer—if indeed it be not a phantom that such things are done—he could not mix aloe leaves with tea or red lead in the pepper; if he practised any other kind of business, he could not for a moment condescend to the little petty shifts, called "methods of business." To him it is nothing what is called "business;" it is what is called God's law, he feels that he is not of the world, consequently, he goes against its fashions and its maxims. A singular story is told of a certain Quaker. One day he was bathing in the Thames, and a waterman called out to him, "Ha! there goes the Quaker." "How do you know I'm a Quaker?" "Because you swim against the stream; it is the way the Quakers always do." That is the way Christians always ought to do—to swim against the stream. The Lord's people should not go along with the rest in their worldliness. Their characters should be visibly different. You should be such men that your fellows can recognise you without any difficulty, and say, "Such a man is a Christian."

FOR MEDITATION: When the Christian thinks to himself "But everybody else does it", he is thinking of denying Christ (Ephesians 4: 17,20).

Comfort for the desponding

"Oh that I were as in months past." Job 29: 2
SUGGESTED FURTHER READING: Galatians 4: 11-20

There is such a thing, my dear friends, as your getting into a terribly bad condition through the ministry that you attend. Can it be expected that men should grow in grace when they are never watered with the streams that make glad the city of our God? Can they be supposed to grow strong in the Lord Jesus, when they do not feed on spiritual food? We know some who grumble, Sabbath after Sabbath, and say they can't hear such and such a minister. Why don't you buy an ear-trumpet then? Ah! But I mean, that I can't hear him to my soul's profit. Then do not go to hear him, if you have tried for a long while and don't get any profit. I always think that a man who grumbles as he goes out of chapel ought not to be pitied, but whipped, for he can stay away if he likes, and go where he will be pleased. There are plenty of places where the sheep may feed in their own manner; and everyone is bound to go where he gets the pasture most suited to his soul. But you are not bound to run away directly your minister dies, as many of you did before you came here. You should not run away from the ship directly the storm comes, and the captain is gone, and you find her not exactly sea-worthy; stand by her, begin caulking her, God will send you a captain, there will be fine weather by and by, and all will be right. But very frequently a bad minister starves God's people into walking skeletons, so that you can tell all their bones; and who wonders that they starve out their minister, when they get no nourishment from his ministrations.

FOR MEDITATION: God provides leaders to build up his people so that they can go on to build up one another (Ephesians 4: 11-12). The absence of the leader will show whether the flock can stand on their own feet in the Lord (Philippians 1: 27; Colossians 2: 5).

SERMON NO. 51

Preaching! Man's privilege and God's power!

"For Herod feared John, knowing that he was a just man and an holy, and observed him; and when he heard him, he did many things, and heard him gladly." Mark 6: 20.
SUGGESTED FURTHER READING: James 1: 19-25.

If you would hear the word to profit, you must hear it **obediently**. You must hear it as James and John did, when the master said "Follow me," and they left their nets and their boats and they followed him. You must do the word as well as hear it, yielding up your hearts to its sway, being willing to walk in the road which it maps, to follow the path which it lays before you. Hearing it obediently, you must also hear it **personally** for yourselves, not for others, but for yourselves alone. You must be as Zaccheus, who was in the sycamore tree, and the Master said, "Zaccheus, make haste and come down; for today I must abide at thy house." The word will never bless you till it comes home directly to yourself. You must be as Mary, who when the Master spoke to her she did not know his voice, till he said unto her, "Mary", and she said, "Rabboni." There must be an individual hearing of the truth, and a reception of it for yourself in your own heart. Then, too, you must hear the truth **penitently**. You must be as that Mary, who when she listened to the word, must needs go and wash the feet of Jesus with her tears, and wipe them with the hairs of her head. There must be tears for your many sins, a true confession of your guilt before God. But above all you must hear it **believingly**. The word must not be unto you as mere sound, but as matter of fact. You must be as Lydia, whose heart the Lord opened; or as the trembling gaoler, who believed on the Lord Jesus with all his house and was baptized immediately. You must be as the thief, who could pray, "Lord, remember me," and who could believe the precious promise given, "Today shalt thou be with me in Paradise."

FOR MEDITATION: To want to hear the preaching of God's Word and to enjoy hearing it are good things as far as they go, but by themselves they do not go far enough (Ezekiel 33: 30-32).

SERMON NO. 347

A woman's memorial

"Verily I say unto you, Wheresoever this gospel shall be preached in the whole world, there shall also this, that this woman hath done, be told for a memorial of her." Matthew 26: 13.
SUGGESTED FURTHER READING: I Corinthians I: 26-31

The evangelists are of course the historians of the time of Christ; but what strange historians they are! They leave out just that which worldly ones would write, and they record just that which the worldly would have passed over. What historian would have thought of recording the story of the widow and her two mites? Would a Hume or a Smollet have spared half a page for such an incident? Or think you that even a Macaulay could have found it in his pen to write down a story of an eccentric woman, who broke an alabaster box of precious ointment upon the head of Jesus? But so it is. Jesus values things, not by their glare and glitter, but by their intrinsic value. He bids his historians store up, not the things which shall dazzle men, but those which shall instruct and teach them in their spirits. Christ values a matter, not by its exterior, but by the motive which dictated it, by the love which shines from it. O singular historian! You have passed by much that Herod did; you tell us little of the glories of his temple; you tell us little of Pilate, and that little not to his credit; you treat with neglect the battles that are passing over the face of the earth; the grandeur of Caesar does not entice you from your simple story. But you continue to tell these little things, and wise are you in so doing, for truly these little things, when put into the scales of wisdom, weigh more than those monstrous bubbles of which the world delights to read.

FOR MEDITATION: God usually bypasses those who look great to the world and in their own eyes; he desires people who are after his own heart, however inconspicuous they are in the world's sight (I Samuel 16: 7; Luke 3: 1-2).

Satan's banquet

"The governor of the feast called the bridegroom, And saith unto him, Every man at the beginning doth set forth good wine; and when men have well drunk, then that which is worse; but thou hast kept the good wine until now." John 2: 9-10
SUGGESTED FURTHER READING: Psalm 55: 12-23

The governor of the feast said more than he intended to say, or rather, there is more truth in what he said than he himself imagined. This is the established rule all the world over: "the good wine first, and when men have well drunk, then that which is worse." It is the rule with men; and have not hundreds of disappointed hearts bewailed it? Friendship first—the oily tongue, the words softer than butter, and afterwards the drawn sword. Ahitophel first presents the lordly dish of love and kindness to David, then afterwards that which is worse, for he forsakes his master, and becomes the counsellor of his rebel son. Judas presents first of all the dish of fair speech and of kindness; the Saviour partook thereof, he walked to the house of God in company with him, and took sweet counsel with him; but afterwards there came the dregs of the wine—"He that eateth bread with me hath lifted up his heel against me." Judas the thief betrayed his Master, bringing forth afterwards "that which is worse." You have found it so with many whom you thought your friends. In the heyday of prosperity, when the sun was shining, and the birds were singing, and all was fair and cheerful with you, they brought forth the good wine; but there came a chilling frost, and nipped your flowers, and the leaves fell from the trees, and your streams were frosted with ice, and then they brought forth that which is worse, they forsook you and fled; they left you in your hour of peril, and taught you that great truth, that "Cursed is he that trusteth in man, and maketh flesh his arm."

FOR MEDITATION: Has someone you trusted let you down badly, albeit unintentionally? Christ's first miracle reminds us that man's ways are not God's ways (Isaiah 55: 8); the Christian has a friend who sticks closer than a brother (Proverbs 18: 24) and is assured that the best is still to come (Hebrews 10: 34).

SERMON NO. 225

The warning neglected

"He heard the sound of the trumpet, and took not warning; his blood shall be upon him." Ezekiel 33: 5
SUGGESTED FURTHER READING: Haggai 1: 1-6

Men have got time. It is the want of will, not want of way. You have time, sir, have you not, despite all your business, to spend in pleasure? You have time to read your newspaper—have you not time to read your Bible? You have time to sing a song—have you no time to pray a prayer? Why, you know when farmer Brown met farmer Smith in the market one day, he said to him, "Farmer Smith, I can't think how it is you find time for hunting. Why, man, what with sowing and mowing and reaping and ploughing, and all that, my time is so fully occupied on my farm, that I have no time for hunting." "Ah," said he, "Brown, if you liked hunting as much as I do, if you could not find time, you'd make it." And so it is with religion, the reason why men cannot find time for it is, because they do not like it well enough. If they liked it, they would find time. And besides, what time does it want? What time does it require? Can I not pray to God over my ledger? Can I not snatch a text at my breakfast, and think over it all day? May I not even when I am busy in the affairs of the world, be thinking of my soul, and casting myself upon a Redeemer's blood and atonement? It wants no time. There may be some time required; some time for my private devotions, and for communion with Christ, but when I grow in grace, I shall think it right to have more and more time, the more I can possibly get, the happier I shall be, and I shall never make the excuse that I have not time.

FOR MEDITATION: How much time do you make to spend alone with God each day? What do you do with him for the rest of the day? (Colossians 3: 23).

SERMON NO. 165

Manasseh

"Then Manasseh knew that the Lord he was God." 2 Chronicles 33: 13
SUGGESTED FURTHER READING: Romans 1: 18-25

It takes ten thousand times more faith to be an unbeliever than to be a believer in God's revelation. One man comes to me and tells me I am credulous, because I believe in a great First Cause who created the heavens and the earth, and that God became man and died for sin. I tell him I may be, and no doubt am very credulous, as he conceives credulity, but I conceive that which I believe is in perfect consistency with my reason, and I therefore receive it. "But," saith he, "I am not credulous—not at all." Sir, I say, I should like to ask you one thing. You do not believe the world was created by God. "No." You must be amazingly credulous, then, I am sure. Do you think this Bible exists without being made? If you should say I am credulous, because I believe it had a printer and a binder, I should say that you were infinitely more credulous, if you assured me that it was made at all, and should you begin to tell me one of your theories about creation—that atoms floated through space, and came to a certain shape, I should resign the palm of credulity to you. You believe, perhaps, moreover, that man came to be in this world through the improvement of certain creatures. I have read that you say that there were certain monads—that afterwards they grew into fishes—that these fishes wanted to fly, and then wings grew—that by and by they wanted to crawl, and then legs came, and they became lizards, and by many steps they then became monkeys, and then the monkeys became men, and you believe yourself to be cousin ape to an orang-utan. Now, I may be very credulous, but really not so credulous as you are.

FOR MEDITATION: If Manasseh, the greatest of idolaters (2 Chronicles 33: 3), could be converted and worship the one true God, your most ardent evolutionist neighbours or colleagues can be converted and worship the God who created them!

Free-will—a slave

"And ye will not come unto me, that ye might have life." John 5: 40
SUGGESTED FURTHER READING: John 6: 60-65

It is certain that men will not come unto Christ, that they might have life. We might prove this from many texts of Scripture, but we will take one parable. You remember the parable where a certain king had a feast for his son, and invited a great number to come; the oxen and fatlings were killed, and he sent his messengers inviting many to the supper. Did they go to the feast? No; but they all, with one accord, began to make excuse. One said he had married a wife, and therefore he could not come, whereas he might have brought her with him. Another had bought a yoke of oxen, and went to prove them; but the feast was in the night-time and he could not prove his oxen in the dark. Another had bought a piece of land, and wanted to see it; but I should not think he went to see it with a lantern. So they all made excuses and would not come. Well the king was determined to have the feast; so he said, "Go into the highways and hedges," and invite them— stop! Not invite—"compel them to come in;" for even the ragged fellows in the hedges would never have come unless they were compelled. Take another parable; a certain man had a vineyard; at the appointed season he sent one of his servants for his rent. What did they do to him? They beat that servant. He sent another; and they stoned him. He sent another and they killed him. And, at last, he said "I will send them my son, they will reverence him." But what did they do? They said, "This is the heir, let us kill him, and cast him out of the vineyard." So they did. It is the same with all men by nature. The Son of God came, yet men rejected him.

FOR MEDITATION: When you thank God for your salvation, do you give him all the credit for your conversion as well (John 15: 16)?

SERMON NO.52

Christ our passover

"For even Christ our passover is sacrificed for us." 1 Corinthians 5: 7
SUGGESTED FURTHER READING: John 6: 25-35

Some of you, my friends, who are true Christians, live too much on your changing feelings, on your experiences and evidences. Now, that is all wrong. That is just as if a worshipper had gone to the tabernacle and begun eating one of the coats that were worn by the priest. When a man lives on Christ's righteousness, it is the same as eating Christ's dress. When a man lives on his feelings, that is as much as if the child of God should live on some tokens that he received in the sanctuary that were never meant for food, but only to comfort him a little. What the Christian lives on is not Christ's righteousness, but Christ; he does not live on Christ's pardon, but on Christ; and on Christ he lives daily, on nearness to Christ. Oh! I do love Christ-preaching. It is not the doctrine of justification that does my heart good, it is Christ, the justifier; it is not pardon that so much makes the Christian's heart rejoice, it is Christ the pardoner; it is not election that I love half so much as my being chosen in Christ before the worlds began; it is not final perseverance that I love so much as the thought that in Christ my life is hid, and that since he gives unto his sheep eternal life, they shall never perish, neither shall any man pluck them out of his hand. Take care, Christian, to eat the Paschal Lamb and nothing else. I tell thee man, if thou eatest that alone, it will be like bread to thee—thy soul's best food. If thou livest on anything else but the Saviour, thou art like one who seeks to live on some weed that grows in the desert, instead of eating the manna that comes down from heaven. Jesus is the manna.

FOR MEDITATION: This communion sermon reminds us that if we sideline Christ in our Christianity, we are left with little more than an inanity—the best of what remains, even the Lord's Supper or the doctrines of grace, will be empty if in them we fail to "remember Jesus Christ" (2 Timothy 2: 8).

SERMON NO. 54

Consolation in Christ

"If there be therefore any consolation in Christ, if any comfort of love, if any fellowship of the Spirit, if any bowels and mercies." Philippians 2: 1
SUGGESTED FURTHER READING: John 16: 7-15

The Holy Spirit, during the present dispensation, is revealed to us as the Comforter. It is the Spirit's business to console and cheer the hearts of God's people. He does convince of sin; he does illuminate and instruct; but still the main part of his business lies in making glad the hearts of the renewed, in confirming the weak, and lifting up all those that be bowed down. Whatever the Holy Spirit may not be, he is evermore the Comforter to the church; and this age is peculiarly the dispensation of the Holy Spirit, in which Christ cheers us not by his personal presence, as he shall do by-and-by, but by the indwelling and constant abiding of the Holy Spirit the Comforter. Now, mark you, as the Holy Spirit is the Comforter, Christ is the comfort. The Holy Spirit consoles, but Christ is the consolation. If I may use the figure, the Holy Spirit is the Physician, but Christ is the medicine. He heals the wound, but it is by applying the holy ointment of Christ's name and grace. He takes not of his own things, but of the things of Christ. We are not consoled today by new revelations, but by the old revelation explained, enforced, and lit up with new splendour by the presence and power of the Holy Spirit the Comforter. If we give to the Holy Spirit the Greek name of Paraclete, as we sometimes do, then our heart confers on our blessed Lord Jesus the title of the Paraclesis. If the one be the Comforter, the other is the comfort.

FOR MEDITATION: Many of the errors taught about God the Holy Spirit would come to nothing if God's people understood the Scriptural teaching on the relationships between the three persons of the Trinity. May the Holy Spirit help us to grow in the knowledge of the only true God and Jesus Christ whom he has sent (John 17: 3).

Dilemma and deliverance

"Thou, Lord, hast not forsaken them that seek thee." Psalm 9: 10
SUGGESTED FURTHER READING: Psalm 23

If we could but once believe the doctrine that the child of God might fall from grace and perish everlastingly, we might, indeed, shut up our Bible in despair. To what purpose would my preaching be—the preaching of a rickety gospel like that? To what purpose your faith—a faith in a God that cannot and would not carry on to the end? To what use the blood of Christ, if it were shed in vain, and did not bring the blood-bought ones securely home? To what purpose the Spirit, if he were not omnipotent enough to overcome our wandering, to arrest our sins and make us perfect, and present us faultless before the throne of God at last? That doctrine of the final perseverance of the saints is, I believe, as thoroughly bound up with the standing or falling of the gospel, as is the article of justification by faith. Give that up and I see no gospel left; I see no beauty in religion that is worthy of my acceptance, or that deserves my admiration. An unchanging God, an everlasting covenant, a sure mercy, these are the things that my soul delights in, and I know your hearts love to feed upon them. But take these away, and what have we? We have a foundation of wood, hay, straw, and stubble. We have nothing solid. We have a fort of earthworks, a mud hovel through which the thief may break and steal away our treasures. No, this foundation stands sure —"The Lord knoweth them that are his;" and he will certainly bring them all to his right hand at last in glory everlasting.

FOR MEDITATION: If the truly converted man can be lost, Jesus must have meant "lend" when he said "give", "temporary" when he said "eternal" and "perhaps" when he said "never" (John 10: 28). Uncertainty is the hallmark of man-made religion.

Compel them to come in

"Compel them to come in." Luke 14: 23
SUGGESTED FURTHER READING: John 3: 31-36

I beseech you by him that liveth and was dead, and is alive for evermore, consider my master's message which he instructs me now to address you. But do you spurn it? Do you still refuse it? Then I must change my tone a minute. I will not merely tell you the message, and invite you as I do with all earnestness, and sincere affection—I will go further. Sinner, in God's name, I command you to repent and believe. Do you ask me my authority? I am an ambassador of heaven. My credentials, some of them secret, and in my own heart; and others of them open before you this day in the seals of my ministry, sitting and standing in this hall, where God has given me many souls for my hire. As God the everlasting one has given me a commission to preach his gospel, I command you to believe in the Lord Jesus Christ; not on my own authority, but on the authority of him who said, "Go ye into all the world and preach the gospel to every creature;" and then he annexed this solemn sanction, "He that believeth and is baptised shall be saved, but he that believeth not shall be damned." Reject my message, and remember "He that despised Moses' law died without mercy under two or three witnesses: of how much sorer punishment, suppose ye, shall he be thought worthy, who hath trodden under foot the Son of God." An ambassador is not to stand below the man with whom he deals, for we stand higher. If the minister chooses to take his proper rank, girded with the omnipotence of God, and anointed with his holy unction, he is to command men, and speak with all authority compelling them to come in: "command, exhort, rebuke with all longsuffering."

FOR MEDITATION: Do we regard the Gospel as a take-it or leave-it option? The opposite of trusting in Christ is disobedience (Romans 1: 5 and 16: 26).

The Destroyer destroyed

"That through death he might destroy him that had the power of death, that is, the devil." Hebrews 2: 14

SUGGESTED FURTHER READING: Genesis 3: 1-15

At last the day arrived; it was telegraphed to the court of hell that at last Christ would die. They rung their bells with hellish mirth and joy. "He will die now," said he; "Judas has taken the thirty pieces of silver. Let those scribes and Pharisees get him, they will no more let him go than the spider will a poor unfortunate fly. He is safe now." And the devil laughed for very glee, when he saw the Saviour stand before Pilate's bar. And when it was said, "Let him be crucified," then his joy knew no bounds, except that bound which his own misery must ever set to it. As far as he could, he revelled in what was to him a delightful thought, that the Lord of glory was about to die. In death, as Christ was seen of angels, he was seen of devils too; and that dreary march from Pilate's palace to the cross was one which devils saw with extraordinary interest. And when they saw him on the cross, there stood the exulting fiend, smiling to himself. "Ah! I have the King of Glory now in my dominions; I have the power of death, and I have the power over the Lord Jesus." He exerted that power, till the Lord Jesus had to cry out in bitter anguish, "My God, my God, why hast thou forsaken me?" But, how short-lived was hellish victory! How brief was the Satanic triumph! He died; and "It is finished!" shook the gates of hell. Down from the cross the conqueror leaped, pursued the fiend with thunder-bolts of wrath; swift to the shades of hell the fiend did fly, and swift descending went the conqueror after him.

FOR MEDITATION: The powers of darkness enjoyed only an hour of apparent victory over the Lord Jesus Christ (Luke 22: 53), but it resulted in his victory procession with them on public display as his captives (Colossians 2: 15).

Turn or burn

"If he turn not, he will whet his sword; he hath bent his bow, and made it ready." Psalm 7: 12
SUGGESTED FURTHER READING: 2 Thessalonians 1: 5-12

God has a sword, and he will punish man on account of his iniquity. This evil generation has laboured to take away from God the sword of his justice; they have endeavoured to prove to themselves that God will "clear the guilty," and will by no means "punish iniquity, transgression and sin." Two hundred years ago the predominant strain of the pulpit was one of terror: it was like Mount Sinai, it thundered forth the dreadful wrath of God, and from the lips of a Baxter or a Bunyan, you heard most terrible sermons, full to the brim with warnings of judgment to come. Perhaps some of the Puritan fathers may have gone too far, and have given too great a prominence to the terrors of the Lord in their ministry: but the age in which we live has sought to forget those terrors altogether, and if we dare to tell men that God will punish them for their sins, it is charged upon us that we want to bully them into religion, and if we faithfully and honestly tell our hearers that sin must bring after it certain destruction, it is said that we are attempting to frighten them into goodness. Now we care not what men mockingly impute to us; we feel it our duty, when men sin, to tell them they shall be punished, and so long as the world will not give up its sin we feel we must not cease our warnings. But the cry of the age is, that God is merciful, that God is love. Who said he was not? But remember, it is equally true, God is just, severely and inflexibly just. He were not God, if he were not just; he could not be merciful if he were not just.

FOR MEDITATION: The "meek and lowly" Lord Jesus Christ spoke often of judgment because of his care for the souls of men and his longing for them to repent and find rest (Matthew 11: 20-30).

SERMON NO. 106

The feast of the Lord

"The governor of the feast called the bridegroom, And saith unto him, Every man at the beginning doth set forth good wine; and when men have well drunk, then that which is worse: but thou hast kept the good wine until now." John 2: 9-10
SUGGESTED FURTHER READING: Psalm 73

If the Christian has the best wine to come, why should he envy the unbeliever? David did; he was discontented when he saw the prosperity of the wicked, and you and I are often tempted to do it; but you know what we ought to say when we see the wicked prosper, when we see them happy and full of delights of sinful pleasure. We ought to say, "My good wine is to come; I can bear that you should have your turn; my turn will come afterwards; I can be put off with these things, and lie with Lazarus at the gate, while the dogs lick my sores; my turn is to come, when the angels shall carry me into Abraham's bosom, and your turn is to come too, when in hell you lift up your eyes, being in torments." Christian, what more shall I say to you?—though there be a thousand lessons to learn from this, the best wine is kept to the last. Take heed to yourself, that you also keep your good wine until the last. The further you go on the road, seek to bring to your Saviour the more acceptable sacrifice. You had little faith years ago: man! Bring out the good wine now! Seek to have more faith. Your Master is better to you every day and you shall see him to be the best of all Masters and friends. Seek to be better to your Master every day; be more generous to his cause, more active to labour for him, more kind to his people, more diligent in prayer; and take heed that as you grow in years you grow in grace, so that when you come at last to the river Jordan, and the Master shall give you the best wine, you may also give to him the best wine.

FOR MEDITATION: In which direction is your Christian life going at the moment—forwards (Philippians 3: 13), backwards (Galatians 5: 7) or nowhere (1 Corinthians 3: 1-3)?

The Exodus

"And it came to pass at the end of the four hundred and thirty years, even the self same day it came to pass, that all the hosts of the Lord went out from the land of Egypt." Exodus 12: 41
SUGGESTED FURTHER READING: 1 Corinthians 10: 1-11

It is our firm conviction and increasing belief, that the historical books of Scripture were intended to teach us spiritual things by types and figures. We believe that every portion of Scripture history is not only a faithful transcript of what did actually happen, but also a shadow of what happens spiritually in the dealings of God with his people, or in the dispensations of his grace towards the world at large. We do not look upon the historical books of Scripture as being mere rolls of history, such as profane authors might have written, but we regard them as being most true and infallible records of the past, and also most bright and glorious foreshadowings of the future, or else most wondrous metaphors and marvellous illustrations of things which are verily received among us, and most truly felt in the Christian heart. We may be wrong—we believe we are not; at any rate, the very error has given us instruction, and our mistake has afforded us comfort. We look upon the book of Exodus as being a book of types of the deliverances which God will give to his elect people; not only as a history of what he has done, in bringing them out of Egypt by smiting the first-born, leading them through the Red Sea, and guiding them through the wilderness, but also as a picture of his faithful dealings with all his people, whom by the blood of Christ he separates from the Egyptians, and by his strong and mighty hand takes out of the house of their bondage and out of the land of their slavery.

FOR MEDITATION: Are you getting as much out of the Old Testament as you should? It is full of the Lord Jesus Christ (Luke 24: 27)! While it may be wrong and confusing to see types in every verse or action, if you major on the types which are identified and applied in the New Testament you cannot go far wrong.

The wailing of Risca

"Suddenly are my tents spoiled, and my curtains in a moment."
Jeremiah 4: 20
SUGGESTED FURTHER READING: Luke 12: 35-48

Live while you live; while it is called today, work, for the night cometh
wherein no man can work. And let us learn never to do anything which we
would not wish to be found doing if we were to die. We are sometimes asked
by young people whether they may go to the theatre, whether they may
dance, or whether they may do this or that. You may do anything which you
would not be ashamed to be doing when Christ shall come. You may do
anything which you would not blush to be found doing if the hand of death
should smite you; but if you would dread to die in any spot, go not there; if
you would not wish to enter the presence of your God with such-and-such a
word upon your lip, utter not that word; or if there would be a thought that
would be uncongenial to the judgment-day, seek not to think that thought.
So act that you may feel you can take your shroud with you wherever you go.
Happy is he that dies in his pulpit. Blessed is the man that dies in his daily
business, for he is found with his loins girt about him serving his Master;
but, unhappy must he be to whom death comes as an intruder, and finds him
engaged in that which he will blush to have ever touched, when God shall
appear in judgment. Power supreme; thou everlasting king; permit not
death to intrude upon an ill-spent hour, but find me rapt in meditation high;
singing my great Creator; proclaiming the love of Jesus, or lifting up my
heart in prayer for myself and my fellow-sinners.

FOR MEDITATION: Life contains a final moment when it will be impossible to
explain away or cover up something inappropriate.

NOTE: This sermon was occasioned by a mine explosion, in which some two
hundred or so miners were killed, at Risca, near Newport in South Wales.
Spurgeon had often gone to the Vale of Risca to rest and preach.

The Minister's farewell

"Wherefore I take you to record this day, that I am pure from the blood of all men. For I have not shunned to declare unto you all the counsel of God." Acts 20: 26-27
SUGGESTED FURTHER READING: Titus 2: 7-15

I have seen the young believer, just saved from sin, happy in his early Christian career, and walking humbly with his God. But evil has crept in, disguised in the mantle of truth. The finger of partial blindness was laid upon his eyes, and only one doctrine could be seen. Sovereignty was seen, but not responsibility. The minister once beloved was hated; he who had been honest to preach God's word, was accounted as the offscouring of all things. And what became the effect? The very reverse of good and gracious. Bigotry replaced love; bitterness lived where once there had been a loveliness of character. I could point you to innumerable instances where harping upon any one particular doctrine, has driven men to excess of bigotry and bitterness. And when a man has once come there, he is ready enough for sin of any kind to which the devil may please to tempt him. There is a necessity that the whole gospel should be preached, or else the spirits, even of Christians, will become marred and maimed. I have known men diligent for Christ, labouring to win souls with both hands; and suddenly they have espoused one particular doctrine and not the whole truth and they have subsided into lethargy. On the other hand where men have only taken the practical side of truth, and left out the doctrinal, too many professors have run over into legality; have talked as if they were to be saved by works, and have almost forgotten that grace by which they were called. They are like the Galatians, they have been bewitched by what they have heard. The believer in Christ, if he is to be kept pure, simple, holy, charitable, Christ-like, is only to be kept so by a preaching of the whole truth as it is in Jesus.

FOR MEDITATION: Doctrine should lead to practice; practice should spring from doctrine (Romans 12: 1; Ephesians 4: 1). Do you seek to hear and apply the whole counsel of God in your life (James 1: 22)?

NOTE: This was Spurgeon's farewell sermon at the Royal Surrey Gardens Music Hall.

SERMON NO. 289

The blood

"When I see the blood, I will pass over you." Exodus 12: 13
SUGGESTED FURTHER READING: 1 Corinthians 15: 12-22

The blood of Jesus Christ is blood that has been accepted. Christ died—he was buried; but neither heaven nor earth could tell whether God had accepted the ransom. There was wanted God's seal upon the great Magna Carta of man's salvation, and that seal was put, in that hour when God summoned the angel, and commanded him to descend from heaven and roll away the stone. Christ was put in the prison house of the grave, as a hostage for his people. Until God had signed the warrant for acquittal of all his people, Christ must abide in the bonds of death. He did not attempt to break his prison; he did not come out illegally, by wrenching down the bars of his dungeon; he waited: he folded up the napkin, laying it by itself: he laid the grave-clothes in a separate place; he waited, waited patiently, and at last down from the skies, like the flash of a meteor, the angel descended, touched the stone and rolled it away; and when Christ came out, rising from the dead in the glory of his Father's power, then was the seal put upon the great charter of our redemption. The blood was accepted, and sin was forgiven. And now, soul, it is not possible for God to reject you, if you come this day to him, pleading the blood of Christ. God cannot—and here we speak with reverence too—the everlasting God cannot reject a sinner who pleads the blood of Christ: for if he did so, it would be to deny himself, and to contradict all his former acts. He has accepted blood, and he will accept it.

FOR MEDITATION: Are you still stuck at the point of asking "What proves the resurrection"? Or have you advanced to consider what the resurrection proves (Romans 4: 25; Acts 17: 31)?

The Holy Spirit and the one church

"These be they who separate themselves, sensual, having not the Spirit."
Jude 19
SUGGESTED FURTHER READING: Romans 8: 5-13

The Holy Spirit when he comes in the heart comes like water. That is to say, he comes to purify the soul. He that is to-day as foul as he was before his pretended conversion is a hypocrite and a liar; he that this day loves sin and lives in it just as he was accustomed to do, let him know that the truth is not in him, but he hath received the strong delusion to believe a lie: God's people are a holy people; God's Spirit works by love, and purifies the soul. Once let it get into our hearts, and it will have no rest till it has turned every sin out. God's Holy Spirit and man's sin cannot live together peaceably; they may both be in the same heart, but they cannot both reign there, nor can they both be quiet there; for "the Spirit lusteth against the flesh, and the flesh lusteth against the Spirit;" they cannot rest, but there will be a perpetual warring in the soul, so that the Christian will have to cry, "O wretched man that I am! Who shall deliver me from the body of this death?" But in due time the Spirit will drive out all sin, and will present us blameless before the throne of his Majesty with exceeding great joy. Now, answer this question for thyself, and not for another man. Hast thou received this Spirit? Answer me.

FOR MEDITATION: When the Holy Spirit enters a person at the new birth, he begins to change that person for the better; but that involves declaring war on the flesh (Galatians 5: 17). An intensified awareness of one's sinfulness can be very distressing (Romans 7: 24), but the believer can take courage in the knowledge that God is at work. Those who know nothing of these experiences since professing conversion should examine their professed faith, no matter what other experiences of the Spirit they may claim to have had.

Faith

"Without faith it is impossible to please God." Hebrews 11:6
SUGGESTED FURTHER READING: Hebrews 3: 12–4: 2

I may know a thing, and yet not believe it. Therefore assent must go with faith: that is to say, what we know we must also agree with, as being most certainly the will of God. Now, with faith, it is necessary that I should not only read the Scriptures and understand them, but that I should receive them in my soul as being the very truth of the living God, and should devoutly, with my whole heart, receive the whole of Scripture as being inspired of the most High, and the whole of the doctrine which he requires me to believe for my salvation. You are not allowed to divide the Scriptures, and to believe what you please; you are not allowed to believe the Scriptures with a half-heartedness, for if you do this wilfully, you have not the faith which looks alone to Christ. True faith gives its full assent to the Scriptures; it takes a page and says, "No matter what is in the page, I believe it;" it turns over the next chapter and says, "Here are some things hard to be understood, which they that are unlearned and unstable do ignore, as they do also the other Scriptures, to their destruction; but hard though it be, I believe it." It sees the Trinity; it cannot understand the Trinity in Unity, but it believes it. It sees an atoning sacrifice; there is something difficult in the thought, but it believes it; and whatever it be which it sees in revelation, it devoutly puts its lips to the book, and says, "I love it all; I give my full, free and hearty assent to every word of it, whether it be the threatening or the promise, the proverb, the precept, or the blessing. I believe that since it is all the word of God it is all most assuredly true."

FOR MEDITATION: Faith enables us to accept much which we cannot explain—"Through faith we understand" (Hebrews 11: 3): "Believing is seeing". Nothing else can fill the gap left by a lack of faith.

SERMON NO. 107

Perfection in faith

"For by one offering he hath perfected for ever them that are sanctified."
Hebrews 10: 14
SUGGESTED FURTHER READING: 2 Timothy 2: 20-26

We could not have access to God unless on the footing of perfection; for God cannot walk and talk with imperfect creatures. But we are perfect; not in character, for we are still sinners; but we are perfected through the blood of Jesus Christ, so that God can allow us to have access to him as perfected creatures. We may come boldly, because being sprinkled with the blood, God does not look on us as unholy and unclean, otherwise he could not allow us to come to his mercy seat; but he looks upon us as being perfected for ever through the one sacrifice of Christ. That is one thing. The other is this. We are the vessels of God's temple; he has chosen us to be like the golden pots of his sanctuary; but God could not accept a worship which was offered to him in unholy vessels. Those vessels, therefore, were made perfect by being sprinkled with blood. God could not accept the praise which comes from your unholy heart; he could not accept the song which springs from your uncircumcised lips, nor the faith which arises from your doubting soul, unless he had taken the great precaution to sprinkle you with the blood of Christ; and now, whatever he uses you for, he uses you as a perfect instrument, regarding you as being perfect in Christ Jesus. That, again, is the meaning of the text, and the same meaning, only a different phase of it. And, the last meaning is, that the sacrifices of the Jews did not give believing Jews peace of conscience for any length of time; they had to come again, and again, and again, because they felt that those sacrifices did not present to them a perfect justification before God. But behold, beloved, you and I are complete in Jesus. We have no need of any other sacrifice. All others we disclaim. He hath perfected us for ever. We may set our conscience at ease, because we are truly, really, and everlastingly accepted in him.

FOR MEDITATION: Being accepted in Christ enables us to serve God acceptably.

Heaven

"The things which God hath prepared for them that love him. "
1 Corinthians 2: 9
SUGGESTED FURTHER READING: Matthew 26: 26-29

One of the places where you may most of all expect to see heaven is at the Lord's table. There are some of you, my dearly beloved, who absent yourselves from the supper of the Lord on earth; let me tell you in God's name, that you are not only sinning against God, but robbing yourselves of a most inestimable privilege. If there is one season in which the soul gets into closer communion with Christ than another, it is at the Lord's table. How often have we sung there:

"Can I Gethsemane forget?
Or there thy conflicts see,
Thine agony and bloody sweat,
And not remember thee?

Remember thee and all thy pains,
And all thy love to me,
Yes, while a pulse, or breath remains,
I will remember thee."

And then you see what an easy transition it is to heaven:

"And when these failing lips grow dumb,
And thought and memory flee;
When thou shalt in thy kingdom come,
Jesus, remember me."

O my erring brethren, you who live on, unbaptised, and who receive not this sacred supper, I tell you they will not save you—most assuredly they will not, and if you are not saved before you receive them they will be an injury to you; but if you are the Lord's people, why need you stay away? I tell you, the Lord's table is so high a place that you can see heaven from it very often. You get so near the cross there, you breathe so near the cross, that your sight becomes clearer, and the air brighter, and you can see more of heaven there than anywhere else. Christian, do not neglect the supper of your Lord; for if you do, he will hide heaven from you, in a measure.

FOR MEDITATION: When you come to the Lord's Table, do you look forward to the future in anticipation as well as to the past in gratitude (1 Corinthians 11: 26)?

SERMON NO. 56

A blow at self-righteousness

"If I justify myself, mine own mouth shall condemn me; if I say, I am perfect, it shall also prove me perverse." Job 9: 20
SUGGESTED FURTHER READING: 1 Corinthians 15: 1-4

Let me just utter a solemn sentence which you may consider at your leisure. If you trust to your faith and to your repentance, you will be as much lost as if you trusted to your good works or trusted to your sins. The ground of your salvation is not faith, but Christ; it is not repentance, but Christ. If I trust my trust of Christ, I am lost. My business is to trust Christ; to rest on him; to depend, not on what the Spirit has done in me, but on what Christ did for me, when he hung upon the tree. Now be it known unto you, that when Christ died, he took the sins of all his people upon his head, and there and then they all ceased to be. At the moment when Christ died, the sins of all his redeemed were blotted out. He did then suffer all that they ought to have suffered; he paid all their debts; and their sins were actually and positively lifted that day from their shoulders to his shoulders, for "the Lord hath laid on him the iniquity of us all." And now, if you believe in Jesus, there is not a sin remaining upon you, for your sin was laid on Christ; Christ was punished for your sins before they were committed, and as Kent says:

"Here's pardon full for sin that's past,
It matters not how black their cast;
And oh! my soul with wonder view,
For sins to come here's pardon too."

Blessed privilege of the believer! But if you live and die unbelievers, know this, that all your sins lie on your own shoulders.

FOR MEDITATION: To boast of the sincerest faith and the most thorough-going repentance is to exhibit the most sophisticated form of self-righteousness. Repentance and faith are both gifts from God so that sinners can receive his greatest gift, the Lord Jesus Christ (John 1: 12).

SERMON NO. 350

The inexhaustible barrel

"And the barrel of meal wasted not, neither did the cruse of oil fail, according to the word of the Lord, which he spake by Elijah."
1 Kings 17: 16
SUGGESTED FURTHER READING: 1 Peter 5: 6-11

If God saves us, it will be a trying matter. All the way to heaven, we shall only get there by the skin of our teeth. We shall not go to heaven sailing along with sails swelling in the breeze, like sea birds with their fair white wings, but we shall proceed with sails torn to ribbons, with masts creaking, and the ship's pumps at work both by night and day. We shall reach the city at the shutting of the gate, but not an hour before. O believer, thy Lord will bring thee safe to the end of thy pilgrimage; but mark, thou wilt never have one particle of strength to waste in wantonness upon the road. There will be enough to get thee up the hill Difficulty, but only enough then by climbing on your hands and knees. You will have strength enough to fight Apollyon, but when the battle is over your arm will have no strength remaining. Your trials will be so many, that if you had only one trial more, it would be like the last straw that breaks the camel's back. But, nevertheless, though God's love should thus try you all the journey through, your faith will bear the trying, for while God dashes you down to the earth with one hand in providence, he will lift you up with the other in grace. You will have consolation and affliction weighed out in equal degree, ounce for ounce, and grain for grain; you will be like the Israelite in the wilderness, if you gather much manna, you will have nothing over; while blessed be God, if you gather little you shall have no lack. You shall have daily grace for daily trials.

FOR MEDITATION: The Christian does not need to go looking for problems—they are as fundamental to the Christian faith as any major doctrine (Acts 14: 22); but the Christian receives from God the ability to endure (1 Corinthians 10: 13).

Love

"We love him, because he first loved us." 1 John 4: 19
SUGGESTED FURTHER READING: 1 John 3: 14-18

We have known many Christians who have forgotten much of their love to Christ when they have risen in the world. "Ah!" said a woman, who desired to do much for Christ in poverty, and who had had a great sum left her, "I cannot do as much as I used to do." "But how is that?" said one. Said she, "When I had a meagre purse I had an overflowing heart, and now I have an overflowing purse I have only a meagre heart." It is a sad temptation for some men to get rich. They were content to go to the meeting-house and mix with the ignoble congregation, while they had but little; they have grown rich, there is a Turkey carpet in the drawing-room, they have arrangements now too splendid to permit them to invite the poor of the flock, as once they did, and Christ Jesus is not so fashionable as to allow them to introduce any religious topic when they meet with their new friends. Besides this, they say they are now obliged to pay this visit and that visit, and they must spend so much time upon attire, and in maintaining their station and respectability, they cannot find time to pray as they did. The house of God has to be neglected for the party, and Christ has less of their heart than ever he had. "Is this thy kindness to thy friend?" And hast thou risen so high that thou art ashamed of Christ? And art thou grown so rich, that Christ in his poverty is despised? Alas! Poor wealth! Alas! Base wealth! Alas! Vile wealth! It would be well for thee if it should be all swept away, if a descent to poverty should be a restoration to the ardency of thine affection.

FOR MEDITATION: If success in the world goes to our hearts it can do others much good (1 Timothy 6: 17-19); if it goes to our heads it can do us much harm (1 Timothy 6: 9-10).

The first Christmas carol

"Glory to God in the highest, and on earth peace, good will toward men."
Luke 2: 14
SUGGESTED FURTHER READING: Romans 14: 5-9

I wish everybody that keeps Christmas this year, would keep it as the angels kept it. There are many persons who, when they talk about keeping Christmas, mean by that the cutting of the bands of their religion for one day in the year, as if Christ were the Lord of misrule, as if the birth of Christ should be celebrated like the orgies of Bacchus. There are some very religious people, that on Christmas would never forget to go to church in the morning; they believe Christmas to be nearly as holy as Sunday, for they reverence the tradition of the elders. Yet their way of spending the rest of the day is very remarkable; for if they see their way straight up stairs to their bed at night, it must be by accident. They would not consider they had kept Christmas in a proper manner, if they did not verge on gluttony and drunkenness. There are many who think Christmas cannot possibly be kept, except there be a great shout of merriment and mirth in the house, and added to that the boisterousness of sin. Now, my brethren, although we, as successors of the Puritans, will not keep the day in any religious sense whatever, attaching nothing more to it than to any other day: believing that every day may be a Christmas for ought we know, and wishing to make every day Christmas, if we can, yet we must try to set an example to others how to behave on that day; and specially since the angels gave glory to God: let us do the same. Once more the angels said, "Peace to men": let us labour if we can to make peace next Christmas day.

FOR MEDITATION: The unconverted cannot understand why Christians do not join them in their wild Christmas celebrations (1 Peter 4: 3-4); those who celebrate the event without being able to give a sensible reason for doing so, are providing us with wonderful opportunities to give a reason for the hope that is within us (1 Peter 3: 15).

SERMON NO. 168

Going home—a Christmas sermon

"Go home to thy friends, and tell them how great things the Lord hath done for thee, and hath had compassion on thee." Mark 5: 19
SUGGESTED FURTHER READING: 2 Kings 7: 3-9

First, **tell it truthfully**. Do not tell more than you know; do not tell John Bunyan's experience, when you ought to tell your own. Do not tell your mother you have felt what only Rutherford felt. Tell her no more than the truth. Tell your experience truthfully; for perhaps one single fly in the pot of ointment will spoil it, and one statement you may make which is not true may ruin it all. Tell the story truthfully.

In the next place, **tell it very humbly**. I have said that before. Do not intrude yourselves upon those who are older, and know more; but tell your story humbly; not as a preacher, not ex-cathedra, but as a friend and as a son.

Next, **tell it very earnestly**. Let them see you mean it. Do not talk about religion flippantly; you will do no good if you do. Do not make puns on texts; do not quote Scripture by way of joke: if you do, you may talk till you are dumb, you will do no good, if you in the least degree give them occasion to laugh by laughing at holy things yourself. Tell it very earnestly.

And then, **tell it very devoutly**. Do not try to tell your tale to man till you have told it first to God. When you are at home on Christmas Day, let no one see your face till God has seen it. Be up in the morning, wrestle with God; and if your friends are not converted, wrestle with God for them; and then you will find it easy work to wrestle with them for God. Seek, if you can, to get them one by one, and tell them the story. Do not be afraid; only think of the good you may possibly do.

FOR MEDITATION: Many of us will be with unconverted friends or relatives over Christmas. May Spurgeon's four points help each of us to speak of "the Son of God, who loved me, and gave himself for me" (Galatians 2: 20).

SERMON NO. 109

Plenteous redemption

"With him is plenteous redemption." Psalm 130: 7
SUGGESTED FURTHER READING: Galatians 4: 1-7

This "plenteous redemption" is plenteous, because it is enough for all the distresses of the saints. Your wants are almost infinite; but this atonement is quite so. Your troubles are almost unutterable; but this atonement is quite unutterable. Your needs you can scarce tell; but this redemption I know you cannot tell. Believe, then, that it is "plenteous redemption." O believing sinner, what a sweet comfort it is for you, that there is "plenteous redemption," and that you have a lot in it. You will most certainly be brought safely home, by Jesus' grace. Are you seeking Christ; or rather, do you know yourselves to be sinners? If you do, I have authority from God to say to every one who will confess his sins, that Christ has redeemed him. "This is a faithful saying, and worthy of all acceptation, that Christ Jesus came into the world to save sinners, of whom I am chief." Are you a sinner? I do not mean a sham sinner; there are lots of them about, but I have no gospel to preach to them just now. I do not mean one of those hypocritical sinners, who cry, "Yes, I am a sinner,"—who are sinners out of compliment, and do not mean it. I will preach another thing to you: I will preach against your self-righteousness another day; but I shall not preach anything to you just now about Christ, for he "came not to call the righteous, but sinners to repentance." But are you a sinner, in the bona fide sense of the word? Do you know yourself to be a lost, ruined, undone, sinner? Then in God's name I urge you to believe this—that Christ has died to save you.

FOR MEDITATION: We spend money to buy presents for others; Christ came to spend His lifeblood to buy sinners back for God. Christmas means nothing without the Christ; Christmas means nothing without Easter (Mark 10: 45).

SERMON NO. 351

The incarnation and birth of Christ

"But thou, Bethlehem Ephratah, though thou be little among the thousands of Judah, yet out of thee shall he come forth unto me that is to be ruler in Israel; whose goings forth have been from old, from everlasting." Micah 5: 2
SUGGESTED FURTHER READING: Hebrews 10: 5-7

"Go," saith the Father, "and thy Father's blessing on thy head!" Then comes the unrobing. How do angels crowd around to see the Son of God take off his robes! He laid aside his crown; he said, "My father, I am Lord over all, blessed for ever, but I will lay my crown aside, and be as mortal men are." He strips himself of his bright vest of glory; "Father," he says, "I will wear a robe of clay, just such as men wear." Then he takes off all those jewels wherewith he was glorified; he lays aside his starry mantles and robes of light, to dress himself in the simple garments of the peasant of Galilee. What a solemn disrobing that must have been! And next, can you picture the dismissal! The angels attend the Saviour through the streets, until they approach the doors; when an angel cries, "Lift up your heads, O ye gates, and be ye lifted up ye everlasting doors, and let the king of glory through!" I think the angels must have wept when they lost the company of Jesus— when the Sun of heaven bereaved them of all its light. But they went after him. They descended with him; and when his spirit entered into flesh, and he became a babe, he was attended by that mighty host of angels, who after they had been with him to Bethlehem's manger, and seen him safely laid on his mother's breast, in their journey upwards appeared to the shepherds and told them that he was born king of the Jews. The Father sent him! Contemplate that subject. Let your soul get hold of it, and in every period of his life think that he suffered what the Father willed; that every step of his life was marked with the approval of the great I AM.

FOR MEDITATION: When we think of the birth of the Son of God, our eyes are rightly focused on earth. But are we in danger of forgetting God the Father in heaven, the one who so loved the world that he gave his only-begotten Son (John 3: 16)? May we remember to give "Glory to God in the highest" (Luke 2: 14).

SERMON NO. 57

A Merry Christmas

"And his sons went and feasted in their houses, every one his day; and sent and called for their three sisters to eat and to drink with them. And it was so, when the days of their feasting were gone about, that Job sent and sanctified them, and rose up early in the morning, and offered burnt offerings according to the number of them all: for Job said, It may be that my sons have sinned, and cursed God in their hearts. Thus did Job continually." Job 1: 4-5
SUGGESTED FURTHER READING: Nehemiah 8: 9-12

The text gives a licence. Now, ye souls who would deny to your fellow-men all sorts of mirth, come and listen to the merry bell of this text, while it gives a licence to the righteous especially—a licence that they meet together in their houses, and eat and drink, and praise their God. In Cromwell's days, the Puritans thought it an ungodly thing for men to keep Christmas. They, therefore, tried to put it down, and the common crier went through the street, announcing that Christmas was henceforth no more to be kept, it being a popish, if not a heathenish ceremony. Now, you do not suppose that after the crier had made the proclamation, any living Englishman took any notice of it; at least, I can scarcely imagine that any did, except to laugh at it; for it is idle thus to strain at a gnat and swallow a camel. Although we do not keep the fast as papists, not even as a commemorative festival, yet there is something in old associations that makes us enjoy the day in which a man may shake off the cares of business, and relax with his little ones. God forbid I should be such a Puritan as to proclaim the annihilation of any day of rest which falls to the lot of the labouring man. I wish there were half a dozen holidays in the year. I wish there were more opportunities for the poor to rest; though I would not have as many saint's days as there are in Romish countries; yet, if we had but one or two more days in which the poor man's household, and the rich man's family might meet together, it might perhaps be better for us. However, I am quite certain that all the preaching in the world will not put Christmas down.

FOR MEDITATION: Perhaps you are completely opposed to the keeping of Christmas! That is your right! But you can still benefit from the holiday and show the joy of the Lord to those who are going to be with you.

SERMON NO. 352

A Christmas question

"For unto us a child is born, unto us a Son is given." Isaiah 9: 6
SUGGESTED FURTHER READING: Luke 2: 8-20

Why are we sad? I am looking upon faces just now that appear the very reverse of gloomy, but maybe the smile covers an aching heart. Brother and sister, why are we sad this morning, if unto us a child is born, if unto us a Son is given? Listen to the cry! It is "Harvest home! Harvest home!" See the maidens as they dance, and the young men as they make merry. And why is this mirth? Because they are storing the precious fruits of the earth, they are gathering together into their barns wheat which will soon be consumed. And what, brothers and sisters, have we the bread which endureth to eternal life and are we unhappy? Does the worldling rejoice when his corn is increased, and do we not rejoice when, "Unto us a child is born, and unto us a Son is given?" Listen yonder! What means the firing of the Tower guns? Why all this ringing of bells in the church steeples, as if all London were mad with joy? There is a prince born; therefore there is this salute, and therefore are the bells ringing. Ah, Christians, ring the bells of your hearts, fire the salute of your most joyous songs, "For unto us a child is born, unto us a Son is given." Dance, O my heart, and ring out peals of gladness! Ye drops of blood within my veins, dance every one of you! Oh! All my nerves become harp strings, and let gratitude touch you with angelic fingers! And thou, my tongue, shout—shout to his praise, who hath said to you: "Unto you a child is born, unto you a Son is given." Wipe that tear away! Come, stop that sighing! Hush your murmuring. What matters your poverty? "Unto you a child is born." What matters your sickness? "Unto you a Son is given." What matters your sin? For this child shall take the sin away, and this Son shall wash and make you fit for heaven.

FOR MEDITATION: God sent his only begotten Son to be born as a child, so that sinners could be born again and become the children of God. The deepest sadness belongs to all who still refuse to trust in the Lord Jesus Christ as their Saviour (John 1: 12-13).

The vanguard and rear guard of the Church

"The Lord will go before you; and the God of Israel will be your rereward." Isaiah 52: 12
SUGGESTED FURTHER READING: Ezra 8: 21-23 and 31-32

We shall soon launch into another year, and hitherto we have found our years to be years of trouble. We have had mercies, but still we find this house of our pilgrimage is not an abiding city, not a mansion of peace and comfort. Perhaps we are trembling to go forward. Foreseeing trouble, we know not how we shall be able to endure to the end. We are standing here and pausing for a while, sitting down upon the stone of our Ebenezer to rest ourselves, gazing dubiously into the future, saying, "Alas! What shall I do? Surely, I shall one day fall by the hand of the enemy." Brother, arise, arise; anoint your head, and wash your face, and fast no longer; let this sweet morsel now cheer you; put this cup to your lips, and let your eyes be enlightened: "The Lord Jehovah will go before you." He has gone before you already. Your future path has all been marked out in the great decrees of his predestination. You shall not tread a step which is not mapped out in the great chart of God's decree. Your troubles have been already weighed for you in the scales of his love; your labour is already set aside for you to accomplish by the hand of his wisdom. Depend upon it, your:-

"Times of trial and of grief,
Times of triumph and relief,

All shall come and last and end
As shall please your heavenly Friend."

Remember, you are not a child of chance. If you were, you might indeed fear. You will go nowhere next year except where God shall send you.

FOR MEDITATION: Fear of the future and fear of the unknown still have to be faced by the believer. But the Christian has the remedy to such fear—a great God who knows the future and who leads the way (Acts 20: 22-24; Hebrews 11: 8-10).

SERMON NO. 230

"What have I done?"

"What have I done?" Jeremiah 8: 6
SUGGESTED FURTHER READING: 2 Peter 1: 3-8

What hast thou done? I hear thee reply, "I have done nothing to save myself; for that was done for me in the eternal covenant, from before the foundation of the world. I have done nothing to make a righteousness for myself, for Christ said, "It is finished;" I have done nothing to procure heaven by my merits, for all that Jesus did for me before I was born." But say, brother, what hast thou done for him who died to save thy wretched soul? What hast thou done for his church? What hast thou done for the salvation of the world? What has thou done to promote thine own spiritual growth in grace? Ah! I might hit some of you that are true Christians very hard here; but I will leave you with your God. God will chastise his own children. I will, however, put a pointed question. Are there not many Christians now present who cannot recollect that they have been the means of the salvation of one soul during this year? Come, now; turn back. Have you any reason to believe that directly or indirectly you have been made the means this year of the salvation of a soul? I will go further. There are some of you who are old Christians, and I will ask you this question: Have you any reason to believe that ever since you were converted you have ever been the means of the salvation of a soul? It was reckoned in the East, in the times of the patriarchs, to be a disgrace to a woman that she had no children; but what disgrace it is to a Christian to have no spiritual children—to have none born unto God by his instrumentality! And yet there are some of you here that have been spiritually barren, and have never brought one convert to Christ; you have not one star in your crown of glory, and must wear a starless crown in heaven.

FOR MEDITATION: While the self-righteous makes the fatal mistake of thinking that good deeds lead to salvation, the saved can make the sad mistake of forgetting that salvation is supposed to lead to good deeds (Ephesians 2: 8-10).

Heavenly worship

"And I looked, and, lo, a Lamb stood on the Mount Sion, and with him an hundred forty and four thousand, having his Father's name written in their foreheads. And I heard a voice from heaven, as the voice of many waters, and as the voice of a great thunder: and I heard the voice of harpers harping with their harps: And they sung as it were a new song before the throne, and before the four beasts, and the elders: and no man could learn that song but the hundred and forty and four thousand, which were redeemed from the earth." Revelation 14: 1-3
SUGGESTED FURTHER READING: Revelation 5: 6-10

Why is the song said to be a new song? It will be a new song, because the saints were never in such a position before as they will be when they sing this new song. They are in heaven now; but the scene of our text is something more than heaven. It refers to the time when all the chosen race shall meet around the throne, when the last battle shall have been fought, and the last warrior shall have gained his crown. It is not now that they are singing, but it is in the glorious time to come, when all the hundred and forty and four thousand—or rather, the number typified by that number—will be all safely housed and all secure. I can conceive the period. Time was—eternity now reigns. The voice of God exclaims, "Are my beloved all safe?" The angel flies through paradise and returns with this message, "Yes, they are." "Is Fearful safe? Is Feeble-mind safe? Is Ready-to-Halt safe? Is Despondency safe?" "Yes, O King, they are," says he. "Shut the gates," says the Almighty, "they have been open night and day; shut them now." Then, when all of them shall be there, then will be the time when the shout shall be louder than many waters, and the song shall begin which will never end.

FOR MEDITATION: The old year is about to be replaced by a new year, but that will soon grow old and fade away. Revelation speaks of the former things passing away (21: 4), and the old serpent being cast out and bound (12: 9 and 20: 2). All that remains is new and remains new throughout eternity—a new song, a new heaven, a new earth, new Jerusalem—all things new (21: 1-5).

SERMON NO. 110

The cleansing of the leper

"And if a leprosy break out abroad in the skin, and the leprosy cover all the skin of him that hath the plague from his hand even to his foot, wheresoever the priest looketh; Then the priest shall consider: and, behold, if the leprosy have covered all his flesh, he shall pronounce him clean that hath the plague: it is all turned white: he is clean."
Leviticus 13: 12-13
SUGGESTED FURTHER READING: Colossians 3: 5-14

Sinner, if you are to be saved, Christ must do it all; but when once you have faith in Christ, then you must be washed; then must you cease from sin, and then by the Holy Spirit's power you shall be enabled to do so. What was ineffective before shall become mighty enough now, through the life which God has put into you. The washing with water by the word, and the cleansing of yourself from dead works, shall become an effectual and mighty duty. You shall be made holy, and walk in white, in the purity wherewith Christ has endowed you. The shaving off of his hair was fitly to represent how all the old things were to pass away, and everything was to become new. All the white hair was to be cut off, as you read in Leviticus 14: 9: "He shall shave all the hair off his head, and his beard, and his eyebrows." There was not a remnant or relic left of the old state in which the hair was white; all was to be given up. So it is with the sinner. When he is once pardoned, once cleansed, then he begins to cut off the old habits, his old prides, his old joys. The beard on which the hoary Jew prided himself was to come off, and the eyebrows which seem to be necessary to make the countenance look decent, were all to be taken away. So it is with the pardoned man. He did nothing before, he does everything now. He knew that good works were of no benefit to him in his carnal state, but now he becomes so strict that he will shave off every hair of his old state. Not one darling lust shall be left, not one iniquity shall be spared, all must be cut away.

FOR MEDITATION: Very soon many will be breaking their New Year's resolutions! The Christian is already a new creation in Christ (2 Corinthians 5: 17), a new person with a new nature. May God give us grace and strength to be what we are in Christ.

SERMON NO. 353

Canaan on earth

"For the land, whither thou goest in to possess it, is not as the land of Egypt, from whence ye came out, where thou sowedst thy seed, and wateredst it with thy foot, as a garden of herbs: But the land, whither ye go to possess it, is a land of hills and valleys, and drinketh water of the rain of heaven: A land which the Lord thy God careth for: the eyes of the Lord thy God are always upon it, from the beginning of the year, even unto the end of the year." Deuteronomy 11: 10-12
SUGGESTED FURTHER READING: Psalm 139: 1-12

We have come now, beloved, to the end of another year—to the threshold of another period of time, and have marched another year's journey through the wilderness. Come, now! In reading this verse over, can you say Amen to it? "The eyes of the Lord thy God are always upon you, from the beginning of the year even unto the end of the year." Some of you say, "I have had deep troubles this year." "I have lost a friend," says one. "Ah!" says another, "I have been impoverished this year." "I have been slandered", cries another. "I have been exceedingly vexed and grieved", says another. "I have been persecuted," says another. Well, beloved, take the year altogether—the ups and the downs, the troubles and the joys, the hills and the valleys altogether, and what have you to say about it? You may say, "Surely goodness and mercy have followed me all the days of my life, and I will dwell in the house of the Lord for ever." Do not pick out one day in the year, and say it was a bad day, but take all the year round, let it revolve in all its grandeur. Judge between things that differ; and then what will you say? "Ah! Bless the Lord! He hath done all things well; my soul, and all that is within me, bless his holy name!" And you know why all things have been well. It is because the eyes of the Lord have been upon you all the year.

FOR MEDITATION: Are you glad that God sees you through and through every moment of your life? This should bring terror to the unbeliever (Hebrews 4: 13) but great comfort to God's people in the hour of distress (Genesis 16: 13; Exodus 2: 25).

SERMON NO. 58

Watch-night Service

"Arise, cry out in the night: in the beginning of the watches pour out thine heart like water before the face of the Lord." Lamentations 2: 19
SUGGESTED FURTHER READING: Psalm 90: 1-12 (an exposition of which was given earlier in the service)

Dear friends, may grace be given unto you, that ye may be able to pour out your hearts this night! Remember, my hearers, it may seem a light thing for us to assemble tonight at such an hour, but listen for one moment to the ticking of that clock!...... It is the beating of the pulse of eternity. You hear the ticking of that clock!—It is the footstep of death pursuing you. Each time the clock ticks, death's footsteps are falling on the ground close behind you. You will soon enter another year. This year will have gone in a few seconds. 1855 is almost gone; where will the next year be spent, my friends? One has been spent on earth; where will you spend the next? "In heaven!" says one, "I trust." Another murmurs, "Perhaps I shall spend mine in hell!" Ah! Solemn is the thought, but before that clock strikes twelve, some here may be in hell; and, blessed be the name of God, some of us may be in heaven! But oh do you know how to estimate your time, my hearers? Do you know how to measure your days? Oh! I have not words to speak tonight. Do you know that every hour you are nearing the tomb? That every hour you are nearing judgment? That the archangel is flapping his wings every second of your life, and, trumpet at his mouth, is approaching you? That you do not live stationary lives, but always going on, on, on, towards the grave? Do you know where the stream of life is hastening some of you? To the rapids—to the rapids of woe and destruction! What shall the end of those be who obey not the gospel of God? You will not have so many years to live as you had last year!

FOR MEDITATION: The march of time is a terrible enemy to all who persist in unbelief, but the Christian sees things differently—"now is our salvation nearer than when we believed. The night is far spent, the day is at hand" (Romans 13: 11-12).
Spurgeon must have the last word: "Now, my friends, in the highest and best sense, I wish you all a happy New Year."

SERMON NO. 59

Summary of Subject Index

Subject Index

God the Son—His Work

God the Holy Spirit

Section 2   Man in his natural sinful state

Subject Index

Subject Index

Section 8   **Times & Seasons**

Section 9   **Death & the future state**

Scripture Index

Scripture Index

Scripture Index

Scripture Index

Location of numbers (In order of appearance)

New Park Street Chapel, Southwark (101)

1-6, 10, 28-38, 41-83, 86, 87, 89, 91, 93, 95, 97, 99-101, 103, 117, 121, 125, 147, 157, 174, 178, 180, 217, 220, 226, 232, 239, 244, 254, 262, 282, 284, 310, 319-325, 337, 362, 364

Exeter Hall, Strand (94)

7-9, 11-27, 84, 85, 88, 90, 92, 96, 98, 102, 108, 219, 221, 290-309, 311, 313, 315-318, 326-330, 333-336, 338-341, 343-361, 363, 365-368

A Field, King Edward's Road, Hackney (2)

39/40 (Tuesday 4/9/1855)

Maberley Chapel, Kingsland (1)

94 (Monday 25/8/1856 - on behalf of the Metropolitan Benefit Societies' Asylum)

The Music Hall, Royal Surrey Gardens (157)

104-107, 109-116, 118-120, 122-124, 126-146, 148-153, 156, 158-173, 175-177, 179, 181-191, 193-197, 200-216, 218, 222-225, 227-231, 233-238, 240-243, 245-253, 255-261, 263-267, 271-281, 283, 285-289

The Crystal Palace, Sydenham (2)

154/155 (Wednesday 7/10/1857)

Bloomsbury Chapel (1)

192 (Tuesday 4/5/1858 - on behalf of the Sunday School Union)

The Grand Stand, Epsom Race Course (2)

198, 199 (both Friday 11/6/1858)

The New (Metropolitan) Tabernacle (5)

268-270, 331, 332 (Tuesdays 16/8/1859 & 21/8/1860 respectively)

Surrey Chapel, Blackfriars Road (1)

312 (Thursday 3/5/1860 - on behalf of the Religious Tract Society)

The Tabernacle, Moorfields (1)

314 (Wednesday 9/5/1860 - on behalf of the London Missionary Society)

Tottenham Court Road Chapel (1)

342 (Undated)

Other weekday sermons: 59,78,99 (on behalf of The Aged Pilgrim's Friend Society), 178,190 (on behalf of The Baptist Missionary Society). Undated: 351,360. All other sermons were preached on the Lord's Day. No 65 being on behalf of the Baptist Fund for the relief of Poor Ministers. No 76 again for the Baptist Missionary Society.

Time of Numbers

The vast majority of sermons are those preached in the **morning,** including all 157 numbers relating to the Royal Surrey Gardens Music Hall. Sermons preached at other times of the day are as follows:
Evening (56 including 32 at New Park Street Chapel & 17 at Exeter Hall)

2, 5, 15, 23, 25, 27, 39/40, 49, 54, 78, 84, 85, 88, 90, 92, 96, 98, 99, 102, 108, 121, 125, 147, 157, 174, 178, 180, 192, 199, 217, 219, 221, 226, 232, 239, 244, 254, 262, 282, 310, 312, 314, 319-325, 337, 342, 351, 362, 364, 367

Night - 59 (Watchnight Service)

Afternoon - 94,198
Day-meetings - 154/155,268-270,331/332

Dates

The sermons as printed contain a few obvious discrepancies :

No 59 (Watchnight Service Tuesday 31 December 1855) must have been on Monday - the previous sermon was preached on Sunday 30 December.

Nos 72 and 73 are both dated Sunday morning 30 march 1856 and both contain internal references to being preached in the morning. External sources confirm that no 72 is correctly dated and that no 73 was not the evening sermon; one possibility is that no 73 was preached on Sunday morning 6 April 1856 which is not otherwise represented.

No 149 (Sunday 31 August 1857) must have been on August 30th - the previous sermon is dated 23 August and the following 6 September.

No 296 (Sunday 26 January 1860) must have been on the 29th - the previous sermon is dated 22 January and the following 5 February.

No 309 is dated Sunday morning 22 April 1860; nos.322 and 324 are both dated Sunday evening 22 April 1860. No 322 refers back to the morning sermon no.309; it is clear that no.324 is incorrectly dated, but it is not possible to ascertain the correct date.

Notably Used Sermons

In the Prefaces to volumes 3-7 Spurgeon selects the following numbers which were particularly used of God :

169, 171, 174, 184, 193, 195, 202, 227, 228, 231, 236, 244, 246, 275, 279, 280, 291, 293, 296, 301, 304, 317, 333, 336, 349, 351, 353, 361, 362.

Contents of Volumes

Vol. 1 nos. 1-53;
Vol. 2 nos. 54-106;
Vol. 3 nos. 107-164;
Vol. 4 nos. 165-224;
Vol. 5 nos. 225-285;
Vol. 6 nos. 286-347;
Vol. 7 nos. 348-368 (plus continuation).